About this book

The war of 1948 is known to Israelis as the "War of Independence". But for Palestinians, the war is forever the *Nakba*, "The Catastrophe". The conflict led to the creation of the state of Israel and resulted in the destruction of much of Palestinian society by Zionist forces. Approximately 90 per cent of the Palestinians who lived in the major part of Palestine upon which Israel was established became refugees. The minority of Palestinians – 160,000 – who remained behind, are one of the main subjects of this book. Many of them were forced out of their homes and became second-class citizens of the state of Israel. As such, they were subject to a system of military administration between 1948 and 1966 by a government that confiscated the bulk of their lands.

For the Palestinians, both refugees and non-refugees, the traumatic events of 1948 have become central to Palestinian history, memory and identity. Moreover, in recent years Palestinians have been producing memories of the *Nakba*, compiling and recording oral history and holding annual commemorations designed to preserve the memory of the catastrophe, while emphasising the link between refugee rights, identity and memory. In the absence of a rich source of Palestinian documentary records, oral history and interviews with internally displaced Palestinians are a critical and natural source for constructing a more comprehensible narrative of their experiences.

This collection is dedicated to the memory of Edward W. Said (1935–2003), whose voice articulated the aspirations of the disenfranchised, the oppressed and the marginalised, and whose message was humanist and universal, extending beyond Palestine to touch wide audiences.

Catastrophe Remembered

Palestine, Israel and the Internal Refugees

**Essays in Memory of
Edward W. Said (1935–2003)**

Edited by
Nur Masalha

Zed Books

LONDON AND NEW YORK

Catastrophe Remembered was first published by Zed Books Ltd,
7 Cynthia Street, London N1 9JF, UK and Room 400, 175 Fifth Avenue,
New York, NY 10010, USA in 2005
www.zedbooks.co.uk

Editorial Copyright © Nur Masalha 2005
Copyright © Individual Contributors 2005

Cover designed by Andrew Corbett
Set in 10½/13 pt Garamond by Long House, Cumbria, UK
Printed and bound in Malta by Gutenberg Press

Distributed in the USA exclusively by Palgrave Macmillan, a division of
St Martin's Press, LLC, 175 Fifth Avenue, New York, NY 10010

A catalogue record for this book is available from the British Library

US Cataloging-in-Publication Data
is available from the Library of Congress

ISBN 1 84277 622 3 (cased)
ISBN 1 84277 623 1 (limp)

Contents

Part I • Evolving Israeli Policies and Indigenous Resistance

Part II • Palestinian Oral History and Memory

PART III • Human Rights and International Protection

Notes on Contributors

Professor Naseer H. Aruri is Chancellor Professor (Emeritus) of Political Science at the University of Massachusetts at Dartmouth. He is Chair of the Board of Directors of the Trans-Arab Research Institute (Boston), and a member of the Board of Directors of the newly established International Institute of Criminal Investigations (The Hague). He is a member of the Independent Palestinian Commission for the Protection of Citizens' Rights, and a founding member of the Arab Organisation for Human Rights. He was also a member of the board of directors of Human Rights Watch/Middle East, 1990–1992, and a three-term member of the board of directors of Amnesty International, USA, 1984–1990. His latest book is: *Dishonest Broker: The US Role in Israel and Palestine* (Cambridge, MA: South End Press, 2003).

Professor Isma'el Abu-Sa'ad is a senior lecturer in the Department of Education at the University of Ben-Gurion, Beer Sheba. He is the author of many articles on the Palestinian Bedouin of the Negev. His co-edited books include *The Influence of Settlement on Substance Use and Abuse among Nomadic Populations in Israel and Kenya* (Nirp Research for Policy Series 7) (2002) and *The Future of Indigenous Peoples: Strategies for Survival and Development* (2003).

Nihad Boqa'i is a leading expert on the Palestinian refugees and internally displaced persons and a researcher at the Badil Resource Center for Palestinian Residency and Refugee Rights, Bethlehem, Palestine.

Eitan Bronstein is Chair of Zochrot (*zochrot* means "to remember" in Hebrew), the only Israeli organisation that campaigns to raise awareness of the Palestinian *Nakba* in both Jewish society and Israeli schools.

Zochrot also posts signs on the sites of destroyed Palestinian villages.

Dr Hillel Cohen was born in Jerusalem in 1961. He covered Palestinian affairs for the Jerusalem-based Hebrew magazine *Kol Ha'ir* (1992–99). He was Research Fellow in the Department of War Studies, King's College, London (2002–03) and Research Fellow at the Truman Institute, Hebrew University of Jerusalem (1998–2004). He has a PhD from the Hebrew University (in 2002) and an MA from the same university on the Palestinian internal refugees in Israel. He is currently teaching in the Department of Middle Eastern Studies, Hebrew University. His book *Present Absentees* (in Hebrew) was published in 2000, and an updated version was published in Arabic in Beirut in 2003. His book *An Army of Shadows: Palestinian Collaborators in the Service of Zionism 1917–1948* (in Hebrew) was published in Jerusalem in 2004.

Jonathan Cook is a writer and freelance journalist living in Nazareth. He has contributed to, among other publications, the *Guardian* (London), *International Herald Tribune* (Paris), *Le Monde Diplomatique* (Paris) and *Al-Ahram Weekly On-Line* (Cairo).

William Dalrymple is a Scottish writer and historian. His book *White Mughals* won the Wolfson Prize for History 2003 and the Scottish Book of the Year Prize, and was shortlisted for the PEN History Award. He wrote the highly acclaimed bestseller *In Xanadu*. The book won the 1990 Yorkshire Post Best First Work Award and a Scottish Arts Council Spring Book Award; it was also shortlisted for the John Llewellyn Rhys Memorial Prize. In 1989 Dalrymple moved to Delhi where he lived for six years researching his second book, *City of Djinns*, which won the 1994 Thomas Cook Travel Book Award and the *Sunday Times* Young British Writer of the Year Award. *From the Holy Mountain*, his acclaimed study of the demise of Christianity in its Middle Eastern homeland, was awarded the Scottish Arts Council Autumn Book Award for 1997; it was also shortlisted for the 1998 Thomas Cook Award, the John Llewellyn Rhys Prize and the Duff Cooper Prize. A collection of his writings about India, *The Age of Kali*, was published in 1998. He is a Fellow of the Royal Society of Literature and of the Royal Asiatic Society, and in 2002 was awarded the Mungo Park Medal by the Royal Scottish Geographical Society for his "outstanding contribution to travel literature".

Isabelle Humphries is currently studying for a PhD at St Mary's College, University of Surrey, on the Palestinian internal refugees in Galilee. She has an MA in Middle East Politics from Durham University and has worked for three years with Palestinian NGOs, and as a freelance writer, on both sides of the 1967 border.

Dr Mahmoud 'Issa is a Palestinian refugee from the village of Lubya, Galilee, and is currently based in Denmark. He worked for the Danish Refugee Council as a Counsellor and Senior Researcher. He is also the author of many articles on the oral history of the Palestinian refugees.

Dr Nur Masalha is a senior lecturer and the Director of the Holy Land Research Project at St Mary's College, University of Surrey, as well as the editor of *Holy Land Studies: A Multidisciplinary Journal*. His books include: *Expulsion of the Palestinians: The Concept of 'Transfer' in Zionist Political Thought, 1882–1948* (Washington DC: Institute for Palestine Studies, 1992); *The Palestinians in Israel: Is Israel the State of All Its Citizens and "Absentees"?* (Haifa: Galilee Centre for Social Research, 1993); *A Land Without a People* (London: Faber and Faber, 1997); *Imperial Israel and the Palestinians* (London: Pluto Press, 2000); and *The Politics of Denial* (London: Pluto Press, 2003).

Dr Ilan Pappé is a senior lecturer in the Department of Political Science at Haifa University and Chair of the Emile Touma Institute, Haifa, Israel. His books include *The Making of the Arab–Israeli Conflict, 1948–1951* (London: I. B. Tauris, 1992); *The Israel/Palestine Question* (London: Routledge, 1999); *A Modern History of Palestine: One Land, Two Peoples* (Cambridge: Cambridge University Press, 2004).

Terry Rempel is Coordinator of Research and Information at the Badil Resource Center for Palestinian Residency and Refugee Rights, Bethlehem. (address: PO Box 728, Bethlehem, Palestine). He is also a research fellow at the School of Historical, Political and Sociological Studies, University of Exeter. His recent publications include "Temporary Protection as an Instrument for Implementing the Right of Return for Palestinian Refugees", *Boston University International Law Journal*, Vol. 22 (Spring 2004), pp.1-162, co-authored with Susan M. Akram.

Acknowledgements

I am particularly grateful to Isabelle Humphries who has helped me greatly with this project, with source material, ideas, criticism, discussions and practical assistance. Other friends and colleagues have also helped me with ideas and logistics. Among them I would like to thank the late Michael Prior, Ilan Pappé, Naseer Aruri, As'ad Ghanem, 'Abbas Shiblak, Muhsin Yusif, Sari Hanafi, Michael Hayes, Anna Hardman, Bashir Abu-Manneh, Terry Rempel, Nihad Boqa'i, Mahmoud 'Issa, Isma'el Abu-Sa'ad, Ahmad Sa'di, Eitan Bronstein, William Dalrymple, Jonathan Cook, Hillel Cohen, the late Michael Adams, Maisa Hourani, and Peter Colvin. I am also deeply indebted to my wife, Dr Stephanie Cronin, for her moral support, editorial assistance and perceptive comments. Of course I alone am responsible for this book and its deficiencies.

Foreword • Edward W. Said, Scholar-Activist

Naseer H. Aruri

It is only fitting that this collection, dealing with Palestinian internal refugees, identity and memory, oral history, indigenous rights, and international protection, is dedicated to the memory of Edward W. Said. At least half of the collection deals with Palestinian oral history and memory, which, together with issues such as the Palestinian *Nakba* (catastrophe), indigenous rights and international protection, right of return, and eventually the one-state solution, constituted much of Said's concerns, expressed in numerous oral and written works that span the past three decades. Indeed, Said played a key, if not indispensable, role in transforming the international discourse on all these issues.

The voice of Professor Edward W. Said articulated the aspirations of the disenfranchised, the oppressed, the marginalised, and the voiceless, whose predicament he presented in ways that no one else could. He was, after all, a voice for the ideas, hopes and visions that diverse oppressed and indigenous people came to hold dear and cherish. His message was humanist, universal, and conciliatory, focusing on, but also extending beyond Palestine to touch a wide audience and to resonate in the hearts of all those for whom the pursuit of justice and human dignity was a compelling priority.

Edward was one of the twentieth century's greatest thinkers, who has who has left a unique and indelible legacy in numerous fields and across many disciplines: he was an internationally renowned literary and cultural critic, a philosopher of history, a music critic, a Middle East specialist, a political theorist, an activist, and a most deeply humane voice of conscience. Rarely does one come across someone who combines such an exceptional diversity of talents, devotion to principles and just causes, boundless energy, intellectual resources, and analytical prowess.

Edward's great writings appear in 26 languages in the most prestigious and widely read periodicals, newspapers and scholarly journals. He authored more than 20 books and over 250 articles and presented at least 50 endowed lectures in the last 25 years of his life. In addition to having served as University professor at Columbia University (the highest academic rank), he had been a visiting professor at Yale, Harvard, and Johns Hopkins as well as a fellow at numerous centres of learning and advanced studies around the world. He was general editor of a book series for Harvard University Press titled Convergences: Inventories of the Present. He wrote a regular music column for the *Nation*, and a regular column for *Al-Ahram* in Cairo, as well as contributing articles to many other journals, magazines, and newspapers, including *Le Monde Diplomatique*, the *London Review of Books*, and other prestigious publications.

It was this rich diversity and his ground-breaking contributions that gave Edward his unique character. One readily sees in his many writings the interplay of politics, culture, psychology, and the arts – in his works *Orientalism, Culture and Imperialism, After the Last Sky, Representations of the Intellectual, Covering Islam*, and *Beginnings*, as well as his books on the Palestine question and Oslo, among others.

One of his everlasting contributions is likely to be his demonstration of how the justification for empire building was embedded in the Western cultural imagination during the age of empire, and how even today the imperial legacy colours relations between the West and the formerly colonised world, at all levels. His comprehension that all cultures are interdependent, and consequently that the West and its former subjects must recognise that the true human community is global, also testifies to the genius of Edward.

Together with a few colleagues, he was responsible for creating the basis for post-colonial studies as a new discipline. He provided the linguistic and methodological tools to help us understand the nature of imperialism and its malignant impact on colonial societies throughout the world. His articulation of the relationship, indeed the linkage, between culture and power marks another of his major contributions to knowledge. In both, *Orientalism* and *Culture and Imperialism*, he demonstrates how the concept of empire was ever-present in the literary works of the age. The falsely claimed knowledge of the "orient" created a perspective that enabled the West to exercise power over the East, spreading its hegemony in destructive ways that distorted the political development of colonial societies and fragmented their very existence. So central is the emphasis on culture in Edward's work that he founded an entirely new school of thought for the study of imperialism that integrated major diverse disciplines into a coherent analytic paradigm focusing on culture and power.

In addition to Edward Said the world-renowned scholar, there was also Edward Said the enthusiastic activist. "Scholar-activist" is indeed a hyphenated description rarely-applied to people of Said's stature. Although Edward's manner, appearance and lifestyle were seemingly aristocratic, his writings, lectures and activism consolidated an integral relationship between the academy and civil society. Edward was the scholar-activist *par excellence*. He bridged the gap between the underprivileged and the ivory tower. He took up the cause of Palestine in venues that are usually closed to the underprivileged: the lecture theatres, the concert stages, the highbrow journals, the principal television shows, the numerous occasions honouring him and celebrating his work worldwide. Thus, in many ways, he allowed Palestine to ride on his coat-tails rather than the other way around.

He did not detach himself from the politics of Palestine, and this required him to travel to distant and sometimes not easily accessible places, sleeping in simple hotels, putting up with mundane and sometimes intolerably sectarian discussions, subjecting himself to tedious arrangements, and having to endure on occasion endless speeches filled with bombast and triumphalist declarations. This is not to say that such politics was the hallmark of the Palestinian national movement to which he belonged, but simply to underscore the rare tolerance of an inevitable dimension of *all* politics by a scholarly giant for whom such endeavours could be very taxing.

Edward Said was described by the *New York Times* as "one of the most influential literary and cultural critics in the world". Yet he did not hesitate to lend his name to the Palestine National Council, our parliament in exile, with all its pitfalls, tedious procedures, and monotonous discussions. For him, it was still the only available representative forum for a people who suffered physical and legal fragmentation, in addition to dispossession and disenfranchisement.

Edward was typically described as "the conscience of Palestine", having delivered the kind of eloquent message perhaps unheard since that of the late Fayez Sayegh. Like Fayez, he was an independent, who lent his name to Palestine, the idea, the nation, the identity, not to this or that Palestinian "front" or *tantheem*. Referring to some Palestinian intellectuals who headed new non-governmental organisations, he once told me: "We don't have to have shops (*dakakeen*) – we're independent."

Edward's message was so universal and straightforward that, on occasion, it provoked the wrath of strange bedfellows, who could not deal with his fierce nationalism, conciliatory demeanour, and empathy for both Jewish suffering and Palestinian misery at the same time. Like Gandhi's position on Zionism, Edward's opposition to the Zionist project and adherence to the "requirements of justice" did not stand in contradiction to his expressed sympathy for "the life-long persecution of the Jews".

That reality was underscored by the fact that Edward's Israeli-Argentinian friend Daniel Barenboim, the distinguished pianist and Chief Conductor for Life of the Staatskapelle Berlin, played four pieces of Edward's favourite music at his funeral in Riverside Church near the Columbia campus, where he had lived and taught for four decades. Together, for the previous five years, Barenboim and Said had organised the East-West Divan Workshop in order to train young Arab and Israeli musicians. That project will remain forever a testimony to the fact that the future of Palestine must be charted by a joint struggle for equal co-existence, the only alternative to oppression and perpetual conflict.

Those who described Edward in the 1980s as Arafat's spokesperson in New York forgot to add that Edward was never a mouthpiece for anybody. Nor was he a speechwriter for Arafat when he wrote his famous "Gun and Olive Branch" General Assembly speech in 1974, or when in Algiers he drafted the Palestinian Declaration of Independence (1988). These were Palestinian documents reflecting the spirit of the age.

When Arafat abandoned the Palestinian consensus, opting for the open-ended Oslo agreement, Edward could not tolerate that new low in the lengthening record of Palestinian concessions. Edward's sharp criticism spared neither Arafat nor his associates, whom he publicly named as complicit. I will never forget Edward referring to these Palestinian intellectuals and luminaries by name at a panel we shared together during the mid-nineties in Washington. On that occasion, Edward's rebuke of Arafat's pandering to Washington included certain words that elicited a shy smile from Edward's daughter sitting in the front seat as well as a disclaimer from the president of the Arab-American organisation sponsoring the event. Edward said: "Even Adeed of Somalia told the Americans to f__ themselves." The break with Arafat resulted in the banning of Edward's books in Arafat's domain, Edward's native homeland.

It is rather ironical that Edward's battle against leukaemia and what some have described as "the cancer of Oslo" began two years prior to the "historic handshake" of Yitzhak Rabin and Yasser Arafat at the White House on 13 September 1993, ushering in the ill-fated Oslo process. In the context of the anticipated Madrid Conference held in October/November 1991 under the auspices of the US and the ailing USSR, which opened up fruitless negotiations between Israel and the Palestinians in Washington for the next eleven months, Edward invited a group of us to a meeting in London on 6 September 1991, one of his "what is to be done" sessions that he would convene when the going was rough. Sadly, he received the ominous news of his leukaemia during that very session. He had invited some twenty-four Palestinians from four continents to put our heads together in order to face yet another challenge. At our opening session, Edward outlined the goals of the meeting:

> The PLO is in bad shape, but we are not focusing on criticism now. We are not here to discuss strategies of the peace conference, and how to reform the PLO. We need to coordinate our efforts … and create a model of cooperative work … Can we lift an inch of the occupation? There is a need to connect Israel with the occupation … we need to share knowledge and experience, to create a permanent network to acquire resources, to provide a model for others – a collective will to make a difference, … to de-legitimise the occupation.

At that meeting, a speaker from the African National Congress, invited by Edward, helped set the tone: "When we began to relate to the diplomatic dimension in 1989 because the world was changing and insisting on peaceful resolution, we did not abandon the struggle, the people." The message was very clear: You do not sign away your national rights under the guise of negotiations. Whatever Edward and we said in the next several months was ignored. Arafat was no longer willing to listen to Edward's advice. After all, Arafat's appearance at the White House in September 1993, itself an act of surrender, was misconstrued by Arafat as a sign of a final arrival. There was no longer any need for principled interlocutors such as Edward Said or his friends. The Palestinian leadership was embracing its own brand of autocracy: the Oslo agreement was "examined" by fewer than six Palestinians.

Shortly afterwards, Edward's worst suspicions were confirmed. A truncated, divided Palestinian state is not what the Palestinian people have struggled for. An independent state within the Oslo framework is not likely to succeed either. The Oslo agreement was merely a diplomatic cover for additional Israeli territorial expansionism under "peaceful conditions". Meanwhile, the privations and hardships associated with Palestinians' status as either refugees or an occupied population, or second-class citizens would continue to retard Palestinian political development despite all the trappings of statehood. (The Palestinian Authority created a president without executive power, a council without legislative powers, courts with insignificant jurisdiction, an over-blown civilian bureaucracy prone to corruption, and a pervasive military apparatus focused on suppressing dissent.)

Edward Said realised that any realistic alternative to Oslo must guarantee the removal of the incapacities inflicted on the Palestinians in the three spheres (those living in the 1967 occupied territories of the West Bank, Gaza and East Jerusalem those inside Israel and the 4 million exiles). No degree of independence or liberation could be meaningful without removing the legal, social, and economic disabilities that both set the Palestinians apart and divide them into three segments. That would require a determined systematic and protracted struggle, combining the three segments of the Palestinian people jointly with Israeli Jews who wish to be neither master of another people, nor privileged in an apartheid system, nor colonial settlers denying the existence of the indigenous natives of the land, nor wishing their disappearance.

The goal of the struggle would have to be anchored in humanitarian and customary international law, which upholds the right of return and self-determination. It would be based on the equal protection under the law in any such unified state – as in the 14th amendment to the US Constitution: the illegality of any disparity or classification in protection of the law, the end of group segregation, and its removal from the social, economic and legal fabrics of society. Equality for every single human being in Palestine-Israel would be the motto of the new struggle. Redress of the 1948 grievances would have to be effected. Ethnic cleansing cannot be wiped away by documents such as the Beilin–Abu Mazin agreement (1994), or the Beilin–'Abed Rabbo agreement (also known as the Geneva Initiative of 2004), which negates the rights of the Palestinian refugees to return and restitution of property.

Such a joint Palestinian–Israeli struggle, of course, would be bound to collide with the interests of the major players – in Washington, in Tel Aviv, and in Ramallah. For it would signal that US domination of Middle East diplomacy had failed. It would serve as an indictment of Zionism – the classical Labour version of Rabin, Peres, and Barak, as well as the revisionist brand of Jabotinsky, Begin, Netanyahu, and Sharon. It would serve as an indictment of the narrow brand of Palestinian nationalism, which seemed either unwilling or unable to re-examine the past with all its errors, pitfalls and misconceptions.

Some have branded this kind of joint Palestinian–Israeli struggle as unrealistic, and the goal as idealistic or utopian. That vision, however, has more prospects for success than the 1993–2000 open-ended formula, whose interpretations continued to exact higher energies than its application, and whose future was doomed by a suspension of international law, by grotesque power inequality, and by the steadily eroding interest on the part of the self-styled peacemaker in reaching a principled compromise.

Only when this struggle can take place in the context of a broadened critique of the concept of Zionism inside Israel and world Jewish communities in order to include the Jewish mainstream and penetrate the consciousness of the average Israeli Jew, will the so-called peace process begin to assume truly peaceful dimensions. Only when the Palestinians decide to rediscover and reconstruct their idea of a democratic secular state framework, and transform it from an empty slogan into a viable programme that can be adapted to present realities, will the hope for real peace be rekindled. Call it a bi-national solution, or a federal system, or a cantonal system on the Swiss model, the common denominators are still equal rights, equal citizenship, plurality, co-existence and common humanity.

Having realised the effective demise of the two-state solution, Edward, like many others, began to realise the fact that Oslo's architects have inadvertently set the stage for a single non-sectarian state in all of Palestine. From that moment onward, he became a principal voice for a pluralist existence in historic Palestine. Such a vision can derive only from a long-term common Arab–Jewish struggle for equality, expressed within a single, secular, democratic republic. In that regard, he wrote the following in the *Christian Science Monitor* of 27 May 1997:

> The whole idea of trying to produce two states is at an end. The Oslo peace process is really in tatters ... The lives of Israelis and Palestinians are hopelessly intertwined. There is no way to separate them. You can have fantasy and denial or put people in ghettos. However, in reality there is a common history. Therefore, we have to find a way to live together. It may take 50 years. However, the Israeli experience will gradually turn back towards the world they really live in, the Islamic Arab world. In addition, that can only come through Palestinians.

In an interview with David Barsamian, Said again endorsed secular bi-nationalism, not only as a desirable outcome, but also as a necessary reality:

> Of course, on the West Bank, the settlers and Palestinians interact, through antipathy and hostility, but physically they're in the same place. This is something that cannot be changed by pulling people back to separate boundaries or separate states ... Then there is the demographic reality: by the year 2010, there will be demographic parity between the two, Palestinians and Israelis. The South Africans, in a country twenty times bigger than Israel, could not for long maintain apartheid. In addition, it is unlikely that a place like Israel – which is surrounded on all sides by Arab states – is going to be able to maintain what is, in effect, a system of apartheid for Palestinians. So, although a bi-national state now seems like a totally long shot and completely utopian, not to say to many people a crazy idea, it is the one idea that will allow people to live with – and not exterminate – each other.[1]

Such a state would be based on Edward Said's concept of identity. His particular concept was so unique and so original as to merit a brief mention. It reflects his universalism, his non-ethnic, non-sectarian perspective, which made him a citizen of the world. His definition of the term "Palestinian" was anyone who identifies with the suffering of the Palestinians, who resists the constraints of what Oslo's "final status settlement" really meant, and, finally, who participates in the liberation struggle:

> … we stand firm on the matter of identity as something more signifi-
> cant and politically democratic than mere residence and subservience
> to what Israel offers us. What we ask for as Palestinians is the right to
> be citizens and not just numbers in the ultimately losing game being
> played by the Oslo participants. It is worth pointing out moreover that
> Israelis will also be the losers if they accept the narrow-minded and
> ungenerous definition of the Palestinians as a subject people confined
> to a "homeland" being manipulated by their government. In a decade,
> there will be demographic parity between Jews and Arabs in historical
> Palestine. Better that we accommodate to each other sooner rather
> than later as full members of a binational secular state than go on
> fighting what has been demeaningly called a shepherd's war between
> feuding tribes. To choose that identity is to make history. Not to
> choose is to disappear.

Perhaps the best way to honour Edward's legacy is to work as diligently as he did in the defence of justice and freedom, and to resolve not to be intimidated by the vulgar pressures, the stereotypical attempts to silence our voices. Since he became inflicted with this horrible illness twelve years ago, he never let it deter him from writing, travelling and contributing. His unwavering commitment to the universal values that must govern just societies was the hallmark of his scholarship and activism. What made this epitome of the scholar-activist so special was that he never succumbed to the seduction of accommodation with those in power. He always remained true to his ideals and principles no matter the personal cost. Edward's life would have been easier had he chosen to be a detached intellectual, not having to endure the threats on his life, and the vicious attacks on his character by those who wished to censor his pen and silence his powerful voice. Those attacks were in essence a tribute to his humanity, valour, and perseverance. The ideals and principles he so ably articulated are expressed in various forms and different styles by the authors of this anthology, and will surely live on and be a source of inspiration for all freedom-loving people in our day, and for generations to come.

Notes

1 David Barsamian, "Edward W. Said", *The Progressive* (April 1999), p. 35.
2 Edward Said, 'By Birth or By Choice?" *Al-Ahram Weekly On-Line*, 28 October–3 November, 1999, issue 453, at http://weekly.ahram.org.eg/1999/453/op2.htm

Introduction
Nur Masalha

The *Nakba*, Oral History and Collective Memory

The 1948 Palestine War is known to Palestinians as the *Nakba*, the "disaster" or "catastrophe".[1] The war, which led to the creation of the state of Israel on 78 per cent of historic Palestine, resulted in the destruction of much of Palestinian society, and much of the Arab landscape, by the Zionist Yishuv, a predominantly European settler community immigrated into Palestine in the period between 1882 and 1948. From the territory occupied by the Israelis in 1948, about 90 per cent of the Palestinians were driven out – many by psychological warfare and/or military pressure and a very large number at gunpoint. The war simply provided the opportunity and the necessary background for the creation of a Jewish state largely free of Arabs. It concentrated Jewish-Zionist minds, and provided the security, military and strategic explanations and justifications for purging the Jewish state and dispossessing the Palestinian people.[2] Today some 70 per cent of Palestinians are refugees; there are over 4 million Palestinian refugees in the Middle East and many more worldwide. In 1948 the minority of Palestinians – 160,000 – who remained behind (many of them internally displaced) became second-class citizens of the state of Israel, subject to a system of military administration by a government that had confiscated the bulk of their lands. The gross and ongoing discrimination against the 1 million Palestinian citizens of Israel – and the fact that Israel continues to confiscate their land – the facts of the *Nakba*, Israel's responsibility for ethnic cleansing, the ocean of suffering of the Palestinian (internal and external) refugees, and the grotesque and continuing violation of international law, morality and human decency by the Israeli government, are some of the issues addressed in this collection.

Contributors to this collection include well-known authors and leading experts in the field of internal displacement. Structurally and thematically the collection consists of three major parts. Part One deals with evolving Israeli policies towards the internally displaced from 1948 to the present. Part Two focuses on Palestinian oral history and memory, including the oral history of the Palestinian peasantry (*fellahin*),[3] and addresses issues such as the status of the scores of "unrecognised villages" symbolised by 'Ayn Hawd (see Chapter 8 by Jonathan Cook), and Israeli-Jewish awareness of the *Nakba*. Part Three explores the issues of indigenous refugee rights and international protection, including international dimensions of the internal refugee question and durable solutions.

Methodologically the collection reflects two distinct approaches to the issue of internal displacement. The first – reflected in the first four chapters – examines evolving Israeli policies towards the internal refugees and indigenous resistance to these policies. The second approach – in chapters 5, 6, 7 and 9 – largely reflects a "history from below" or "from the ground up" approach, giving space to the perspective of the participants rather than that of the "policy-makers". The perspectives of the internally displaced are presented by incorporating original and geographically extensive oral history interviews with internal refugees, conducted by Isabelle Humphries, Mahmoud 'Issa, Hillel Cohen, Jonathan Cook, William Dalrymple and Nihad Boqa'i, and supplemented by existing published testimonies, as well as published research by Palestinian historians. The collection draws on two sets of original research in addition to an extensive range of new historiography. The first is a collection of oral testimony from internal refugees. The second consists of hitherto unexamined Israeli archival documentation. Overall the research in this collection reflects diverse sources, including published and unpublished Israeli archival documents, memoirs, collections of oral history, and interviews with the Palestinian internal refugees themselves and the use of secondary works, including recent works by Palestinian and Israeli "new historians".

The founding myths of Zionism and the state of Israel, which dictated the conceptual removal of Palestinians before, during and after their physical removal in 1948, and the invention of euphemisms such as *transfer* and *present absentees*, have been extensively discussed elsewhere.[4] The focus of this collection is on internally displaced Palestinians, who are dealt with within the wider context of the *Nakba*, collective memory and identity. While some contributors to the collection view the struggle of internally displaced Palestinians inside Israel essentially as a civil rights struggle and within the context of Israeli-Palestinian identity (Hillel Cohen, for instance), other contributors highlight the Palestinian collective national dimension of the refugee question inside Israel and link it to the wider Palestinian refugee issue (Ilan Pappé, Terry Rempel, Isabelle Humphries and Nihad Boqa'i). In general, however, the collection asserts that the Palestinian *Nakba* was collective, and that individual solutions for a few thousand internally displaced Palestinians inside Israel will not suffice. There is a need to address the questions of land and property that have symbolic, religious, national, cultural and economic significance for the Palestinian community inside Israel as a whole.

Contributors to this collection agree that the traumatic events of 1948 are, inevitably, central to both the Palestinian society of today and Palestinian history, memory and collective identity. Palestinians, hardly surprisingly, perceive their tragedy as something unique: after all the *Nakba* brought about a catastrophic rupture in modern Palestinian history. Palestinian author Salman Abu Sitta's description of the *Nakba* is a case in point:

> The Palestinian *Nakba* is unsurpassed in history. For a country to be occupied by a foreign minority, emptied almost entirely of its people, its physical and cultural landmarks obliterated, its destruction hailed as a miraculous act of God and a victory for freedom and civilised values, all done according to a premeditated plan, meticulously executed, financially and politically supported from abroad, and still maintained today, is no doubt unique.[5]

Although the ocean of *Nakba* suffering is bound to be perceived as unique by Palestinians, it is, however, resonant with all extreme human suffering, including historic Jewish suffering in Europe. This suggestion is not designed to minimise the scale and magnitude of the *Shoah* (Holocaust), or by some leap of the imagination to compare it to the *Nakba* in Palestine. However both the *Nakba* and ongoing Palestinian suffering are surely a reminder of the reality of the suffering of Jews in Europe. Some observers have remarked that it is precisely because of the Jewish *Shoah* that the truth about the *Nakba* and the continuing horrific suffering of the Palestinian people have remained largely invisible to enlightened public opinion in the West.[6] Of course acknowledging the truth of what took place in Europe can never morally justify the uprooting of another people outside Europe and the destruction of historic Palestine.

For Palestinians a main reason for the continuation of the Israeli–Palestinian conflict is the failure of the Israeli state to acknowledge the 1948 ethnic cleansing and dispossession of over 750,000 indigenous inhabitants of Palestine and their descendants. So long as this historical truth is denied or excluded, there can be no peace, no reconciliation in the Middle East. Clearly, therefore, recognition of the *Nakba* is central to the future of Palestine and Israel; recognition of the historic injury and injustice that were visited upon the Palestinians is a prerequisite for a just solution. Remembering the *Nakba* is also vital, because its most salient by-product was the Palestine refugee problem, the greatest and the most enduring refugee problem in the world.

This collection is dedicated to the memory of Professor Edward W. Said (1935–2003), one of the twentieth century's foremost public intellectuals, whose voice articulated the aspirations of the disenfranchised, the oppressed and the marginalised, and whose message was humanist and universal, extending beyond Palestine to touch wide audiences. The chapters focus on four categories of internally displaced Palestinians in Israel and the 1967 Occupied Territories. They deal with evolving Israeli policies towards internally displaced Palestinians and explore issues such as *Nakba* memory and identity, Palestinian oral history, and indigenous rights. In the last two decades we have had major contributions by Palestinian authors, some of whose accounts have been based on the oral history of the refugees themselves. Palestinian authors have also been producing data and memories of the *Nakba*,[7] compiling and recording oral history and holding annual commemorations designed to preserve the memory of the Catastrophe, while emphasising the link between refugee rights, collective identity and memory and the challenge of return. This collection, like many of Said's seminal works, is an outcome of the Palestinian experience, of dispossession and dislocation, of exile and indigenous resistance. In fact it was Said who was the first to locate the Palestinian catastrophe in a wider perspective. His critical strength was in juxtaposing the Palestinian *Nakba*, and all its horrors, with its *denial*, not only in Israel, but also in the West. In many of his works, Said exposed the Western media's attempts to sideline, if not altogether eliminate from the public domain, the tragedy of Palestine.

No less important was the way Said related directly to the historian's method in discussing the meaning and significance of the "historical document". When taking part in a two-day conference of Israeli and Palestinian historians (including Ilan Pappé, Benny Morris, Itamar Rabinowitch, Zeev Sternhell, Elias Sanbar, and myself) in Paris in 1998, Said explained in a few sentences to the attentive public at large, and to the less attentive Israeli historians in particular, what a "historical document" is.[8] The Israeli historians taking part in the Paris conference (especially Morris and Rabinowitch) expressed their almost religious belief that they were both ideologically and empirically impartial, and declared that the only reliable sources for the reconstruction of the 1948 war were in the Israeli Defence Force (IDF) archives and its documents. Said made clear that a report by a soldier from 1948 is as much an interpretation, and quite often manipulation, of the reality as any other human recollection of the same event; it was never the reality itself. By this he pointed us to the vitality and significance of oral history in the reconstruction of the past. The most horrific aspects of the *Nakba* – the dozens of massacres that accompanied the ethnic cleansing – as well as a detailed description of what "ethnic cleansing" had been from the point of view of the one "ethnically cleansed" – can only be known when such a historiographical approach is adopted.[9] Edward Said's continuing legacy is also reflected in the collection.

In the context of rural and peasant Palestinian society, oral history is a particularly useful methodology; 66 per cent of the Palestinian population in 1944 was agrarian with a literacy rate, when last officially estimated, of only 15 per cent.[10] Moreover the *Nakba*, and the political instability and repression faced by the dispersed Palestinian communities since 1948 have also impeded Palestinian researches and studies.[11] In *Palestinian Identity*, Palestinian historian Rashid Khalidi argues that modern Palestinian historiography has suffered from "inherent historical biases" and that "The views and exploits of those able to read and write are perhaps naturally more frequently recorded by historians, with their tendency to favour written records, than those of the illiterate."[12] In the absence of a rich source of contemporary Palestinian documentary records, oral history and interviews with Palestinian (internal and external) refugees are a valuable and indeed essential source for constructing a more comprehensible narrative of the experience of Palestinian refugees and internally displaced Palestinians across the Green Line (the pre-1967 border).

While Louis Starr notes that memory is "fallible, ego distorts and contradictions sometimes go unresolved", nevertheless

> Problems of evaluation are not markedly different from those inherent in the use of letters, diaries, and other primary sources…. the scholar must test the evidence in an oral history memoir for internal consistency and, whenever possible, by corroboration from other sources, often including the oral history memoirs of others on the same topic.[13]

Taken as a whole, Palestinian oral history and refugee recollections give a good idea of reality. However in the case of the Palestinian *Nakba*, oral history is not merely a choice of methodology. Rather its use can represent a decision as to whether to record any history at all.[14] Oral history is the major means of reconstructing the history of the Palestinian refugees and internally displaced Palestinians as seen from the perspective of primary subjects. Thus, incorporating Palestinian oral history is a major part of this collection. In fact more than half the collection deals with Palestinian oral history and memory, which, together with issues such as the *Nakba*, indigenous rights and international protection, the "right of return" of the Palestinian refugees, and a just solution in Palestine-Israel, constituted much of Edward Said's concerns.

Oral history has been of similar importance in the recollection and collective memorisation and memorialisation of the *Shoah*. In Israel the national memorial at *Yad va-Shem*, the "Holocaust Martyrs' and Heroes' Remembrance" institution, is predominantly based on oral history and millions of pages of testimony. It was established in 1953 by a Knesset act and located in west Jerusalem. According to its website, *Yad va-Shem* is a vast, sprawling complex of tree-studded walkways leading to museums, exhibits, archives, monuments, sculptures, and memorials. It has been entrusted with documenting the history of the Jewish people during the Holocaust period, preserving the memory and story of each of the 6 million victims, and imparting the legacy of the Holocaust to generations to come through its archives, library, school, museums and recognition of the "Righteous Among the Nations". The archive collection of *Yad va-Shem* comprises 62 million pages of documents and nearly 267,500 photographs, along with thousands of films and videotaped testimonies of survivors. The Hall of Names is a "tribute to the victims by remembering them not as anonymous numbers but as individual human beings". The "Pages of Testimony" are symbolic gravestones, which record names and biographical data of millions of martyrs, as submitted by family members and friends. To date *Yad va-Shem* has computerised 3.2 million names of Holocaust victims, compiled from approximately 2 million pages of testimony and various other lists. The collections of *Yad va-Shem* include tens of thousands of testimonies dictated, recorded or videotaped by survivors of the *Shoah* in Israel and elsewhere. The testimonies are in all the languages spoken by the survivors. A second type of testimony consists of the forms filled out by survivors or relatives of the victims containing information about individual victims, such as their names, place and date of birth, place of residence, vocation, place and circum-stances of death and so on. 2 million pages of testimony have been digitised in order to make them accessible to the public in the institution's Central Database of *Shoah* Victims' Names which went on online in September 2004.[15]

In recent years organisations set up by Palestinians inside Israel have waged a never-ending battle for the preservation of both *Nakba* memory and the cultural and material heritage of the refugees (see Chapter 1 by Nur Masalha and Chapter 3 by Nihad Boqa'i).[16] However, in contrast to the Israeli national memorial at *Yad va-Shem*, there is no *Nakba* museum, no *Nakba* Hall of Names, no Central Database of *Nakba* Victims' Names, no tombstones or monuments for the hundreds of Palestinian villages and towns ethnically cleansed and destroyed in 1948. What is more chilling, furthermore, is the fact that the Dayr Yasin massacre of 9 April 1948 took place within sight of the place that became *Yad va-Shem*; only a mile from where Jewish martyrs are memorialised lie the Palestinian martyrs of Dayr Yasin whose graves are unknown and unmarked. In fact *Yad va-Shem* itself is situated on the lands of Dayr Yasin, as is the city of Jerusalem's western (Jewish) cemetery.[17] Indeed the irony of *Yad va-Shem* and Dayr Yasin is breathtaking; very few Israelis and visitors to *Yad va-Shem* go to Dayr Yasin, and in dedication ceremonies at *Yad va-Shem* no one ever looks to the north and remembers Dayr Yasin.[18] The case of Zochrot, a grassroots Israeli organisation for raising Israeli-Jewish awareness of the Palestinian *Nakba* and refugee rights – whose activities are described by Eitan Bronstein in Chapter 9 – shows that a growing numbers of Israeli Jews regard the commemoration of the *Nakba* and implementation of the "right of return" for Palestinians as the only road to a lasting peace and reconciliation in Palestine-Israel. However the views of Zochrot activists and supporters are not typical of Israeli attitudes towards the victims of the *Nakba*-attitudes that have been extensively discussed in my work *The Politics of Denial*.[19]

While for Palestinians Dayr Yasin has remained a potent symbol of the collective *Nakba*, in Israel the ghosts of Dayr Yasin, Lubya (Chapter 7 by Mahmoud 'Issa), Kafr Bir'im (Chapter 6 by William Dalrymple) and the hundreds of villages destroyed in 1948, are completely suppressed or simply bulldozed over. 'Azmi Bishara, a leading Israeli-Palestinian intellectual and a member of the Israeli Knesset, writes:

> The villages that no longer exist were forced out of [Israeli] public awareness, away from the signposts of memory. They received new names – of Jewish settlements – but traces [of their past] were left behind, like the *sabr* bushes,[20] or the stones from fences or bricks from the demolished houses … The Arab villages have no tombstones and there are no monuments to them. There will be no equality and there will be no democracy [in Israel], and there will be no historic compromise [between Israelis and Palestinians] until they receive their tombstones. The Jewish site cast out utterly the other, the "local" i.e., the other who was in that place. The response of the [Israel-Jewish] Left to the [Palestinian use of the] nomenclature of the collective memory was that this matter must be removed from the [Jewish-Arab national] compromise, [that] there is no room in the compromise of history. History itself will prove that it must be part of the compromise – in order for the victim to forgive, he must be recognized as a victim.[21]

Categories of Internally Displaced Palestinians[22]

Categorisation and definition of the internal refugees/internally displaced Palestinians across the Green Line have to be understood against the background of three different political entities and three different historical periods: Mandatory Palestine, the State of Israel, the 1967 Occupied Territories. Delineating the difference between "refugees" and "internally displaced persons" is further complicated both by the lack of internationally recognised boundaries between Israel and Palestine and by the fact that the Israeli legislator does not recognise the term *refugee* (*laji* in Arabic, *palit* in Hebrew) as far as the Palestinian Arab inside Israel is concerned.[23] There are, however, four distinct categories of internally displaced Palestinians across the Green Line – the first and second categories are often referred to as *present absentees* (see below):

(a) *1948 internally displaced Palestinians in Israel*: The largest group of internally displaced Palestinians is located inside Israel and consists of Palestinians originally displaced and dispossessed of their homes and lands during the 1948 war or immediately after. Almost all chapters in this book address this category.

(b) *Post-1948 internally displaced Palestinians*: A second and smaller group consists of those Palestinians inside Israel who have been displaced since 1948 due, primarily, to internal transfer and eviction, land expropriation, and house demolition. A large sector of this group is comprised of Palestinian Bedouins and is dealt with in Chapter 4 on forcible relocation and sedentarisation by Isma'el Abu-Sa'ad.

(c) *1967 internally displaced Palestinians*: A third category of internally displaced persons is comprised of those Palestinians displaced within the West Bank, including east Jerusalem, and the Gaza Strip during the 1967 war. This does not include 1967 Palestinian refugees who are often referred to as "1967 displaced persons" due to the fact that at the time of their displacement the West Bank was under Jordanian control – that is, they did not cross an "international border" to seek shelter in Jordan.

(d) *Post-1967 internally displaced Palestinians*: The fourth category of internally displaced Palestinians are those Palestinians displaced within the West Bank, east Jerusalem, and the Gaza Strip after 1967 by means of land expropriation, house demolition, revocation of residency rights in Jerusalem, and other forms of internal transfer including, more recently, forced separation along ethnic, religious and national lines. This group also includes a large number of Bedouin. The last two groups are dealt with in Chapter 11 by Terry Rempel.

To complicate matters of categorisation and definition, Palestinians internally displaced from west to east Jerusalem in 1948, for example, were considered "refugees" because of the creation of a functional "border" between the two sides of the city, namely the 1949 armistice line. Setting aside the legal implications of Israel's military occupation of the West Bank (including east Jerusalem), and the Gaza Strip, the removal of the physical barrier between west and east Jerusalem in 1967 would suggest that 1948 refugees from western Jerusalem residing in the eastern part of the city were no longer refugees but "internally displaced persons".

Conflicting Estimates and Lack of Data[24]

There are no precise statistics on the internally displaced Palestinians either in Israel or in the 1967 Occupied Territories. Overall the data on the internally displaced Palestinians and their social and economic conditions have serious shortcomings. As with other groups of internally displaced persons worldwide, there is a lack of comprehensive and systematic data. There is no registration system for internally displaced Palestinians[25] and official data on the current status of Palestinians inside Israel and in the 1967 Occupied Territories do not distinguish between internally displaced Palestinians and the general Palestinian population. As with refugees, it may be assumed that internally displaced Palestinians have relatively lower standards of living than Palestinians who are not displaced. However recent surveys of the 1967 Occupied Territories suggest that Israel's military response to the second Palestinian uprising (*intifada*) has led to a narrowing of the socio-economic gap between refugees and non-refugees.[26] Nevertheless distinctions between refugees and non-refugees remain according to area of residence – that is, between camp populations and non-camp populations. In general, data on the current status of internally displaced Palestinians is characterised both by its uneven quality and its uncertainty and is derived largely from historical documents, news reports, and human rights documentation.

Estimates of the total number of internally displaced Palestinians inside Israel and in the 1967 Occupied Territories vary according to source, available data, and applicable definition of internally displaced persons. According to Terry Rempel of the Badil Center for Palestinian Residency and Refugee Rights in Bethlehem, there are approximately 260,000 1948 internally displaced Palestinians (category A described above), who comprise around one-quarter of the total Palestinian population inside Israel.[27] This estimate, however, does not include those displaced and forcibly relocated after 1948,[28] especially the Bedouins in the Negev (discussed in Chapter 4 by Abu-Sa'ad), and the inhabitants of urban areas such as Haifa and Acre, who were permitted to return to their cities of origin but denied the right to repossess their homes and properties. Also not included are Palestinians who were transferred after 1949 from outlying village settlements (*khirba*) to the village proper in the Wadi 'Ara valley and Palestinians who remained in their villages but lost their lands. Taking into consideration all these categories, according to

Rempel, the total number of internally displaced Palestinians inside Israel today exceeds 300,000–350,000 persons.[29]

Rempel's figures for category A are in harmony with estimates made by Israeli-Palestinian researchers and by 'Adalah (Justice), the Legal Centre for Arab Minority Rights in Israel.[30] There are, however, few estimates for the three categories of B C and D internally displaced Palestinians described above. Conservative estimates for these three categories are as follows: 75,000 Palestinians internally displaced in Israel after 1948;[31] 10,000 1967 internally displaced Palestinians;[32] and, 50,000–100,000 Palestinians displaced internally in the West Bank, east Jerusalem, and the Gaza Strip after 1967.[33] According to Rempel, the total size of the internally displaced population inside Israel and the 1967 Occupied Territories may be as high as 450,000 persons.[34]

Israeli-Jewish authors such Hillel Cohen, Charles Kamen and Meron Benvenisti, on the other hand – although critical of Israeli policies towards the internal refugees – have suggested more conservative estimates of the numbers of internally displaced Palestinians inside Israel They also tend to rely, in part, on official Israeli documents which put the number of internal refugees in 1951 at 23,000 to 35,000, located mainly in the Galilee, constituting 15 to 20 per cent of the total Arab population in Israel.[35] These figures, however, were only for urban and rural refugees and did not include the Bedouin in the Negev, many of whom were forced to leave their places of residence for areas determined by the Israeli army (Chapter 4). Hillel Cohen, in Chapter 2, puts the current figures for internally displaced Palestinians in Israel at 150,000–170,000. He also argues that in 1950 there were about 25,000–30,000 internally displaced Palestinians out of a total 160,000 Palestinians in Israel and that there is no reason to think that their overall proportion in the population has increased since then; hence, their current proportion is about 15 per cent of the Palestinian population in Israel. A small-scale census conducted by Sami Smooha, of Haifa University, in the 1980s came up with the same result. Although higher figures are put forward, in Cohen's opinion, they are the result of:

(a) including the Bedouin of the Negev who were forcibly relocated in 1949–51;

(b) including other groups of *present absentees*, such as villagers from the Little Triangle, whose lands were transferred to the Israeli Custodian

of Absentees Properties before the Rhodes Truce Agreements of
1949, and who ended up losing their lands, although remaining in
their villages of origin;
(c) including refugees from cities (mainly from Haifa) who returned to
their cities, but not to their original houses;
(d) the existence of a specific Israeli document which cites the figure of
40,000 internal refugees in 1950, and on which some writers have
based their assessment. But this figure also includes Jewish internal
refugees from the old city of Jerusalem, Gush 'Etzion and other
Jewish groups. Therefore, according to Cohen, this 1950 figure of
40,000 cannot be the basis for calculating the number of internally
displaced Palestinians in Israel.[36]

Although Israeli, Palestinian and international organisations have
devoted considerable attention to the question of how many Palestinian
refugees were outside Israel after 1948, there has been very little public
concern regarding the number of those Palestinians who became internal
refugees in Israel. The Israeli population censuses carried out in 1948 and
in 1961 did not include questions designed to distinguish between Israeli
Arabs who had become internally displaced and those who had not. This
lack of attention to the internal refugees was deliberate. It is also consistent with the general neglect suffered by the Palestinian citizens of Israel.
Another reason for the lack of official Israeli statistics was the unwillingness on the part of official circles to draw attention to the existence of the
internal refugees and their awkward situation by providing a means of
identifying them. The identification of their problem would have served
as a reminder that the Palestinian refugee problem created in 1948 also
existed within Israel, although its scope, in comparison with the wider
Palestinian refugee problem (the problem of those 750,000 Palestinian
refugees who in 1948 were driven out from the would-be Jewish state,
and their descendants), was limited, and its nature unique.[37]

Israeli Policies, Indigenous Resistance and Peacemaking

In the 1950s the internally displaced Palestinians inside Israel were considered – with kafkaesque irony by the Israeli bureaucracy – as *present
absentees* (*nifkadim nokhahim*[38]) under the Absentees' Property Law of 1950
(which is discussed in Chapter 1).[39] They were *present* physically but legally

and conceptually *absent* in relation to their homes and lands of origin. Acquiring the paradoxical title of *present absentees*, the internally displaced had their property and homes taken by the state, making them refugees and exiles within their own homeland. Most of them had been forced under military orders to leave their villages during the 1948–49 war; they had locked their doors, taken their keys and land deeds, and planned to return as soon as the Israel army allowed. Internal movements of the Palestinian population during 1948–49 continued for many months and in 1950 Palestinians were still being expelled by Israeli forces from localities where they had managed to hang on for two years.[40] Other evictions carried out in the post-1948–49 period were designed to break up areas of Arab concentration under the pretext of security needs.[41] The Palestinian internal refugees inside Israel are *present absentees* because most of them have never left the country, remaining through the 1948-49 war and the years following.[42] According to unjust laws passed to gain Arab land for the state, especially the Absentees' Property Law of 1950, they are considered *absentees* because they left their original villages, regardless of the reason. Although the 1948 internally displaced Palestinians were eventually accorded Israeli citizenship under the 1952 Israeli Nationality Law, as *present absentees* they – and their children – have been systematically prevented from returning to their homes and lands or regaining their property. Successive policies adopted by the Jewish state – military and diplomatic, legal and political – were aimed at consolidating the power and domination of Israel's Jewish majority. A key element in this effort was the prevention of the return of Palestinian refugees – residing inside and outside the borders of the state of Israel – to their ancestral homes and properties. This objective has served until today as a guiding premise underlying Israeli policy concerning the internal refugees.

The *present absentees* have found themselves in a unique situation. Despite their historical, geographic, cultural and national ties with the Palestinian people, they are internal refugees in their own homeland and their special situation is shared with the Palestinian community in Israel. They hold Israeli citizenship, a fact that distinguishes them from all other Palestinian refugee communities in the region. In addition, the "internal refugees" have been conspicuous by their long absence from the international agenda and the denial of international refugee aid to them; UNRWA's operations in Israel were discontinued in July 1952. Sharing common memories of their towns and villages of origins, they have formed a distinct group among the Israeli Palestinians: "a minority within the minority". They formed a separate social category which was very noticeable in the Arab villages and towns, and the Arabic word for "refugee", *laji*, became commonly used among the Arabs in Israel to refer to the "internally displaced".[43] The vast majority of them are Muslim (about 90 per cent) and the remainder are Christians; the Druze are not represented among the internally displaced refugees since no Druze permanently left their villages.[44] The internally displaced differ from the Palestinian "external refugees" in another respect: they came exclusively from rural agricultural areas, whereas the "external refugees" originated from both urban and rural populations.[45]

In terms of their geographical distribution, the overwhelming majority of the internally displaced originated from, and currently live (like most of the Palestinians in Israel) in the northern part of the country, in the Palestine mandatory government districts of Safad, Acre, Haifa, Baysan and Tiberias.[46] A study carried out by Charles Kamen in the mid-1980s found that a substantial number of the residents of completely destroyed villages in the northern part of the country, such as al-Mujaydil, al-Damun, al-Birwa, Iqrit, Kafr Bir'im, al-Ruways, Haditha, Ma'lul, al-Muftakhara, al-Mansura and Qumiya, remained in Israel.[47] To this list one should add other destroyed villages such Hittin, Nimrin, al-Shajara, 'Arab al-Khisas, 'Arab al-Baqqara, al-Kabri, al-Zib, al-Bassa, 'Amqa, al-Shaykh Dawud, al-Ghabisiyya, al-Farradiyya, al-Manshiyya, Mi'ar, al-Nahr, Suhmata, Tarbikha, Umm al-Faraj, and Saffuriyya. The latter's former residents, for instance, currently occupy a whole quarter in Nazareth. Apparently the internally displaced Palestinians inside Israel are currently residing in around eighty villages and towns; their movements caused the Arab populations of various localities in Israel to increase or decrease. Most of them had found temporary places of asylum in, and were eventually absorbed into, the remaining nearby Arab localities, situated on average between three and sixteen kilometres from their original place of residence.[48] In his study Kamen found that half of the inhabitants of Judyada are refugees, as are one-third of the population of Majd al-Korum, and almost one-third of that of Rama and Jish; one-fourth of the population of Nazareth,[49] Kafr Yasif and Yafa (near Nazareth) are refugees.[50] Also a few of the internally displaced today live in the most impoverished and overcrowded neighbourhoods of what are now "mixed towns" – the previously Arab towns of Jaffa, Acre, Lydda and Ramle.[51]

It should be pointed out that the desire among many of the internally displaced to return to their "original" homes and "personal territory" is not just based on nostalgia for the past or yearning for the "lost paradise" but rather is derived from existential and day-to-day problems, including the pressing need for housing among the internal refugees and their descendants and the ever-shrinking land surface areas available to Arab villages and towns in Israel.[52]

The history, rights and needs of Palestinian internal refugees have been excluded from recent Middle East peacemaking efforts. In Chapter 9 ("The *Nakba* in Hebrew") Eitan Bronstein calls on Jewish-Israelis to assess critically the role played by their leaders in the destruction of historic Palestine and in violations of basic human rights and international law. In the concluding Chapters 10 and 11 Israeli historian Ilan Pappé and Terry Rempel both draw attention to the fact that, although the situation of the internal refugees has remained off the agenda of Israeli–Palestinian negotiations, it is, however, generally viewed as an integral part of the overall Palestine refugee question. Moreover, although they are an integral part of both the Palestinian national minority in Israel and the Palestinian people, their continued existence as a separate social category, and as refugees in their own homeland, make them potential candidates for special concern.

The indigenous struggle to publicise the truth about the *Nakba* and the refugees, and to institutionalise *Nakba* commemoration, have been vital ways of keeping the hope for peace with justice alive. The growing cooperation in this regard of Palestinians and Israeli Jews, through grass-roots organisations like Ittijah and Zochrot, and through the Haifa Right of Return conference of 26–28 March 2004, which attracted more than 300 people of whom about a hundred were Israeli Jews, were two heartening examples. But there is also a need for various projects such as educational workshops on the *Nakba*, a *Nakba* Museum and the institutionalisation of a *Nakba* Memorial Day. It is also hoped that this collection will be a major contribution to the struggle for protecting the *Nakba* memory against its denial in Israel and around the world, and for relocating the right of return at the centre of peacemaking in the Middle East. Clearly there is a need for a new approach to peacemaking in Palestine-Israel based on a recognition that the root cause of the Israeli–Palestinian conflict is the *Nakba* during which hundreds of thousands of Palestinians were ethnically cleansed and dispossessed. Righting of the wrongs inflicted in the *Nakba*, and redressing the evils inflicted on the Palestinians ever since, would allow, for the first time, both citizens and returnees to enjoy a normal and peaceful life on a democratic and equal basis in Palestine-Israel. Israeli historian Pappé elaborates on this point by calling for Israeli accountability for the *Nakba*. There can be no peace in the region until there is accountability, acknowledgement and acceptance of Israel's role in the continuing conflict between Israelis and Palestinians. Rempel, furthermore, draws attention to the role of public participation in peacemaking, and the inclusion of international human rights principles and the recognition of refugee rights in successful peace agreements.

Notes

1 One of the first to label it *Nakba* was Constantine Zurayk distinguished philosopher of Arab history and liberal intellectual, in his book *Ma'na al-Nakba* (The Meaning of the Disaster), a self-critical analysis of the socio-economic causes of the Arab defeat in 1948, written immediately after the 1948 war. An English edition was published in 1956 under the title: *Palestine: The Meaning of the Disaster* (Beirut: Khayat, 1956). The term also became the title of the monumental work of Palestinian historian 'Arif Al-'Arif, *Al-Nakba: Nakbat Bayt al-Maqdis Wal-Firdaws al-Mafqud 1947–1952* (*The Disaster: The Disaster of Jerusalem and the Lost Paradise 1947–52*), 6 volumes (Beirut and Sidon, Lebanon: al-Maktaba al-'Asriyya, 1958–1960 [Arabic]).

2 For extensive discussion of Zionist expulsion and ethnic cleansing policies in 1948, see my works, *Expulsion of the Palestinians: The Concept of "Transfer" in Zionist Political Thought, 1882–1948* (Washington DC: Institute for Palestine Studies, 1992); *A Land Without a People* (London: Faber and Faber, 1997); *The Politics of Denial: Israel and the Palestinian Refugee Problem* (London: Pluto Press, 2003).

3 Singular *fellah*, the word used in Arabic for "ploughman" or "tiller", the word used in Arabic-speaking countries to designate peasantry.

4 See my works *Expulsion of the Palestinians*; *A Land Without a People*; *The Politics of Denial*; and *Imperial Israel and the Palestinians* (London: Pluto Press, 2003); also Gabriel Piterberg, "Erasure," *New Left Review* 10 (July–August 2001), at: http://www.newleftreview.net/NLR24402.shtml#_edn23 (accessed on 16 September 2004).

5 Salman Abu Sitta, *The Palestinian Nakba 1948: The Register of Depopulated Localities in Palestine* (London: Palestinian Return Centre, 1998), p.5.

6 See, for instance Uri Davis, *Apartheid Israel: Possibilities for the Struggle Within* (London and New York: Zed Books, 2003), p. 18.

7 Examples include my work *Expulsion of the Palestinians*; Walid Khalidi, *All That Remains* (Washington DC: Institute for Palestine Studies, 1992); Abu Sitta, *The Palestinian Nakba 1948*.

8 Ilan Pappé, "Palestine and Truth, Culture and Imperialism: The Legacy of Edward W. Said", *Holy Land Studies: A Multidisciplinary Journal* 2, No.2 (March 2004), p.137.

9 'Ibid.

10 Rose Esber, "*War and Displacement in Mandate Palestine 29 November 1947 to 15 May 1948*", Unpublished History thesis, SOAS, University of London, March 2003, p.22.

11 Rashid Khalidi, *Palestinian Identity: The Construction of Modern National Consciousness* (New York: Columbia University Press, 1997), p.89.

12 Khalidi, *Palestinian Identity*, p.89.

13 Louis Starr, "Oral History", in David K. Dunaway and Willa K. Baurn (eds.), *Oral History: An Interdisciplinary Anthology* (Tennessee: American Association for State and Local History, 1984), pp.4-5.

14 For further discussion see, Esber, *War and Displacement in Mandate Palestine*.

15 Yad va-Shem website at:
    http://www.yad-vashem.org.il/about_yad/ index_about_yad.html.

16 See also Gideon Levy, "Twilight Zone/Social Studies Lesson", *Haaretz*, 31 March 2004, at:
    http://www.haaretz.com/hasen/spages/410906.html; Meron Benvenisti, *Sacred Landscape: The Buried History of the Holy Land Since 1948* (Berkeley: University of California Press, 2000), pp.267-9.

17 Davis, *Apartheid Israel*, p.35.

18 Daniel McGowan, "Deir Yassin Remembered" in *Remembering Deir Yassin: The Future of Israel and Palestine*, edited by Daniel McGowan and Marc H. Ellis (New York: Olive Branch Press, 1998), pp.6-7.

19 See note 2.

20 *Sabr* is the Arabic name for a type of cactus that flourishes in Palestine.

21 'Azmi Bishara, "Between Place and Space", *Studio* [Hebrew] 37, October 1992, quoted in Meron Benvenisti, *Sacred Landscape*, p.267.

22 The editor gratefully acknowledges the very useful information provided by Terry Rempel, of Badil Resource Center in Bethlehem, on the various categories of internally displaced Palestinians.

23 Davis, *Apartheid Israel*, p.100.

24 Some of the data on the Palestinians displaced inside Israel and in the 1967 Occupied Territories were provided by Terry Rempel and Hillel Cohen.

25 Early registration and census information exists for 1948 internally displaced Palestinians. Internally displaced Palestinians requiring assistance were originally registered with the UN Relief and Works Agency for Palestine Refugees (UNRWA). Initial registration files for 1948 internally displaced include six boxes consisting of 11,304 family cards and 5,155 correction cards. Each card contains the names, ages, sex, occupation, past address, and "distribution centre" to which the family was attached. For more details on the UNRWA registration system see Salim Tamari and Elia Zureik, "UNRWA Archives on Palestinian Refugees", *Reinterpreting the Historical Record: The Uses of Palestinian Refugee Archives for Social Science Research and Policy Analysis* (Jerusalem: Institute of Jerusalem Studies and

Institute for Palestine Studies, 2001), pp.25-60.

26 See *Palestinian Public Perceptions on Their Living Conditions, The Role of International and Local Aid during the Second Intifada*, Report VI. Geneva: Graduate Institute of Development Studies, University of Geneva, September 2003.

27 Derived from initial registration figures from UNRWA in *Report of the Director of the United Nations Relief and Works Agency for Palestine Refugees in the Near East*. UN Doc. A/1905, 30 June 1951 and the average annual growth rate of the Palestinian population inside Israel between 1950 and 2001. For further estimates, see Wakim Wakim, *"Lajiun fil Watan: Al-Hadirun al-Ghaibun fi Israel"* [Refugees in the Homeland: Present Absentees in Israel], *Majallat al-Dirasat al-Filastiniyah* 45/46 (Winter/Spring 2001 [Arabic]); *Profile of Internal Displacement: Israel* – Compilation of information available in the Global Internally Displaced Database of the Norwegian Refugee Council (as of 14 January 2002). Geneva: Norwegian Refugee Council/Global Internally Displaced Project, 2002.

28 Badil Resource Center (2002) puts the number of the internally displaced in the post-1948 period at 75,000.

29 Information provided by Rempel.

30 In 1988 the Israeli-Palestinian sociologist Majid al-Haj, of Haifa University, put the figure at 200,000. Majid al-Haj, "The Arab Internal Refugees: The Emergence of a Minority Within the Minorities", *Immigrants and Minorities* 7, no.2 (1988), pp.149-65; Majid al-Haj, "Adjustment Patterns of the Arab Internal refugees in Israel", *Internal Migration* 24, no.3 (1986), pp.651-73. 'Adalah-Legal Centre for Arab Minority Rights in Israel, History of the Arabs in Israel, at: http://www.adalah.org/ histlegal.htm (accessed on 20 November 2000). See also Riad Beidas, "The Internally Displaced – Seeking Return Within One's Own Land: An Interview with Wakim Wakim", *Journal of Palestine Studies*, 31, no. 1 (Autumn 2001), p.33. Various estimates of the internally displaced are based on a report by the Director of the United Nations Relief and Works Agency for Palestine Refugees in the Near East, and on the annual birth rate of the Muslims in Israel which reached 4.2 per cent in the period between 1950 and 2001 (Israel Central Bureau of Statistics, 2002, Statistical Abstract of Israel, No.53. cited in Badil 2003). The Badil Resource Center (2003) estimates the number of internally displaced who were displaced in 1948 at only approximately 274,000 in 2002 (around 285,000 in 2003). Some Palestinian researchers give "higher" estimates. Ramzi Rabah estimates the number of the internally displaced inside Israel as 300,000 persons in 1996, while Uri Davis put the figure at 250,000; Davis, *Apartheid Israel*, p.100.

31 The majority are Bedouins forced off large tracts of land in the Negev and living in "unrecognised villages" or concentrated into so-called development towns. The remaining displaced persons include other Palestinians who were transferred by the government during the late 1940s and early 1950s; Palestinians displaced by land expropriation; and Palestinians displaced as a result of house demolition. It is unclear how many affected families have not been able to return to their homes of origin and remain displaced.

32 The majority are persons displaced internally from the villages of 'Imwas, Yalu,

Bayt Nuba, Bayt Marsam, Bayt 'Awa, Habla and Jiftlik, as well as from the city of Qalqilya and the old city of Jerusalem, including the entire Mughrabi quarter. It is unclear how many affected families remain internally displaced. See Masalha, *A Land Without a People*, pp.80-90; Masalha, *The Politics of Denial*, pp.189-211.

33 This figure includes persons deprived of residency status in eastern Jerusalem and Palestinians displaced as a result of land expropriation and house demolition. It is unclear how many affected families have not been able to return to their homes of origin and remain displaced. See also *Profile of Internal Displacement: Palestinian Territories: Compilation of the Information*, available in the Global Internally Displaced Database of the Norwegian Refugee Council (as of 29 July 2003) (Geneva: Norwegian Refugee Council/Global Internally Displaced Project, 2003).

34 Information provided by Rempel.

35 Hillel Cohen puts the figure at 15 per cent. See his work *Hanifkadim Hanokhahim: Haplitim Hafalastinayyim Beyisrael Mea$z$ 1948* [The Present Absentees: The Palestinian Refugees in Israel Since 1948] (Jerusalem. The Van Leer Institute and the Institute for Israeli-Arab Studies, 2000 [Hebrew]); see also David Grossman, *Nokhahim Nifkadim* [Present Absentees] (Tel Aviv: Kibbutz Meuhad Publications, 1992 [Hebrew]), p.15. An English edition was published (London: Jonathan Cape, 1993), entitled *Sleeping on a Wire*. Charles Kamen wrote that in 1948–49 the number was approximately 23,000. Charles S. Kamen, "After the Catastrophe I: The Arabs in Israel", *Middle Eastern Studies* 23, no. 4 (October 1987), pp.468-70. Meron Benvenisti puts the number at 30,000 to 35,000, or 17 to 20 per cent of all Palestinian residents of Israel. Benvenisti, *Sacred Landscape*, pp. 200201. The Israeli estimates rely on a document of the Ministry Of Labour of 29 June 1952, Israel State Archives, Ministry of Labour files, 6178/2924, and also a Jewish National Fund census for 1949–50 dated 15 February 1950 from the Central Zionist Archives (Jerusalem), file KKI, 5/18875.

36 Personal communication, dated 4 January 2004.

37 Kamen, "After the Catastrophe I", p.466.

38 See, for instance, Cohen, *Hanifkadim Hanokhahim*. The Israeli author David Grossman described Israeli-Palestinians in 1992 as *"Nokhahim Nifkadim"* ("Present Absentees") in terms of their political and social power. David Grossman, *Nokhahim Nifkadim* [Present Absentees] (Tel Aviv: Kibbutz Meuhad Publications, 1992 [Hebrew]).

39 The term relates to the status of the internally displaced under Israel's 1950 Absentees' Property Law, *Laws of the State of Israel*, Vol.4, Ordinances, 5710 (1949/50), pp.68-82. The original draft law was amended to prevent internally displaced Palestinians and those refugees in the West Bank and Gaza Strip from returning to their homes. In the case of the latter, Israeli officials were concerned that if the West Bank and Gaza Strip fell under Israeli jurisdiction in the future, Israel would be obligated to allow the refugees to return to their homes. For critical comments on the law, see Tom Segev, *1949: The First Israelis* (New York: The Free Press, 1986), p.80, and Alina Korn, "The Arab Minority in Israel during the Military Government (1948–1966)". unpublished PhD dissertation, the Hebrew University of Jerusalem, 1991, pp.91-6 [Hebrew]); Piterberg, "Erasure".

40 Charles S. Kamen, "After the Catastrophe I: The Arabs in Israel", *Middle Eastern Studies* 23, no.4 (October 1987), p.466.

41 *Discrimination Diary, 25 May 2000*, The Arab Association for Human Rights, at: http://www.arabhra.org/dd/dd225.htm (accessed on 8 December 2001).

42 Although there is no possibility of arriving at a reliable estimate of the number of "returnees", a study conducted by Majid al-Haj found that 45 per cent of the original 37,500 "internal refugees" first moved to neighbouring Arab countries, before returning back to Israel shortly after 1948. Majid Al-Haj, "The Arab Internal Refugees in Israel: The Emergence of a Minority Within the Minority", in Ian Lustick (ed.) *Palestinians under Israeli Rule* (New York: Garland Publishing Inc., 1994), pp.5-6.

43 Nearly 50 per cent of the marriages of the internally displaced take place within their original community. Majid Al-Haj, "The Arab Internal Refugees in Israel, pp.5-6 and 16. See also Ahmad Ashkar, "Internal Refugees: Their Inalienable Right to Return", *News From Within* 9, no.8 (August 1995), p.14-17; Kamen, "After the Catastrophe I", p.467.

44 al-Haj, "The Arab Internal Refugees in Israel", p.9.

45 Ibid.

46 Kamen, "After the Catastrophe I", p.470.

47 Ibid., p.471.

48 al-Haj, "The Arab Internal Refugees in Israel", pp.5-6.

49 In April 1949, Nazareth, eight months after it was captured, had 5,222 refugees; an additional 7,334 refugees were found in the surrounding villages. Most of the refugees in Nazareth had come from towns or from large villages: one-third came from Haifa, and slightly less than one-quarter (or 1,200) came from al-Mujaydil, five kilometres south of Nazareth, whose inhabitants had been expelled to the town after the village had been captured. Ten per cent of the Nazareth refugees were from Tiberias, and a similar proportion (560 persons) came from 'Illut, a village which lay five kilometres to the west. 42 families of refugees were from Baysan. Only the refugees from Haifa, 'Illut and Na'ura (six person) had the possibility of returning to their former localities. Charles S. Kamen, "After the Catastrophe II: The Arabs in Israel, 1948–51", *Middle Eastern Studies*, 24, no.1 (January 1988), pp.78-9.

50 Kamen, 'After the Catastrophe I', p.474.

51 Joseph Schechla, "The Invisible People Come to Light: Israel's 'Internally Displaced' and the 'Unrecognized Villages'", *Journal of Palestine Studies* 31, no.1 (Autumn 2001), p.22.

52 Beidas, "The Internally Displaced", p.34.

PART ONE
Evolving Israeli Policies and
Indigenous Resistance

1
Present Absentees and Indigenous Resistance
Nur Masalha

Israeli Policies During the Post-*Nakba* Period
The Military Administration (1948–66)
Historically, a combination of military–strategic, demographic-land settlement, and Zionist ideological considerations governed Israel's land policies during the post-*Nakba* period towards the Palestinian citizens of Israel, including the internally displaced. The internal refugees, who constitute some 25 per cent of the total of 1 million Palestinian citizens of Israel, are described by Israeli law as *present absentees*. Land and settlement expansion, in particular, have always been at the heart of the conflict between the Zionist immigrants/settlers and the native Palestinians. Prior to the 1948 *Nakba* ("Catastrophe") the Palestinian community had been overwhelmingly rural; the Palestinians had been the overwhelming majority in the country and had owned much of the land, while the Jewish community in Palestine (the Yishuv) had been (in 1947) about one-third of the total population and had owned about 6 per cent of the land. Hence the quest for land had underpinned the Zionist project in the pre-1948 period. In a sense, in the post-*Nakba* period the Israeli state's long-lasting battle against the Palestinian community inside Israel was a battle for "more land". This battle essentially was dictated by the Jewish state's premises and fundamentals:

(a) the "ingathering" of the world's Jews in Israel (*kibbutz galoyut*);
(b) the acquisition, takeover and conquest of land (*kibbush haadama*);
(c) the consolidation of Jewish demography in a state created exclusively for the Jews – who mostly had yet to arrive in Israel – at the expense of the displaced, "transferred" and internally relocated Palestinians;

(d) Jewish "population dispersion" throughout the country (*pezur ochlosiya*);

(e) Judaisation of the Galilee (*yehud hagalil*).

The establishment of Israel in 1948 did not alter Zionism's premises and fundamentals with regard to the Palestinian community remaining under Israeli control. Indeed, the principal objectives of the Israeli state, as defined in terms of its Zionist ideology, have been the fulfilment of the Jewish majority's aspirations, and those of would-be Jewish immigrants, frequently at the expense of the aspirations of the Palestinian community (including the internal refugees).

For the remaining Palestinian citizens of Israel, their attachment to the land of their ancestors can hardly be overstated. Prior to the *Nakba*, Palestinian society was overwhelmingly rural, agriculture was the major source of livelihood, and farming the land was the backbone of the Palestinian economy. For the indigenous inhabitants of Palestine, the land was a means of livelihood, a symbol of identity, survival and security in the face of the 1948 expulsions, dispossession and dispersal of their compatriots. The issue of land use and development has always been crucially important for the survival of the Palestinian community inside Israel. Dispossession by land expropriation is probably the most significant aspect of the policy of deprivation pursued by Israel against this national community. Predicated on the Zionist premise of more land for the Jewish would-be newcomers and settlers, Israel's policy of land confiscation destroyed the livelihood of many Israeli Arabs, severely curtailed the development of Arab localities, and threatened to undermine the very survival of a territorially based Palestinian community in Israel.

The *Nakba* brought enormous disruption to the economy of the remaining Palestinian population in Israel, including the internally displaced. The outcome of the 1948–49 war and the cease-fire agreements between Israel and the Arab countries of 1949 left Israel in control of over 5 million acres of Palestinian land, mostly belonging to the external refugees; the property of the internally displaced consisted of about 300,000 *dunums* of land, which the Israeli state declared to be "absentee property".[1] Soon after the 1948 war, the Israeli authorities confiscated nearly 1 million acres of Palestinian refugee land.[2] First the Israeli state took over the land of the "external refugees", who were barred from returning, whilst the remaining Palestinian community was subsequently subjected to laws and regulations that effectively deprived it of most of its land. The history of expropriation began immediately after 1948. The massive drive to take over Arab land, belonging to Palestinian (internal and external) refugees, has been conducted according to strict legality. The land was expropriated by the authority of laws passed by the Israeli parliament, and transferred to Jewish control and ownership.[3] In 1955, the then Arab affairs editor for the Israeli daily *Haaretz*, Moshe Keren, described this process as "wholesale robbery in legal guise. Hundreds of thousands of *dunams* [*sic*] were taken away from the Arab minority".[4]

The Palestinian citizens inside Israel, including the internal refugees, were subjected to a repressive Military Administration for some eighteen years (1948–66). Many observers do not realise that the state of emergency declared in Israel in 1948 is still in effect. Although direct military government, which had applied to the Arab areas of Israel, was abolished in 1966, the Defence (Emergency) Regulations, originally enacted by the British mandatory authorities in 1945, were retained by the Knesset in a special law, and the state of emergency has never been lifted completely. The Regulations, subject to certain amendments, have remained in force until the present day. Moreover since the termination of the Military Administration, Israeli governments have continued legislative and administrative procedures aimed at confiscating lands of the destroyed villages in order to prevent the return of the internally displaced.

The Defence (Emergency) Regulations, which were the primary legal instrument for political repression inside Israel, provided the legal basis for the system of direct military rule imposed on Arab (and only Arab) citizens of Israel during the post-*Nakba* period; in fact the Military Administration existed only in the areas in which the majority of Israel's Arab population resided. Under the Regulations the authorities can still declare closed military areas, confiscate land, close down newspapers, detain people without trial, and even expel them.[5] An Emergency Article for the Exploitation of Uncultivated Land (1948) permitted Israel's Minister of Agriculture to seize Arab property that was uncultivated. Seizures were effected by enclosing an area under the Defence (Emergency) Regulations, thus preventing its cultivation and enabling its expropriation. Lands falling under this category were leased by the Custodian of Absentees' Property to Jewish settlers and farmers, old and new.[6] Furthermore the imposition of martial law and military administration in the period between 1948 and 1966 had an enormous impact on the internally displaced and the remaining Palestinian population in Israel. In 1948 the Israeli Provisional State Council (the forerunner of the Knesset), in search of international recognition for the newly proclaimed state, included in the "Independence Charter" a promise that the Jewish state would "uphold the full social and political equality of all its citizens, without distinction of religion, race, and sex". What, in fact, took place was exactly the opposite. After its establishment, Israel treated the Palestinians still remaining within its frontiers almost as foreigners. It swiftly imposed a military administration in the areas inhabited by the Palestinian community, expropriated over half of the lands of this "non-Jewish" population, and pursued various policies of demographic containment, political control and systematic discrimination in all spheres of life.

Officially the purpose of imposing martial law and the Military Administration on Israel's Palestinian community was security. However, their establishment was intended to serve a number of both stated and concealed objectives:

(a) The first objective was to prevent the return of the Palestinian refugees ("external refugees") to their homes, villages and towns in Israel. "In the process other Arabs who had not infiltrated the country were sometimes driven out as well."[7]

(b) The second and third goals were specifically aimed at the internal refugees; the second goal was "to evacuate semi-abandoned [Arab] neighborhoods and villages as well as some which had not been abandoned – and to transfer their inhabitants to other parts of the country. Some were evacuated from a 'security cordon' along the borders, and others were removed in order to make room for Jews."[8]

(c) The third purpose was to reduce the overall number of the internal refugees in the state of Israel;

(d) The fourth goal was to maintain control and supervision over the Israeli Palestinian citizens, who were separated and isolated from the Jewish population.[9]

To reduce the overall number of internally displaced persons in the state of Israel in the post-1948 period the Military Administration carried out many incidents of expulsion, especially from the Galilee and the Triangle after the latter's annexation to Israel in May 1949, following the Rhodes agreement signed with Jordan on 3 April 1949. For instance, in late May or early June 1949, 4,000 internal refugees were expelled by the Military Administration from the Triangle across the border into the West Bank. The military governor of the central area, Lieutenant Colonel Emmanuel Markovsky, reported to the head of the Military Administration, General Elimelech Avner, on 30 June 1949:

> Upon our entry into the area [the Triangle] and the proclamation of [Israel's] rule in it, we announced that we will not recognise the [internal] refugees as being entitled to reside in the area or any aid and benefit. We prohibited their employment in any work … we banned organising permanent aid for them. When we received authorisation to transfer them across the border, the action was implemented in full within a week.

Markovsky added that after the Military Administration put pressure on "representatives" of the Triangle's villages (possibly certain *mukhtar*s), the latter agreed to assist in the process. In conclusion, Markovsky wrote: "In retrospect, this action proved that a fair and forceful rule in the [Israeli Arab] villages gives the possibility of implementing tasks in full, and fortifies Israel's rule." In the same year, some 1,000 people from the village of Baqa al-Gharbiyya in the Triangle (presumably many of them internal refugees) were expelled by Israel across the border into the West Bank.

In early February 1951, the residents of thirteen small Arab villages in Wadi 'Ara were expelled over the border. On 17 November of the same year the inhabitants of the village of Khirbat al-Buwayshat in the Triangle were expelled and their houses were dynamited by the army. Earlier, in 1949, some 700 people from Kafr Yasif village in the Galilee were trucked to the Jordanian border and ordered to cross it. These internal refugees had never left the Galilee during the 1948 war, but simply had fled their homes in adjoining villages and moved to Kafr Yasif. In a Knesset debate on 8 March 1949, Arab Knesset member Tawfiq Tubi strongly protested against this large single expulsion of internally displaced persons. He stated:

> The forced evacuation of Arab villages has also been carried out by the Israeli authorities. Only a few weeks ago 700 people who had

taken refuge in the village of [Kafr] Yasif during the [1948] war were taken to the Iraqi front [on the northern West Bank border with Israel] in trucks and forced to cross the lines to 'Abdullah.

In mid-April 1949, the US consul in Jerusalem reported that "several hundred" Galilee Arabs (some of the internal refugees) had been expelled by the Israeli army across the border, together with some Palestinian refugees who had "infiltrated" back to their villages. Such expulsions often were carried out with brutality. One kibbutz woman wrote anonymously to the newspaper '*Al-Hamishmar* of witnessing such "infiltrators", men, women and children blindfolded, being trucked out:

> Those of us standing nearby had witnessed no bad behaviour on the part of the Arabs, who sat frightened, almost one on top of the other. But the soldiers were quick to teach us what they meant by "order". "The expert" jumped up and began to … hit [the Arabs] across their blindfolded eyes and when he had finished, he stamped on all of them and then, in the end, laughed uproariously and with satisfaction at his heroism. We were shocked by this despicable act. I ask, does this not remind us exactly of the Nazi acts towards the Jews?

On 31 May 1950 the Israeli army transported about 120 internal refugees in two crowded trucks to a point near the edge of Wadi Araba, a hot desert wasteland astride the Israeli-Jordanian frontier between the Dead Sea and the Gulf of Aqaba. The refugees were ordered to cross to Jordan, with the soldiers "firing bursts over their heads to urge them forward". While most of the expellees made it, as many as thirty-six "may be assumed … [to have] perished from thirst and starvation", the British minister to Amman, Kirkbride, wrote.[10] The survivors, who were questioned in Jordan, were found to be:

> Members of divided families who infiltrated across the line to find their relatives, or who fled from what is now Israeli territory when the Jews arrived there, abandoning money and valuables in their homes; … Refugees caught *en route* from Gaza to Jordan; … [and] Arabs living in their homes in Israel, with whom the Jews have become displeased for some reason or other.

The issue of both the "internally displaced" Palestinian and the "external refugees" remained a major preoccupation for the Military Administration. On 24 March 1949, Prime Minister David Ben-Gurion appointed a committee that was directed to submit to him recom-mendations on whether the Military Administration should be abolished, or, alternatively, whether any changes in its policies towards the Palestinian community and the internal refugees ought to be carried out. By determining the composition of the committee, Ben-Gurion seemed to have ensured the outcome of its investigations. The committee was headed by General Elimelech Avner, who was the head of the Military Administration, and its two other members were Major Michael Hanegbi, the Military Governor of the Negev, and Yehoshu'a Palmon of the Foreign Ministry. In its report, submitted to the Prime Minister on 3 May 1949, the committee stressed that the continuation of a forceful military administration was essential for security, demographic, and land settlement reasons and for dealing with the question of refugees within Israel. The committee maintained, *inter alia*, that comprehensive and effective supervision over the Arab population was needed in order to:

(a) find "a solution to the problem of the Arab refugees who are present within the boundaries of the state [because the problem of internal refugees] requires the transfer [of Arab communities] from one place to another, the concentration of land for their resettlement, the transfer of [Arab] workers to employment centres, [and] directed [Jewish] settlement policies. ... The implementation of all these requires a regime with military character, which is not subject to the rules of normal procedures";

(b) "[facilitate] greatly the implementation of the desired demographic and land policies, and the process of populating [with Jews] the abandoned Arab villages and towns".

(c) prevent "infiltration" of Palestinian [external] refugees back to their homes and villages;

(d) prevent the Palestinian community from becoming a fifth column.[11]

In October 1952, Ben-Gurion asked then minister-without-portfolio Pinhas Lavon (later defence minister) to look into the functioning of the Military Administration. Lavon's report, which was presented a few weeks later, criticised the Military Administration as inefficient and harbouring much corruption. Lavon also attempted to deal with claims he heard from army General Staff representatives, who had asserted that the reason for the difficulties and inefficiency of the Military Administration was the lack of a consistent policy towards the Palestinian community and the internally displaced. This inconsistency, according to the army, was the result of the activities of civilian ministries among the Arab population, in parallel with army activities. The army, Lavon wrote, wanted exclusive and total authority in dealing with the Arab community. However, he recommended that the army's demand should not be accepted, although he opposed abolition of the Military Administration and the Defence (Emergency) Regulations. Lavon's report was most telling:

> The claim about the "lack of a consistent policy" [made by repre-sentatives of the General Staff] is based on the demand to [adopt] a policy which would lead to the emigration of the Arab residents from the territory of the State of Israel. ... Such emigration is undoubtedly desirable, but it is doubtful whether it would be possible to achieve that – the emigration of tens of thousands of Arabs – with the means available to a Military Government in time of peace, in a democratic state, which is open to criticism, supervision, and is in need of world's sympathy. The harm [resulting] from half measures is clear, and their benefit is doubtful. Absolutely effective means [which would bring about the total departure of the Arab minority] cannot be pursued by the state of Israel, without the shaking of its international position.

While describing the idea of a wholesale mass exodus of the Arab community as "desirable" but not practicable for international as well as domestic reasons, Lavon, like most Israeli ministers and senior officials, was still in favour of an active policy of encouraging "voluntary" transfer:

> The above explanation does not come [however] to weaken or belittle the efforts being made in order to obtain the consent of Arab residents [Israeli citizens] to emigrate to foreign countries. Such plans deserve encouragement and full support from the [official] institu-tions concerned. The required financial investment is certainly worth-while, and it is desirable that the treasury [Finance Ministry] ought actively to enter into details [of these plans].[12]

The institution of the Military Administration, together with the imposition of the Defence (Emergency) Regulations, empowered the military governors to close off the Arab localities and to restrict entry or exit only to those who had been issued permits by the military authorities. These Regulations also enabled the Israeli authorities to evict and deport people from their villages and towns; to place individuals under administrative detention for indefinite periods without trial; and to impose fines and penalties without due process.[13] Although the Regulations themselves made no distinction between Jew and Arab, there is no doubt that the primary use of most of the powers in these Regulations was to impose restrictions on the Palestinian citizens of Israel[14] and regulate the residence of the majority of them and their descendants. Regulation 125 in effect legalises the expropriation of Arab land, giving local military commanders the right to declare any region under their jurisdiction a "closed area".[15] As Professor David Kretzmer of the Hebrew University pointed out, "in the discussion of institutional discrimination [against the Arabs in Israel], during the time of the military government many of the rules applying to closed areas were only applied to Arabs while Jews were allowed to move in and out of the areas freely".[16] The military governors, in particular, were authorised to close Arab areas in order to prevent internal refugees from returning to their homes and lands that had been confiscated by the state and taken over by new and old Jewish settlements.[17] Yehoshu'a Palmon of the Foreign Ministry suggested in a letter to the Custodian of Absentees' Property, Zalman Lifschitz of the Prime Minister's Office, and the attorney general that "in the cases in which [internal] refugees want to sell their property in their former place of residence and leave the country, we should encourage them to do that".[18] Copies of the letter were sent to the foreign minister, the Military Administration, and Yosef Weitz. A year later, Palmon, then advisor on Arab affairs in the Prime Minister's Office, wrote a letter to foreign minister Moshe Sharett in which he expounded his views on the prickly issue of the property of the *present absentees*:

> Arab residents of Israel, who, from a social, religious, or cultural viewpoint, are not inclined to remain in Israel, after they would receive all or a respectable part of the compensation for their property, and their hope for what they had not received [their actual property] was lost, they would look for and find a way to leave the country.[19]

Dispossession by land expropriation: the Absentees' Property Law of 1950

The issue of continuing land expropriation is possibly the most explosive in the relationship between the Palestinian community inside Israel and the Jewish state. It is an issue that has caused tremendous resentment and bitterness among the Palestinian citizens of Israel and has galvanised them into action. This action reached a peak in the Land Day of 30 March 1976, a day which began as a peaceful general strike and culminated in a confrontation with the Israeli border police in the course of which six Palestinians were shot dead.[20] Since 1976, 30 March has become a "national day" of commemoration and protests of the Palestinian community – protests that are mainly directly against the state's policies of land expropriation and land use. An important memorandum presented by Hanna Naqqara, an Israeli-Palestinian attorney and a leading expert on land affairs, to the Arab Popular Congress in Nazareth held on 17 February 1979 exposed the impact of Israeli land policies on the internally displaced:

> Tens of thousands of [Israeli?] Arabs are still far away from their destroyed villages and stolen lands. There is an army of local refugees from Saffuriyya, al-Mujaydil, Ma'lul, Hittin, Nimrin, al-Shajara, 'Arab al-Khisas, 'Arab al-Baqqarah, al-Kabri, al-Mansura, al-Zib, al-Bassa, 'Amqa, Shaykh Dawud, al-Birwa, al-Damun, al-Ruways, al-Ghabisiyya, Iqrit, Kafr Bir'im, 'Anan, Farradiyya, al-Manshiyya, Mi'ar, Sha'b, al-Nahr, al-Sai'ra, Suhmata, Tarbikha, Umm al-Faraj, and others. This army of local refugees was created by the policies of consecutive ethnic governments, existing and working for the eviction of native people and the planting of a new people.[21]

The most recent impact of these land policies was the crisis in Umm al-Fahem, an Arab town in the Wadi 'Ara region, which began in May 1998 when the Israeli government announced that it was expanding a nearby military facility, in the process expropriating 4,500 acres of local Arab agricultural land.[22] In the three days of rioting that followed the local demonstration of 27 September 1998, over 400 Arab residents were injured in clashes with the border police.[23]

Since 1948 Israel has enacted some thirty statutes that expropriated and transferred land from Palestinian citizens to state (Jewish) ownership.[24] There is little doubt, however, that the major expropriations of lands belonging to Palestinians (internal and external refugees) were carried out under the Absentees' Property Law, 1950.[25] This statute was used after 1948 to transfer Palestinian properties to Jewish hands *via* the Custodian of Absentees' Property, who subsequently transferred them to the Israeli Development Authority. The law was preceded by the Defence (Emergency) Regulations dealing with "absentees' property". On the face of it, the declared objective of the Absentees' Property Law of 1950 was to "protect" the property of *absentee* owners, and to facilitate use of this property for the development of the Israeli economy and the state.[26] In reality, however, under this law, with all its amendments, millions of *dunums* of Palestinian refugee land and billions of dollars' worth of Arab property were seized by the state of Israel.[27]

The law directs the Finance Minister to appoint a Custodian of Absentees' Property and Section 4(a)(1) provides that "all absentees' property is hereby vested in the Custodian as from the day of publication of this appointment or the day on which it became absentee's property, whichever is the later date."[28] The law gives far-reaching powers to the Custodian of Absentees' Property, with severe consequences for the Palestinian landowner whose property was deemed "absentee property"; it empowers the Custodian to take care of the absentee's property, manage it, and expel occupants who, in the Custodian's opinion, have no right to occupy it. The law does not give the "absentee" (internal or external refugee) the right to return to his property. Instead it gives the Custodian the power, at his sole discretion, and on the recommendation of a special committee, to release/sell vested property. Where the vested property has been sold, "the property sold becomes released property and passes into the ownership of the purchaser and the consideration which the Custodian has received becomes held property" (Section 28 (c).[29]

The most important provision in the law is the definition of the term "absentees' property". Section 1 defines the term "absentee" as follows:

(a) "absentee" means –
  (1) a person who, at any time during the period between the 16th Kislev, 5708 (29 November, 1947) and the day on which a declaration is published, under section 9(d) of the Law and Administration Ordinance, (5708-1948), that the state of emergency declared by the Provisional Council of the State on the 10th of Iyar, 5708 (19th May, 1948) has ceased to exist, was the legal owner of any property situated in the area of Israel or enjoyed or held it, whether by himself or through another, and who at any time during the said period –
    (i) was a national or citizen of the Lebanon, Egypt, Syria,

Saudi-Arabia, Trans-Jordan, Iraq or the Yemen, or

(ii) was in one of these countries or in any part of Palestine outside the area of Israel or

(iii) was a Palestinian citizen and left his ordinary place of residence in Palestine

(a) for a place outside Palestine before the 27th Av, 5708 (1st September, 1948); or

(b) for a place in Palestine held at the time by forces which sought to prevent the establishment of the State of Israel or which fought against it after its establishment;

(2) a body of persons which, at any time during the period specified in paragraph (1), was a legal owner of any property situated in the area of Israel or enjoyed or held such property, whether by itself or through another, and all the members, partners, shareholders, directors or managers of which are absentees within the meaning of paragraph (1), or the management of the business of which is otherwise decisively controlled by such absentees, or all the capital of which is in the hands of such absentees.[30]

Critical examination of this definition reveals that a person may be an "absentee" under the law, even though he was present in Israel when his property was deemed to have become "absentees' property". In other words, if a person was an "absentee" at any time between 29 November 1947 and 1 September 1948, his property becomes "absentees' property", whether he is still an absentee or not.[31] While that applied in absentia to those Palestinian refugees outside Jewish-occupied Palestine, it also provided for the legal dispossession of those Palestinian citizens of Israel who had never left the newly created state or those Palestinians who were reabsorbed into Israel as a result of the armistice agreements of 1949. Consequently most of the internally displaced have become *present absentees* by virtue of the fact that they had properties confiscated; very few of them have ever recovered any property.

In 1948, each Arab village had on average approximately 2,280 acres of arable land; by 1974 this was reduced to 500 acres.[32] Between 1948 and 1990 the Israeli-Palestinians (including the internal refugees) lost close to 1 million acres of land;[33] during the first four decades of the state 80 per cent of the lands owned by Palestinians living in Israel were confiscated and put at the exclusive disposal of Jewish citizens.[34] Through a series of legal measures, expropriations continue even today, with minimal financial compensation based on undervalued assessments (decided unilaterally and with no relation to market value), which, in any case, many internal refugees refused.[35] As a result of this massive land seizure and the state's land use and planning policies within the Green Line, 93 per cent of the land is owned by the state and the Jewish National Fund (JNF);[36] according to a series of law passed in the early 1960s (especially the Basic Law: Israel Lands and the Israel Lands Authority Law),[37] almost all the land in Israel came to be owned by the state (93 per cent). Yet when the state assumed control (in the form of the Israel Lands Authority), it agreed to continue to abide by the JNF's mandate for those lands that were once administered by the JNF whose primary purpose has always been to facilitate the control of land as the "perpetual property of the Jewish people".[38] In effect those lands, originally belonging to Palestinian (external) refugees and *present absentees*, are currently held "in perpetuity by the Jewish people" – not the citizens of Israel – a distinction that excludes the Arab citizens from ownership and land use.

Furthermore the Israel Lands Authority (ILA) continues internally to transfer lands to the JNF – 12,500 acres in 1991, and 10,000 acres in 1998 are but recent examples.[39] In reality the line between the Israel Lands Authority and the JNF is a thin one, as the JNF nominates six of the thirteen members of the ILA's Board (the rest are government officials). Professor Amnon Rubinstein, writing in *Haaretz* of 13 October 1991, critically remarked: "These transfers present a grave problem, because lands that were intended for use by all Israeli citizens were handed over to an agency that sells and leases land only to Jews". By self-definition, these lands, whether controlled by the ILA or the JNF, are utilised almost exclusively for the fulfilment of the Zionist goals of Jewish settlement and population dispersion. Inevitably, this land use policy has resulted in the massive dispossession of the Palestinian community, including the internal refugees.[40] Although the Palestinian citizens of Israel constitute 20 per cent of the total population, they control *only* 2 per cent of the municipal jurisdictional areas in the country.[41] Right Reverend Riah Abu al-'Assal of Nazareth (enthroned in 1998 as the Anglican Bishop of Jerusalem), had this to say:

> In 1948, 16.5 dunams [*sic*] were allowed per capita for the Arab minority. Today about 0.5 dunam [*sic*] is allowed. We have no more space to bury our dead … I am not exaggerating. I live in a town called Nazareth which has become the most crowded town in the country

... In the Greek Orthodox Cemetery in Nazareth – and the Greek Orthodox community numbers over 11,000 people – they dig up the graves of those who died ten years ago to bury the newly dead.[42]

The Struggle for "Return" of Kafr Bir'im[43] and Iqrit (1948–2005)

The most famous case of the internally displaced involved the inhabitants of the two villages Kafr Bir'im and Iqrit, who were forcibly evicted by the Israeli army in November 1948 and never allowed to return. This case also illustrates the strong desire among many of the internally displaced persons to return to their "original" homes and "personal" territory. Termed the "uprooted" (*ha'akurim*) in the Israeli press, the Christian inhabitants of Iqrit and Kafr Bir'im in northern Galilee and their descendants are part of the approximately 250,000 internally displaced Palestinians who were dispossessed by the Israeli army in 1948 and were not allowed to go back to their homes. In 1948 Iqrit and Kafr Bir'im were considered "friendly" villages; their inhabitants did not take up arms against Israel. The villagers were "evicted" by the Israeli army on 6 November 1948 and transferred to various Arab villages in Galilee, including Jish and Ramah. The history of these evicted villagers is one of "broken promises";[44] initially the Israeli army asked the residents of Iqrit and Kafr Bir'im to leave their villages because of "security concerns" along the Israeli–Lebanese border (Kafr Biri'm was located about two miles from the Israeli–Lebanese border and nine miles east of Iqrit). Apparently their residents complied with the order after receiving explicit assurances from both the Galilee District military commander, Elisha Shultz, and the then Minister for Minorities, Bechor Shitrit, that they would be permitted to return within two weeks.[45] But this promise, which ran counter to Israel's general policy at the time of creating Arab-free "security zones" along the borders of the state, was not kept. In *Israel's Border Wars, 1949–1956*, Israeli historian Benny Morris discusses the issue of "Expelling Border Communities [Israeli Arabs] and Nudging Back the Borders":

> At the end of 1948 ... Israel decided to clear its border areas of Arab villages, to a depth of five or ten kilometres. The motive of the policy – initially implemented at the beginning of November along the Lebanese border – was military: Arab villages along the border – just

behind IDF positions and patrol roads, constituted a threat. They could receive and assist Arab troops and irregulars should the Arabs renew the war; harbour saboteurs and spies; and serve as way stations for infiltrating returnees [Palestinian refugees], thieves, and smugglers. Partly depopulated villages, such as Tarshiha in the Galilee, beckoned infiltrators [returning refugees] bent on resettlement. And some semi-abandoned border villages, such as Zakariya, in the Jerusalem Corridor, were a socio-economic burden on the state since the young adult males were mostly dead, incarcerated, or had fled to Jordan, while the old, the women, and the children of the village lived off government hand-outs. Lastly, the authorities wanted as small an Arab minority as possible in the new Jewish state.

In part, these border-area transfers were designed to hamper infiltration [of Palestinian refugees] into Israel.[46]

On 21 June 1949 the leaders of Kafr Bir'im met with Shitrit, who asked them to be "patient". But nothing happened for two years. Having lost faith in the Israeli government, the villagers on 30 August 1951 filed a claim in the High Court of Justice, requesting the government return of their land. The High Court issued a conditional order on 8 October, ordering the government to explain why the villagers had not been allowed to return.[47] In response, in November the army, using the Defence (Emergency) Regulations, declared Kafr Bir'im "a closed area" for security reasons, requiring a special permit to enter. A month later while the case of Iqrit was still before the High Court, the army issued retroactive expulsion orders and its sappers systematically blew up every house in the village. The High Court issued its final ruling on the Kafr Bir'im case on 18 January 1952, declaring that in the light of the military actions, the villagers of Kafr Bir'im would need to obtain special permits in order to return home – permits which the army refused to issue. On 4 August 1953 the finance ministry stepped in, officially confiscating the lands of Kafr Bir'im for the purpose of "development", using the legal pretext that the lands were "abandoned and uncultivated by the owners". Finally on 16 and 17 September the army destroyed the remaining houses of Kafr Bir'im.[48] The lands of the two villages were confiscated, declared "state lands", and leased to Jewish agricultural and urban settlements. A similar process took place in several Arab villages in Israel.

The villagers of Iqrit and Kafr Bir'im were not permitted to return because, according to prime minister Golda Meir in 1972, allowing them to do so might set a precedent for other, similarly uprooted internal refugees.[49] Apparently monetary compensation was subsequently offered by the Israeli government to the inhabitants of Kafr Bir'im and Iqrit, only to be turned down by the majority of them.[50] When their hopes of return were frustrated, they took action through the Israeli courts, through lobbying and through peaceful demonstrations; their legal and political struggle, and the struggle of their descendants, to return to their homes and original lands has stretched out to more than half a century. There are four main reasons why the case of Iqrit and Kafr Bir'im became a *cause célèbre*:

- the tenacity of the villagers, their perseverance and direct action, their effective lobbying activities and legal struggle, stretching over half a century; they never gave up hope or ceased their efforts;
- the mobilisation of Christian churches in the Holy Land and the effective use of their international connections;
- the formation of grassroots local organisations from an early stage designed to campaign specifically for the rights of the villagers, such as the Committee for the Uprooted of Kafr Bir'im and the Public Committee of Iqrit and Kafr Bir'im;
- the perception among liberal Zionist-Israelis, who have expressed sympathy for the villagers, that their case was "unique", and as such would not be taken as a "precedent" to allow other internal refugees to return to the homes and original lands.

The affair of Kafr Bir'im and Iqrit often burst into the open and provoked controversy inside Israel and soul-searching among Jews and non-Jews in the West. On 23 July 1972, after a long cabinet session discussing whether or not to allow the "uprooted" of the two villages to return, the Israeli ministers voted against; the government of Golda Meir gave no official reasons for its decision.[51] This decision attracted the interest of the Western press, with many articles and editorials sympathetic to the dispossessed villagers and highly critical of the Israeli government appearing in the *New York Times* (4 September and 22 October), the *Guardian* (16 August), and *Christian Science Monitor* (12 and 26 August). An indication of the impact of the demands of the inhabitants of the two villages on American Jewish opinion is suggested by an article in the American Jewish Congress journal, the *Congress Bi-*

weekly, by Chaim Waxman. Acknowledging that the case of the villagers had received some coverage in the United States, and critical of the handling of the case by the Israeli government, Waxman expressed the fear that the government's refusal to allow the villagers to return could become a major weapon in the arsenals of critics of Zionism and Israel.[52] Israeli journalist Amos Elon wrote in October 1972:

> The question of the repatriation of a few hundred Israeli Arabs to the now ruined villages [of Kafr Bir'im and Iqrit] has revealed a deep soul-searching ... the passion and occasional viciousness of this last debate surpasses any within recent memory.[53]

Later in the year the Labour government announced the abolition of all "closed areas" laws within the Green Line, a decision that was officially put into effect on 31 December 1972. The next day defence minister Moshe Dayan reimposed Defence (Emergency) Regulations on Iqrit and Kafr Bir'im, making them "closed areas" with the villagers still requiring a permit in order to enter them.[54] Four months later, on 1 April 1973, near Hadera in Israel, some 7,000 Israeli Palestinians and Jews took part in an open-air solidarity meeting with the internal refugees of the two villages.[55]

Things began to improve under the pragmatic coalition of Labour–Meretz, which came to power in 1992. A year later, a ministerial committee under Minister of Justice David Libai was formed to deal with the issue of Kafr Bir'im and Iqrit. Two years later, in December 1995, it announced its recommendations, proposing to settle the case if the residents of the villages agreed to the following:

- partial return: about 600 families to be allowed back; eligibility would be restricted to heads of households who lived in one of the villages and owned a house there on 6 November 1948, as well as two adult descendants per household;
- the land would still be under the control of the Finance Ministry;
- only a small parcel of land would be leased to returning households: only 600 *dunums* were to be set aside for each village (less than 10 per cent of the two villages' original land);
- villagers would forgo land and property restitution;
- villagers would not engage in agriculture.

The committee declared that solution to be representative of the "generous good-will of the Israeli government".[56]

These recommendations were never implemented. Though seeing the committee's recommendations as a step in the right direction, the villagers from Iqrit and Kafr Bir'im, who by then numbered 8,000 persons with claims to thousands of *dunums* of land, rejected the decision. In 1948 Kafr Bir'im had a population of about 950, while Iqrit had about 500 inhabitants. According to the *Village Statistics, 1945* of the British mandatory government, Kafr Bir'im lands had consisted of 12,244 *dunums*, while Iqrit had 711 *dunums*.[57] According to Kamel Ya'aqub, of the Committee for the Uprooted of Kafr Bir'im, there were three problems with the government's decision: it limits the number of the villagers who can return; the land stays under State control; it does not return all the land which the villagers farmed, land in use by neighbouring Jewish settlements. As one villager from Bir'im explained: "How do they expect me to decide which two sons will return with me? What should I say to the other six members of my family?"[58] The villagers demanded more land (having lost more land through expropriation after 1948) and insisted that all their descendants be allowed back, while Jewish settlements in the area urged that less land be handed back to the Arab villagers.

Another committee of senior Israeli officials, formed in early 1996 in response to the ongoing villagers' campaign, amended the recommendations of December 1995 by removing the two descendants restriction; it also suggested that the government should consider expansion of the two villages' boundaries if necessary. No action was taken. A petition filed by the Iqrit villagers in late 1996 was still pending in 1999–2000 before the High Court of Justice: the villagers wanted at least the court to order that the ministerial committee recommendations be implemented. On 2 December 1998, the Knesset defeated a private members' bill, submitted by liberal member Dedi Tzucker (Meretz), to allow the villagers to return. However even those liberal Israelis who have supported the villagers' struggle to return to Iqrit and Kafr Bir'im believe that the case is unique and should not be taken as a precedent to allow other internal refugees to return to their villages and homes. However the issue remained unresolved under the governments of Binyamin Netanyahu and Ehud Barak. On 10 October 2001 the deliberations of the government of Ariel Sharon about whether to respect the 1951 High Court ruling and allow the villagers of Iqrit and Kafr Bir'im to return to their homes and properties finally came to an end, when the "security cabinet" of Ariel Sharon decided against their return because of "security concern" and because it "would set a precedent for other displaced Palestinians who all demand to return to their homes and lands". The cabinet decision showed that little had changed in Israel's land policies since 1971, when the then prime minister Golda Meir issued a similar decision. In late October 2001, in response to the Sharon cabinet's decision, the Public Committee of Iqrit and Kafr Bir'im organised a mass protest at the church of Iqrit followed by a public rally in the village in which the Catholic bishop Butrus Mu'alem, the head of the Higher Arab Monitoring Committee, and hundreds of people from Arab towns and villages in the Galilee participated.[59] Bishop Mu'alem said that he would present the case of the two villages to the Pope at their meeting in Rome in early November, although he hoped that the Israeli government would begin to tackle the problem, helping the villagers to return to their original land, before the problem became an international issue.[60]

The official response of the Israeli cabinet to the 1996 petition was to be considered by the High Court in a hearing scheduled for early November 2001, although the prospects of a successful outcome for the residents of Iqrit and Kafr Bir'im in the Israeli legal system appeared to be slim.[61] However there are several reasons why the villagers to Kafr Bir'im and Iqrit have been more successful than other internally displaced communities in Israel in attracting support and sympathy for their cause, including strong attachment to their personal territory, never giving up hope of returning or ceasing their efforts. It was also the mobilisation of many Christian churches in the Holy Land and abroad in support of their case that made it a *cause célèbre*. Another important factor has been their cohesive and distinct village organisations, which have made of the refugee communities of Kafr Bir'im and Iqrit a model for other internally displaced communities to imitate.[62]

"Politics from Below" and Direct Action: ADRID

Although the issue of the internal refugees is still conspicuous by its absence from both the international agenda and the Israeli–Palestinian peace negotiations, the early and mid-1990s witnessed a major turning point in the struggle of the internal refugees to regain their lands and properties. The 1990s introduced two major factors into the debate over the fate of the internal refugees: the impact of the Madrid and Oslo peace processes on the internal refugees,[63] both positive and negative; and the formation, for the first time since 1948, of a nationwide organisation: the National Association for the Defence of the Rights of the Internally Displaced (ADRID)[64] which has emerged gradually since in the early 1990s also under the impact of the Israeli–Palestinian peace process. ADRID is an umbrella organisation whose three principal aims are: (a) promoting the right of return of the internal refugees to their original villages and the rejection of compensation as an alternative to return; (b) uniting the efforts and activities of the various local and village committees of internal refugees within the framework of ADRID; (c) conducting public relations campaigns on behalf of the internally displaced directed at Israeli (Jewish and Arab) and international audiences.[65] ADRID was founded in 1992, shortly after the Madrid Peace Conference of October 1991, because according to one of its founders, Ahmad Ashkar, "the convening of the Madrid Conference convinced us beyond the shadow of a doubt that the PLO and Arab countries had abandoned the Arabs of [19]48 [i.e., Israeli-Palestinians]. Therefore, we decided to take matters into our hands."[66] The leader of ADRID, Wakim Wakim – a Galilee-based lawyer who himself comes from a family of internal refugees originating from the (destroyed) village of al-Bassa – had this to say in an interview in December 2002:

> We began just after the Madrid Conference. Needless to say, we were very upset with the Palestinian delegation for not raising the issue of the internally displaced, and our fear of exclusion from the PLO's strategy led us to take action by forming a committee to prepare for the peace conference announced by Madrid. Before our initiative, there were already a number of local committees that had been working on their own, representing the inhabitants of specific destroyed villages, such as Iqrit and [Kafr] Bir'im. There was also a committee for Saffuriyya (the Committee to Preserve the Heritage of Saffuriyya),[67] the Hittin Committee, and a few others.[68]

The beginnings of ADRID were the early 1990s, when a very small number of activists from several local village committees held their first joint meeting, at the end of which they announced the establishment of a standing committee for the defence of the rights of the internally displaced. The committee, aiming to unify local efforts and to make its issue a common cause rather than a separate issue of each village, for the next three years organised lectures and panel discussions in various Arab schools and localities around Israel. Then on 11 March 1995 they held their first nationwide conference at Qasr al-Salam, near Tamra in western Galilee, with the participation of some 280 delegates representing thirty-nine destroyed villages and various groups of the internally displaced. The conference, which became a major turning point, crucially transformed the standing committee into a nationwide organisation, ADRID, and issued a public statement which rejected "all alternatives to the right of return". Significantly, however, it was only in May 2000 that ADRID was registered as a non-governmental organisation (NGO).[69] Since then, the association has continued to operate under two slightly different names: one highlighting its delicate legal position in Israel and the other (ADRID), emphasising its national Palestinian character. Interestingly, though, because the overwhelming majority of the internally displaced originated from, and currently live in, the northern part of the country, the activities of ADRID are largely concentrated in the north of the country.

Nakba Memory and Commemoration

Since 1948 Israel's refugee strategy towards the internal refugees has consisted of a series of practical measures, including the suppressing of *Nakba* memory, the denial of restitution of property and involuntary resettlement. The victims – in this case internally displaced Israeli-Arab citizens – became "victimisers", a threat to Israel's demographic security and ethnic domination. The struggle of the Palestinian citizens of Israel (including the *present absentees*) for a multicultural, democratic and inclusive state – a state of all its citizens – became a threat to the very central Zionist ethnic project of Judaising Palestine-Israel. Israel's refugee strategy of turning history on its head, however, has clearly failed. In fact the more the state policies were focused on suppressing *Nakba* memory and dissolving the internal refugee problem, the more the indigenous resistance to that policy became stronger and the more visible *Nakba* commemoration and actual direct action became. *Nakba* memory and active participation in rituals of commemoration, driven by a very sense of historical injustice, is far stronger among the third generation of *present absentees* than the first and second. Although Palestinians – unlike the Israelis – are denied statehood and state archives, they have, especially in the last two decades, been recording the de-Arabisation of Palestine and producing and making public their memories of the *Nakba*. Palestinian historians have begun compiling and recording oral histories, Palestinian public figures and intellectuals have been writing memoirs, and rituals of commemoration have developed that preserve what happened and convey its memory to those who only experienced the after-effects of the catastrophe. Moreover Palestinian films have been made, historical accounts have been written, and refugee art has been exhibited.

More crucially, in recent years there has been an awakening of all sorts, including the participation of Palestinian communities in Israel in the commemoration of the *Nakba* to an extent that was unseen in years past. This was partly because of the activities of ADRID which, since its foundation in the 1990s, has had a number of major successes. It was the first Arab organisation in Israel to articulate successfully the nationwide demands of the internal refugees. To that end it has conducted a widely publicised campaign of direct action. This has included commemorative and mass rallies, regular marches to, and cultural activities on the lands of, destroyed villages (such as Saffuriyya, Suhmata, al-Ghabisiyya, al-Birwa, Ma'lul, Lubya, Hittin), as well the restoration of holy sites (mosques, churches and cemeteries) in these villages. There is also a certain amount of cooperation between ADRID and the Islamic Movement in Israel; a great deal of the joint activity on the ground is carried out through the Al-Aqsa Association for the Preservation of Consecrated Islamic Property, whose headquarters are located in the town of Umm al-Fahem, led by the Islamic Movement in Israel. In addition to ADRID and the Al-Aqsa Association, several grassroots organisations promote *Nakba* awareness and civil rights activities throughout the country, including 'Adalah ("Justice") – the Legal Centre for Arab Minority Rights in Israel; Ittijah – Union of Arab Community Based Associations;[70] and Zochrot – the Hebrew word for *Nakba*.[71] While ADRID, 'Adalah and Ittijah are all secular organisations representing both Palestinian Christians and Palestinian Muslims in Israel, the Al-Aqsa Association is a faith-based organisation which focuses primarily on sites sacred to Islam that were left unattended, vandalised and even desecrated after the *Nakba*. The Al-Aqsa Association looks after old cemeteries and mosques, and campaigns for the release and restoration of mosques existing in abandoned (almost completely destroyed) villages.[72]

Another significant success has been in uniting a large number of

Arab mayors, Arab members of the Knesset and practically all Arab political parties and national institutions in Israel (operating under the umbrella of the Higher Arab Monitoring Committee:[73] in support of the demands of the internal refugees.[74] One of the largest and most successful mass rallies ever organised by the ADRID was held on 11 March 2000 in the sports hall of the municipality of Nazareth, the largest Arab town in Israel. It was attended by some 850 participants, including the mayor of Nazareth Ramiz Jarayseh, Muhammad Zaydan (the head of the Higher Arab Monitoring Committee), 'Abdul-Karim al-Zraykhi of the PLO Refugee Department, activists from displaced communities, representatives of Arab political parties and institutions in Israel, as well as solidarity delegations from the occupied Golan Heights and refugee camps in the West Bank. The speakers emphasised two common themes: (a) the determination of Palestinian refugees in general and internally displaced in particular to continue the struggle for the "right of return"; (b) the need for united political action towards a solution of the Palestinian refugee problem, based on the implementation of international law and UN resolutions, especially Resolution 194.

Speaking on behalf of ADRID, Wakim Wakim presented its manifesto and pointed out that:

- ADRID called for the return of the internally displaced to their homes and property, in accordance with UN Resolution 194. It also called for the abolition of the Law of Absentees' Property and other laws providing for ethnic discrimination against the Arab citizens of Israel.
- while ADRID is the representative of the internally displaced in Israel, the PLO is the sole (overall) representative of the Palestinian people, including external and internal refugees;
- ADRID called for the maintenance of the sacred sites (mosques, churches and cemeteries) in all destroyed villages and the protection of other Arab sites of historical significance;
- any future political agreement signed by the PLO with Israel that excludes the "right of return" would be considered null and void by the Palestinian refugees and internally displaced;
- Israel continues to violate the basic rights of its Palestinian citizens: their right to property is denied; some Israeli leaders even question their right to vote in the elections to the Knesset and be represented in parliament;
- ADRID demands broad support for the internally displaced from all

Palestinian social and political institutions, and for the immediate adoption of the cause of the internally displaced persons in Israel by the Palestinian leadership;

- ADRID calls for a joint and intensive effort at documentation of Palestinian eviction and displacement during the 1948 *Nakba*.[75]

The manifesto of ADRID and its political activities underline the fact that one of its paramount objectives has been to try to create a linkage between the desire among many of the internal refugees to return to their original villages and regain their land – a desire partly derived from existential and day-to-day problems, including the pressing need for housing among the internal refugees and their descendants – and the wider Palestinian national struggle for the right to return under international law and UN resolutions.[76] A 1986 study of three refugee communities living in the Galilee (Shafa'amr, Tarshiha and Kabul) by Professor Majid al-Haj, of Haifa University, had found that many of the internally displaced had begun to lose hope that their eviction from their homes was only temporary.[77] However many of them continued to demand that their case be resolved in any final settlement reached between Israel and the Palestinians. Since the mid-1990s, however, the internal refugees, as a result of the effective nation-wide activities of ADRID, have been receiving considerable media attention both inside and outside Israel.

Despite constant harassment from, and various restrictions imposed by, the Israeli authorities and police, visits to destroyed villages, public rallies for the commemoration of the *Nakba*, and protest marches, coordinated by ADRID, have become a regular event.[78] On 12 May 1997, the forty-ninth anniversary of the creation of the state of Israel, thousands of Arab citizens, including many internal refugees, responded to calls by ADRID and took part in protest action, processions and commemorations, conducted under the slogan "Give the Internal Refugees Back their Lands".[79] On 28 March 1998, while Israel was preparing to celebrate its fiftieth anniversary, thousands of internal refugees held a protest procession from the village of Shaykh Dannun in the foothills of the western Galilee mountains to the ruins of the al-Ghabisiyya – a neighbouring abandoned village whose land ownership and use (together with two smaller neighbouring villages) in the mid-1940s was 11,786 *dunums*.[80] The protesters carried placards with the names of Palestinian villages destroyed in 1948 and called on the Israeli government to let them go back to their villages and lands. These protests turned out to be the start of many events undertaken by the Palestinian citizens of Israel to mark the fiftieth anniversary of the *Nakba*.[81]

Calls to boycott all celebrations of the independence of Israel and replace them by public rallies for the commemoration of the 1948 Palestinian *Nakba* have become a regular feature of the tactics of ADRID in recent years. Success for this tactic came in May 2000 when the Palestinian community in Israel issued, for the first time, a united call for a public boycott of the celebrations of Israel's "Independence Day" (14 May) – a boycott led by ADRID in coordination with the Higher Arab Monitoring Committee. When an "independence celebration" was staged by the Israeli authorities in the Arab town of Shafa'amr on 7 May, it was met by a Palestinian counter-demonstration which led to violent clashes with the Israeli police and resulted in twenty Arab injuries and thirty arrests.[82] A May 2000 statement issued by ADRID under the title "Their Independence Day – The Day of Our *Nakba*", read:

> We the internally displaced Palestinians suffer a double pain. We have remained near our destroyed villages and towns. With pain we listen to the silent prayers of our mosques and the silent call of our church bells – silenced since our eviction and transformed into stables for the settlers' cattle and sites of prostitution and drug abuse. They desecrate the cemeteries of our ancestors who, for 52 years, have not stopped appealing to our conscience and the conscience of humanity.[83]

It is hardly surprising that these calls and protests were treated by the Israeli authorities as acts of nationalist subversion, and that the Israeli police intervened to prevent grassroots activists from marching into abandoned villages and the ruins of places of Muslim and Christian worship. In fact officials of the Israel Land Authorities have embarked on a large-scale operation to fence off abandoned Palestinian buildings and sites and have erected large signs warning against "trespassing".[84]

In April–May 2004, as Israel began to celebrate its fifty-sixth. Independence Day, internally displaced Palestinians began to com-memorate their *Nakba*, the destruction of pre-1948 Palestinian society. One depopulated village is Endor, located southeast of Nazareth in the Galilee area of Israel. A visit to the village on 27 April was part of the commemoration of the *Nakba* organised by ADRID. Apparently all that remains of Endor are the walls of 75 houses abandoned in 1948. Endor then had a population of some 620 Palestinian Arabs who owned 10,414 *dunums* of land in the area. ADRID's commemoration ceremonies on 27 April were followed by a public rally, the seventh annual Right of Return March and a visit to Endor in the afternoon. ADRID's commemoration activities were supported by other Arab NGOs and by human rights organisations such as Zochrot, an Israeli organisation for raising Jewish-Israeli awareness of the *Nakba* and Palestinian refugee rights. Zochrot was also to hold a public discussion in Tel Aviv on the question of celebrating independence *versus* the *Nakba*. [85]

Conclusion

Raising awareness of their plight at both local and international levels has remained central to the struggle of the internal refugees to bring about the implementation of international resolutions and the fulfilment of their right to return to their destroyed villages. As Israel remains unwilling to concede these rights, support from human rights organisations and the international community will be crucial in the years ahead. Moreover until the internally displaced are allowed to return to their homes and original lands, it would be difficult to see how the state of Israel can begin to address fundamental issues such as democracy and equality for all citizens irrespective of religious, ethnic or racial affiliation.

The emergence of local Palestinian organisations, at both village and nationwide levels, has proved to be vitally important; since the early 1990s, the internally displaced have become better organised and more effective politically, mainly through the formation of civil society organisations and NGOs, including ADRID.[86] The emergence of these organisations since the early 1990s, their mass protests and activities inside the destroyed villages, together with the direct action of older, well-established Arab organisations in Israel (such as the Committee for the Uprooted of Kafr Bir'im, the Committee for the Defence of Arab Lands and the Higher Arab Monitoring Committee) have had some impact, attracting attention in the Hebrew press in Israel and, more importantly, support from international human rights organisations. Both the UN Human Rights Committee and the UN Committee on Economic, Social and Cultural Rights severely criticised Israel in 1998 for its land policies and for its treatment of the Arab citizens *and present absentees*. Israel's policies were described by the Committee on Economic, Social and Cultural Rights as an institutionalised form of discrimination and a serious breach of Israel's obligations under international law, and, more specifically, the International Covenant on Economic, Social and Cultural Rights of 1966. Addressing the issue under articles 16 and 17 of the Covenant, the UN Committee on Economic, Social and Cultural Rights, in its report of December 1998, expressed

> its concern over the plight of an estimated 200,000 uprooted "*present absentees*", Palestinian Arab citizens of Israel most of whom were forced to leave their villages during the 1948 war on the understanding that they would be allowed by the Government of Israel to return after the war. Although a few have been given back their property, the vast majority continue to be displaced and dispossessed within the State because their lands were confiscated and not returned to them.

On the issue of land use and land policies pursued by semi-official Zionist agencies in Israel, the UN Human Rights Committee and the UN Committee on Economic, Social and Cultural Rights expressed its

> concern that excessive emphasis upon the State as a "Jewish State" encourages discrimination and accords a second-class status to its non-Jewish citizens. The Committee notes with concern that the Government of Israel does not accord equal rights to its Arab citizens, although they comprise over 19 percent of the total population. ... The Committee notes with grave concern that the Status Law of 1952 authorizes the World Zionist Organization/Jewish Agency and its subsidiaries, including the Jewish National Fund, to control most of the land in Israel, since these institutions are chartered to benefit Jews exclusively. Despite the fact that the institutions are chartered under private law, the State of Israel nevertheless has a decisive influence on their policies and thus remains responsible for their activities. A State party cannot divest itself of its obligations under the Covenant by privatizing governmental functions. The Committee takes the view that large-scale and systematic confiscation of Palestinian land and property by the State, and the transfer of that property to these agencies, constitute an institutionalized form of discrimination because these agencies by definition would deny the use of these properties to non-Jews. Thus, these practices constitute a breach of

Israel's obligations under the Covenant.[87]

Conscious of the Palestinian Authority's propensity for making concessions without consulting the refugees,[88] ADRID and other Palestinian civil rights groups in Israel refused to have the Palestinian leadership assume responsibility for the internal refugees.[89] On 8 January 2001 the Hebrew daily *Haaretz* published an article entitled: "Also the Refugees in Israel Want to Return Home":

> Representatives of the "internal refugees" (the "uprooted") have recently renewed their appeal to the Palestinian leadership. They called on senior [representatives] of the [Palestinian] Authority not to conduct negotiations in their name with regard to their demand to return home.

According to *Haaretz*, the secretary of ADRID, Wakim Wakim, stated that he and his colleagues were concerned that then PA President Yasser 'Arafat would be willing to make far-reaching concessions to Israel with regard to the right of return. Instead of being represented in the final status talks by the PA, the internal refugees were seeking to conduct legal, public and political struggles within the Israeli system. The "internally displaced", Wakim explained, felt they had a better chance of realising the dream of return than the 1948 external refugees, because, being Israeli citizens, they were better placed to utilise the Israeli legal tools available. Wakim added:

> The government of Israel must remember that, even if it were to succeed in imposing a semblance of settlement on the Palestinian Authority that would dissolve the question of the right of return, it [the government] would have to continue facing our demands – to fulfil our rights as citizens.[90]

Since the early 1990s the struggle against the denial of the *Nakba* in Israel has become a major struggle for the Palestinian community in general and the *present absentees* in particular. The Palestinian community in Israel has associated, in a way that it did not previously, its collective and individual memories of the 1948 catastrophe with the general Palestinian plight and with its own predicament. This association has been manifested in an array of symbolic events such as memorial services during *Nakba* commemoration day, organising tours and marches to abandoned and destroyed Palestinian villages in Israel, regular seminars on the past and extensive interviews with *Nakba* survivors in the Arabic press in Israel.[91] Several organisations set up by Palestinian citizens of Israel and internally displaced refugees (including ADRID, the Al-Aqsa Association, 'Adalah and Ittijah) have waged effective and partially successful grassroots and legal campaigns for the preservation of the *Nakba* memory and the material and cultural heritage of the refugees.[92] However only the winning of this battle for the "signposts of memory" will help bring peace and reconciliation to Palestine-Israel.

Notes

1 Majid al-Haj, "The Arab Internal Refugees in Israel: The Emergence of a Minority Within the Minority", in Ian Lustick (ed.), *Palestinians under Israeli Rule* (New York: Garland Publishing Inc., 1994), p.9.
2 David Gilmour, *Dispossessed: The Ordeal of the Palestinians* (London: Sphere Books, 1982), p.101.
3 For selected Israeli laws affecting Arab land ownership, see Oren Yiftachel, *Planning a Mixed Region in Israel* (Aldershot, England: Avebury, 1992), appendix 1, p.313.
4 Quoted in Ian Lustick, *Arabs in the Jewish State* (Austin and London: University of Texas Press, 1980), pp.175-6.
5 Riad Beidas, "The Internally Displaced – Seeking Return Within One's Own Land: An Interview with Wakim Wakim", *Journal of Palestine Studies* 31, no.1 (Autumn 2001), p.36.
6 Simha Flapan, *The Birth of Israel: Myths and Realities* (New York: Pantheon Books, 1997), p.107.
7 Tom Segev, *1949: The First Israelis* (New York: The Free Press, 1986), p.52.
8 Ibid.
9 Ibid.
10 Quoted in Benny Morris, *Israel's Border Wars, 1949–1956* (Oxford: Clarendon Press, Revised edition, 1997), pp. 157-8.
11 See Israeli State Archives (ISA), Foreign Ministry, 2401/19a.
12 For Lavon's report, see ISA, Foreign Ministry, 2401/19a.
13 Segev, *1949: The First Israelis*, p.51.
14 David Kretzmer, *The Legal Status of the Arabs in Israel* (Boulder, San Francisco: Westview Press, 1990), p.141.
15 For further discussion of the specific case of Kafr Bir'im and Iqrit, see below and Chapter 6.
16 Kretzmer, *The Legal Status of the Arabs in Israel*, p.142.
17 See Penny Maddrell, *The Bedouin of the Negev* (London: The Minority Rights Group, Report No.81, 1990), p.7.
18 ISA, Foreign Ministry, 2401/21.

19   ISA, Foreign Ministry, 2401/21b.

20   Kretzmer, *The Legal Status of the Arabs in Israel*, pp.50-1; Hussein Abu Hussein and Fiona McKay, *Access Denied: Palestinian Land Rights in Israel* (London: Zed Books, 2003), p.87; Meron Benvenisti, *Sacred Landscape: The Buried History of the Holy Land since 1948* (Berkeley: University of California Press, 2000), p.226.

21   Cited in the manifesto of the National Committee for the Defence of the Internally Displaced Palestinians in Israel, Badil Resource Center, at: http://www.badil.org/Publications/Press/2000/manifesto.htm (accessed on 25 May 2005). The names of the villages have been systematised in line with the transliteration system adopted by the editor.

22   One acre equals four *dunums*.

23   *Discrimination Diary, 25 February 2000*, The Arab Association for Human Rights, at: http://www.arabhra.org/dd/dd225.htm (accessed on 8 December 2001).

24   Yiftachel, *Planning a Mixed Region in Israel*, appendix 1, p.313; Uri Davis, *Apartheid Israel: The Possibilities for Struggle Within* (London and New York: Zed Books, 2003), pp.40-7, 99-104; Abu Hussein and McKay, *Access Denied;* Usama Halabi, "The Impact of the Jewishness of the State of Israel on the Status and Rights of the Arab Citizens in Israel", in Nur Masalha (ed.), *The Palestinians in Israel: Is Israel the State of all its Citizens and "Absentees"?* (Nazareth: the Galilee Centre for Social Research, 1993), pp.22-5.

25   In Hebrew Hok Nikhsie Nifkadim.

26   See the address of the Chairman of the Knesset Finance Committee, who presented the bill to the Knesset, in *Divrie Haknesset* [Israeli Parliament's Proceedings] 868-70, 27 February 1950.

27   Benvenisti, *Sacred Landscape*, p.158.

28   Quoted in Kretzmer, *The Legal Status of the Arabs in Israel*, p.56; Halabi, "The Impact of the Jewishness of the State of Israel on the Status and Rights of the Arab Citizens in Israel", pp.22-5.

29   Kretzmer, *The Legal Status of the Arabs in Israel*, p.56.

30   Ibid., pp.56-7.

31   Ibid., p.57.

32   Gilmour, *Dispossessed*, p.108.

33   Benjamin Beit-Hallahmi, *Original Sins* (London: Pluto Press, 1992), p.91.

34   'Adalah, *History of the Palestinians in Israel*, at: http://www.adalah.org/ background.shtml (accessed on 3 November 2001).

35   Al-Haj, "The Arab Internal Refugees in Israel", p.9; Beidas, "The Internally Displaced – Seeking Return Within One's Own Land", p.33.

36   *Discrimination Diary, 21 October 1999*, Arab Association for Human Rights, at http://www.arabhra.org/dd/dd10-21.htm (accessed on 8 December 2001). Professor 'Uzi Ornan estimates that 95 percent of the lands within the Green Line are classified as state land. Cited in Noam Chomsky, *Socialist Revolution* 5 (1975), pp.45-6. For further discussion of land alienation and its effect on Arabs, see Elia Zureik, *The Palestinians in Israel* (London: Routledge & Kegan Paul, 1979), pp.115–22; Ran Kislev, "Land Expropriations: History of Oppression", *New Outlook* (September–October 1976), pp.23-32.

37 Abu Hussein and McKay, *Access Denied*, p.16, and chapters five and six; Davis, *Apartheid Israel*, p.190.

38 In 1953 the JNF reiterated that its primary mission was to acquire lands "for the purpose of settling Jews on the said lands and property". Kretzmer, *The Legal Status of the Arabs in Israel*, pp.61-73

39 See article by Amnon Rubinstein, in *Haaretz*, 13 October 1999.

40 Henry Rosenfeld, "The Class Situation of the Arab National Minority in Israel", *Comparative Studies in Society and History* 20, no.3 (July 1978), p.400. Professor 'Uzi Ornan estimates that 95 per cent of the lands within the Green Line are classified as state land. Cited in Noam Chomsky, *Socialist Revolution* 5 (1975), pp. 45-6. For further discussion of land alienation and its effect on Arabs, see Elia Zureik, *The Palestinians in Israel* (London: Routledge & Kegan Paul, 1979), pp.115-22; Ran Kislev, "Land Expropriations: History of Oppression", *New Outlook* (September–October 1976), pp.23-32.

41 Benvenisti, *Sacred Landscape*, p.226.

42 Riah Abu Al-Assal, "Zionism: As It Is in Israel for an Arab", in *Judaism or Zionism?* (London: Zed Books, 1986), p.172.

43 See also Chapter 6 on Kafr Bir'im.

44 Joseph L. Ryan, "Refugees Within Israel: The Case of the Villagers of Kafr Iqrit and Bir'im", *Journal of Palestine Studies* II, no.4 (Summer 1993), p.59-60; *Christian Science Monitor*, 12 August 1972.

45 *Discrimination Diary, 20 December 1999*, the Arab Association for Human Rights, at: http://www.arabhra.org/dd/dd1219.htm (accessed on 8 December 2001).

46 Morris, *Israel's Border Wars*, p.148.

47 *Discrimination Diary, 20 December 1999*, the Arab Association for Human Rights, at: http://www.arabhra.org/dd/dd1219.htm (accessed on 8 December 2001).

48 Ibid.

49 Ibid.

50 Ryan, "Refugees Within Israel", pp.64-5.

51 *Jerusalem Post*, 24 July 1972.

52 Ryan, "Refugees Within Israel", p.55.

53 Amos Elon, "Two Arab Towns that Plumb Israel's Conscience", *New York Times Magazine*, 22 October 1972, p.44.

54 *Discrimination Diary, 20 December 1999*, the Arab Association for Human Rights, at: http://www.arabhra.org/dd/dd1219.htm (accessed on 8 December 2001).

55 Ryan, "Refugees Within Israel", p.55.

56 *Discrimination Diary, 20 December 1999*, the Arab Association for Human Rights, at: http://www.arabhra.org/dd/dd1219.htm (accessed on 8 December 2001).

57 *Village Statistics, 1945* (Beirut: PLO Research Centre edition, 1970), pp.40, 70.

58 *Discrimination Diary, 20 December 1999*, the Arab Association for Human Rights, at: http://www.arabhra.org/dd/dd1219.htm (accessed on 8 December 2001).

59 *Fasl al-Maqal*, 26 October 2001.

60 *Al-Ittihad*, 21 October 2001.

61 "Israel's Racist Land Policies Remain Unchanged: Government Rejects Return of Internally Displaced Palestinian Villagers of Iqrit and Bir'im", at: Badil

Resource Center, 11 October 2001 (E53/2001).

62 Al-Haj, "The Arab Internal Refugees in Israel", p.13.

63 Hillel Cohen, *Hanifkadim Hanokhahim: Haplitim Hafalastinayyim Beyisrael Meaz 1948* [The Present Absentees: The Palestinian Refugees in Israel Since 1948], (Jerusalem: Centre for the Study of Arab Society in Israel, Van Leer Institute, 2000 [Hebrew]), p.12.

64 In Arabic *"al-Lajna al-Qutriyya Li-Difai' 'an Huquq al-Muhajjarin fi Israeel"*.

65 Wakim Wakim, *Haq al-'Awda Lemuhajri al-Dahkil Haq Ghair Qabil Littasarrof* [The Right of Return of the Internally Displaced is an Inalienable Right] (Haifa: Initiating Committee for the Defence of the Rights of the Displaced in Israel, 1995), p.2.

66 Ahmad Ashkar, "Internal Refugees: Their Inalienable Right to Return", *News from Within* 11, no. (August 1995), pp.14-7.

67 A destroyed village near Nazareth; an entire and very crowded quarter in the city is inhabited by displaced people from Saffuriyya.

68 Beidas, "The Internally Displaced – Seeking Return Within One's Own Land", p.35.

69 Beidas, "The Internally Displaced – Seeking Return Within One's Own Land", p.36

70 See, for instance, Ittijah's newsletter, issue no.31 (18 June 2004), at: http://www.ittijah.org/newsletter/newsletter04_06_18.html (accessed on 28 September 2004).

71 See Chapter 9.

72 Cohen, *Hanifkadim Hanokhahim*, p.14; Benvenisti, *Sacred Landscape*, pp.267-69.

73 In Arabic, *"Lajnat al-Mutaba'a al-'Ulya"*.

74 Cohen, *Hanifkadim Hanokhahim*, p.13. See also interview with 'Azmi Bishara, leader of al-Tajamu'a al-Watani al-Dimuqrati, in *Haaretz*, 12 June 1996; statements by the Mayor of Umm al-Fahem, Raid Salah, in *Sawt al-Haq Wal-Hurriyya*, 31 March 1995.

75 The manifesto of the National Committee for the Defence of the Internally Displaced Palestinians in Israel, Badil Resource Center, at: http://www.badil.org/Press/2000/manifesto.htm (accessed on 15 December 2001); Statement by the National Committee for the Defence of Internally Displaced Palestinians in Israel, Badil Resource Center, 13 March 2000, at: http://www.badil.org/Press/2000/ press93-00.htm (accessed on 15 December 2001); *Internally Displaced Palestinians in Israel Reaffirm: We Demand to Return to Our Homes and Property*, Badil Resource Center, 13 March 2000, at: http://www.badil.org/Press/2000/press93-00.htm (accessed on 15 December 2001).

76 Beidas, "The Internally Displaced-Seeking Return Within One's Own Land", p.34.

77 Al-Haj, "The Arab Internal Refugees in Israel," p.8.

78 Ashkar, "Internal Refugees: Their Inalienable Right to Return", pp.14–7; *Al-Ayyam* (Ramallah), 14 May 1997.

79 *Al-Ayyam* (Ramallah), 14 May 1997.

80 Al-Ghabisiyya was occupied on 20–21 May 1948. The village surrendered
formally and its population was expelled sometime during the following days or
weeks. Al-Ghabisiyya and other two neighbouring villages, Shaykh Dannun and
Shaykh Dawud, were evacuated. Those inhabitants from al-Ghabisiyya who had
not sought refuge in Lebanon were joined by other internally displaced from
villages such as al-Nahr, al-Tall, Umm al-Faraj, 'Amqa, and Kuwaykat and ended
up in the repopulated village of Shaykh Dannun which in 1973 had a population
of 1000. The only landmark that remains today in al-Ghabisiyya is the mosque
and the debris of houses, terraces and village cemetery can be see amidst a thick
forest of cypress tree that was planed on the village site and part of the land. The
Jewish settlement of Netiv Hashayara uses the adjacent non-forested land for
agriculture. Walid Khalidi (ed.), *All That Remains: The Palestinian Villages Occupied
and Depopulated by Israel in 1948* (Washington DC: Institute for Palestine Studies,
1992), pp.13-15; Morris, *The Birth of the Palestinian Refugee Problem*, pp.124–5.
81 *Haaretz*, 29 March 1998.
82 *Palestinians in Israel Boycott Israeli Independence Celebrations: Statement by the National
Committee for the Defence of Internally Displaced Palestinians in Israel*, Badil Resource
Center, 9 May 2000, at: http://www.badil.org/Press/2000/press101-00.htm
(accessed on 15 December 2001); Benvenisti, *Sacred Landscape*, p.268.
83 *Palestinians in Israel Boycott Israeli Independence Celebrations: Statement by the National
Committee for the Defence of Internally Displaced Palestinians in Israel*, Badil Resource
Center, 9 May 2000, at: http://www.badil.org/Press/2000/press101-00.htm
(accessed on 15 December 2001);
84 Benvenisti, *Sacred Landscape*, p.268.
85 "Internally displaced Palestinians commemorate 1948 *Nakba* by visit to
destroyed village with 3,000-year history", BADIL Resource Center for
Palestinian Residency and Refugee Rights Press release, 20 April 2004.
86 Ashkar, "Internal Refugees: Their Inalienable Right to Return", pp.14-17.
87 *Concluding Observations of the Committee on Economic, Social and Cultural Rights, Israel,
UN Economic and Social Council*, General, E/C.12/1/Add.27, 4 December 1998,
at: http://www.hri.ca/fortherecord1999/docu.../e-c12-1-add27.ht (accessed on
8 December 2001.) The full text of the International Covenant on Economic,
Social and Cultural Rights, at: http://www.tufts.edu/departments/fletcher/
multi/ texts/BH497.txt11/12/2001.
88 See, for instance, Yasir Arafat, "The Palestinian Vision of Peace" (Op-Ed), 3
February 2002, pp. 4 and 15.
89 Naseer Aruri, "The Right of Return and its Detractors" in Michael Prior (ed.),
Speaking the Truth About Zionism ad Israel (London: Melisende, 2004), pp.220–21.
90 Uri Nir, "Also the Refugees in Israel Want to Return Home", *Haaretz*, 8 January
2001, pp.1 and 13a.
91 Ilan Pappé, "Demons of the Nakbah", *Al-Ahram Weekly* Online, no.586, 16–22
May 2002.
92 Benvenisti, *Sacred Landscape*, pp.267-9.

2
The State of Israel *versus* the Palestinian Internal Refugees

Hillel Cohen

The internal refugees in Israel are Palestinians who were uprooted from their villages in the course of the 1948 war, but found refuge within the borders of the state and became its citizens. From 1948 up until today, they have continuously voiced their demand to return to their villages, only to be met by the refusal of all Israeli governments. For the most part, the internal refugees' lands were allocated to Jewish settlement. While constituting a part of the general refugee problem, the moral, political and practical controversy about the internal refugees is one of the most concrete expressions of the structural conflict between the state of Israel and its Arab citizens.

This chapter aims to analyse the relations between the state of Israel and the Palestinian internal refugees in the context of the struggle over "refugee identity" from the 1948 war onwards. After introducing the roots of the problem of the internal refugees and the legal mechanisms through which Israel took over their lands, the chapter deals with the Israeli policy of abolishing their identity, and the resistance of groups within these communities. Since the early 1990s we have witnessed a revival of the "refugee identity", which will be presented and analysed at the end of the chapter.[1]

The Roots of the Problem and the Denial of Return

The roots of this phenomenon are to be found in the way in which Palestinian Arabs were uprooted from areas conquered by Jewish forces in the 1948 war. Terrified by the advancing Israeli army, whole communities had left their villages and sought refuge in neighbouring villages which had not yet been conquered, or in large towns, which they believed would never be taken by the Israelis. But most of these villages and towns were indeed conquered, and their inhabitants, as well as their "guests", were uprooted. In the rare cases where the host communities stayed in place, the refugees from the neighbouring villages stayed with them, or at least tried to.[2] That was the case with thousands of villagers from the eastern Galilee, who concentrated in the town of Nazareth prior to its occupation. The same goes for many refugees who, relying on the close ties between the Druze leadership and the Israeli army, fled to Druze villages, hoping they would be allowed to stay. Many others found asylum in villages that later surrendered to the Israeli army without battle, and became part of the new state of Israel with their inhabitants.[3]

The reaction of the Israeli Defence Force (IDF), as reported by Israeli officials, was to drive the refugees who remained in the state of Israel over the border, in order to prevent them from returning to their villages. Thousands of refugees were thus expelled from the region of al-Ramah and al-Buqay'a (in the northern mountains of Galilee) and from the town of al-Majdal (now Ashkelon, in the southern coast).[4] Similarly, Israel pressured inhabitants of villages in the Arab Triangle to leave their homes prior to the allocation of this area to the state of Israel according to the Israeli–Jordan Rhodes Agreement of 1949.[5]

In spite of the forced expulsions, according to official estimates some 25,000 internal refugees remained within the borders of the newborn state, mainly in the Galilee, constituting about one-sixth of the total Arab population.[6] Unable to carry out extensive acts of deportation after the war, Israel now had to tackle the task of preventing the internal refugees from returning to their villages and reoccupying their lands.

Israel justified its refusal to allow the return of the internal refugees to their villages and lands in three ways. The first was its determination to expand Jewish settlement. In this context the uprooting of Arab residents was seen as a golden opportunity, after years of restrictions on Jewish land acquisition. The expected mass immigration of Jewish refugees from all over the world increased the need for land. Existing settlements were also demanding more agricultural land.[7] Thus in the course of the war old and new immigrants were settled in abandoned Arab villages,[8] whose populations were at that time external or internal refugees. In that period, among other such projects, kibbutz Megiddo was established on the lands of Lajjun, some of whose residents moved to Umm al-Fahem.

Kibbutz Yas'ur in western Galilee was established on the lands of al-Birwa, whose residents moved to Majd al-Kurum, al-Maker and Judayda, while kibbutz Beit Ha'emek was established on the lands of Kuwaykat in western Galilee, some of whose former residents found refuge in Abu Sinan.[9] The settlement of new immigrants in abandoned Arab villages would continue during the 1950s.

The second justification was security. The dominant concept amongst the Israeli leadership at the time was that the Palestinians and the Arab states were preparing themselves for a second round of warfare in order to remove the disgrace of their defeat in 1948 and destroy the state of Israel. The Arab citizens of Israel were perceived as a "fifth column" – waiting for such a move and preparing to help it. This assumption resulted in the evacuation of Arab villages from border areas (Iqrit and Kafr Bir'im were the best-known examples). Thus the Bedouins of the Zubaydat tribe in lower Galilee were evacuated under the accusation that they were delivering intelligence information from Jordan to Lebanon. Residents of small villages in the Arab Triangle were transferred to larger villages.[10] The same kind of reasoning led to the decision to forbid resettlement of abandoned villages. Instead, the internal refugees were concentrated in towns or villages and were distanced from strategically important areas, such as main roads and highways.

The third reason can be seen as vengefulness or, alternatively, as a refusal to reward those who were seen as the aggressors. The Jewish community perceived the 1948 war as one that was forced on its peace-loving members. In its aftermath many of them supported an "iron fist" policy towards the Arab citizens, and particularly toward villagers who had participated actively in the fighting. Those who started the war, was the consensus, had to pay the price. Moreover, some believed that allowing the internal refugees to return to their villages in spite of their past aggression would be perceived by the Arab population as an indication of weakness and would cause them to disparage the state of Israel. This notion is illustrated by prime minister David Ben-Gurion's reply to a question put by the communist member of the Knesset (Israeli parliament) Tawfik Tubi: "The village of al-Birwa is an abandoned village destroyed in the battles. Its residents co-operated with the Qawaqji militia [the Israeli common term for the "Salvation Army" organised by the Arab League to support the Palestinians]. The IDF and the government dealt generously with them and permitted them to stay in villages near al-Birwa and to be residents of Israel."[11]

After the war, which took the life of 6,000 Jews – 1 per cent of the Jewish population – the Zionist leadership saw no moral fault in refusing to allow the internal refugees to return home. Permitting them to remain in nearby villages was presented as a humanitarian gesture. The refugees were to remain in the villages in which they had found refuge. Israel, aided by the United Nations Relief and Worker Agency for Palestine Refugees (UNWRA), provided basic welfare in food and housing, while the refugees' land was settled by Jews.

The Appropriation of Land: Legal Mechanisms

Parallel to the denial of return, the state authorities began to undertake legislative measures designed to establish legally the appropriation of the refugees' lands. In June 1948, the first version of regulations transferring the lands of the refugees to the ownership of the state was published. Toward the end of 1949 the terms of a more comprehensive law – the Law of Absentees' Property – were drafted for presentation to the Knesset. The newly established Authority for the Rehabilitation of the Refugees, composed of experts in land and Arab affairs, worked to define the internal refugees, along with all others, as absentees, and to have their lands given to the state. In October 1949, at the sixth meeting of the Committee for Refugee Affairs, the prime minister's advisor Zalman Lif (Lifschitz) said, "The revised law would also include evacuated Arabs. According to the law every Arab who was not in his place of residence on a certain date, whatever the reason (flight, evacuation, transfer), is considered an absentee."[12]

In 1950, the Knesset accepted the Law of Absentees' Property, replacing emergency regulations on the subject. The definition of an absentee included "every Israeli citizen who left his regular residence in Israel (a) to a place outside Israel before 1.9.48 or (b) for a place in Israel which was at that time occupied by forces which sought to prevent the establishment of the state of Israel or fought against it after its establishment".[13] Thus the internal refugees were defined as absentees even though they were present in the State on the relevant date, and are legal citizens. This anomalous situation granted them (along with additional population groups) the title 'present absentees' since in spite of their physical presence in the country they are legally considered as absentees and their property is taken from them and transferred to the

Custodian of Absentees' Property.[14] The legislation denied the internal refugees any possibility of winning legal assistance and made the transfer of their assets to the state completely legal. Appeals to the Supreme Court, based on claims that their leaving of residence was temporary, now became irrelevant.

Along with this legislation, the authorities encouraged the absorption of the refugees in the villages to which they had fled. They were given priority in leasing abandoned lands in places where they were concentrated. In a few villages such as al-Makr, Judayda and Sha'ab in western Galilee, and Wadi al-Hamam and 'Akbara in eastern Galilee houses were built for the internal refugees, but only on condition that they sign a document renouncing their assets in their villages of origin. Despite initial resistance, some refugees eventually agreed to settle in these villages.[15]

The 1952 Land Acquisition Law (LAL) gave absolute and retroactive confirmation to the transfer of the lands of the internal refugees to state ownership, including the lands of refugees who from a legal point of view were not absentees, for example those who had left their villages for others already conquered by the IDF, or who were sheltering near their village. The law also determined a compensation mechanism for the internal refugees, in money or alternative lands. From a legal point of view this was a sort of watershed; from now on the state could legally take over any Arab-owned land without facing appeal. It was left to persuade the refugees to accept the compensation money, to make them sign a document renouncing any claim to their lands, and to help them resettle in one of the populated villages.

Landlessness: Stages in State–Refugee Relations

The introduction of the LAL marked a new era for the internal refugees. Alongside the 1952 decision to transfer the authorities of UNRWA regarding the refugees to the Israeli government, the new law ended the period of the creation of the refugee problem and the appropriation of refugees' lands. The vast majority of internal refugees were now dwelling in temporary housing in the outskirts of villages in the Galilee and the Triangle.

The law heralded the second phase of relations between Israel and the internal refugees, which lasted until 1958. From here on, there was no more forced transferring of Arab citizens, and no more land allocation by the state without some legal procedure. A reparation mechanism in the framework of the LAL was established during these years, yet most of the refugees upheld their demand to return to their villages while only a few agreed to give up their original homes and lands. During this period the refugees still perceived the prospect of returning to their villages as realistic. Only a tiny minority of them started to build permanent houses, frequently without permits. Towards the end of the period, families of internal refugees who had dispersed to different parts of Israel began to move voluntarily to one chosen "temporary" village in order to live alongside each other. In retrospect, this could be seen as a first sign of their coming to terms with the fact that they would probably not be allowed to reunite in their original home.

The third period, from 1958 to 1967, marked the settlement of the internal refugees in the villages in which they were absorbed. The reason for their tendency to accept permanent settlement at that time is triple. First, they realised that the refugee problem was not likely to be resolved by a "second round" of war between Israel and the Arab states, especially in light of Egypt's defeat in the 1956 Suez War. A second reason was the improvement and updating of the state's reparation mechanism, involving paying higher sums to the refugees in return for their lands and speeding up public building in the villages where they were living. The final reason was the extensive use by Israel of the internal refugees' lands, which deepened the refugees' recognition that they would never get them back.

A new era began after the 1967 war, when the issue of the internal refugees was almost entirely removed from the public agenda. The main reason for this was that the burning personal problems of most of the refugees had been settled: both of those who accepted reparations and of those who managed to cope by themselves. Public attention was now drawn to the territories conquered in 1967, and their inhabitants. This development was reflected in Knesset debates. Until 1967 the demand for the return of the internal refugees to their villages was raised in almost every Knesset session. After 1967 the subject was hardly mentioned.[16]

In recent years, and most intensively since the 1990s, the subject has once again emerged on the public agenda of the Arab population in Israel. The Arab parties and the Hadash party[17] demanded a solution to the problem in their election platforms of 1996 and 1999. Local refugee committees in dozens of villages, presided over by a national committee, strive to strengthen the identity of refugees, to preserve the memory of the lost villages and to raise the demand for return. The decision to hold the national ceremony marking fifty years of the *Nakba* (the Palestinian disaster of 1948) in the abandoned village of al-Ghabisiyya in western Galilee, under the slogan of returning the internal refugees to their villages, could be seen as characteristic of the renewed interest in this issue. Commemorating the *Nakba* in abandoned villages at the initiative of the national refugee committee has become a tradition among Palestinian citizens of Israel in recent years.

The Israeli State and the Uprooting of Refugee Identity

The activities of refugee committees provide the clearest indication of the revival of refugee identity among the internal refugees. This relatively new phenomenon is viewed unfavourably by the state of Israel, which spent years trying to uproot this identity. In effect, over and above the legislation aimed at appropriating the lands of the internal refugees, the main state activity regarding this population was in the realm of identity. This is not a special characteristic of state activity among the refugees: state intervention in creating and neutralising sub-identities[18] constituted a central element in controlling and supervising the population. Through varied leucocratic and legal means, including the use of force, the state authorities acted to uproot the collective refugee identity of this population on the assumption that this would weaken the refugees' demand to return to their villages of origin.

Analysing "refugee identity" is essential to comprehend this point fully, and it reveals that this identity has two aspects: positive and negative. The positive aspect is being native to a certain settlement that no longer exists, cherishing its abandoned pathways, destroyed houses and lost scents. This aspect of identity can be called "I was there". It was pointedly expressed by Mahmoud 'Issa in his research on the refugees of the village of Lubya (which was located on the Tiberias–Nazareth road): "For youngsters, middle-aged or old, Lubya constitutes a basic identity image, a source to relate to in thought and sub-consciously, a model of cultural framework".[19] The other aspect of refugee identity is the negative one, the self-conception, and the image of oneself in the eyes of others as a refugee, a foreigner who doesn't belong to his present place of dwelling.

It is an image that could be summed in the notion: "I am not from here". This notion is expressed through a sense of alienation from the place of refuge, sometimes stressed by rejection projected by the absorbing community. This characteristic of identity was shown by Hasan Musa in the mid-1980s in his research concerning internal refugees from four Galilee villages. He found that 28 out of 80 internal refugees who were asked about their sentiments reported feelings of alienation and of being outsiders.[20]

Israel's main struggle was naturally directed against the positive identity, which preserved the connection between the refugees and their original villages. The action taken by the state consisted of physical activity aimed directly at the refugees and their lands, and indirect activity intended to influence both their consciousness and the general public discourse on the issue. The direct activity consisted of preventing the refugees from approaching their abandoned villages, as well as providing reparations or alternative housing.

Prevention of any approach to the abandoned villages was primarily intended to create a complete break between the refugees and their villages, in order to enable the handing over of their lands to Jewish settlement. Accordingly, the first activity was the total evacuation of the abandoned villages (in most of them between five and ten per cent of the original residents had remained).[21] Subsequently the authorities were strict about repeatedly evacuating refugees who tried to get hold of their lands; IDF units patrolled the abandoned villages in order to make sure that the residents did not return. Anyone found in the abandoned villages was removed to neighbouring villages or expelled from the country.[22] In 1951 the sites of the abandoned villages were declared security areas, permitting legal measures to be taken against anyone entering them.[23] This was an intermediary step toward turning them into Jewish villages.

However, even after the transfer of the lands to Jewish settlement, the state continued to ensure that the refugees would be cut off from their former lands. The relevant Israeli authorities laid down that "under no circumstances must land be leased to Arabs formerly from that village, or originally from there". Moreover, they were not permitted to work, even as labourers, in their former lands. In addition, Jews or Arabs leasing land in an abandoned village had to undertake not to employ refugees whose origins were in that village.[24]

The new generation born after the war, the authorities thought, would be unable to develop an emotional connection to the parental village, or claim "I am from there". Neither could the older generation go to their place of origin and point concretely at their homes. The destruction of the villages at a later stage was to symbolise forever the lack of any prospect of materialising the refugees' yearning to return home. Nevertheless, the authorities assumed that even this was not enough if the "community of memory" remained intact.

This was why the reparation mechanism was put into force. Internal refugees were put under enormous pressure to accept compensation arrangements and give up their land. But most internal refugees abstained from demanding reparation for their lost lands. They perceived such an agreement as cutting themselves off from the ideal of return, from personal, communal and national points of view. Moreover, this norm of refusal constituted a principle, which united the refugees and preserved their identity. Breaking it would lead to the disintegration of their communities. Conscious of all that, the Israeli establishment strove to split the refugee consensus. The Israeli authorities realised that undermining the holy principle of "no compensation" would break the social solidarity of the refugees and their collective identity. This explains why the Israeli authorities decided in September 1954 to seek individual refugees who would agree to accept reparations. They thought this was the way to break the opposition of the refugee community to the proposed arrangement.[25] As shown by data from the Israel Land Authority, this activity proved fruitful.[26] The number of internal refugees requesting reparations and giving up their land constantly grew, and the refugee identity began to disintegrate. Moreover, the state's success in spreading the refugees in different villages hastened the collapse of the old community frameworks that had preserved the refugee identity.

Alongside those activities, the state kept trying to penetrate the refugee consciousness. In his book *Imagined Communities*, Benedict Anderson explains the role of population census, maps and museums in the construction of national identities.[27] The same institutions were used by Israel for uprooting the refugee identity. Israel did not mention the origins of the internal refugees in the formal statistics. They were not included in the UNWRA registry, and the abandoned villages did not appear on maps. It goes without saying that no museum was established in Israel to commemorate life in the villages which no longer existed.

The use of maps in this context is particularly noteworthy. After the removal of the names of abandoned Palestinian villages from maps, only a few of them could be located in updated topographical maps. This is true also for remains of villages on which Jewish villages were not established. I have noted how in 1952 the internal refugees were removed from the UNWRA scrolls. In Israeli population censuses, the refugees are registered as belonging in their villages of refuge not of origin, emphasising the message that they are no longer connected to the latter.

In Israeli Arab schools, neither the *Nakba* and the refugee problem in general, nor that of the internal refugees in particular, have been part of the curriculum. Teachers trying to present these issues were subjected to the scrutiny of the security services. A religious education teacher in Acre said, "The government robbed us of our lands and drove us from our villages though the holy books of three faiths – the Jewish, the Muslim and the Christian – state that it is forbidden to plunder the lands of the poor." His words were relayed to the security service which passed them on to the Ministry of Education.[28]

In the mid-1980s, it looked as if the goal of uprooting the refugee identity had been achieved. In his conclusions to a research project published in 1986, Professor Majid al-Haj, of Haifa University, wrote: "There is nothing distinguishing the refugees from other Arabs in the general community. Unlike refugees in other places, who established voluntary societies and other social frameworks, the internal Arab refugees have no organisational frameworks of any sort".[29] Similarly, Alexander Bligh could present the settlement of the refugees in the state of Israel as a successful example of such a resettlement project.[30] Al-Haj observed, however, that half of his interviewees reported a "feeling of being a refugee" although this had no concrete expression, at least not in the position taken by these refugees toward Israeli society or the state's establishment.[31]

The Refugee Identity: Reawakening and Opposition

The reality described above changed completely in the early 1990s. The political discourse of the Palestinians in Israel regarding the internal refugees was in upheaval. The reawakening of the refugee identity invoked identification among the masses. This process kept accelerating with the establishment of over twenty local associations of internal refugees, roofed by a national committee.

The speedy revival of the "refugee identity" shows that even without social, institutional and organisational frameworks, it was preserved not only by the first generation, the refugees themselves, but by their descendants as well. It proves that an internal stratum maintained itself over the years in spite of governmental policies. We can assume that the preservation of the refugee identity was fed during the first years by the struggle of those displaced to return to their original villages, and was later reinforced by the alienation felt by the refugees in their new homes.

This feeling of alienation was the result of the objective situation in these villages, aggravated by a shortage of land. "I generally try to forget I am a refugee", al-Haj quotes one of his interviewees, "but when I see the local people going with their families to their fields, while I, like the other refugees, have no property, I feel very strongly that I am different from the other sons of the village." Many other interviewees expressed similar sentiments.

In this situation it is no wonder that the negative refugee identity was preserved into the second generation. But the refugee committees established in the 1990s are not satisfied with only this part of the refugee identity. Most of their activity aims to reconstruct the positive components of refugee identity. Committee activists, along with some members of the second and third refugee generations, are renewing physical contact with the abandoned villages through work camps and restoration activities, thus strengthening refugee consciousness and identity. Those activities challenge to an extent the measures taken by the state along the years, regarding maps, museums (or, in fact, their absence), and population censuses. The participation of members of second and third generations in those activities helps to strengthen their contact with their villages of origin and does away in practice with the separation the state had tried to enforce.

In addition, the refugee identity is being strengthened by a series of symbolic and educational means intended to construct a new discourse. In recent years quite a few books concerning the abandoned villages have been published by Palestinian citizens of Israel and in other Palestinian communities. Some, like *All That Remains: The Palestinian Villages Occupied and Depopulated by Israel in 1948*, edited by Walid Khalidi, document all the villages,[32] while the majority survey particular villages or districts in pre-1948 Palestine. Written by refugees, internal or external, in the framework of academic research or as a private initiative, these books constitute a mobile written museum.

The refugees committees are now planning a census of Israel's internal refugees. In addition to strengthening identity, this will constitute the factual basis for planned legal and public struggles. Another move aimed at reconstituting lost communities is the rehabilitation of those who accepted reparations in the past. This reflects an attempt to develop a new discourse in which those who accepted compensation in the past would not be excluded from their communities.

All in all, it appears that the attempts by the Israeli establishment to neutralise refugee identity have failed, just as the supreme goal for which it strove – the creation of an Arab-Israeli identity cut off from the maternal Palestinian identity – did not succeed. Perhaps these failures show how limited external factors are in the process of the crystallisation of identity.

However, in order to present a full picture, one must examine the reawakening of the Palestinian refugee identity in Israel in its historical context, along with the beginning of negotiations between Israel and the Palestinian political leadership. As the political dialogue proceeded, it seemed that the contradiction between the focal points of identity among Palestinians in Israel – Israeli civic identity on one hand and Palestinian national identity on the other – was diminished. This process brought about a strengthening of Israeli identity among the Palestinians in Israel (along with, and not instead of, their Palestinian identity). The strengthening of the Israeli component of the identity of the Palestinians in Israel has been acknowledged by the PLO and the Israeli government who agreed not to include the internal refugee problem in the discussion (yet to take place in the unforeseeable future) of the general Palestinian refugee problem. The internal refugees have decided to carry on with their struggle as Israeli citizens, demanding the correction of an injustice done to them. The internal refugees, like the other Palestinian citizens of Israel, hoped that the peace process would encourage Israel to come to terms with them as well as with the PLO and the Palestinians in the occupied territories and the diaspora.[33]

Another explanation for the renewal of the internal refugees' struggle is suggested by Professor Arnon Sofer, of Haifa University. Sofer believes that it is a result of a feeling among Israeli Arabs that Israeli sovereignty in areas of dense Arab population was weakened through prolonged Israeli compromise. He claims that the demands of the

Palestinian internal refugees are part of a process aiming to transform Israel from a Jewish state to a "state of all its citizens".[34] According to this Israeli-Jewish attitude, strengthening the Palestinian identity of Arab-Israeli citizens, like the reinforcement of refugee identity, represents a threat to the Jewish-Zionist identity of Israel.

The demographic factor should also be considered. As years went by, the refugees' descendants were more and more distressed by the problem of land shortage. Israel kept appropriating land from villages that were not destroyed during the 1948 war. However, the land and housing problems of the internal refugees (especially those who refused to accept reparations) were much graver than those of the rest of the population. The hope voiced by activists that the lands could be returned by means of a political struggle gave some refugees new hope.

The above-mentioned factors complement one another, and each had its influence on the revival of the refugee identity. Nevertheless, in spite of this revival of identity, and activities in the abandoned villages, it is still too early to determine to what extent the revival incorporates the whole refugee population (some villages have not organised at all, others have only symbolic representation). Neither is it clear to what extent they will persist in their struggle and how successful it will be. The answers to those questions depend greatly on the position to be adopted by the state. For the time being, one can hardly observe any sign of change to Israel's old policies opposing any expression of the right of return for refugees, internal or external. The growing tension between Israel and the Palestinian Authority since the eruption of the al-Aqsa Intifada, as well as the crisis of trust between the state and its Arab citizens in the wake of the events of October 2000, have only resulted up to now in a strengthening of the Jewish-Israeli position rejecting any change in the status quo. Hence the Israeli cabinet decision in October 2001 not to allow the Iqrit and Kafr Bir'im refugees to return to their homes (contrary to former recommendations). To justify that decision, it was argued that in spite of the special circumstances of those refugees, their return would set a precedent, strengthening the demands of return voiced by other internal refugees all over the country.

The failure of negotiations between Israel and the Palestinians at Camp David (July 2000), which was explained in the official Israeli political discourse as stemming from Palestinian obstinacy over the "right of return", only increased Israeli opposition to any concessions for the internal refugees. The reasoning for that approach varies between explanations regarding security, and a declared wish to maintain the Jewish-Zionist character of the state.

Naturally, the internal refugee committees are conscious of the fears of the Jewish public and the Israeli establishment concerning their demands, and are aware that there is little hope of achieving a return to the pre-1948 situation. Therefore, in general, they are not demanding to get all their land back, but only the portions of land that are not worked or settled. According to their initial surveys, a substantial part of the lands in many abandoned villages is deserted. However, even limiting their demands did not yield a change in the state's position. Most of the committees' activities are therefore directed at present toward internal organisational work and raising the subject of the internal refugees within the overall Israeli political discourse.

To conclude, during the past decade the internal refugees have undergone two major political developments. The first was their re-establishment of their collective refugee identity as a tool of activity, and the second was coming to terms with their status as Israeli citizens, hence defining their struggle as a civic rather than a national one (though some would regard it as a "national minority" problem). To their dismay, they have witnessed no significant change in the attitude of Israeli governments towards their demands. Furthermore, the current crisis in the Israeli–Palestinian relationship in general, and between Israel and its Arab citizens in particular, has led Israel to harden even further its position regarding their problem. It seems at the moment that only a process of reconciliation between Israel, the Palestinians and the Palestinian citizens of Israel might enable a change in the Israeli point of view on this matter. Without such a change, the problem of the internal refugees will remain unsolved.

Notes

1 A version of this chapter was first published in *Refuge* 21, No.2 (February 2003). The author and editor would like to thank the journal for the permission to publish it in this collection with some minor modifications.

2 Only 20 per cent of the Palestinian population in the area that became the state of Israel have remained within the borders of the state. 80 per cent were uprooted; they settled mainly in Jordan (including the area that would be annexed

by it in 1950, the so-called West Bank), Gaza Strip, Lebanon and Syria.

3 "Report of the activities of the military government in Nazareth and region, 17 July 1948 to 17 October 1948", Israel State Archives, Jerusalem (herein: ISA) Foreign Office files, 2564/11.

4 See also Chapter 9.

5 For further material on the expulsion and evacuation of internal refugees during and after the war, see Hillel Cohen, *Hanifkadim Hanokhahim: Haplitim Hafalastinayyim BeYisrael Meaz 1948* [*Present Absentees: Palestinian Refugees in Israel Since 1948*], (Jerusalem: Centre for the Study of Arab Society in Israel, Van Leer Institute, 2000), pp.37-41 [in Hebrew]).

6 This figure includes only urban and rural refugees and does not include the Bedouin in the Negev, many of whom were forced to leave their places of residence for areas determined by the IDF. The sources are a document of the Ministry of Labour of 29 June 1952, ISA, Ministry of Labour files, 6178/2924, and also a Jewish National Fund census for 1949–50 dated 15 February 1950 from the Central Zionist Archives (hereafter: CZA), file KKL 5/18875.

7 For example, the committee of western Galilee settlements demanded that "all abandoned land" north of the Acre-Safad road shall be available for dividing up between western Galilee Jewish settlements. It claimed that plans for resettling refugees on these lands would damage the development possibilities of their settlements. See its letter to the Ministry of Agriculture and others in ISA, Ministry of Agriculture files, 581/2180 and the reply of the Ministry of Agriculture, which did not wholly accept its position.

8 Benny Morris, *The Birth of the Palestinian Refugee Problem, 1947–1949* (Tel-Aviv: 'Am 'Oved, 1991 [in Hebrew]), pp.28-30.

9 See Hillel Cohen, "On one expulsion which was prevented", *Mitsad Sheni* (May 1999), pp.28-30 [in Hebrew]. The article deals with an initiative in January 1949 to expel the refugees of Kuwaykat on the grounds that they removed the Israeli flag from the gate of kibbutz Beit Ha'emek.

10 "Minute of the third sitting of the Transfer Committee, March 1949". ISA, Ministry of Minorities files, 1322/22. The evacuation of small villages from the the Triangle continued for two years after the war, see the meeting of the Committee for Refugee Affairs 11 January 1950, IDF Archives, file 721/2-843 and also the Communist daily *al-Ittihad,* 10 February 1951.

11 *Divrei Haknesset* [Israeli Parliament's proceedings] 1 (1949), p.1634.

12 "A minute of the sixth meeting of the Committee for Refugee Affairs", 12 October 1949, IDF Archives (hereafter: IDFA), file 721/2-83.

13 The proposed law is found in the *Divrei Haknesset* [Israeli Parliament's Proceedings] 2 (1950), p.921.

14 The term "present absentees" first appeared in print in an article by Aharon Liskovsky, "Present Absentees in Israel", *Ha-Mizrah He-Hadash* 10 (1960), pp.187-90 [in Hebrew].

15 "Report of the Authority for settling Arab refugees", 1 August 1950, CZA, file KKL 5/18875.

16 This does not mean that the subject was not dealt with at various levels,

community or family, but these are outside our present study.

17 Hadash – the Democratic Front For Peace and Equality is a Jewish–Arab party based on members of the Israeli communist party and independent activists.

18 The term "sub-identity", is intended to refer to identities constituting part of a wider identity, without reference to the degree of importance or centrality of each of these sub-identities for the people belonging to them. Thus for example the overall Palestinian identity includes Christian and Muslim Palestinians and also Palestinians in the Diaspora, in the state of Israel, in the areas of the Palestinian National Authority, etc.

19 Mahmoud 'Issa, "Decoding the silencing process in modern Palestinian historiography", paper presented to the conference "Worlds and Visions, Perspectives on the Middle East Today", 5, December 1997, University of Rhus, Denmark.

20 Hasan Musa, "Geographic Distribution of the Arab Refugees in their Homelands: The Galilee Area, 1948–1987" (Haifa: MA thesis submitted to Haifa University, 1988 [in Hebrew]). Musa suggests that we should differentiate between a sense of "strangeness" and a sense of being a refugee, finding that among those who reported that they have a sense of being a refugee, there are people who feel like "locals" and others who feel like foreigners. This can be explained when we deconstruct the "refugee identity" into a negative component ("I am not from here") and a positive one ("I am from there").

21 This component figure for the percentage of Arabs remaining in the western Galilee after the 1948 war was sent from the official in charge of the western Galilee in the Ministry of Agriculture, Aharon Dror, to the Executive of the Ministry, September 1949, ISA, Ministry of Agriculture files, 2174/546.

22 On the decision to expel the refugees from Saffuriya, see "The transfer of an Arab population" [the military governor of the Galilee, January 1949], ISA, Ministry of Minorities files, 279/59. The use of the Minorities' Brigade stems not only from the need for Arabic speakers but also from the policy of deepening the ethnic rifts within the Arab community.

23 The Military Governor in Galilee declared abandoned villages as closed military areas during 1951. IDFA, file 7/54-54.

24 Letter from the Adviser to the Prime Minister on Arab Affairs, Yehoshu'a Palmon, to the Military Governors, 28 February 1950. ISA, Ministry of Agriculture files, 2181/5821. See also a letter from the Military Governor of the Galilee to the office of the Custodian of Enemy Property, 13 July 1950, IDFA, file 68/55-68.

25 "Summary of the first meeting of the Regional Galilee Committee", 2 September 1954, ISA, Israeli Police files, 2314/6.

26 Cohen, *Hanifkadim Hanokhahim*, pp.86-9.

27 Benedict Anderson, *Imagined Communities: Reflections on the Origin and Spread of Nationalism* (London: Verso, 1991).

28 ISA, Ministry of Education files, 236/17.

29 Majid al-Haj, "Adjustment Patterns of the Arab Refugees in Israel", *International Migration* 24, No.3 (1986), p.657.

30 Alexander Bligh, "Israel and the Refugee Problem: From Exodus to Resettlement 1948–1952", *Middle Eastern Studies* 34 (1998), pp.123-47.

31 Al-Haj, "Adjustment Patterns of the Arab Refugees in Israel", p.659.

32 Walid Khalidi, *All That Remains: The Palestinian Villages Occupied and Depopulated by Israel in 1948* (Washington DC: Institute for Palestine Studies, 1992).

33. Conversations with the activists of the internal refugees' committees, Wakim Wakim and Dawud Bader, Nahariya and Shaykh Dannun, July 1996.

34 Arnon Sofer, "The Israeli Arabs and the Peace Process", *Nativ* 51, No.4 (April 1996), p.134 [in Hebrew]).

3
Patterns of Internal Displacement, Social Adjustment and the Challenge of Return

Nihad Boqa'i

Internally displaced Palestinians in Israel are part of the larger Palestinian refugee population displaced/expelled from villages and homes during the 1948 war in Palestine, and over a few years following. During the 1948 *Nakba* most of the displaced Palestinians were forced into surrounding Arab states and the Palestinian territories that did not fall under Israeli control (i.e. the West Bank and Gaza Strip). As with the estimated 750,000–900,000 Palestinian refugees who were displaced from more than 500 depopulated villages[2] beyond the borders of the new state, Israel also refused to allow internally displaced Palestinians (IDPs, or internal refugees), to return to their homes and villages.[1]

The displacement of Palestinians did not end with the 1948 war, and the Israeli authorities continued to transfer and displace Palestinians during the 1950s. At the same time, Israeli military forces destroyed most of the depopulated Palestinian villages,[2] and declared these villages "closed military zones" to prevent displaced Palestinians from returning. In addition, the Israeli authorities planted forests in the depopulated villages in order to "conceal" Palestinian existence. In most cases, the Israeli government established Zionist-Jewish settlements on the land of these villages,[3] some of which took the names of the original Palestinian villages. For example, the Jewish settlement that replaced the destroyed Bayt Dajan village was named Beit Dagan, kibbutz "Sa'sa' " was built on Sa'sa' village; cooperative Moshav settlement of "Amka" on the land of 'Amqa village; and moshav "Elanit" (tree in Hebrew) on the land of "al-Shajara" (tree in Arabic) village (Wakim 2001a). It should be noted that the internally displaced Palestinians (IDPs) are one of the unfortunate categories of Palestinian refugees whose status, officially speaking, has not been registered. The state of Israel has never acknowledged the IDPs as a separate category, or even their status as "refugees" or so-called IDPs. Unlike the majority of Palestinian refugees who are registered by the United Nations Relief and Works Agency for Palestine Refugees (UNRWA), there exists no registration system for internally displaced Palestinians.

The overwhelming majority of the 1948 internally displaced Pales-tinians (90 per cent), are located in the north of Israel (Kamen 1984). In total, some 162 Palestinian villages in the north were depopulated during the war. However, displaced Palestinians who remained within Israel originally come from approximately 44 villages only. Of those 44 villages, 10 villages had a population of more than 500 people, 17 of 100–500 persons, and 17 other villages had populations of less than 100 persons (Kamen 1984). It is estimated that 47 out of the 70 original Palestinian villages remaining after the war,[4] in addition to the cities, provided shelter for internally displaced Palestinians. Today, the IDPs reside in most of the Palestinian villages and towns inside Israel, in some of which they comprise the majority of the population. Despite the fact that some IDPs also reside in Palestinian towns such as Nazareth and Shafa'amr, and cities with a mixed Jewish–Arab community such as Haifa, Acre, Lydda, Ramle and Jaffa, the vast majority of the displaced people live in host Palestinian villages which are near their villages of origin.

Patterns of Displacement

Patterns of displacement during the 1948 war, and in its aftermath, give an indication of the initial reaction of displaced Palestinians to the crisis of displacement from their villages. Patterns should be understood not as separate sub-movements, but as a reflection of political, economic and social conditions facing the displaced. These patterns proved to have a major impact on the life of displaced people within the boundaries of the host village.

The character and patterns of displacement, in addition to the collec-tivity of the villages and the extended families (*hamulas*) of those displaced, resulted in a collective movement of displacement; in some cases, for example, all the depopulated village residents were moved together from one place to another (Al-Haj 1994). The two main patterns of displacement, direct and indirect movements to the place of refuge, are both characterised by the above-mentioned collective action. The first pattern, characterised by *direct* displacement to the "permanent" places of refuge, such as the neighbouring Arab states, looks more "organised" and less chaotic; the second pattern, however, was characterised by *indirect* displacement (3–4 successive displacements on average) according to the sequence of the occupation of the Palestinian villages by Zionist forces and Israeli troops in 1948 (Sa'id 1992). Most of the IDPs moved from one place of refuge to another. In his survey of three host villages in Galilee, Palestinian sociologist Majid al-Haj (1994) concluded that half of the IDPs that he interviewed moved to another host village inside the areas that became the state of Israel before their movement to the current host village. Only one-third of the surveyed displaced Palestinians moved directly to the current host village. Patterns of indirect displacement have been "continuous and severe" and have spread out over a longer period of time than the direct movement to the place of refuge.

In some cases, tension among the villagers affected their solidarity and families' considerations, especially when the village, such as al-Kabri in the Galilee (Morris 1987), was attacked by Zionist forces several times before its eventual occupation and depopulation. Each attack was followed by the displacement of a number of families to other "safer" places (Roberts 2000).

In general, Palestinians, like most of the displaced worldwide, did not know where their exact and final place of refuge would be. The majority of the refugees interviewed or surveyed in different studies expressed their inability during the displacement period to determine their final resting place (Hanafi 2001; Yahya 1998 for example). The first and urgent need of the displaced persons, who had fled from their places of origin during armed conflict or under threat of violence, had been to escape the immediate danger. Determining their place of refuge was only a secondary priority. In addition to this, determining the place of refuge was conditioned by other factors, like the reaction of the host communities and the activities of the "national" authorities (the Israeli authorities in the case of the IDPs).

The Israeli authorities played a major role not only in the displacements, but also in determining the direction of movement of those displaced from the villages. This Israeli involvement continued after 1948, through several plans to transfer/expel Palestinian villagers outside the Armistice lines (that is, to the West Bank and Gaza Strip, and the Arab states) (Masalha 1997; Morris 1987), or inside the Armistice lines, on the pretext of military and security "reasons" (Cohen 2000). The process of external and internal population transfer was carried out to facilitate a programme of repopulation of specific areas in the new state with Jewish settlements, and annexation of more Palestinian land. With these goals in mind, the Israeli authorities carried out, for instance, the transfer and relocation of Palestinians from the villages of Iqrit, Kafr Bir'im, al-Ghabisiyya, Krad al-Baqqara and Krad al-Ghannama in the post-1948 period and throughout the early 1950s. Some villagers were expelled to Lebanon and Syria; others were transferred and resettled in nearby Palestinian villages in Galilee. The Israeli authorities relocated the inhabitants from al-Rihaniyya village to the Kafr Kama host village, and from the village of Tarshiha residents were moved to the host village of Mi'ilya (Cohen 2000).

At the same time, the Israeli military forced the Bedouin of the Negev to abandon their traditional nomadic lifestyle; almost 11,000 Bedouins were concentrated in designated zones in the north of the Negev (Abu-Rabia' 1999). In order to facilitate Zionist land confiscation and the colonisation process in the Negev, the Bedouin have been forced over the years into seven townships. From 95 tribes that lived in the Negev before 1948, there remained only 11 tribes after the 1948 *Nakba* (Badil 2002a). During the 1950s, the transfer of the Negev Bedouins continued to the Arab states and the Palestinian territories then under the rule of the Hashemite kingdom of Jordan (Masalha 1997). In 1957, for example, Israel expelled the "'Arab al-Syaj" tribe; in 1981, following Camp David, the Israeli government displaced thousands of Bedouins from the "Tal al-Meleh" tribe.[5]

During the early period the Israeli authorities worked towards resettling hundreds of Palestinians in the Arab host villages.[6] Most of the authorities' activities were focused on "official" and "semi-official" shelter villages chosen to resettle Palestinians transferred from other villages. These villages, mainly "empty", that is, depopulated villages, are located in the Galilee and include the villages of 'Akbara, and Wadi al-Hamam in Safad district, and Sha'ab, Shaykh Dannun, Judayda, al-Maker and al-Mazra'a in Acre district (Cohen 2000). The Israeli authorities operated also in some "non-official" shelter villages such as Kabul and al-Rayna in the Galilee.

In a few cases, the Israeli authorities helped displaced Palestinians to rent empty homes in host villages[7] or, in other cases, to register the houses of "secondary occupation" as permanent property of the IDPs in exchange for ceding their rights in their villages of origin. These cases include, for example, IDPs in al-Jish host village in April 1961 (Sa'id 1992). At the same time, the authorities built tens of housing units in designated shelter villages in order to resolve partially the housing problems faced by the IDPs.[8] However, these housing units made little impact on overall IDP housing needs after the war. In order to acquire government-constructed units, moreover, displaced people were asked to cede their housing and property rights in their villages of origin. In addition, most of the land dedicated to government-constructed housing was confiscated from the Palestinian host villages.[9] In sum, few IDPs benefited from the limited housing programme in the host villages, and those who did benefit often faced social rejection by other displaced communities.

At the same time as Israel was involved in forcibly displacing, trans-ferring and resettling displaced Palestinians, the latter were looking as much as possible for places of refuge that could provide a socio-cultural environment similar to that in their village of origin. Displaced families were hosted by their relatives in nearby villages, most of which would have had similar socio-cultural environment to the depopulated village. In 'Arraba host village in the Galilee, for example, 44 of 68 displaced families surveyed chose the village to host them because they had relatives and family there (Sa'id 1992). Re-uniting with other displaced families from the village of origin was another factor for mobility to a certain village rather than another, according to some displaced families.

Religion was a very important socio-cultural element in choosing places of refuge, especially for the displaced Christian minority (some 10 per cent of the total internally displaced population (Kamen 1984). Palestinians displaced from the Christian village of Kafr Bir'im, for instance, found refuge in the Christian village of al-Jish. The Muslim Tamra host village, on the other hand, took in displaced Palestinian Muslims from the de-populated villages of al-Damun, al-Ruways, and al-Birwa.

Religion was a less important consideration in religiously "mixed" host localities. Nazareth, for example, a largely Christian city pre-*Nakba*, absorbed a large percentage of displaced Palestinian Muslims. Interestingly, displaced Muslim preferred to live in areas of the city periphery considered Muslim neighbourhoods, in areas such as Safafri neighbourhood (named after the depopulated village of Saffuriyya), or the eastern neighbourhood which was closer to rural life. The few displaced Christians who came to the city preferred to live in the centre and the Christian neighbourhoods (Sa'id 1992).

In the first years of displacement socio-cultural factors such as family considerations, geographic distance and religion affected the choice of a refuge. It was only in the latter part of the 1950s and the early 1960s that economic considerations began to influence the choice. This was when people realised that the period of displacement would not be short as they had expected and hoped. Economic conditions in the host villages were miserable in general, because of restrictions on freedom of movement, the effects of the war on the Palestinian economy, and the limited resources in the villages. Approximately one-third of the displaced people who came to the larger host town of Shafa'amr during late 1950s and the early 1960s, were driven there by economic considerations (al-Haj 1994).

"Refugee" Identity and Patterns of Adjustment in the Host Villages

After 1948 the Palestinian refugees, including the IDPs, had to deal with a new challenge: how could the Palestinian *fellahin* (peasants)[10] who had lived for generations in their own village live outside its borders? And what adjustments were needed by the displaced collectively and individually in order to cope with their new reality?

During the first years of displacement, while most of the displaced Palestinians believed that they would return to their villages of origin after a while, they tried to reproduce the life of the village of origin as much as possible within the place of refuge. This behaviour, observed within the Palestinian host villages and also in refugee communities abroad, was linked directly to the centrality of the family and the village as socio-cultural and economic structures in the Palestinian *fellah* life. It can also be seen as a defensive reaction to sudden and forced displacement, and suspicious "external" environments, in this case the host Palestinian communities. Reproducing socio-cultural structures that existed in the pre-*Nakba* era functions as a response to the external hostility, engendering solidarity and security and empowering the displaced group of the same origin.

As researchers have previously discussed, "village and family" in Palestinian *fellahi* culture, as in other Arab *fellahi* societies, are main "defensive lines" for members from "strangers", providing security but also existing as socio-cultural structures and central units in the Palestinian *fellah* identity. Anthropologist Rosemary Sayigh (1979) points out that the solidarity of the Palestinians in the villages provided three essential needs: first, defending the village residents from external dangers: second, unifying people into a system of socially owned lands; and third, providing an environment where villagers could live their own socio-cultural life.

The weakness of the central authority in Palestine in the Ottoman and British periods strengthened the autonomy of the Palestinian village. Internal village factors such as the long-term stability of four or five extended families living in the village, socio-economic homogeneity, and lack of significant movement between the villages and urban centres, also contributed to individual village identity and autonomy. Interestingly, while the *Nakba* led to the collapse of social structures such as the village and the *hamulas* (extended families), paradoxically in the context of dispossession and exile the need of the individual for these social structures grew. Patterns of displacement of the Palestinians in 1948, and subsequent collective movement of the dispossessed to places of refuge, are partly based on the social structures in the village of origin, i.e. the *hamula* and the village.

Displaced people moved subsequently from one host village to another in order to rejoin their families. Displaced *fellahi* families who tried to reunite themselves in "exile" succeeded only partially, owing to their disconnection from the land that represented the material base for the patriarchal system and family hierarchy. The reuniting of displaced families was never fully completed in the post-*Nakba* era. The collapse of the village and the dispersion of the family in various places of refuge have had a negative influence on the power of these social structures over their members. Other factors meant that even when reuniting was possible, displaced people from the same village of origin were still dispersed in certain "centres" of refuge. Displaced people from Umm al-Zinat village in Haifa district have dispersed to different host villages and towns, such Umm al-Fahem, Daliyat al-Karmel, al-Furaydis, al-Rayna and Yafa. In the West Bank, displaced people from the same village have dispersed into different refugee camps such as Nur Shams, Jenin, Tulkarem, Balata and al-Jalazon. Displaced people from al-Ghabisiyya village have dispersed mainly to the host villages of Shaykh Dannun and al-Mazra'a, and in Lebanon to certain refugee camps such as Burj al-Barajneh, 'Ayn al-Helweh, and Nahr al-Barid (Roberts 2000). In other cases individual families also have dispersed over more than one place of refuge.

Reproducing the lifestyle of the village of origin within the place of refuge, in addition to other factors discussed below, led displaced people to be geographically separated from the communities in the host villages. Most of the IDPs lived in segregated or separate areas and neighbourhoods within the host villages; these areas mainly located in the periphery of the host village, have been named after the village of origin, following a similar pattern to Palestinian refugees outside the state (Sha'aban 2002; Roberts 2000). The majority of the IDPs from the village of Mi'ar who live in the host village of Kabul in the Galilee, for example, live in the "Mi'ari" neighbourhood. Other "Mi'ari" neighbourhoods are located in Sha'ab and 'Arraba host villages. In Nazareth, the "Safafri" neighbourhood is named after the nearby depopulated village of Saffuriyya. In some cases, displaced neighbourhoods (or part) within the host villages were named after a large displaced family living in it. In Judayda host village, for example, the "Barawneh" neighbourhood (displaced people from al-Birwa village of origin), is also called "Kayyaliyya", based on the name of the large family of "Kayyal" that lives there.

While the separation of refugees from the host society had already taken place in the refugee camp context, refugees also created internal neighbourhoods according to villages of origin. Refugees in Burj al-Barajneh in Lebanon, for instance, stated that belonging to the village of origin played a major role in the distribution of the refugees in the camp. Palestinians from distinct villages chose to live in a certain neighbourhood inside the camp owing to its being named after their village of origin. In the camp, there are six main neighbourhoods named after villages of origin: al-Ghabisiyya, al-Kabri, Sha'ab, Kuwaykat, Shaykh Dawud, and Tarshiha (Roberts 2000). Thus, in the context of reproducing the village of origin, refugees from other villages, as well as members of the host societies, are considered part of the "external environment".

Separation is also a result of the nature of displacement itself. Being geographically separated is one of the most common characteristics of displaced refugee and immigrant communities worldwide. Disadvantaged or weak groups often find security and solidarity in the presence of other members of the same group; add to this the structure of the Palestinian village as host place based on the *hamula* and distinction between sects, which plays a chief role in the spatial organisation of the village. Each extended family, or *hamula*, has a separate neighbourhood according to the village structure (every village consisted of 3–4 *hamulas*, hence 3–4 neighbourhoods). In only a few cases, displaced persons succeeded in living in the village centre, and this happened when locals were displaced too, or when they left their homes at a later time to live in new houses outside the overcrowded centre.

Geographical separation of the displaced within the boundaries of the host village, in general, could facilitate reunion in specific places, and re-activate, even if only partly, their social networks from the village of origin. Living in specific neighbourhoods based on the village of origin provided the *Nakba* generation with a space to tell the younger generation about the village of origin. However, separation did have a negative influence on relations with the locals in the host village, because there was seldom any social interaction with the locals, especially once it became obvious that the displacement would be long term. While separated neighbourhoods existed based on the village of origin both in Palestinian host villages in Israel and in the refugee camps in exile, there is a key difference between the two "separations". Refugees in camps share the same status of refugees even though they originate from different villages. Inside the Palestinian host villages in Israel, however, there is a dichotomous separation between "locals" and "strangers/refugees" that is determined by the origin of the host village residents.

During the first years of refuge, displaced people experienced a process of themselves being "renamed" after their village of origin, and not only their neighbourhoods in the host villages. The name of "Damuni", for example, was given to all the IDPs from the depopulated village of al-Damun, not only in the Palestinian host villages inside Israel, but also in exile and especially in the refugee camps which had no local hosts. This process in turn enhanced the affinity of displaced people (based on the village of origin) within the Palestinian/Arab social structure (Al-Haj 1994). Renaming the displaced people within the contexts both of the Palestinian host village and the refugee camp aimed mainly to empower the reunion of the displaced villagers from the same place, on the one hand, and to distinguish the displaced people from other social categories – locals and displaced people from other displaced villages – on the other.

Despite certain differences between host villages, a general pattern emerged of a divide between host villagers and the displaced. In most host Palestinian villages, the dichotomous line between "locals" and "refugees" is evident. Clear geographic separation, competition over limited power and important resources, the displaced families' tendency to keep their own socio-cultural uniqueness as "people from …" in addition to the locals' unwillingness to accept the displaced people as equal members in the village at large, all contribute to the divide. It should be noted that the social structure of the Palestinian village itself is "rich" in social distinctions. In addition to the local/refugee dichotomy, and the hierarchies among the displaced people themselves based on village of origin, there exist other social distinctions among different religious communities/sects (such as Muslims, Christians and Druze), and different social communities (such as *fellahin*, Bedouins, and urban), and families and *hamulas*.

It should be noted, however, that during the first stage of displacement, displaced people did not face major social obstacles, primarily due to the fact that local Palestinian residents in the host villages considered assistance of displaced people as a national and moral duty. Furthermore, displaced persons as well as locals had the same feeling of being "victims" of the 1948 war. Palestinian refugees in the Arab countries, on the other hand, were poorly treated by the local Arab citizens and the authorities.[11] Locals and displaced people in Israel viewed their situation as temporary, and their return as a matter of time. Tension between displaced people and locals arose, however, when IDPs started to build "permanent houses" in the host villages (Cabaha and Brazilai 1996). At that point locals perceived the situation as a danger to their village.

"Renaming" of the displaced people after their villages of origin had a central role in this social distinction, of defining a displaced group as a separate category not only from the locals but also from other displaced categories in the same host village. While naming after the village of origin is acceptable among the displaced communities, and even encouraged, the term *"refugees"* applied by the locals to all displaced communities in the village is not universally acceptable among displaced people themselves.[12] According to the displaced people, categorising all displaced communities under one category of "*refugees*" without taking into considerations the socio-cultural differences among displaced people from different villages of origin reflects confusion and humiliation. In addition, the term "*refugee*" holds a negative social meaning, especially for the younger generations of the displaced who never experienced displacement. The term thus represents for them "homelessness", "poverty" and estrangement" from their place of origin. In fact, in most cases, displaced people from certain villages of origin are very similar to the locals socio-culturally when compared to other displaced people from other villages of origin. The "renaming" after the village of origin, therefore, is a result not only of the displaced people's tendency to reproduce their lifestyle and reactivate their social structures in the pre-*Nakba* era, but also of their desire to avoid negative categorisation under the status of refugees.

Some characteristics of the villages from the pre-*Nakba* period accompanied the displaced people to the host villages (and also into exile). The stability of the Palestinian villages and their autonomy in this period led to a basic stereotyping of the village in the public consciousness of the region. Each village "gained" special characteristics and developed a special accent – people can tell where a person comes from by their accent. These characteristics also reinforce the social distinctions within the host village in the post-*Nakba* period.

The intensity of the social distinction inside the ,host village is dependent on two main aspects. The first is the degree of homogeneity within the host village. When the host village is more homogenous culturally and socially, the social distinction between the locals and the displaced people becomes more pronounced. The most evident social distinction is "locals" and "refugees". When the shelter village was more "heterogeneous", the IDPs had more opportunities to integrate within the social structure of the village (Cabaha and Brazilai 1996). The second aspect is the size of the displaced population in the host village. Social distinction was less evident in those villages where displaced people were a majority of the population. In Shaykh Dannun host village (Galilee), for example, the majority of the inhabitants were IDPs from the depopulated village of al-Ghabisiyya; there, the social integration within the shelter village was more evident (Al-Haj 1994; Musa 1988).

Dawud Bader, the coordinator of the National Association for the Defense of the Rights of the Internally Displaced in Israel (ADRID), is internally displaced from al-Ghabisiyya and now lives in Shaykh Dannun host village. Bader states:

> Shaykh Dannun, for example, includes displaced persons from the depopulated villages of al-Ghabisiyya, 'Amqa, Kuwaykat, al-Nahr, Umm al-Faraj, in addition to the residents from Shaykh Dannun itself and Shaykh Dawud [a village close to Shaykh Dannun]. The relationship between the residents in the village is equal, and there is no distinction between the displaced people and the non-displaced people. The residents of the village also lost their lands and houses, and had to pay for their lands in order to build their houses again. However in other [host] villages such as Tamra and Shafa'amr, the social distinction is clearly apparent. There, the displaced people are living around the old village, in homogenous neighbourhoods, which led in some cases to tension between displaced and non-displaced people ...[13]

The most evident distinction between the locals and the displaced is best articulated in those host villages where displaced people are considered more of a genuine threat to local residents, such as Tamra and Shafa'amr, through exercising greater political power on the political centre of the village by being a small majority (such as 'Ibillin and Yafa host villages) or a large minority (such as Judayda al-Maker host village). In those host villages IDPs are often one of the causes of local socio-political conflicts. It should be noted, in relation to the political participation of the displaced people in the host village, that during the first stage of displacement, in which the IDPs as a group were not yet organised locally, the IDPs adopted a neutral stance towards local conflicts (Cabaha and Brazilai 1996). This position led to a dynamic where the local population offered more benefits to the IDPs in order to win their support.

In addition to the participation of some displaced people in national political parties such as the Democratic Front for Peace and Equality (DFPE), the Islamic Movement and the National Democratic Assembly (NDA) or Balad, some of the IDPs participated in local elections for the local councils of the host villages as members of the local parties pertinent to the village of origin. In Yafa host village, for example, displaced people from the depopulated village of Ma'lul participated in elections during the 1990s under the banner of the "Ma'lul refugees" party.

These local refugee parties often focused on issues of interest or concern to all the Palestinian population in Israel and not only refugees (questions of equality and integration) as a means to attract political support from local parties. In some cases, the "refugee parties" attained key positions in the local councils. In the 1999 elections for the local councils, the "Future party", the official name of the party of the displaced Mi'ari in Sha'ab village, attained one mandate among nine mandates for the local council. Another party that represented categories of the displaced Bedouins (from Krad al-Baqqara and Krad al-Ghannama depopulated villages) in the village of Sha'ab attained two mandates. The candidate for the Mi'ari party stated after the elections:

> My united village sons …
> as son of this blessed village, I grew up belonging to Sha'ab, I do as much as I can to serve my village and its residents….since the first day of my election as a member in Sha'ab local council I put in front of my eyes only one aim: to work in the interests of my village, regardless of all the familial and political considerations. Today, my brothers and sisters, we are working in constant strong steps towards the building of a better future for Sha'ab village and its residents, in all the fields, culture, education and the infrastructure that started since our first day in the local council.[14]

In only a few cases was the mayor of the local council of the host village a displaced person. In all these cases displaced candidates were from national parties such as DFPE or the Islamic Movement, and not from independent local refugee parties. In the mid-1980s, Hashim Mahamid (from al-Lajjun village in origin, and a DFPE candidate) became the mayor of the Umm al-Fahem host town. In Jaljulya host village, *shaykh* Tawfik Khatib (from Kharish village in origin, and candidate of the Islamic Movement) won in the 1990s. In Judayda host village (Judayda and al-Maker united their local councils later), 'Afif Kayyal (from al-Birwa village of origin and candidate of DFPE) won during the 1990s and also in the November 2003 local elections. In Tamra host village, 'Adel Abu al-Haija (from al-Ruways, and candidate of the DFPE) won the local elections of November 2003.

Voting patterns in village council elections, in general, reflect the strong loyalty of the individual to the interests of the family. Parties of the displaced people are used as an "alternative" to the advantage of larger families compared to local families. Large displaced families are more free to make "external" alliances with other families or to join the national political parties in the village and not only the parties of the displaced. the family as a collective, therefore, continues to exist despite the fact that the younger generations of the displaced people are more educated and economically independent from patriarchal control.

The role and character of the Palestinian family has changed since the *Nakba*: the nature of displacement and the new "reality" under Israeli rule, together with the lack of Palestinian national institutions, has led to a concentration in already existing social networks such as family and sect, by empowering security and solidarity among the network members. Family (and also village and sect) got a new function after the *Nakba*, created by the paradox of Israeli citizenship and Palestinian national identity for Palestinians inside Israel. *Hamula* politics became more linked to the Israeli civil identity than to the Palestinian national identity through providing a sense of belonging for Israeli-Palestinian individuals that Israeli citizenship alone cannot provide.

At the same time, the Israeli authorities (like the British mandatory authorities before them) reinforced the role of the *hamula* among Palestinians, including displaced people, as one of the mechanisms of control over Palestinians in general. The *hamula* became the main vehicle for providing "conformity and loyalty" to the state of Israel, which in turn provided services and infrastructure for the *hamula* (Lustick 1980). Democratic participation on the national and the local levels gave the *hamula* opportunities to empower itself during the elections.

However, the role of the family has changed gradually, and its power has been reduced. The power of the "traditional" social networks in the Palestinian villages appears mainly in the internal elections in the villages and in cases of clashes between two *hamula*s (Stendel 1992). Four indicators show the decrease of the power of the family in the context of the Palestinian village inside Israel: the decrease of the larger families' influence on their members; the decrease in the number of the nuclear families; the decline in the influence of "traditional" leaders (such as the *mukhtars*) and the economic developments in the Palestinian community (Lustick 1980).

The Israeli authorities, although interested in empowering the family as a controlling mechanism and as an alternative to their national identity for the Palestinians inside Israel, indirectly weakened the family structure through preventing Palestinian peasants from cultivating their lands in the post-1948 period. Land dispossession in the Palestinian villages gradually led displaced people (and also the locals) to join the Israeli job market as part-time and unskilled labourers, a process of de-agriculturalisation that was also a controlling mechanism adopted by the state to control the Palestinians through economic dependence.[15] Through "de-agriculturalisation", the Israeli authorities succeeded in transfering the economic power from the Palestinian village to the Jewish urban centres. This created a landless working class within the villages as most of the village income came as wages from outside the village boundaries. Land ceased to be the centre of family life in the Palestinian village (Stendel 1992). The *hamula* stopped being both a production and a consumption unit, as had been the case in the pre-*Nakba* period.

Economic integration of the displaced people after the *Nakba*, therefore, was quicker than the process of social integration. The degree of dispossession experienced by the IDPs was one of the reasons for their economic underdevelopment and their inferior status in the social class structure in the first years of displacement, and the limited resources accessible to the IDPs precluded the possibility of social and economic integration in the host village (Al-Haj 1986). The reliance of both displaced and local Palestinians on the Israeli economy through de-agriculturalisation, gradually reduced the economic gaps between locals and the displaced.

It should be noted that in the first years of displacement the economic status of the IDPs was not so different from that of other Palestinians in comparison to Palestinian refugees in exile, especially since the confiscation of Palestinian land continued in those Palestinian villages that remained after 1948. Due to the 1948 war, the Palestinian economy in general collapsed entirely, and in particular the village economy (not to mention the political and social structure of Palestinian society).[16] Numerous international organisations that offered services and assistance to Palestinian refugees and the IDPs in Israel, such as the International Committee of the Red Cross (ICRC), and the UN Relief and Works Agency for Palestine Refugees (UNRWA), (which was established in 1950 and offered assistance to the IDPs until 1952) had to offer assistance to non-displaced people too (Cohen 2000).

The end of military rule over Israeli-Palestinians in 1966, and the

Israeli occupation of the West Bank and Gaza Strip in 1967, opened Palestinian markets to Israeli goods. This led to an economic improvement for the Palestinian minority, including the displaced. While the economic gap between the IDPs and the locals in the Palestinian villages started to vanish, the general economic gap between the Israeli-Palestinians in general and the Israeli-Jewish sector remained.

Palestinians in Israel, including the internally displaced, were influenced by the economic developments that occurred in the external sphere, and as the weakest category in the Israeli economy, they were always the first victims of economic crisis. In the last quarter of 2000, and with the beginning of the second (al-Aqsa) Intifada, 20 Palestinian villages and towns were among the first 25 villages and towns in Israel with higher than 10 per cent unemployment.[17] A significant proportion of these towns and villages included high numbers of displaced persons. In 2002 more than 40 per cent of Palestinians in Israel had incomes below the official Israeli poverty line (Badil 2002a). Within the host villages, however, displaced people did succeed over time in setting up shops and local markets. Most of them were enthusiastic about social and economic integration within their village of refuge to the extent that they did not describe their stores as "refugee stores" (Cabaha and Brazilai 1996).

In general, while displaced people succeeded during the first period of displacement in reproducing in the host village the lifestyle of their village of origin, long-term displacement and differences between displaced generations developed over time so that two different patterns emerged: belonging and estrangement.

Improvement in the economic status of the displaced and social interaction through shared social customs and infrastructure within the host village (be it schooling or personal friendships or football matches or weddings) encouraged a sense of belonging among the IDPs, especially for the younger generations.[18] Later generations saw the host village as less of a stopgap solution than the first displaced generation. Those born in the host village emphasise their belonging to both village of origin and host village.

Cabaha and Brazilai (1996) discovered that almost 70 per cent of the third generation of their survey felt they belonged to the host village, while still holding on to the belief in their "right to return" to their village of origin. The majority of the second generation (80 per cent) also expressed their "right to return"; however, in contrast with the third generation they had mixed feelings about belonging to the host village. Younger generations expressed their willingness to participate in the social life of the host village, seeing themselves more as "sons of the place" (Sa'id 1992). Despite the fact that the neighbourhoods were named after the village of origin, creating a "new" identity for the displaced people in the host villages, the impact of the village of origin on the daily life of displaced people is limited compared to that of the host village. As a result, in the past two decades more and more displaced people have moved to live in mixed neighbourhoods with locals, beyond the separate neighbourhoods of the displaced.

Despite greater interaction with the host village, social differences, geographical segregation and rejection by local people continued to engender a sense of estrangement beyond the first generation. Some members of the second and third generation see the village of origin as a "shelter" from the host village, which rejects their full and equal integration (Sa'id 1999). The connection between estrangement and social distinction is very strong and visible. In the host villages where the displaced people are the majority (such as Shaykh Dannun), estrangement becomes less visible among the displaced (Al-Haj 1994; Musa 1988).

In the Village of Origin

While the social struggle of the displaced people in the host village centres mainly on dealing with "daily" issues and living conditions, their political struggle in regard to the village of origin is directed more against the Israeli authorities. Village of origin has become a major symbol providing "legitimacy" for the displaced people, providing an identity for them within the host village. Crucially the village of origin shapes the perception of both the past and the future, and more specifically the question of memory and desire to return.

The village of origin and the activities around it embody elements of protest and resistance directed against both the Israeli authorities and the "status quo" in the host village. Through their activities, displaced people express more interest in the past and the future than in the present, as part of an ongoing "displacement narrative" that can only be brought to an end through return to the village of origin.

The Legal and Political Struggle for Return

Internally displaced people inside Israel have a long history of struggle to return to their villages of origin. The "right of return" remains a key consensus among displaced people in particular and Palestinians in Israel in general. At the same time however, the displaced people's struggle for return, like other national struggles, has developed since 1948. Through different means, through creating different "narratives" around the village of origin, and even different meanings of the "return" itself, displaced people developed their struggle to return, taking into consideration both their social and economic development within the host village and political developments within the Palestinian national arena.

The struggle for return, in effect, began at the end of the 1948 war. Displaced families and refugee villagers in Syria and Lebanon and in the host villages in Israel tried spontaneously to return to their villages by crossing the armistice lines, often in the middle of the night, despite the threats issued by the Israeli government against returnees (referred to as "infiltrators"). The Israeli army killed or deported most of these persons outside the armistice lines (Masalha 1997; Morris 1987).[19] In order to prevent displaced persons and refugees returning, the army declared the de-populated villages as "closed military zones" under the emergency regulations, article 1251. Such orders legalised the deportation of all residents of these villages, which included villages from whom the majority, but not all, of the population had been displaced in the war.[20] The Israeli state archives dealing with the military rule period are full of the reports of "illegal entrance" to the depopulated villages, and the deportation of returnees outside Israeli borders (Cohen 2000).

During the first period of displacement, displaced people (as well as local Palestinian villagers and Arab host governments) believed that return was simply a matter of time. This perception had two causes. First, the displaced people estimated that the newly established Jewish state was only temporary, the liberation of Palestine and their eventual return would be achieved when the Arab nations would come to liberate Palestine. Second, displaced Palestinians did not realise that their displacement was not incidental, but integral to the Zionist agenda, and consequently they could not accept that the Israeli authorities would never allow them to return to their villages of origin.

Israeli displacement activities continued throughout the 1950s, not only outside the armistice lines, but also involving population "transfer" within the existing Palestinian villages, or to certain de-populated villages, such as the relocation of Bedouins from Krad al-Baqqara and Krad al-Ghannama to the depopulated village of Sha'ab in the 1950s. These steps, designed to create officially sanctioned shelter villages, would lead the displaced villagers to try to return to their village of origin. For security reasons, and in order to reduce the high concentration of displaced people in one place of refuge, Israel permitted IDPs to return to some cities of origin in specific cases, namely IDPs from the cities of Haifa, Acre and Jaffa. However these IDPs were not permitted to repossess their homes and property. They were only allowed to look for new housing in their localities of origin (Cohen 2000; Kamen 1984).[21]

At the same time, the post-*Nakba* period led to the development of a "new" leadership consisting of persons who were linked to the Zionist ruling parties, mostly prior to the *Nakba*. The new leadership, mainly village *mukhtars* and various dignitaries, who were also *hamula*-based leaders, would be employed for many years as the main mediators between the Israeli authorities and the Palestinians, including displaced people. They would also function as one of the Israeli mechanisms of control of Palestinians. These *mukhtars* and dignitaries tried to facilitate the repatriation of displaced people (often relatives of the same dignitaries) to their villages of origin by sending letters to Israeli government ministries in the names of the displaced people themselves. The letters often dwelled on the good relationship between the residents of the village of origin and their Jewish neighbours before 1948, and their desire to live in peace under Israeli rule. These attempts aimed mainly to "resolve" the problems of specific groups of displaced people, and not the whole problem of the IDPs in Israel. These types of letter were sent separately to David Ben-Gurion, then prime minister and the defence minister, and also to Bechor Shitrit, then Minister for Minorities, by displaced people from different places of refuge, such as displaced people from Haifa and Tiberias who moved to Nazareth host city, and those from Suhmata (Galilee) in Buqay'a host village (Cohen 2000). In a letter that was sent by the IDPs from Mi'ar depopulated village to Shitrit, for instance, the displaced villagers wrote:

We left the village based on the incorrect information that the Israeli army would kill men, children and women ... and when we tried to return, we were prevented from doing so by the army of Qawaqji[23] ... we did not participate in the [1948] war, and we request our return in the name of justice and humanity...[22]

The Israeli response to these letters was always negative. At the same time, the Israeli government announced its willingness to assist the IDPs, but only on condition of resettlement in new host villages. In response to Israeli rejectionism, some of the displaced villagers took their case to the Israeli High Court.

Internally displaced villagers from al-Ghabisiyya initially succeeded in getting a decision from the court on 30 November 1951, allowing them to return to their village of origin. However, the military authorities, fearing that this decision would create a "legal" precedent for return of the displaced, decided to declare the village of al-Ghabisiyya a "closed military zone" under the Defence (Emergency) Regulations (Article 1251) of the British mandatory period. Publishing this announcement in the Israeli Official Gazette shortly before the Israeli High Court could publish its own ruling on al-Ghabisiyya, the military prevented the legal return of the displaced. When the same displaced villagers readdressed the High Court, the court ruled that "since the residents did not go back before the [government] decision was published in the Official Gazette, they could not go back after its publication".[23]

The displaced of Qarrada (Ashkar 2000) and Iqrit and Kafr Bir'im found themselves in a similar position. Iqrit residents moved to al-Rama village in October 1948 "for two weeks", based on an agreement between the village's *mukhtar* and elders and the military authorities. When the military authorities refused to allow the villagers to return to Iqrit, they addressed the Israeli High Court, which ruled in favour of return.[24] Subsequently, however, on 24 December 1951 the Israeli military destroyed the whole village bar the church, and declared the village site a closed military zone. At the end of October 1972, when Defence Minister Moshe Dayan announced that "closed military zones" would be opened, he excluded the villages of Iqrit and Kafr Bir'im (Ozacky-Lazar 1993). The village of Kafr Bir'im had been occupied in October 1948, when its residents received orders in writing to leave the place in 48 hours. Most of the residents moved to al-Jish host village, and Israeli-Jewish settlers moved to the village and set up kibbutz Bir'am on its lands in June 1949. In August 1951, some of the displaced people from Kafr Bir'im went to the High Court, which subsequently ruled in favour of allowing the residents to return to the village.[25] However, in January 1952, the High Court issue a new ruling cancelling the previous one, based on the claim that the residents had no official permission to return to their village of origin. In September 1953, the Israeli army destroyed all the houses in the village (Sa'id 1999).

The apparent inability of the High Court to enforce its decisions on the return of the displaced people against the might of the military resulted in a decline in the number of appeals by displaced people to the courts. Displaced villagers from Iqrit and Kafr Bir'im, however, continue their legal-political struggle to this day.

A nationwide political struggle to address the problem of internal refugees by allowing them to return to their villages of origin was led by the Israeli Communist Party (ICP), then the only Israeli party active among the Palestinians inside Israel. Despite the fact that political activity during the period of military rule – which lasted until 1966 – was highly restricted and Israeli-Palestinian politicians were threatened and even jailed by the Israeli authorities, the ICP continued to demand repatriation of displaced people. In March 1949, member of the Knesset Tawfik Tubi, who represented the ICP, stated in the Israeli parliament:

> 6,000 refugees are living today in Nazareth, in catastrophic conditions, while their villages of origin, al-Mujaydil, 'Illut, Ma'lul, are only 4km from Nazareth. Thousands of refugees in the state of Israel are waiting to return to their empty villages, such as al-Birwa, al-Damun, Iqrit … Many of the Arab *fellahin* and the house owners who live in Israel have the right to own their property and their houses, a right they are denied because of the illegal implementation of the "Abandoned Areas Ordinance" [of 1948].[26]

But the demands of the ICP Knesset members also were rejected by the Israeli government, even when these demands were confined to a limited number of displaced. At the same time, the official Arabic-language newspaper of the ICP, *al-Ittihad*, reported almost weekly on the problems encountered by the IDPs and on their wish to return to their homes and villages of origin. In November 1948, for example, *al-Ittihad* demanded that displaced persons from the depopulated village of 'Ilut be allowed to return to their village of origin:

> It is clear that 'Ilut residents didn't want to leave their village ... and with the winter coming soon, 'Ilut residents will face the danger of death from starvation and cold, although the solution to their problem is so clear. (*al-Ittihad*, 15 November 1948, cited in Sa'id 1999)

In addition to its parliamentary activities and its news coverage in *al-Ittihad*, during the late 1950s and early 1960s, the ICP organised many activities such as marches and public protests among the displaced people, designed to mobilise support for the right to return to their villages of origin (Sa'id 1999). Israeli historian Hillel Cohen (2000), who has studied the history of Palestinian internal refugees in Israel, highlighted the key role played by the ICP in the post-*Nakba* period in support of the IDPs' struggle: "in addition to the injustice of Israeli proposals to resolve the problem of the displaced persons inside Israel, [the ICP's campaigns] were the main reason for the displaced persons' rejection of the idea of resettlement in the first years of the displacement". Despite the fact that the ICP could achieve very little on the ground, the party's campaigns led to greater support among displaced people for the ICP (Sa'id 1999). Later, with the establishment of the Land Movement (Harakat al-Arad) in Israel in July 1964, the new radical nationalist movement called for the right of return for all Palestinian refugees (internal and external), an end to house demolitions, and the right of internal refugees to visit their villages of origin, particularly during religious holidays (Sa'id 1999).

The lack of Palestinian national leadership and institutions enabled the Israeli authorities to make the issue of the IDPs humanitarian rather than political. Throughout the 1950s and 1960s the struggle for return conducted by the displaced themselves was mainly local, focusing on specific villages of origin. By the end of the 1960s the intensity of debate among the IDPs regarding return to their villages of origin had declined for several reasons: the traumatic Israeli conquest of the West Bank and Gaza Strip in June 1967; the reorientation of the struggle of the Palestinian citizens inside Israel towards more "urgent" and immediate struggles, such as land confiscations and institutional discrimination by the Israeli state; the failure of the attempts to persuade the Israeli authorities to allow them to return; and improvements in the economic situation of the displaced in the host villages in comparision with the early years of displacement. All these factors pushed return further down the political agenda. According to the Knesset proceedings (*Divrei Haknesset*), there was also a significant drop in statements made by Palestinian Knesset members during the 1970s and 1980s on matters related to the IDPs and their desire to return to their villages of origin (Cohen 2000).

During the 1970s and 1980s, the Israeli authorities appeared to have succeeded in concealing the reality of the internal refugees and in suppressing their right to return to their villages of origin. The same period also witnessed fewer governmental efforts to address the IDP problem. During the 1970s, when Palestinians inside Israel began to organise nationwide campaigns, the displaced people and their struggle to return was not made a priority issue. Various nationwide organisations were established, including "Arab students' committees" within Israeli universities, the National Union for Arab Students (in 1975), the National Union for Secondary Schools Pupils, the National Committee of the Arab Local Councils (in 1974), and the National Committee for the Defence of the Land (in 1975). The few committees of the displaced that existed in this period all operated on the local level and focused on specific villages of origin; no nationwide campaign on behalf of the displaced existed.

The problem of the IDPs in general and their struggle for return in particular were concealed during the 1970s and 1980s behind the wider political demands of the Palestinian national movement inside Israel, which focused from June 1967 on two major issues: Israeli withdrawal from the 1967 Occupied Territories and the establishment of an independent Palestinian state in the West Bank and Gaza Strip; full equality for the Palestinian citizens of Israel. However, the same historical period witnessed an increase in academic research on the IDPs and villages of origin inside Israel. According to Israeli anthropologist Dan Rabinowitz (1998), academic writing – especially ethnographic, sociological and historical works – have had a strong impact on the cultural, social, historical and political development of the Palestinians (including the refugees) and on their ability to construct and articulate a separate and vibrant identity. The subsequent "rediscovery" of the internally displaced Palestinians occurs simultaneously with the increase in academic output, especially that produced and written by the

Palestinians themselves.

The early 1990s witnessed the beginning of negotiations between the Israeli Labour government and the PLO, leading to the signing of the Oslo Agreement in September 1993, and the establishment of the Palestinian Authority in the Occupied Territories. The 1990s were characterised by the emergence of a massive campaign for return in Israel, led by the IDPs themselves, and more specifically by the second and (even third) generation of internal (and external) refugees.

Displaced activists argue that this massive campaign for the "right of return" was linked directly to the fact that the Oslo peace process had completely ignored their rights. Despite differences between the Palestinian internal refugees in Israel and Palestinian refugees in the West Bank and Gaza Strip, their responses to the flaws of the Oslo peace process were similar (Gasner-Jaradat 2000). Popular committees were established in both places in order to protect the rights of the refugees and the IDPs. This was the first time that the internal refugees set up committees ("by refugees and for refugees") to lobby for their rights at the national level. During the latter part of the 1990s, "return committees and organisations" were also established in the Arab countries (including Lebanon, Syria and Jordan) as well as in Europe and North America. The emergence of this huge campaign reflected a crisis of representation at the Palestinian national level. The Oslo process, according to the "return activists", marginalised the right of return of the Palestinian refugees and IDPs. Amir Makhoul, Director of Ittijah, the Union of Arab Associations inside Israel, had this to say:

> [The] Oslo [process] led each Palestinian constituency to search for its future separately, far from a durable solution for all Palestinians, and made it impossible to address the Palestinians as one political centre. But [Oslo also] fixed the idea that the [Palestinian] National Authority interests are opposed to the real interests of two constituencies of the Palestinian people: the refugees and Palestinians inside Israel. (Makhoul 1999)

Paradoxically, however, one of the positive effects of the Oslo process, in relation to the refugees and IDPs, was that the process engendered increased interest in and awareness of this issue. As the different parties searched for solutions to the conflict, there was a need to study the major "obstacles" for peace between the Palestinians and the Israelis, particularly the refugee question (Sayigh 1998). Moreover, the refugees themselves have had the opportunity to articulate their point of view, their needs and their rights.

In April 1992, the IDPs inside Israel organised the first national public meeting at which they established a "follow-up committee" campaigning for the rights of the internal refugees. The committee emphasised that the IDPs were part of the Palestinian people, and protested against the PLO negotiations with the Israeli government – negotiations which completely ignored their "right of return". The committee also demanded implementation of UN resolutions related to the Palestinian refugees, especially General Assembly Resolution 194(III) of 11 December 1948 (Wakim 2001b). Three years later, the follow-up committee called for a conference on the IDPs in the village of 'Ibillin (March 1995). Representatives of some 28 depopulated villages (some 280 persons in total) participated in the meeting (Cohen 2000).[27] The participants decided to establish a "National Association for the Defense of the Rights of Internally Displaced" Palestinians inside Israel, or ADRID (officially registered with the Israeli Ministry of Justice as an NGO in 1998). ADRID consisted of representatives of tens villages of origin. A few days later, a nationwide Follow-up Committee of the Palestinian citizens inside Israel announced its support for the IDPs and declared ADRID as a "legitimate" representative forum of the IDPs in Israel (Wakim 2001b). Wakim Wakim, Secretary-General of ADRID and a second-generation internal refugee from al-Bassa village, had this to say:

> The important and historical resolution to establish the National Association [ADRID] as the legitimate representative of the IDPs in Israel [was adopted] in order to stop Israeli plans, supported by Arabs and the international community, against Palestinians, to deny their right of return and of self-determination [i.e., a Palestinian state] that we totally reject. (Wakim 2001b)

ADRID called upon the Israeli government to implement UN Resolution 194, to allow the IDPs and the external refugees to return to their homes and villages of origin. The committee began active campaigning, organising many activities in the villages of origin, among the most prominent being the organisation of annual marches to the villages. ADRID began to collect material for archives on individual villages, and to set up collaborative projects with Arab members of the Knesset and Arab political parties. ADRID also encouraged the establishment of various individual local village committees (Gasner-Jaradat 2000).

As a result, during the Israeli general election of 1996 all Israeli-Palestinian political parties supported in their manifestos the demand of the internally displaced to return to their villages of origin. Key political parties such as the Democratic Front for Peace and Equality (Hadash) (DFPE), the National Democratic Assembly (NDA) and the Islamic Movement, as well as smaller political parties such as Abnaa al-Balad and the Democratic Action Organisation (Da'im), all called for return. Party newspapers, such as *al-Ittihad*, *Sawt al-Haq Wa al-Huriyya*, *Fasl al-Maqal* and *al-Watan*, covered the question of the "right of return" extensively (Sa'id 1999). This was a significant development from the 1992 general election, when a demand for return was not mentioned by any Palestinian political party inside Israel (Cohen 2000). Moreover, by the late 1990s, some of the Israeli-Jewish left-wing groups, such as Ta'ayush, Gush Shalom, Bat Shalom and Zochrot, had begun to address the "right of return" of the displaced people.[28] The Palestinian community in Israel themselves continued to support the struggle of the displaced people. Palestinian sociologist Elia Zureik (1999) showed that more than 90 per cent of the Palestinians inside Israel thought that Israel should permit the IDPs to return to their villages of origin.[29]

The 1990s witnessed the establishment – in addition to ADRID – of a large number of individual village committees, such as those of Suhmata and Saffuriyya (1993), al-Damun (1996), al-Ghabisiyya, Mi'ar, al-Birwa, Lubya, Umm al-Zinat, 'Amqa and al-Bassa. Most of the local committees are also affiliated to ADRID.[30] The local committees consisted of displaced persons from the second and third generations, but are not based on family networks. Local committee activities are based around the core work of organising visits and voluntary work within villages and often the publication of pamphlets on the villages of origin. Some committees (including those of Hittin, al-Ghabisiyya, Iqrit and Kafr Bir'im) have also organised prayers in mosques and churches in support of the internal refugees (Sa'id 1999; *al-Ittihad*, 3 March 2002). Some run specific projects: for example, the committees of Suhmata and Saffuriyya both conducted surveys of the displaced population and their distribution inside Israel (Sa'id 1999).

In March 2000, ADRID organised a second nationwide conference in

Nazareth, with the participation of local refugee committees, Israeli-Palestinian political parties, and even representatives of the PLO. The final declaration of the conference reaffirmed the statements made at the first nationwide conference in 'Ibillin in 1995, including the "right of return" of the IDPs and refugees to the villages of origin (Wakim 2001b). During the same year more local committees joined ADRID. These include the committees of Daliyat al-Rawha, Miska, and 'Ayn al-Zaytun (Badil 2002b).

Since 2000, ADRID has worked closely with other Palestinian refugee committees and organisations in the West Bank, on the basis of shared principles, including UN Resolution 194. ADRID has participated in international conferences working in full coordination with other Palestinian refugee organisations (Badil 2001, 2002b). Moreover, ADRID cooperated with refugee groups to organise joint activities, such as the International Day of Solidarity with the Palestinian refugees in 2001. In 2001 ADRID also organised a major march in Nazareth.[31] Between October 2000 and November 2003, ADRID took part in four international meetings between Palestinian refugee committees and organisations held respectively in Cyprus, Brussels, Copenhagen and London.[32] One of the main outcomes of these meetings was the establishment of the Palestinian Right of Return Coalition as an international umbrella for all refugee and IDP organisations worldwide. ADRID has been an active member of this international coalition, and its campaigns on behalf of the Palestinian internal refugees have become a central focus of the international campaign for Palestinian refugee rights.

ADRID also protested against the deliberate exclusion of the rights of the Palestinian refugees and displaced people in Israel from the Israeli–Palestinian negotiation process. The committee led a demonstration in July 2000 in front of the American embassy in Tel Aviv (and a similar one in Nazareth), in protest against the denial of refugee rights at the Camp David Summit.[33] In December 2000, when the two sides announced that the final status talks would resume in the Egyptian port of Taba in January 2001, ADRID issued the following public statement:

> We, the internally displaced Palestinians [in Israel], are fully aware of the fact that the right of return of Palestinians displaced within the "green line", and of the [Palestinian] refugees in the diaspora, is both an individual and a collective right, sacred and inalienable, guaranteed to us by all international laws, humanitarian and human rights conven-

tions, and therefore not subject to negotiations. We therefore alert the Palestinian negotiators, and warn the Israeli leadership, not to gamble with our right of return. Do not trade our right of return for any other issue, and do not sign any agreement which denies this right, directly or indirectly.[34]

ADRID also participated in the campaign to defend refugee rights by sending letters to various parties involved, including the Arab leaders attending the Arab summits in October 2000, and in March 2001, in Amman.[35] ADRID has taken part in grassroots campaigning against political plans that sign away the right of return, such as the Nussiebeh-Ayalon plan of 2002 and the Geneva declaration of October 2003.[36]

Alongside this campaigning, ADRID works to influence Israeli public opinion and also calls on the international community to become involved in efforts to resolve the problem of the Palestinian internal refugees in Israel. At a meeting with the British Parliamentary Labour Council for the Middle East, which had visited Israel-Palestine and other parts of the region in September 2000 to ascertain the attitudes of the Palestinian refugees themselves, ADRID spokesperson, Suleiman Fahmawi, had this to say:

> The ball should not be put in our court, it should be put in the court of the international community. Why does the international community not provide us with a mechanism for return? We are a helpless people, we own nothing, and we don't have the means to implement the right of return. The international community has all required means, such as imposing pressure on Israel. To give you an example of a mechanism: many Palestinians are living in the vicinity of their town of origin. Return can easily be arranged to the land that now lies vacant. (Joint Parliamentary Middle East Council 2002)

In late 2002, competing with 44 NGOs worldwide, ADRID won the international Body Shop award for human rights, together with three other international associations.[37]

The struggle for the return of the Palestinian IDPs in Israel, which grew rapidly during the 1990s, has also been affected to a large extent by the process of strengthening Palestinian civil society inside Israel. Palestinian civil society structures had virtually disappeared in the aftermath of the 1948 *Nakba* and the mass displacement of Palestinians. With the end of military rule inside Israel in 1966, various political and social organisations began to emerge. During the 1990s, an extraordinarily large number of new Palestinian civil society associations, some 656, were officially registered inside Israel. In 1995, an umbrella organisation for Arab NGOs was established: Ittijah, the Union of Arab Associations inside Israel. Today Ittijah directly represents some 55 Israeli-Palestinian associations, and offers additional services to more than 150 Palestinian associations. Approximately, two-thirds of the Ittijah member organisations were established after 1990.[38] Palestinian associations inside the Green Line such as the Al-Aqsa Association, the Galilee Society, the Association of the Forty for the unrecognised villages inside Israel,[39] 'Adalah – the Legal Centre for Arab Minority Rights in Israel – and the Arab Centre for Alternative Planning (AC-AP), support both the displaced themselves and ADRID as a committee.[40]

"Rediscovering" the Village of Origin and Articulating Its "Narrative"

Since the 1948 *Nakba,* the activities of the displaced people have reflected a strong relationship between memory, identity, and the desire to return to the place of origin. These three interconnected dimensions are closely linked to the IDPs' struggle in Israel. "Socialisation" of the place of origin, promoted by many members of the displaced communities, aimed at creating a territorially based identity which centred on the village of origin, and this in turn helped to empower the struggle for return. Most of the activities of the IDPs, therefore, have had a strong physical connection to the place of origin. These activities, such as visits, summer camps and other social and political activities, took place not only within the boundaries of the village of origin, but also outside it. These include printing maps, issuing publications, meeting politicians and local leaders, appealing to the Israeli courts, and articulating the "narrative" of the village of origin. In short, since the *Nakba* the villages of origin have become the most important provider of "legitimacy" for the displaced, and the centre of memory, identity and the struggle for return.

Interestingly, the "quantum leap" in the displaced people's struggle, which is centred on the village of origin, has occurred among the second and third generations of internal refugees. Although these people were born outside the village of origin, and many in the second and third generations expressed attachment to the host village, younger activists from the community have made the village of origin a major project of identity and education, and have expressed a stronger belief in future return than the older generation of refugees.[41] At the same time, however, younger generations have learned from their fathers' unsuccessful attempts to return in the past, taking into consideration the developments that have taken place among Palestinian citizens of Israel. Dawud Bader, ADRID coordinator and a member of the second generation of internal refugees, argues:

> the internally displaced persons in Israel faced difficult experiences and bad conditions in the past. During the early years of military rule, displaced people could only find a shelter to live quietly and to try to advance themselves. Later, and gradually, the younger educated generation became more involved in political and national issues. The displaced persons became more advanced in many fields. They became more involved in confronting the Israeli authorities and their discriminatory policies. Israel doesn't distinguish in its policy between displaced persons and non-displaced persons in the fields of land confiscation and ethnic-national discrimination.[42]

History and memory became a central component of the displaced struggle. Younger generations began to reconstruct the collective memory of the village of origin through various means. Until recently, history and memory for the older generation had only existed in oral form, and within the social context of the host village. Younger generations, on the other hand, have been trying to articulate and "institutionalise" memory since the early 1990s. In this context, the IDPs have been more fortunate than the Palestinian refugees in the diaspora, owing to the possibility of physical access to the villages of origin which provides IDPs with the opportunity to "experience the village of origin". Wakim Wakim, Secretary-General of ADRID, had this to say:

> Our task is not only to confront the grandsons of Zionism on the issue of displacement, or to rewrite the Palestinian *Nakba* narrative, systematically and comprehensively; it is more than this. We aim to organise the displaced communities through the popular committees and relevant associations, and under the [umbrella] of the Displaced Committee [ADRID], as an organised national forum, and by encouraging the local committees to organise visits [to the villages of

origin], by publishing bulletins to strengthen the belonging of the depopulated village as a microcosmos of Palestine, by organising
summer camps for displaced children, and by protecting the holy sites
in the depopulated villages. (Wakim 2001b)

Visits to the villages of origins, preserving holy sites, holding summer
camps and marches within their boundaries, therefore, have become key
components of the IDPs' strategy to focus on the village of origin. These
activities aim to encourage displaced people to "rediscover" the village of
origin themselves, and to empower their memory, sense of belonging and
identity. During the commemoration of the *Nakba* in 2000, ADRID
organised, in coordination with the local refugee committees, more than
twenty marches and trips to the villages of origin (Badil 2002b).[43] In 2003
most of the IDPs' activities during the commemoration of the *Nakba*
were held in the villages of origin.[44]

The protection and preservation of village Muslim and Christian holy
sites is carried out on both a local and a national level. In March 2002,
displaced people from al-Ghabisiyya organised public prayer in front of
the closed village mosque. The participants had asked the Israeli
authorities to reopen the mosque which has been closed since 1997.[45]
Some of the voluntary and semi-religious activities in the villages of
origin have been carried out by the Islamic-led Al-Aqsa Association,
which has been looking after and cleaning remaining old mosques and
cemeteries. In 1994, the Al-Aqsa Association presided over the voluntary
work of restoring the cemetery in the depopulated village of Husha.
Similar activities were also carried out in the old village of Balad al-
Shaykh (Cohen 2000). The Al-Aqsa Association has continued to lobby
for the reopening for prayer of all old mosques in villages of origin. This
campaign has had some successes, including the decision by the Israeli
Ministry for Religious Affairs in the mid-1990s to spend some
NIS300,000 (around $70,000) on repairing mosques in villages of origin
(Sa'id 1999).

Since 1987, displaced persons from Kafr Bir'im village have been
organising annual summer camps on the site of the depopulated Arab
village (Magate 2000). Working in coordination with various Arab
national associations, several village committees have organised summer
camps in the village of origin. During these summer camps, individuals
from the first generation of displacement are often invited to come to
give talks about life in the village before the 1948 *Nakba*. Organisers of

the Kafr Bir'im summer camps summed up the purpose of the events: "It's not to talk about the village, but rather to live it 24 hours a day" (Sa'id 1999).

In 1998 ADRID, in coordination with internal refugee local committees and Israeli-Palestinian national associations, began organising the "Return March" as a major annual national collective event. The Return March is held on the same day as Israeli "Independence Day" – which is marked according to the Hebrew calendar – with the participation of thousands of displaced people and Israeli-Palestinians. Initially the route of the Return March used to include one of the host villages, ending with one of the villages of origin. In 1998, on the fiftieth annual commemoration of the *Nakba*, the march started from the town of Nazareth and ended in the pre-*Nakba* village of Saffuriyya.[46] In 2000 the march began in the host village of Kabul and ended in al-Damun village of origin. In 2001 it began in the host village of Yafa and ended in the Ma'lul village of origin. In 2001 there was also a march to al-Birwa village of origin (Wakim 2001b; Badil 2001), and in 2003 to Umm al-Zinat village of origin.[47] Other national dates around which marches were held included Land Day, and the 1948 date of village occupation, for example a march was held on 28 March 1998 from Shaykh Dannun host village to al-Ghabisiyya village of origin. These marches expressed strong protest against the Israeli authorities' attitudes towards the internal refugees; the symbolic "return" each year to the village of origin on exactly the same day of Israel's "independence" is extremely powerful.

Palestinian national associations inside Israel and local committees of internal refugees have also published booklets and pamphlets focusing on the experience of displacement, on the concept of living as an internal refugee and on the villages of origin.[48] Publications on the villages of origin, especially those focusing on the pre-*Nakba* period, are prepared and produced mostly by the displaced people themselves. These publications tend to emphasise the history of the village of origin in the pre-*Nakba* era, list names of families, names of sites and landmarks, the boundaries of the village, as well as including photos from the pre-1948 period.[49] "Socialisation" of the place of origin, therefore, has been attained by commemorating the suffering of the displaced people and remembering their places of origin. This approach has ensured that "socialisation" processes have become central to the protests and resistance of the internal refugees.

Conclusion

Internally displaced Palestinians in Israel are an integral part of the Palestinian refugee communities. As part of the Palestinian refugee problem, and part of the Palestinian citizens of Israel, their problems as refugees within their homeland must be addressed in the same way as the problems of any other Palestinian constituency. Internal refugees also face challenges in their daily lives within the Israeli-Palestinian host communities, and in the Jewish state of Israel, as a "minority within a minority" – a state that discriminates against them systematically. This reality is partly the outcome of the 1948 *Nakba*. In international legal terminology the distinction between refugees and IDPs is unambiguous; a refugee is one who has crossed international borders, while an IDP is displaced within the same country.[50] However the refugee experience and the identity of the Palestinian IDPs demonstrate that a legal definition does not adequately cover the situation in reality. In the case of the internal refugees the alienation resulting from internal displacement "within one's own homeland" is much in evidence.

Long-term displacement of Palestinians in Israel has resulted in many changes, including social and economic adaptation by the younger generations to their host communities. Over time, most of the IDPs from the younger generations have developed two sets of emotional attachments and commitments, one towards the host village and another towards the village of origin. IDPs feel that there is no contradiction between the two sets of obligations. However, accommodation within the host community cannot provide the internally displaced Palestinians with a comprehensive solution. Return to, and rehabilitation in, the place of origin could provide an alternative. Israeli authorities, however, will continue to reject this option – an intransigent attitude which constitutes the major obstacle for achieving a just and durable solution.

The struggle for return since the early 1990s can be interpreted as an attempt to articulate a new nation-wide awareness among the internally displaced; the struggle and protests have been directed at the Israeli authorities, and in support of the wider Palestinian national cause. Although leading activists among the internally displaced have formed links with other Palestinian refugee groups, their methods and tactics are derived from the local contexts of internal displacement in Israel. The attempts of the displaced activists to politicise their cause, and to make it a Palestinian national issue, was the outcome of the failure of the first generation of internal refugees to achieve repatriation.

Notes

1 For more details on the various estimates of the number of Palestinian refugees, see Badil 2003a. Palestinian historian Walid Khalidi (1992) counts 418 depopulated Palestinian villages; however, Palestinian researcher Salman Abu Sitta (1998) puts their numbers at 531, after adding the Bedouin tribes in the Negev.

2 Some of the mosques, churches and cemeteries still exist in a number of depopulated villages. According to Khalidi (1992), out of 418 depopulated villages surveyed, only seven villages were not completely destroyed; some of these villages were resettled by new Jewish immigrants. These seven villages are Tarbikha in Acre district, Balad al-Shaykh, al-Tira, and 'Ayn Hawd in the Haifa district, and 'Ayn Karim, al-Maliha, and Dayr Yasin in the Jerusalem district.

3 Between October 1948 and August 1949, 109 Jewish settlements were built on the land of depopulated Palestinian villages. See Khalidi (1992).

4 These included Nazareth 3,000-6,000 IDPs; Acre 1,000; Majd al-Kurum 850, al-Rama 550-850, Yafa 370-750, Abu-Sinan 400, Kafr Yassif 400, Kafr Kanna 270-600, Shafa'amr 500. See Kamen (1984).

5 In addition, during the 1980s, 750 families were displaced from the Negev to facilitate the building of a military base. In 1995 the Israeli infrastructure minister ordered the destruction of "al-Hawashleh" village in the Negev and "Arab al-Jahalin". See Cohen (2000); Wakim 2001a; for more details, see Masalha (1997).

6 Until the end of 1950, the authority worked to resettle 204 families (1,020 persons) in the shelter villages, and deported some 1,489 other persons. See Cohen (2000).

7 In 1950, the village department of the Custodian of Absentees' Property announced that it was going to study the question of renting empty houses in the shelter villages to IDPs in twenty villages. Israeli Defense Army Archive, 263/66/2, Cited in Cohen (2000).

8 In the shelter places of Umm al-Fahem, Yamma and Sha'ab and 'Ayn Rafa (near Jerusalem), the Israeli government built some 20 housing units for the IDPs in each shelter place. In Jaljulya 10 housing units were built, in Ramle 45, and in Nazareth more than 200. Cohen (2000).

9 Israeli authorities confiscated, for example, some 56 plots from Tamra host village in the Galilee in October 1958 in order to resettle IDPs. After a few months the government confiscated almost 70 *dunums* in Judayda host village, and 24 *dunums* in al-Jish host village. Cohen (2000).

10 *Fellah* (pl. *fellahin*), the Arabic for "ploughman" or " tiller", is the word used in Arabic-speaking countries to designate peasantry.

11 Sayigh (1979), who studied the Palestinian refugees in Lebanon, argued that the

Palestinian refugees represented to the locals the *Nakba* and the defeat of the Arabs in 1948. The existence of the refugees therefore, in the eyes of the locals reflected the victory of Zionism. Because of differences in the cultural norms, clothes, and religion, locals in Lebanon also viewed the refugees generally as "foreigners", especially throughout the early years.

12 Various studies have shown that the refugees reject the use of the term "refugee" to identify themselves because of its negative social connotation ('Aqel 1992; Yahya 1999). In some cases, the refugees preferred to refer to themselves collectively as "returnees" or "revolutionaries" (Sayigh 1979).

13 Interview with Dawud Bader, 28 October 2002, Shaykh Dannun village.

14 Sha'ab Local Council 2002. *Sha'ab: Services, Honour and Developments.*

15 This process is shown by the percentage of the agriculture workers in the total Palestinian labour force: 49 per cent in 1955, 40 per cent in 1967, 17 per cent in 1977, and 10 per cent in 1984. See Al-Haj (1994).

16 The collapse of the Palestinian economy began with the beginning of the Palestinian rebellion in 1936. While the Zionist-Jewish economy of the Yeshuv experienced considerable development, the Palestinian economy was hit hard by the British Mandate administration. See Kimmerling and Migdal (1998).

17 See *Fasl Al-Maqal*, 29 September 2000; *Al-Ittihad*, 14 October 2000; and *Haaretz*, 18 December 2000.

18 Belonging to the place of refuge through long-term displacement is also relevant to Palestinian refugees in exile, especially in refugee camps such as Burj al-Barajneh (Roberts 2000). See also Hanafi (2002) for further details.

19 For example, on 24 May 1949 the Israeli army deported some 61 persons from the villages of Farradiyya and Samiriyya. The army also deported two families from Mi'ar village who originated from the village of 'Arraba. See Cohen (2000).

20 With the end of the war, many villagers who had remained in villages from which most residents had been displaced or expelled during the war were themselves also expelled. The villages involved included al-Faluja, 'Iraq al-Manshiyya, Farradiyya, 'Anan, Saffuriyya, al-Khalsa, al-Qaytiyya, Khirbat al-Mintar and al-Ghabsiyya. See Morris (1987); Khalidi (1992).

21 In Nazareth, there was a high percentage of IDPs. Inside the city there were more than 4,500 IDPs and in the nearby villages there were an additional 5,000 IDPs. The Israeli government was reluctant to allow such a high population of IDPs to remain in one place. It therefore decided to allow the IDPs from Haifa, Acre and Jaffa to return to the cities. A special ministerial committee recommended that the 560 IDPs from 'Ilut and Hittin should also return, but the army objected to Hittin for "security reasons". The two Bedouin tribes of Krad al-Baqqara and Krad al-Ghannama were "transferred" to Sha'ab village in 1956, which had been empty and declared a "closed military zone". Villagers from Sha'ab, who had been displaced to the nearby villages, were allowed to return to the village. See Cohen (2000); Kamen 1984; Sa'id 1992.

22 State of Israel Archive, Minorities Ministry file, 41/1319, cited in Cohen 2000. The army of Qawaqji was an Arab army of irregulars comprised of different Arab

troops who came to Palestine in 1948.

23 Israeli High Court, file 228/51.

24 Israeli High Court, file 64/51.

25 Israeli High Court, file 195/51.

26 The "Abandoned Areas Ordinance" (1948) in Hebrew is "*Ha-hok le-pekuah 'al harikhush hanatush*" (the Law for Supervising the Abandoned Properties). For Tubi's statement see, *Davrei Haknesset* [Israeli Parliament's Proceedings] 1, 1949, pp.5-84. Other Palestinian members of the Knesset who were linked to Zionist parties voiced similar demands for the return of displaced persons to their villages of origin. See, for example, Seif al-Din al-Zo'bi's statements, *Davrei Haknesset,* 3, 1949, pp.147-149, and Amin Jarjura's statements, *Davrei Haknesset,* 3, 1949, pp 105-6. Cited in Cohen (2000).

27 The first grassroots conference of refugees in the Occupied Territories was held in "al-Fara'a", a former Israeli prison in Nablus, in 1995, and called upon the Palestinian refugees to organise a lobby for return. Other workshops were held in the West Bank and Gaza in 1996; in addition, the "first refugee conference" was held in Dheishe refugee camp, near Bethlehem, in 1996. This grassroots campaign led to the re-activation of the Refugee Affairs Department of the PLO and the establishment of popular committees in each camp of the West Bank and Gaza. Workshops and protest activities continued in the following years. See Gasner-Jaradat (2000).

28 See http://www.NakbaInHebrew.org.

29 At the same time 58 per cent of Palestinians inside Israel supported the return of the Palestinian refugees to Israel, and 22.6 per cent of them supported return to both Israel and the Palestinian state. See Zureik (1999).

30 The committees of Iqrit and Kafr Bir'im, which have conducted a unique legal struggle based on the Israeli High Court rulings on their particular case, have expressed caution with regard to coordination with ADRID and the IDPs in general.

31 Badil press release, 3 April 2001.

32 For further details, see Badil reports on the annual meetings (Badil 2001; 2002b; 2003b).

33 Badil press release, 25 July 2000.

34 ADRID press release, 10 December 2000.

35 Badil press releases, 10 October 2000, and Badil press release, 26 March 2001.

36 For further details, see Boqa'i and Rempel (2003).

37 Badil press release, 5 November 2002.

38 36 out of 54 organisations in total. For further details, see http://www.ittijah.org.

39 The unrecognised villages are Palestinian localities in Israel which the Israeli government does not recognise. They do not receive any services, including electricity, piped water, telephone, postal services and infrastructure. The Association of Forty was established in 1988 on the fortieth anniversary of the *Nakba* and the Universal Declaration of Human Rights. Some of the Palestinians in the unrecognised villages are IDPs, such as the Palestinians from 'Ayn Hawd,

near Haifa. See http://www.assoc40.org . See also Chapter 8.

40 On 27 April 2003, for example, the Arab Centre for Alternative Planning AC-AP, in coordination with ADRID, organised its third annual conference in Nazareth on the Internally Displaced inside Israel, with the participation of international experts on housing rights. Other Palestinian and Israeli researchers took part (Badil press release, 17 March 2003). See also www.ac-ap.org.

41 The majority of the Palestinian younger generation in Israel believed that the solution for the refugees and displaced persons must be based on UN Resolution 194 (67 per cent); only slightly more than 50 per cent of the older generation agreed with this position. The younger generation also believed that it is possible to implement Resolution 194 (67 per cent) – as opposed to only 40 per cent of the older generation. See Zureik (1999).

42 Interview with Dawud Bader, 28 October 2002, Shaykh Dannun village.

43 Most of the IDPs' national activities in the commemoration of the *Nakba* were held under the slogan of "Their Independence. Our *Nakba*". See ADRID press releases, 8 May 2000; 17 April 2001; 14 April 2001.

44 While the village of origin was the centre of the 2003 *Nakba* commemoration activities of the internally displaced people inside Israel, the Palestinian refugees have tried to focus on another "symbol" of *the Nakba*: namely the refugee camp. Approximately half of the 2003 *Nakba* commemoration activities in the West Bank and Gaza Strip took place inside refugee camps. See Boqai' and Rempel (2003).

45 *Al-Ittihad*, 3 March 2002.

46 *Haaretz*, 15 May 1998.

47 ADRID press release, 26 April 2003.

48 In 1998 ADRID published a book written by the Palestinian journalist Wadia 'Awawdeh on this experience and on memory and identity.

49 The local committee of al-Ghabsiyya, in coordination with ADRID, published a pamphlet on the village of al-Ghabsiyya in May 2002, *Al-Ghabisiyya: We Still Have The Keys, The Story of an Uprooted Palestinian Village*. And in May 2003, in coordination with the local committee of Umm al-Zinat, a booklet entitled: *Umm al-Zinat: The Story of an Uprooted Palestinian Village*, was published by ADRID. The displaced committee of al-Damun village of origin published *Al-Damun: My Village* in May 2000.

50 This is also problematic in connection with the Palestinian case, mainly due to the fact that there were no "clear international borders" inside Palestine in 1948. See Badil (2002a).

References

Abu-Rabia', 'Aref. 1999. "Bedouins in the Negev: Displacement, Forced Resettlement and the Natural Zones", *Nashrat al-Hijra al-Qasriyya 5* [Forced Migration Publication], pp.31-33 [Arabic]).

Abu Sitta, Salman. 1998. *The Palestinian Nakba: The Register of Depopulated Localities in Palestine.* (London: The Palestinian Return Centre).

'Aqel, Mahmud. 1992. *'Ayn Bayt 'Alma': Palestinian Refugee Camp, a Study in the Sociology of the Camps* (Jerusalem: Palestinian Academic Society for International Affairs [Arabic]).

Ashkar, Ahmad. 2000. "The Uprooted Palestinian Refugees Inside Israel", *Shaml Newsletter* November (Ramallah, Palestine: Palestinian Diaspora and Refugee Centre).

Badil Resource Center. 2001. *First Annual Strategy Workshop in Cyprus* (Bethlehem, Palestine: Badil Resource Center for Palestinian Residency and Refugee Rights [Arabic]).

—— 2002a. *Internally Displaced Palestinians, International Protection and Durable Solutions.* Badil Information and Discussion Briefs, No.9 (Bethlehem, Palestine: Badil Resource Center for Palestinian Residency and Refugee Rights).

—— 2002b. *Second Annual Workshop, Brussels, Coalition for the Palestinian Right of Return* (Bethlehem, Palestine: Badil Resource Center for Palestinian Residency and Refugee Rights [Arabic]).

—— 2003a. *2002 Survey of Palestinian Refugees and Internally Displaced Persons* (Bethlehem, Palestine: Badil Resource Center for Palestinian Residency and Refugee Rights).

—— 2003b. *Third Annual Strategy Workshop, Copenhagen, Coalition for the Palestinian Right of Return* (Bethlehem, Palestine: Badil Resource Center for Palestinian Residency and Refugee Rights [Arabic]).

Boqai, Nihad and Terry Rempel. 2003. "Our Right of Return is the 'Real Road Map to Peace': Elite vs. Popular Approaches to Resolving the Palestinian Refugee Issue", *Between the Lines* III, Nos.23-24, September; and No.25, December.

Cabaha, Mustafa and Ronit Brazilai. 1996. *Refugees in Their Homeland: The Internal Refugees in State of Israel 1948–1996,* Skirot 'Al Ha'aravim BeYesrael, No.2 (Giv'at Haviva: Institute for Peace Studies [Hebrew]).

Cohen, Hillel. 2000. *The Present Absentees: The Palestinian Refugees in Israel since 1948* (Jerusalem: Centre for the Study of Arab Society in Israel, Van Leer Institute [Hebrew]).

Gasner-Jaradat, Ingrid. 2000. *The Public Campaign for the Defense of the Palestinian Refugee Rights in Historical Palestine.* Badil Information and Discussion Briefs, No.3 (Bethlehem, Palestine: Badil Resource Center for Palestinian Residency and Refugee Rights).

al-Haj, Majid. 1986. "Adjustment Patterns of the Arab Internal Refugees in Israel", *International Migration* 24, No. 3, pp.651-73.

—— 1994. "The Arab Internal Refugees in Israel: The Emergence of a Minority within the Minority", Ian S. Lustick (ed.), *Arab-Israeli Relations: A Collection of Contending Perspectives and Recent Research* (New York and London: Garland Publishing).

Hanafi, Sari. 2001. *Here and There: Towards an Analysis of the Relationship Between the Palestinian Diaspora and the Centre* (Ramallah, Palestine: Muwatin – the Palestinian

Centre for Study of Democracy [Arabic]).

Joint Parliamentary Middle East Councils, Commission of Enquiry – Palestinian Refugees. 2002. *Right of Return* (London: Labour Middle East Council).

Kamen, Charles. 1984. "After the Catastrophe: The Arabs in Israel 1948-1950", *Mahbarot Lamehkar Vebekorit* 10 (Jerusalem), pp.5-91 [Hebrew].

Khalidi, Walid (ed.). 1992. *All That Remains: The Palestinian Villages Occupied and Depopulated by Israel in 1948* (Washington DC: Institute for Palestine Studies).

Lustick, Ian. 1980. *Arabs in the Jewish State* (Austin: University of Texas Press).

Magate, Ilan. 2000. *Bir'im, Enlisted Memory Group,* Skirot 'Al Ha'aravim BeYesrael, No.26. (Giva't Haviva: Institute for Peace Studies [Hebrew]).

Makhoul, Amir. 1999. "*Palestinians in Israel and the Permanent Status*", Speech given at the Annual Ambassadorial Study Day, 7 December 1999, 'Ibillin, organised by Ittijah, at: www.arts.mclill.ca/MEPP/PRRN/papers/misc.html.

Masalha, Nur. 1997. *A Land Without a People: Israel, Transfer and Palestinians 1949–1996* (London: Faber and Faber).

Morris, Benny. 1987. *The Birth of the Palestinian Refugees Problem, 1947–1949* (Cambridge: Cambridge University Press).

Musa, Hasan. 1988. *Geographic Distribution of the Arab Refugees in Their Homelands: The Galilee Area, 1948–1987* (Haifa: MA thesis submitted to Haifa University [Hebrew]).

Ozacky-Lazar, Sarah. 1993. *Iqrit and Bir'im: The Full Story,* Skirot 'Al Ha'aravim BeYesrael, No.10 (Giva't Haviva: Institute for Peace Studies [Hebrew]).

Palestinian Central Bureau of Statistics (PCBS). 2002. *Statistical Abstract of Palestine,* No.3 (Ramallah, Palestine: Palestinian Central Bureau of Statistics).

Rabbah, Ramzi. 1996. *Refugees, the Displaced and the Final Status Negotiations* (Beirut: Dar al-Taqaddum al-'Arabi [Arabic]).

Rabinowitz, Dan. 1998. *Anthropology and the Palestinians* (Jerusalem: Centre for the Study of Arab Society in Israel, Van Leer Institute [Hebrew]).

Roberts, Ribika. 2000. "The Rural Structure of Burj al-Barajneh Refugee Camp", *Nashrat al-Dirasat al-Filastiniyya,* 44, pp.115-135 [Arabic]).

Sa'id, Mahmud. 1992. "The Internal Refugees", *Al-Aswar* 12 (Winter), pp.22-41 [Arabic]).

—— 1999. *The Palestinian Refugees in Israel* (Ramallah, Palestine: Shaml, Palestinian Diaspora and Refugee Centre [Arabic]).

Sayigh, Rosemary. 1979. *Palestinians: From Peasants to Revolutionaries* (London: Zed Books).

—— 1998. "Dis/Solving the Refugee Problem", *Middle East Report* (Summer).

Sha'aban, Hussein. 2002. *Palestinian Refugees in Lebanon: From Hosting to Discrimination* (Jerusalem: PASSIA-Palestinian Academic Society for International Affairs [Arabic]).

Stendel, Ori. 1992. *The Arabs in Israel: Between the Hammer and Anvil* (Jerusalem: Academon – the Hebrew University Student's Publishing House [Hebrew]).

Wakim, Wakim. 2001a. *The Internally Displaced: Refugees in Their Homeland* (Cairo: Centre of Human Rights Studies [Arabic]).

——. 2001b. "Internally Displaced in their Homeland and the Main Stations", *Al-Ittihad* (Special supplement for Land Day, March [Arabic]).

Yahya, 'Adel. 1998. *Palestinian Refugees 1948–1998: Oral History* (Ramallah, Palestine: Palestinian Institute for Cultural Exchange [Arabic]).

Zureik, Elia. 1999. *Public Opinion and Palestinian Refugees* (Ottawa: International Development Research Centre).

4
Forced Sedentarisation, Land Rights and Indigenous Resistance: The Palestinian Bedouin in the Negev
Isma'el Abu-Sa'ad

The Committee [UN Committee on Economic, Social and Cultural Rights] expresses its grave concern about the situation of the Bedouin Palestinians settled in Israel. The number of Bedouins living below the poverty line, their living and housing conditions, their levels of malnutrition, unemployment and infant mortality are all significantly higher than the national averages ... [The unrecognised villages] have no access to water, electricity and sanitation and are subjected on a regular basis to land confiscations, house demolitions, fines for building "illegally", destruction of agricultural fields and trees, and systematic harassment and persecution by the Green Patrol. The Committee notes in particular that the Government's policy of settling Bedouins in seven "townships" has caused high levels of unemployment and loss of livelihood ... (Concluding Observations. Israel, UN Committee on Economic, Social and Cultural Rights, 19th Session, 16 November. 4 December 1998, E/C.12/1/Add.27).

Throughout the Middle East, the desert-dwelling Bedouin have formed an important component of Arab society. As Arab society in general is undergoing many changes, no community has been so dramatically affected as that of the Bedouin. This is particularly true of the Palestinian Bedouin Arab community in Israel. In addition to the changes brought about by the general processes of modernisation, this community has also been greatly affected by the establishment of the state of Israel in 1948, and the subsequent transformation of the existing Palestinian Arab population into a minority in the Western-oriented, Jewish state. This article deals specifically with the evolving Israeli policies toward the Palestinian Bedouin community of the Negev Desert in southern Israel,

numbering over 140,000, who make up 25 per cent of the region's population. In addition, they constitute 10 per cent of the Palestinian Arab
minority in Israel.

Point of Origin: Zionist Policy in the Pre-state Period

The Zionist movement began in Europe in the late nineteenth century
with the goal of establishing a Jewish state in Palestine. It was based on
the premise that Palestine was a territory that belonged exclusively to the
Jewish people due to their presence on the land during biblical times. The
Jewish settlement of Palestine was thus presented as an ideological and
moral project that also provided a solution to the dilemma of anti-
Semitism that had plagued the Jews in their European diaspora communities (Yiftachel 2003). The Zionists also portrayed it as a "land
without a people, for a people without a land" (Masalha 1997). Great
efforts were required to make this fictional depiction of the country a
reality, since at the time of the First Zionist Congress in 1897 the
Palestinian Arabs constituted 95 per cent of the population, and owned
and cultivated most of the country's arable land, while Jews constituted
only 5 per cent of the population and owned 1 per cent of the land (Prior
1999; Khalidi 1992). The Zionists strove both to achieve a Jewish
majority by promoting Jewish immigration to Palestine and to transform
it into a Jewish state by giving it an exclusively Jewish character. David
Ben-Gurion described exactly what he and his fellow Zionists meant by
"a Jewish state":

> When we say "Jewish independence" or a "Jewish state" we mean
> Jewish country, Jewish soil, we mean Jewish labor, we mean Jewish
> economy, Jewish agriculture, Jewish industry, Jewish sea. We mean
> Jewish safety, security, independence, complete independence, as for
> any other free people. (quoted in Lustick 1980: 88)

The Judaisation of the "empty" land became an official policy, as
noted in Israel's first national plan in 1952:

> Modern nations all over the world attempt to decentralize their
> population, so they do not become dependent on central congested
> cities ... In Israel this task is more urgent but also easier ... because
> unlike Britain, we do not require to move existing populations, but
> simply settle new immigrants in the country's *empty regions* [emphasis

added]. Israel can thus decentralize its population to the north, Jerusalem corridor and Negev regions, as part of the only rational way to develop this country (quoted in Yiftachel 2003: 28).

To the early Zionists, the Palestinian Arabs represented a non-European, inferior "other", and their overwhelming numbers in the future Jewish state represented a significant obstacle to the Zionists' quest to establish a sovereign state of their own. A prominent Zionist leader, Israel Zangwill, drawing from the orientalist discourse of the British regarding the indigenous Palestinian Arabs, wrote: "If Lord Shaftesbury was literally inexact in describing Palestine as a country without a people, he was essentially correct, for there is no Arab people living in intimate fusion with the country, utilising its resources and stamping it with characteristic impress; there is at best an Arab encampment" (Masalha 1997: 62). Such pronouncements by leading Zionists promoted the notion of an empty territory – empty, as Masalha explains, not necessarily in the actual absence of inhabitants, but rather, in the sense of a "civilisational barrenness", which was then used to justify Zionist colonisation, and the delegitimisation of the native population as a people, belonging to that particular place (Masalha 1997; Prior 1999).

Again, the Zionist imagery was contradicted by the reality on the ground. The fact that Palestinian Arabs were already cultivating most of the arable land was substantiated by Britain's high commissioner for Palestine, John Chancellor, who in 1930 recommended the total suspension of Jewish immigration and land purchases to protect Arab agriculture on the grounds that all cultivable land was already being utilised, and the arable land now in possession of the indigenous Palestinians could not be sold to Jews without creating a class of landless Arab cultivators (Masalha 1992; Prior 1999; Quigley 1990). Despite the powerful Zionist imagery of the Jewish immigrants "making the desert bloom", this was also true of the Negev Desert in southern Palestine, which was inhabited and extensively cultivated by Palestinian Bedouin. By the mid-1940s, the Negev's Palestinian Bedouin population was estimated at 65,000 to 90,000 and was organised into 95 semi-nomadic tribes (Marx 1967, 1990; Falah 1989; Maddrell 1990; Yiftachel 2003), while the Jewish population consisted of 475 persons, living in four settlements (Prior 1999). The Bedouin were engaged in animal husbandry and non-intensive, seasonal agriculture, and cultivated over two million *dunums* of land, primarily in the northern Negev (Falah 1989; Marx 1990; Yiftachel 2003). Approximately 90 per cent of them earned their living from a mixture of agriculture and pastoralism, and 10 per cent subsisted solely on raising livestock (Falah 1985, 1989).[1]

Despite duplicitous statements made to different audiences claiming that the rights of the indigenous inhabitants of Palestine would be protected and upheld (particularly to gain and maintain European and international support for the Zionist project), the Zionist movement worked toward the goal of removal, or transfer, of the Palestinian Arabs from the territory of their future state. In the 1920s, Zangwill began to campaign openly for transfer, declaring that an "Arab exodus", based on "race redistribution", or a "trek like that of the Boers from Cape Colony" was "literally the only 'way out' of the difficulty of creating a Jewish State in Palestine" (Zangwill 1920: 103, quoted in Prior 1999: 192). Likewise, Joseph Weitz's unedited diary contains the following entry for 20 December 1940:[2]

> Amongst ourselves it must be clear that there is no room for both peoples in this country … After the Arabs are transferred, the country will be wide open for us; with the Arabs staying the country will remain narrow and restricted … [T]he only solution is the Land of Israel, or at least the Western Land of Israel, without Arabs. There is no room for compromise on this point … The only way is to transfer the Arabs from here to neighboring countries, all of them, except perhaps Bethlehem, Nazareth, and Old Jerusalem. Not a single village or a single tribe must be left … Only then will the country be able to absorb millions of Jews and a solution will be found to the Jewish question. (quoted in Masalha 1992: 131-2)

Literally hundreds of statements such as Weitz's were made by Zionists (Said 1979). Palestinian Arabs continued to constitute the majority of the population, and even after four decades of intensive efforts promoting Jewish immigration to Palestine, in 1946 Jews comprised only 30.9 per cent of the population, and owned 6-7 per cent of the land (Hadawi 1991). The pre-state Zionist policy toward the indigenous Palestinian Arab population was aimed at delegitimising, and thus figuratively, and eventually literally, displacing it (Benvenisti 1997; Hadawi 1991; Hever 2002; Lustick 1980; Masalha 1992, 1997; Piterberg 1995; Prior 1999; Raz-Krakotekin 1999). This Zionist ideology of transforming the people, the land and the character of Palestine into a Jewish state has played, and continues to play a defining role in shaping Israeli policies and institutions. I will review how this policy has evolved and been implemented, particularly *vis-à-vis* the Palestinian Bedouin in the Negev, since the 1948 war.

Impact of the 1948 War and the Military Administration

The events immediately prior to, during and after the 1948 War resulted in the exodus/expulsion of over 80 per cent of the Palestinian Arab population in Israeli-held territory. This included the expulsion of roughly 80-85 per cent of the Negev Palestinian Bedouin population to the surrounding territories/countries (West Bank, Gaza, Jordan), which reduced their numbers to approximately 11,000 (Alafenish 1987; Falah 1989; Yiftachel 2003). Of the original 95 tribes inhabiting the Negev, only 19 remained in sufficient numbers to receive official recognition from the Israeli government (Falah 1989).

Senior Zionist statesman Chaim Weitzman, declared this Palestinian exodus "a miraculous simplification of Israel's tasks" (Lustick 1980, p.28), though given the many Zionist plans dealing with the issue of transfer, there is little that is miraculous about this dramatic demographic transformation (Masalha 1992; Prior 1999). The revisionist Israeli historian Simha Flapan (1987) concluded that although Ben-Gurion was careful not to go on record as supporting the "transfer" of the Palestinian Arabs, his ultimate aim to evacuate as many of them as possible from the Jewish state was revealed by the variety of means he used to achieve this purpose. The most decisive of these was the destruction of over 400 entire villages, and the eviction of their inhabitants even if they did not participate in the war.

The Israeli authorities imposed a Military Administration on the areas of the country that were heavily populated with Arabs. The regulations of the Military Administration typified traditional imperialist attitudes for dealing with the native population of a colony. They gave the authorities extensive and extremely rigorous powers, and their enforcement resulted in the nearly complete loss of individual freedoms and property rights. They impinged upon virtually every aspect of life, from control over freedom of speech, movement, the means of transportation, and the press to the expropriation of property (Jiryis 1976).

The most notorious of the military regulations regarding Palestinian rights to property was Article 125, which granted "the military governor the power to proclaim any area or place a forbidden [closed] area ... which no one can enter or leave without ... a written permit from the military commander or his deputy ... failing which he is considered to have committed a crime" (Jiryis 1976:17).

Using these expanded powers, the Israeli authorities took over control of most of the land in the Negev, and deprived the Palestinian Bedouin of the freedom to migrate seasonally with their herds and cultivate their lands (Lustick 1980). Twelve of the nineteen Negev Bedouin tribes were removed from their lands, and the whole population was confined to a specially designated Restricted Area (called the *Siyag*) in the northeastern Negev, which was known for its low fertility, and represented only 10 per cent of the territory the Bedouin had controlled before 1948 (Falah 1989; Yiftachel 2003). Due to the military regulations imposed upon them they could not return to and cultivate their lands, they were isolated from the Palestinian Arab population in other parts of Israel, and they needed special permits to leave their designated sections of the Restricted Area to look for jobs, education, markets, etcetera (Marx 1967). These restrictions represented a form of forced sedentarisation, which virtually ended their traditional way of life.

During the tenure of the Military Administration, the authorities also took great care to prevent the migration of the Bedouin out of the Restricted Area. Bedouin men who were given permits to work in the Jewish sector were not allowed to bring their families with them, thus ensuring their return to the Restricted Area. Even within the Restricted Area, a Bedouin of one tribe could not visit the area of another tribe without the permission of the Military Governor (Marx 1967). The Israeli authority's record during this period was one of intimidation and violence, in which collective punishment against the Negev Bedouin was common. Falah (1985) documented several massacres, as well as several cases of expulsion of Bedouin after the establishment of the state. Jiryis (1976) maintained that, "More than any other group, the Negev Bedouin suffered the full and unrestrained harshness of military rule" (p.122). As one Bedouin Shaykh stated:

> ... the land expropriation and the forced expulsions without com-
> pensation or the right to return ... brought the Bedouin to a situation

which [was] difficult both psychologically and materially, and to a lack of security unlike anything they had previously known. (quoted in Lustick 1980: 13)

Subsequent to their transfer to the Restricted Area, the Negev Bedouin were largely neglected by planning authorities for twenty years. No settlement, agricultural or industrial plans were prepared for this region. As a result, over the course of twenty years, dozens of "spontaneous" Palestinian Bedouin settlements evolved. The seven tribes that had originally lived in the Restricted Area settled on their own lands, while those who had been transferred to the Restricted Area by the government settled in the areas in which they had been placed. These settlements were characterised by tin shacks, cabins or tents because no permanent building activity (for example, stone or concrete structures) was allowed in the Restricted Area (Yiftachel 2003). These "spontaneous" (from the perspective of the state planning authorities) settlements were denied recognition by the government, and as a consequence were also denied basic infrastructure and services, such as electricity, running water and roads (Abu-Saad 2000; Marx 2000; Yiftachel 2003).

Thus, during this period, major Zionist policy objectives were achieved. During the 1948 War and its aftermath, the Palestinian Arab population in the Negev and throughout the country was reduced to a minority. This in itself freed up extensive tracts of land for "Jewish redemption", a process that was expanded during the Military Administration by removing many of the remaining Palestinians from their lands and concentrating them in closed areas, further reducing their land base.

Finally, it must be noted that the Military Administration served, first and foremost, as a tool for consolidating governmental control over the Palestinian Arab minority. This is evidenced by the fact that the Military Administration's regulations were never enforced in the Jewish community. As the State Comptroller reported in 1959:

An order from the military governor declaring an area closed is, in theory, applicable to all citizens without exception whether living in the area or outside it. Thus anyone who enters or leaves a closed area without a written permit from the military governor is in fact committing a criminal offence. In practice, however, Jews are not expected to carry such permits and in general are not prosecuted for breaking the regulations in Article 125 ... There is something wrong in this law, which was drafted to apply to all citizens in the country but is in fact enforced only against some of them (State Comptroller's Report on Security, 1959: 56).

While inconsistent with democratic principles, this one-sided enforcement of military rule was fully consistent with furthering the Zionist aims of creating a Jewish state and increasing Jewish – while decreasing Arab – control over the land.

Nonetheless, as will be shown below, the Bedouin today say that even the previous military government was less damaging and threatening than the policies implemented by the Green Patrol today.

The Expropriation and "Judaisation" of the Land

The "Judaisation" of the land in Palestine has its roots in pre-1948 Zionist settlement methods which attempted to create contiguous chains of segregated Jewish localities, particularly in areas with an Arab majority, such as the Galilee and the northeastern Negev (Yiftachel 1999b). Settlement in these regions was considered one of the valued achievements of Zionist activity. Since the Negev represented nearly 50 per cent of the country's total landmass, the northern portion of which (some 2,560,000 *dunums* or 640,000 acres) consisted of good soil suitable for irrigation, it was central to the Zionist settlement project. As David Ben-Gurion stated:

> Negev land is reserved for Jewish citizens, whenever and whereever they want … We must expel Arabs and take their places … and if we have to use force, then we have force at our disposal not in order to dispossess the Arabs of the Negev, and transfer them, but in order to guarantee our own right to settle in those places. (David Ben-Gurion in a letter to his son, Amos, 5 October 1937, quoted in UN Committee on Economic, Social and Cultural Rights Report 2003: 5)

After its establishment, the Israeli government continued to engage in massive efforts to "Judaise" the land. In some respects the entire country became a frontier, and the glorification associated with settling the frontier assisted in the construction of a unified national Jewish identity, as well as in the actual conquest of the physical space in which that identity could be territorially constructed. These frontier regions were often internal places within the state with predominantly Palestinian populations, over which the government attempted to assert its hegemony (Yiftachel 1999b). The Negev continued to be a major Zionist frontier icon, the Jewish settlement of which was passionately called for by Zionist leaders. Israeli's first prime minister, David Ben-Gurion, claimed that:

> The people of Israel will be tested by the Negev … only by settling and developing the Negev can Israel, as a modern, independent and freedom-seeking nation, rise to the challenge that history put before us … All of us – [Zionist] veterans and [new immigrants], young and old, men and women – should see the Negev as their place and their future and turn southwards. (quoted in Yiftachel 2003: 28-29)

The Judaisation of the land entailed its "de-Arabisation", and thus the relationship between the Palestinian Bedouin and their land was almost entirely expunged from Zionism's official story. Following the war of 1948, David Ben-Gurion appointed a committee whose job was to provide "Hebrew names to all places, mountains, valleys, springs etc., in the Negev". In a letter addressed to the members of the committee, Ben-Gurion wrote the following. "We have to remove the Arabic names for political reasons; as much as we do not recognise the political ownership of the Arabs over the land we also do not recognise their spiritual ownership [of the land] and their names" (*State Archives; Prewar Archive,* C/2613; quoted in Benvenisti 1997: 8-9). As Shamir stated:

> A host of historians, geographers, reporters, engineers, policymakers, and educators emphasize the rootless character of Bedouin life and describe the Bedouin as lacking the fundamental and constructive bond with the soil that marks the transition of humans in nature to humans in society (hence, for example, the distinction between "planned" and "spontaneous" settlements). One aspect of this official story emphasizes the emptiness of the Negev, while another aspect discovers the Bedouin nomads as part of nature. Both aspects ultimately converge into a single trajectory: an empty space that awaits Jewish liberation, and a nomadic culture that awaits civilization. (1996: 236)

The fact that the desert is empty only because the state emptied it, is certainly not acknowledged in the Zionist belief system. Rather, the Zionist version of history, which insists that the Negev was empty and uninhabited, facilitated the enactment of the numerous laws and regulations of land confiscation.

The most dangerous aspect of the land expropriation following the initial wave of expulsion is that it was (and continues to be) done through legal channels and is therefore an "acceptable" and "modern" way of cleansing the space in the Negev. In 1950, the Transfer of Property Law made the government custodian over the property of "absentee owners". Then, in 1953 under the Land Acquisition Law, which was modelled on the Ottoman Land Code of 1858 and which did not officially recognise Bedouin landholdings, the state of Israel expropriated 93 per cent of the Negev land (Yiftachel 2003). It is important to note that it was only after the creation of the state of Israel that the old Ottoman land categories became powerful and effective means for expropriating land. No compensation was offered for these confiscated lands, as the land was required for "positive development needs". Consequently, thousands of Bedouin who were not occupying their lands – as a direct result of their forced transfer to the Restricted Area – lost all of their rights to their land. In the meantime, the lands became a new home for the Jewish agricultural settlements. It is also important to note that as these new Jewish *kibbutzim* and *moshavim* emerged, the Negev Palestinian Bedouin were not permitted to work as labourers in these new settlements during the first decade of the state of Israel, for the jobs were reserved for the new Jewish immigrants (Marx 1967).

Moreover, the classification of Negev Bedouin lands as "state lands" gave their confiscation an unprecedented permanence due to the unique pattern of land ownership in Israel. The Israel Land Authority (ILA) administers state lands in Israel jointly with the Jewish National Fund (JNF), an international non-governmental organisation representing the interests of the Jewish people worldwide, rather than the interests of all citizens of the state of Israel. Nevertheless, the JNF has been given quasi-governmental powers with regard to land administration in Israel. As Yiftachel (1999a) explains:

> Israel created an institutional and legal land system under which confiscated land could not be sold. Further, such land did not merely become state land, but a joint possession of the state and the entire Jewish people. This was achieved by granting extraterritorial organizations, such as the Jewish National Fund, the Jewish Agency and the Zionist Federation, a share of the state's sovereign powers and significant authority in the areas of land, development and settlement. The transfer of land to the hands of unaccountable bodies representing

the "Jewish people" can be likened to a "black hole" into which Arab land enters but cannot be retrieved … Israel's Arab citizens are currently prevented from purchasing, leasing, or using land in around 80 per cent of the country. (Yiftachel 1999a: 372-3).

After the end of the military rule in 1966, some Bedouin attempted to reclaim or return to their lands. According to Falah (1989), the Bedouin used the following four arguments as proof of their ownership of the land: (1) they worked and cultivated the lands for a long period and were in possession of official tax as well as traditional documents; (2) the Turkish government purchased approximately 2,000 *dunums* from the 'Azazmah tribe in 1900 to build the town of Beer-sheba, thereby proving the Bedouin claims to the land; (3) the Israeli authorities recognised the purchasing claims of individual Jews in the Negev before 1948; and (4) the Israeli authorities recognise Bedouin land ownership, but only when they agree to sell it to the state.

Due to the policies of "Judaising the land", the Palestinian Bedouins' attempts to win recognition for their historical land rights through the Israeli justice system have been unsuccessful. The court offers no protection for their lands. For example, in 1974 when the Al-Hawashleh family challenged the confiscation of 36,000 *dunums* (9,000 acres) of their land in order to establish the Jewish town Dimona, the court ruled that this land belonged to the state. Furthermore, the court accepted both arguments made by the state: first, that the Bedouin as nomads had no attachment to the lands and so could not possibly own them; and second, that these were state lands that the Bedouin had invaded (Al-Hawashleh 1974).

Another major land confiscation occurred in 1980. Due to the ever-increasing military needs of Israel, the Israeli army insisted on establishing new airfields and military bases in the Negev to replace those that were closed in the Sinai after the signing of the peace treaty with Egypt. The Law of Requisition of Lands conveniently authorised the expropriation of 82,000 *dunums* of land in the Restricted Area. The compensation offered for these lands was much less than that given to the Jewish settlers who were removed from the Sinai during the same period. Furthermore, the land law mentioned above denied the Bedouin the right of appeal in the court system.

In the nearly sixty years that have passed since Israel's establishment, there has been little or no change in its land policies, despite its lack of success in completely removing the Palestinian presence from the land. According to official government policy, the Bedouin residing on and using their traditional lands are invaders and criminals, as was clearly and openly stated by the former Israeli Minister of Infrastructure, Avigdor Lieberman (himself an immigrant from the former Soviet Union) in 2002:

> We must stop [the Bedouin's] illegal invasion of state land by all means possible. The Bedouin have no regard for our laws; in the process we are losing the last resources of state lands. One of my main missions is to return the power of the [Israel] Land Authority in dealing with the non-Jewish threat to our lands. (quoted in Cook 2002: 2)

The Palestinian Bedouin have no rights to "state lands", despite their status as Israeli citizens, because "state lands" are in actuality "Jewish lands", and the Bedouin are reduced to the illegitimate and dehumanised status of "the non-Jewish threat". After more than half a century as citizens of Israel, they remain illegal invaders, and a threat to the vision of Zionism. A Palestinian Bedouin activist protesting against Israel's land policies described them thus:

> Only in one instance shall the Bedouin Arabs get their full and equal rights in the Jewish State: only if miraculously we'll stop occupying, needing or using any land. Then we shall receive what we truly deserve – full air rights … (minutes of meeting with Avraham Burg, chairman of Israeli Knesset Protocol, 6 December 1997, quoted in Yiftachel 2003: 175).

Despite the government's unrelenting Judaisation/de-Arabisation land policies, the Bedouin continue to resist the confiscation of their land, and the tension involving Palestinian Bedouin land ownership remains a central issue. Ninety five per cent of their land claims have not been settled, covering approximately 800,000 *dunums* (Mana Commission 1997). Half of these lands are in areas settled by Jews. The compromises reached so far between Negev Palestinian Bedouin and the state account for only 30,000 *dunums*. This low figure reflects the slow pace of the Israeli legal system, but also the on-going Palestinian Bedouin resistance to the next stage in the evolution of state policies, which attempted to link the settlement of land disputes with their relocation and urbanisation of the Bedouin (Yiftachel 2003).

Forced Sedentarisation and Urbanisation

In the late 1960s, the government formulated a programme for the resettlement of the Negev Bedouin population into planned, urban-style settlements. The core rationale for the programme of urban settlements derives from the ideological nature of spatial planning in Israel (Falah 1989; Gradus and Stern 1985; Kimmerling 1982; Marx 2000). Dispersion of the Jewish population throughout the land continued to be one of Israel's major national planning goals. Furthermore, the Bedouin's widely dispersed settlement and extensive land use even within the Restricted Area, not to mention their land ownership claims, represented an obstacle to the on-going Zionist conquest and cultivation of "frontier" desert areas (Gradus and Stern 1985; Marx 2000; Yiftachel 2003). Thus, the governmental plan to remove the Bedouin population from the land and settle them in higher density towns was designed to further decrease the extent of their claim on the land and to stem their "spontaneous" settlement activities (Falah 1989; Law-Yone 2003; Marx 2000; Shamir 1996; Yiftachel 2003).

On another level, by the 1960s the rapidly developing Israeli economy required growing numbers of workers (Marx 2000). As such, the unskilled Bedouin workforce, who in urban-style towns would no longer have the land resources to maintain their traditional livelihood, could participate as low-cost workers in the industrial and economic development of the Jewish towns in the Negev. As Moshe Dayan stated:

> We should transform the Bedouins into an urban proletariat – in industry, services, construction, and agriculture. 88 per cent of the Israeli population are not farmers; let the Bedouins be like them. Indeed, this will be a radical move which means that the Bedouin would not live on his land with his herds, but would become an urban person who comes home in the afternoon and puts his slippers on. His children would be accustomed to a father who wears trousers, does not carry a Shabaria [the traditional Bedouin knife] and does not search for vermin in public. The children would go to school with their hair properly combed. This would be a revolution, but it may be fixed within two generations. Without coercion but with govern-mental direction ... this phenomenon of the Bedouins will disappear. (Moshe Dayan, *Haaretz* interview, 13 July 1963)

The government-expressed rationale for this policy has been multi-faceted and often cast in the benevolent light of desiring to "modernise" the Bedouin and enable more efficient provision of services. While this coincides with Falah's (1985) finding that some Middle Eastern countries sedentarised the Bedouin in order to provide them with a level of services and standard of living comparable to those of their general populations, as an explanation it is belied by the fact that an explicitly urban and highly concentrated settlement model was selected. This represented a drastic lifestyle transition for the Bedouin, for which they were in no way prepared. If the goals of the government were in actuality only to modernise and provide the Bedouin with services more efficiently, both of these aims could have been achieved by planning small agricultural villages or cooperatives (such as the Jewish *moshavim* and *kibbutzim*) for the Bedouin, and would have required much less radical change from their traditional lifestyle than urbanisation entailed.

There were, in fact, strong cultural factors that made urban settlements unattractive to the Palestinian Bedouin. As Law-Yone (2003) explained:

Hierarchies of space based on tribal social structure were replaced by repetitive lots of uniform size, shape, and orientation. Gradations of proximity, enclosure, and openness of the desert were replaced by the spatial logic of European urban form. New and strange definitions of private and public spheres were grafted onto a society that had its norms, which were no longer considered valid. (p.181)

Furthermore, aside from the provision of basic services (water, electricity, telephone hook-up, schools and clinics), the towns lacked essential urban characteristics. In his 2002 report, the State Comptroller reported that none of the Bedouin towns had a completed sewage system, despite the fact that the towns had been in existence for many years, and that thousands of families had already paid for establishing this essential system. In four of the seven towns (Hura, Laqyia, Tel-Sheva and Arara) the sewage system was not operational at all. In the words of the State Comptroller (2002: 109):

Reasonably paced implementation of development and infrastructure in the Bedouin towns has not been carried out for many years. The settlements were populated with minimal infrastructure, and subsequently the level of resources invested for establishing and completing the infrastructure was insufficient, particularly with regard to sewage systems, streets and sidewalks. As a result of the many years of neglect in investment in the infrastructure, the settlements are suffering from great negligence. Moreover, there is a severe shortage in the domain of public institutions (e.g. recreational facilities, community centers, libraries, etc.), as well as public parks, sports fields, etc.

Unlike the neighbouring urban settlements in the Jewish sector, the Bedouin towns also lacked intra- and inter-city public transportation services, banks, post offices, public libraries, public parking lots, recreational and cultural centres, etcetera (with the exception of the largest town, Rahat, of over 40,000 inhabitants, which has one bank, one post office, and a cultural centre) (Abu-Saad 2003,1995; Lithwick 2000).

The development of a municipal political system and an urban infrastructure in these localities began at a very low starting point due to the lack of governmental support and investment in these localities (which were administered for many years by non-resident Jewish mayors appointed by the Ministry of the Interior), coupled with the extremely low economic status of the residents. Elections for local authorities in Rahat and Tel-Sheva were held in 1988 and 1992 respectively, because of High Court orders that, for the first time, allowed the residents of the two oldest planned Bedouin towns to exercise the basic right to elect their local community officials. Local council elections in the remaining five Bedouin local authorities were held in 2000, again only after the involvement of the High Court.

At the same time, neither the Bedouin towns nor the "unrecognised villages" were included in the broader development plans for the region. In several key regional plans, both for the Negev and for the Beer Sheva metropolitan area, (including the 1972 District Plan, the 1991 "Negev Front" strategy, the 1995 Beer Sheva Metropolitan Development Plan or the 1998 renewed District Plan), the areas of Palestinian Bedouin settlements were either left blank, as if they were non-existent, or designated for public uses such as sewage plants, recreational forests or industrial zones (Yiftachel 2003). Important new infrastructure developments such as the new Trans-Israel Highway, recently improved rail facilities and even inter-city bus services have taken virtually no account of the Palestinian Bedouin towns and their needs.

The systematic underdevelopment of the government-planned Bedouin towns is evident from the official government document ranking local authorities in Israel according to a socio-economic index

Table 4.1 • Socio-Economic Ranking of Local Authorities

Bedouin Towns	Kseifa	1
	Rahat	2
	Tel-Sheva	3
	Segev Shalom	4
	Arara	5
	Hura	7
	Laqiya	8
Jewish Towns	Dimona	82
	Beer Sheva	115
	Arad	119
	Metar	201
	Omer	209

Note: 1 denotes the lowest ranking among the 210 local authorities in Israel.
Source: *Statistical Abstract of Israel,* 2002

(Statistical Abstract of Israel, 2002), which places the seven towns at the bottom of the list (Table 4.1).

By way of contrast, the neighbouring Jewish towns (Omer, Metar and Lehavim) rank among the highest in the country. Beer Sheba ranks at 115, just over halfway down the list. Dimona, one of the poorer development towns[3], ranks considerably below Beer Sheba, while Arad, one of the more "successful" development towns, ranks slightly higher.

While the urbanisation of the Bedouin suited the policy goal of reducing the Negev Bedouin's *de facto* use of and control over land resources, it is clear that no real attempt has been made by the state to integrate the new Bedouin towns into the national infrastructure in a viable and meaningful sense. They were not given sufficient resources for independent development because Israeli government policy toward the Palestinian minority has consistently aimed at maintaining their dependence upon the Jewish economic and power structures in order to maximise the state's control over them (Lustick 1980).

Non-recognition and Dismantling of Traditional Villages

Over three decades after the initiation of the urban resettlement programme, only half of the Bedouin live in the government-planned towns. The numbers of those refusing to move to the government-planned towns had grown to some 70,000 people, constituting Israel's most marginal and deprived community (Abu-Saad 2000; Shamir 1996; Yiftachel 2003).

In the face of this resistance, the Israeli government is continuing to pursue its two-pronged Judaisation/de-Arabisation policy. As such, it places numerous pressures on the inhabitants of unrecognised localities in an effort to coerce them into moving to the government-planned towns (*Statistical Yearbook of the Negev Bedouin* 1999; Yiftachel 2003). The unrecognised villages and hamlets are denied services such as paved roads, public transportation, electricity, running water, garbage disposal, telephone service, community health facilities, etcetera. Bedouin in the unrecognised villages are also denied licences for building any sort of permanent housing. All forms of housing (except tents) are considered illegal, and are subject to heavy fines and demolition proceedings (Falah, 1989; Maddrell, 1990; Shamir 1996; Yiftachel 2003). From 1992 to 1998, a total of 1,298 buildings were demolished and NIS869,850 (approximately $220,000) in fines were paid, due to the "illegal" status of these buildings (*Statistical Yearbook of the Negev Bedouin* 1999). This policy is being intensified under the Sharon government (UN Committee on Economic, Social and Cultural Rights Report 2003).

The unrecognised villages are denied their own representative authorities and have no official local councils. The effect of this is that they are denied two clear rights: a local authority to provide them with basic services, and the right to elect local representatives.[4] The majority of residents of the unrecognised villages live in areas devoid of any municipal authority. Even those who do live in an area under a municipal authority, such as those villages within the jurisdiction of Jewish regional councils such as Bnei Shimon and Ramat Hanegev, do not receive services from these bodies or vote in their elections. Rather, the residents of the unrecognised villages are governed by a number of administrative structures and units set up especially for the Palestinian Bedouin. These include most notably the Bedouin Development Authority, the Bedouin Education Authority and the Green Patrol.

The Bedouin Development Authority

The Bedouin Development Authority (BDA) was established in 1984 and controls the planning and policy development and implementation for the Palestinian Bedouin community in the Negev. The BDA may have a benevolent-sounding name, but the Palestinian Bedouin community is the only community in Israel to have a special office charged with its development.[5] In this respect it differs from the other Palestinian Arab communities in Israel, most of which were sedentary towns and villages long before Israel's establishment, and have apparently been contained and controlled to the policymakers' satisfaction through normal government channels. But the Palestinian Bedouin in the Negev have persisted in presenting a unique challenge to government policies due to their relatively widespread dispersion and their resistance to the plans for their urbanisation. Thus, all state funding for the Palestinian Bedouin community comes through the BDA office. Even the municipalities of the recognised localities get their budgets through the BDA rather than directly from the various state ministries (Interior, Housing, Infrastructure, etcetera), as is the practice with all other localities (including other Palestinian Arab localities) in Israel.

Administratively, the BDA is a sub-unit of the Israel Lands Administration, which indicates the hidden agenda behind the benevolent name. It receives a large budget to buy land from the Bedouin community, but generally the money goes back to Jerusalem unused.[6] In addition to land resources, the BDA has absolute control over providing access to water for the Negev Bedouin in unrecognised villages. These villages are not connected to the national water system but their inhabitants are given access to water at very high prices in designated central locations, from which they must transport the water to their homes in containers. The BDA operates a very restrictive water policy, using this as another means of encouraging people to leave their land and move to the seven government-sanctioned towns.

The BDA also has a monopoly on all planning for the Bedouin community. Thus it is responsible for opening new neighbourhoods in the seven towns, or establishing new towns. In short, no development may occur for any Negev Bedouin community, whether recognised or unrecognised, if not sanctioned and carried out by the BDA.

The Bedouin Education Authority

The forty-five Bedouin unrecognised villages lack the municipal bodies that would normally provide education services. These services are instead provided through the Bedouin Education Authority (BEA), which was established by the Ministry of Education in 1981. The BEA is responsible for the building, maintenance and renovation of the schools and kindergartens outside the government-planned Bedouin towns. It is also responsible for bussing 12,000 schoolchildren to these 16 schools and 70 kindergartens, as well as to the high schools in the planned towns (since there are no high schools in the unrecognised villages).

Rather than developing the educational services within the unrecognised villages, the BEA primarily works to control the community, awarding services on a discretionary basis as part of the politics of patronage, so that these services are not provided as a right, but as a favour that is dispensed to those who are loyal and withheld from those who are not. This patronage overrides even the planning regulations and results in the provision of services in a manner that is ineffective and irrational (Abu-Saad 2003, 2001; Human Rights Watch 2001).

Since its inception, the BEA has been run by Jewish directors who have worked for the benefit of a close network of clients, and acted in the interests of controlling the community through the provision of education facilities. The patronising and control-oriented attitude of the former BEA director, Moshe Shochat, is well documented. When questioned in an interview given to the *Jewish Week* in July 2001 about the deficiencies in education services within the unrecognised villages, he characterised the community members who were organising to improve their school services as "blood-thirsty Bedouins who commit polygamy, have 30 children and continue to expand their illegal settlements, taking over state land". When questioned about providing indoor plumbing in Bedouin schools, he responded: "In their culture they take care of their needs outdoors. They don't even know how to flush a toilet" (Berman 2001). In response to a public outcry and lawsuit brought against the Ministry of Education and the BEA director, the Ministry of Education's initial response was that it appreciated the BEA director's work with the community and had no authority to dismiss him. On the basis of an internal investigation, the Ministry of Education later announced that it planned to dismiss the BEA director – not because of his racist statements, but rather due to financial irregularities in his administration ('Adalah 2003). Thus, it is clear that the primary role of the BEA is to serve as another means of control over the community, rather than to effectively provide educational services, or to be respectful of and responsive to the needs and concerns of the community.

The Green Patrol

The Green Patrol was established by the Israeli government in 1976 as a paramilitary unit to pressure the Bedouin to move into the urban settlements. Formally, it is presented as a body meant to preserve nature, oversee state lands and protect them from "squatters". In reality, the Green Patrol primarily acts to police, harass and evict the Bedouin living outside the urban settlements (Hazelton 1980; Yiftachel 2003). Herd sizes and grazing areas are very tightly controlled, and the Green Patrol confiscates flocks found in violation of the restrictions. In addition, their tactics include destroying Bedouin dwellings, crops and trees, which are considered "illegal" by the Israeli authorities. While the destruction of crops was usually carried out by tractors, this practice was raised to new heights in February 2002, when the Green Patrol used crop dusters to spray herbicides over and destroy 12,000 *dunums* (3,000 acres) of wheat fields. The decision to destroy the Bedouin crops was made during a meeting of the Governmental Economical Committee of the Knesset (Parliament) by officials from the Ministry of Agriculture, Ministry of Infrastructure, the Green Patrol and the Israeli Land Administration. They claimed that by tending to their agricultural lands, the Bedouin were trespassing on government land (Association for Civil Rights in Israel 2002; Cook 2002; Ornan 2002; Yiftachel 2003). Such action was taken again in March 2003:

> On 4 March 2003 the Israel Lands Administration sent two airplanes loaded with herbicides to spray 1,500 *dunums* (375 acres) of crops being grown by the villagers of the unrecognised village of Abda. Ten children playing in the fields were covered by the toxic spray. Several of them needed treatment for shock after they and their parents thought they had been the victims of a chemical gas strike from Iraq. The Israel Lands Administration (ILA) had not told the villagers of Abda that they were coming to destroy the crops, nor that they would be sending planes armed with herbicides. Elderly people and children who were in the fields were also sprayed. Village residents immediately evacuated those children to the closest clinic at Mitzpe Ramon (a nearby Jewish locality), but the doctor refused to receive them until the [Regional Council of Unrecognised Villages] Vice President contacted the Ministry of Health and Kupat Hulim. (UN Committee on Economic, Social and Cultural Rights Report 2003:14)

This method of crop destruction was again used on 2 April 2003, when airplanes sprayed another 1,300 acres of wheat crops with herbicides (Cook 2003).

Organised Community Resistance

In 1997, the Palestinian Bedouin who lived in the unrecognised villages formed their own regional council as a grassroots community movement; it has drawn up and submitted its own plans for regional development to the Ministry of the Interior. The Interior Ministry did not accept the proposed plan of the Council of Unrecognised Villages for more appropriate, rural settlement models, and has remained intent upon going ahead with the same unsuccessful urban model as before, with only superficial improvements, but it faces serious and organised resistance from the Bedouin community.

In light of the Negev Bedouin's continued resistance to the government's urbanisation policies, the role of the Green Patrol and other paramilitary measures are gaining increasing importance in the governmental effort to de-Arabise the land of the Negev, in some cases directly targeting the leaders of the Bedouin resistance (Cook 2003; UN Committee on Economic, Social and Cultural Rights Report 2003). These measures, which are being intensified under the current government, perhaps foreshadow a fallback to the days immediately before and after the 1948 War when military measures were used to "empty" the land for Jewish settlement.

"Final Closure": Sharon's Plan

In January 2003, the government presented its five-year plan, (also know as Sharon's Plan) for developing the Negev and bringing "final closure" to the Palestinian Bedouin land issue. The plan, of which Sharon was the main author, involves the establishment of seven new Bedouin towns, based on the same concentrated urbanisation models as the existing towns, and fourteen new Jewish settlements. Jews will be offered large subsidies to encourage them to move from the densely populated centre of the country to "settle" the Negev. Land will also be made available to Jewish settlers for the establishment of large, individual ranches and farms, for which the provision of subsidised water and electrification has already been approved by the government (Cook 2003; *Haaretz*, 17 January 2003). The plan also includes a comprehensive strategy to remove the Bedouin in the unrecognised villages from their lands by intensifying the use of coercive measures, such as home demolitions, land confiscation, and forced eviction. The overall plan, with a budget of NIS 1.175 billion (over $250 million), allocates NIS 395 million (a full third of the total budget) for massive reinforcement of the officials and bodies responsible for enforcing planning and construction ordinances in the Negev. The plan includes: the establishment of a new police unit and of special forces to implement government policies *vis-à-vis* the villagers living on their lands and to carry out demolition orders; the allocation of additional funds to the Green Patrol for more personnel, along with new powers to operate against villagers not only in restricted areas (for example, closed military zones and nature reserves), but also in their own living areas and lands; the allocation of additional funds to the Ministry of Interior for enforcing planning and construction ordinances in the Negev, which effectively means intensifying the policy of house demolitions; and the allocation of additional funds to the courts and Ministry of Justice in the Beer-Sheba District to accelerate the processing of demolition orders, including special court sessions and private lawyers hired by the Ministry of Justice solely to prosecute the residents of the unrecognised villages, requiring them to prove their land ownership to the court's satisfaction (UN Committee on Economic, Social and Cultural Rights Report 2003).

The Sharon Plan was developed without the participation of the Bedouin inhabitants of the unrecognised villages. Ehud Olmert, who is the Minister of Industry and Trade, and deputy prime minister, is also in charge of the Israel Lands Administration and has responsibility for the implementation of Sharon's Plan. With regard to Bedouin input into the plan, Olmert stated:

> We are talking about evacuating [the Bedouin] to the new seven towns that we are building for them … We will conduct contacts with them [the Bedouin], however, I assume that they will absolutely oppose [the plan]. We will not be deterred from implementing the decision, because there is no other way we can meet our goals. If it [the plan] required the Bedouin's agreement, it would never be given. It is a question of the government's determination to implement its decisions. (*Haaretz*, 11 April 2003)

Despite the lack of governmental interest in the Bedouin's reaction, the local community organisations together with a group of non-governmental Jewish and Arab organisations sent a detailed letter to prime minister Sharon, critiquing the inequities, inherent violence and non-participative nature of the plan, and suggesting alternative proposals for Negev development and resolution of the land conflict that would treat the Bedouin with equity, as citizens of the state.[7]

Conclusion

A review of Israeli policy toward the Palestinian Bedouin of the Negev reveals that little has changed since the pre-state Zionist goals of Judaising/de-Arabising the land were first established. What has evolved over time are the variety of mechanisms used to implement this policy, which have included expulsions, internal displacement, and massive land confiscation. This was followed by a programme of urbanisation to concentrate the Negev Bedouin into an even smaller geographical area, and the creation of special administrative and enforcement units to deal with Bedouin resistance to this programme. Although there have been some developments within the Israeli intellectual milieu (for example. post-Zionism, revisionist Israeli historians) that have begun to question the previously unassailable morality of the Zionist project, and criticise the on-going Zionist hegemony over Israeli politics and policies, these voices have not yet penetrated the circles of power where policy decisions are made.

What has indeed evolved over the past fifty-some years is the resistance of the Palestinian Arab minority in Israel. Within the past ten years throughout the country, Palestinian human, civil and legal rights organisations have developed that are beginning to document the needs and develop channels for resistance using the legal and civil mechanisms of Israeli society with some measure of success. The Negev Bedouin, who have shown the tenacity typical of the Palestinian people to withstand efforts to remove them from their land, even in the face of great adversity, have also begun to organise their resistance to displacement through the development of their own (albeit unrecognised by the government) regional councils.

The government response to this resistance, particularly under the leadership of Ariel Sharon, has been to intensify the use of coercive measures in order to achieve its goals. The very existence of the Palestinian Arab people has been anathema to the Zionist movement since its inception, and will remain so until the Palestinian people cease to exist, or submit to a diminished, highly controlled existence that somehow ceases to violate Zionist sensibilities. Since neither of these scenarios seems likely, we anticipate an ongoing and increasingly conflict-ridden deadlock between the Israeli government and the Negev's Palestinian Bedouin for as long as the government is unable to relinquish the Zionist dream of Judaising and de-Arabising the land, and resists joining the community of modern democratic nation-states by representing the interests of all its citizens equally.

Notes

1 Based on the 1931 Census of Palestine, 89.3 per cent (42,868 persons) of the Bedouin of the Negev were recorded as living from agriculture, and 10.7 per cent (5,113 persons) were recorded as occupied solely in raising livestock. See Falah (1985).

2 Weitz's original, handwritten diaries are held in the Central Zionist Archives in Jerusalem, and differ from the five volumes he edited and published in 1965, providing another example of how the private face of the Zionist movement, differed from its public face. For a discussion of the differences, see Morris (1999).

3 Developments towns are "frontier" towns that were established by the government to increase the Jewish population in border regions or regions with large Palestinian populations (e.g., western Galilee, northern Negev). They were typically populated with Middle Eastern and North African Jewish immigrants, and tend to have a low socio-economic status. As such, they receive generous development budgets and other economic benefits from the government. Given the Zionist basis for their "development" status, it goes without saying that none of the new Bedouin towns established by the government in the same region were accorded the same status or privileges.

4 The Decree for Local Councils includes two key provisions. First, it is the council's task to concern itself with offering municipal services according to the needs of the residents. According to the Local Council Law, one of the tasks of a local authority is to establish and maintain services, enterprises and institutions, which to its knowledge offer benefits to the public. Similarly, according to Article 3 of the Local Council Law, those who have the right to be elected are those who at the determining day, and for six months previously, have maintained their place of residence in this area.

5 With the exception of a small Bedouin population in the Galilee that makes up a small minority of the Galilee's Palestinian population, and is dealt with through

the same channels as the other Palestinian Arabs in the region.

6   According to the 2001 State Comptroller's Report, of the NIS148 million reserved for buying land from the Bedouin in 1999, NIS131 million was returned to Jerusalem, and NIS9 million was used for administrative purposes.

7   The full text of the letter is as follows:

Mr Ariel Sharon
Prime Minister
Jerusalem
4 May 2003

Dear Mr Ariel Sharon,

Subject: The 5-Year Plan for the Negev Arab Bedouins until 2007 in the Negev

The Forum *Together for Equality and Growth* is made up of non-governmental organisations and representative organisations, of Jews and Arabs, who are all working for the development of the rights of the unrecognised villages' inhabitants, and for the growth of the Negev for Jews and Arabs together.

We commend the development budget allocation for the seven planned towns and we commend the recognition and development of any villages which do not rely on a process of concentrating the rest of the inhabitants of the unrecognised villages into these newly recognised areas. We are deeply disappointed that the suggested plan on which the Cabinet will vote does not provide the vital recognition and services for the villages' inhabitants. Rather this plan proposes land confiscation, population removal and transfer, and the concentration of the Bedouin into confined areas.

Critical Deficiencies of the Plan

1. The Plan was prepared without the participation of the residents of the villages and the proposed evacuation runs contrary to their needs and wellbeing, which are centred on the lands they live on.

2. The new powers of the Green Patrol to operate against villagers within their own living areas and land is a dangerous invasion of their rights to their property.

3. The increase in the budget of the Interior Ministry will be implemented by force, which will mean an increase in house destructions instead of the planning and building investment solutions that would satisfy the needs and the way of life of the residents.

4. The establishment of a Police Unit and Special Forces who would implement the Plan amounts to a criminalisation of villagers because they live on their land.

5. The plan proposes claims funded by the government in courts activated by the government, against the rights of residents to live on their land.

6. The plan proposes the establishment of new individual farms, land reservations, and other settlements on land that is currently unrecognised villages. The government is giving the clear message that these new farms will be Jewish and will replace the existing villages and their inhabitants.

7. We protest against the provision of a budget allocation for the Israeli Land Authority to compensate the villagers who are uprooted and moved off their lands. This provision of a budget is no compensation at all for population transfer. We add once again that 25 per cent of those who live in the Negev are Arab Bedouins and that they live on 2 per cent of the Negev's land.

8. Finally, we must protest the establishment of any local municipality for the villages which is recognised without the participation and agreement of the residents. This concern follows the letter addressed by the Regional Council of the Unrecognised Villages (the Regional Council) to the Interior Minister, Mr Eli Yeshay on 29 October 2002.

We present the following proposals for the Cabinet, to ensure the government of Israel provides equally and acts for the common good of all residents of the Negev.

Proposals for the Cabinet Decision:

1. As a first step, to establish a local municipality on the model which the Regional Council proposed in *Development of Municipal Authority for the Arab Bedouin Unrecognised Villages in the Negev* which was submitted to the Interior Ministry and the planning institutions and was a response to the plan of Mr David Cohen (the Director of the Ministry of Interior regional office).

2. Providing all services without any relation to the Land Settlement, by establishing 20 Services Centers for the 45 different villages on their land. These Services Centers should be established immediately, as a first stage by Exceptional Permit which is within the authority of the Interior Ministry. The established municipal authority will represent the residents and will be responsible for providing services.

3. To freeze the House Demolition measures by recognition of all building and until both sides come to agreement and the village's zoning maps are authorised.

4. To implement immediately the Ministerial Committee for Bedouin Affairs decision from 28 February 2000 which froze the Tama 24/4 Plan that had suggested planning towns such as Mareit. We also propose the closing of the Bedouin Authority for Development, in part because it is the only authority of its kind in Israel.

5. To cancel the areas of the following villages: Al-Mazra'a, Qatamat, Al-Mitaher, Al-Bat, Khelah, Sawea and others from the announcement of the military area. This is according to maps that were prepared by the Regional Council and presented to the Defence Ministry.

6. To change amendment 6 in the population registration (address registration) law and to register residents' addresses according to their historical villages. This is how residents were registered at birth until 1974, and is discussed in the

Regional Council plan *Development of Municipal Authority for the Arab Bedouin Unrecognised Villages in the Negev.*

7. To implement the agreement of January 2001 between the Regional Council and the Ministerial Committee for Arab Affairs, which was signed by the head of committee, the former minister Mr Matan Vilnay.

We convey our thanks in advance for your cooperation,

Sincerely,

Oxfam GB, Al-Ahali, Bimkoum, Jewish Arab Centre for Economic Development, New Israel Fund, Arab Centre for Alternative Planning, Association for Civil Rights in Israel, Arab Association for Human Rights, People and Land, The Follow Up Committee for Arabs in Israel, The Follow Up Committee For Education, Mosawa, Shatil, 'Adalah, Ta'ayush, Coalition for Co-existence in the Negev, Rabbis for Human Rights, Physicians for Human Rights, Sikkuy, The Regional Council for the Unrecognised Villages-Negev

References

Abu-Saad, I. (1991). "Toward an Understanding of Minority Education in Israel: The Case of the Bedouin Arabs of the Negev", *Comparative Education* 27: 235-42.

—— (1995). "Bedouin Arab Education in the Context of Radical Social Change: What is the Future?" *Compare* 25: 149-59.

—— (2000). "Land Issues and Bedouin Urbanisation", *Karkah* 50: 159-69 [Hebrew].

—— (2003). "Israeli 'Development' and Education Policies and their Impact on the Negev Palestinian Bedouin", *Holy Land Studies: Interdisciplinary Journal*, 2 (1): 5-32.

'Adalah (2003). *Education Rights – Palestinian Citizens of Israel* (Shafa'amr: 'Adalah – the Legal Center for Arab Minority Rights in Israel).

Alafenish, S. (1987). "Processes of Change and Continuity in Kinship Systems and Family Ideology in Bedouin Society", *Sociologia Ruralis* 27: 323-40.

Al-Hawashleh. (1974). Civil Appeal 218/74, Salim Al-Hawashleh *vs.* State of Israel, P.D. 38 (3): 141.

Association for Civil Rights in Israel (ACRI) (2002). The Negev Bedouin in Israel – Update (Tel Aviv: ACRI), March.

Benvenisti, M. (1997). "The Hebrew Map", *Teoriya Ve-Bekoret* [*Theory and Criticism*] 11: 7-29 [Hebrew].

Berman, R. (2001). "Bedouin Probe Seen as 'Farce'", *Jewish Week*, 17 August.

Cook, J. (2002). "Israel's Vietnam", *Al-Ahram Weekly* online, Issue No. 598, 8-14 August, at: http://www.ahram.org.eg/weekly/2002/598/index.htm

Cook, J. (May 2003). "Bedouin in the Negev Face New 'Transfer'", *Middle East Research and Information Project* (MERIP) at: www.merip.org

Falah, G. (1985). "The Spatial of Bedouin Sendentarization in Israel", *GeoJournal* 11 (4): 361-8.

Falah, G. (1989). "Israel State Policy Towards Bedouin Sedentarization in the Negev", *Journal of Palestine Studies* 18 (2): 71-90.

Flapan, S. (1987). *The Birth of Israel: Myths and Realities* (New York: Pantheon).

Gradus, Y. and Stern, A. (1985). "From Preconceived to Responsive Planning: Cases of Settlement Design in Arid Environments", in Yehuda Gradus (ed.), *Desert Development: Man and Technology in Sparselands* (Dordrecht, Netherlands: Reidel Publishing Co.): 41-59.

Hadawi, S. (1991). *Bitter Harvest: A Modern History of Palestine* (New York: Olive Branch Press).

Hazleton, L. (1980). "Forgotten Israelis", *New York Review*, 29 May.

Hever, H. (2002). "The Map of Sand: From Hebrew Literature to Israeli Literature", *Teoriya Ve-Bekoret [Theory and Criticism]* 20: 165-190 [Hebrew].

Human Rights Watch (2001). *Second Class: Discrimination Against Palestinian Arab Children in Israel's Schools* (New York: Human Rights Watch).

Jiryis, S. (1976). *The Arabs in Israel* (New York: Monthly Review Press).

Khalidi, W. (1992). *All That Remains: The Palestinian Villages Occupied and Depopulated by Israel in 1948* (Washington, DC: Institute for Palestine Studies).

Kimmerling, B. (1982). "Settlers Without Frontier", *Jerusalem Quarterly* 24: 114-28.

Law-Yone, H. (2003). "From Sedentarization to Urbanization: State Policy Towards Bedouin Society in Israel", in Champagne, D. and Ismael Abu-Saad (eds.), *The Future of Indigenous Peoples: Strategies for Survival and Development* (Los Angeles: American Indian Studies Center, UCLA).

Lithwick, H. (2000). *An Urban Development Strategy for the Negev's Bedouin Community* (Beer Sheba: The Centre for Bedouin Studies and Development, Ben-Gurion University of the Negev).

Lustick, I. (1980). *Arabs in the Jewish State: Israel's Control of a National Minority* (Austin: University of Texas).

Maddrell, P. (1990). *The Beduin of the Negev* (London: Minority Rights Group Report No. 81).

Mana Commission (1997). *Mana Committee Report on Bedouin in Israel* (Jerusalem: Israeli Knesset).

Marx, E. (1967). *The Bedouin of the Negev* (Manchester: Manchester University Press).

—— (1990). "Advocacy in a Bedouin Resettlement Project in the Negev, Israel", in: Salem-Murdock, M., Horowitz, M. and Sella, M. (eds.) *Anthropology and Development in North Africa and the Middle East* (Boulder, Colorado: Westview Press).

—— (2000). "Land and Work: Negev Bedouin Struggle with Israel Bureaucracies", *Nomadic Peoples* 4(2):106-20.

Masalha, N. (1992). *Expulsion of the Palestinians: The Concept of "Transfer" in Zionist Thought, 1882–1948* (Washington DC: Institute for Palestine Studies).

—— (1997). *A Land Without a People: Israel, Transfer and the Palestinians* (London: Faber and Faber).

Morris, B. (1999). *Righteous Victims: A History of the Zionist–Arab Conflict, 1881–1999* (New York: Knopf).

Ornan, U. (2002). "There is another solution", *Haaretz*, 21 April [Hebrew].

Piterberg, G. (1995). "The Nation and its Raconteurs: Orientalism and National Historiography", *Teoriya Ve-Bekoret* [*Theory and Criticism*] 6: 81-104 [Hebrew].

Prior, M. (1999). *Zionism and the State of Israel: A Moral Inquiry* (London: Routledge).

Quigley, J. (1990). *Palestine and Israel: A Challenge to Justice* (Durham, NC: Duke University Press.)

Raz-Krakotzkin, A. (1999). "Orientalism, Jewish Thought and Israeli Society: Some Comments", *Jamaa* 3 (1): 34-60 [Hebrew]).

Said, E. (1979). *The Question of Palestine* (New York: Times Books).

Shamir, R. (1996). "Suspended in Space: Bedouin under the Law of Israel", *Law & Society Review* 30 (2): 231-57.

State Comptroller Report on Security (1959). (Jerusalem: Israel).

State Comptroller Report (2001). (Jerusalem: Israel).

State Comptroller Report No. 52b (2002). (Jerusalem: Israel).

Statistical Abstract of Israel (2002). (Jerusalem: Central Bureau of Statistics).

Statistical Yearbook of the Negev Bedouin (1999). The Centre for Bedouin Studies and Development and The Negev Centre for Regional Development (Beer Sheba: Ben-Gurion University of the Negev).

UN Committee on Economic, Social and Cultural Rights Report (2003). The Unrecognized Villages in the Negev Update: 2003, UN Committee on Economic, Social and Cultural Rights 30th Session – Israel.

Yiftachel, O. (1999a). "'Ethnocracy': The Politics of Judaizing Israel/Palestine", *Constellation: An International Journal of Critical and Democratic Theory*, 6: 364-90.

—— (1999b). "Judaize and Divide: Shaping Spaces in the Israeli 'Ethnocracy' ", *News From Within*, Vol. XV (11).

—— (2003). "Bedouin-Arabs and the Israeli Settler State: Land Policies and Indigenous Resistance", in Champagne, D. and Ismael Abu-Saad (eds.), *The Future of Indigenous Peoples: Strategies for Survival and Development* (Los Angeles: American Indian Studies Centre, UCLA).

Zangwill, I. (1920). *The Voice of Jerusalem* (London: William Heinemann).

PART TWO
Palestinian Oral History and Memory

5
"A Muted Sort of Grief":[1] Tales of Refuge in Nazareth (1948–2005)

Isabelle Humphries

Oral History and Reconstructing the Past

This chapter does not focus on the details of the high politics – the negotiations and Israeli government policy – that created the contemporary limboland in which Palestinian internal refugees live. Instead, gathering threads of stories from Palestinians who have found refuge in Nazareth, this chapter seeks to portray the human, personal experience of exile and internal displacement. Few written sources document everyday life for three generations of displaced villagers in this town, a place that in 1948 found itself a Palestinian island in a Zionist-Jewish defined state. Official historical documents provide dates of village occupation, population statistics and voting patterns, but such figures do not begin to paint the whole picture of half a century in Nazareth.

Despite the suspicion of positivist historians and traditionalists,[2] the work of oral historians in reconstructing the past becomes increasingly respected.[3] Recording individual stories and anecdotes brings to the forefront the lives of those sidelined by traditional history, a history produced by and for a Westernised elite, based on battles and treaties and the biographies of prominent families and military and political leaders. The identity and history of the internally displaced in the Galilee have been maintained through 'the telling of stories, and the passing of knowledge from one generation to the next. While refugees outside had potential access to university and cultural forums that encourage the recording of their history, those who research Palestinian history inside the Jewish state must always struggle against suppression by Zionist cultural and educational institutes. The increasing number of the community involved in documenting stories, through memorial books, films and public festivals, shows the level of importance of this work to the internally displaced. This chapter presents snippets of those stories, describing a life of being present yet "absent" at the same time.

Coffee with Abu Nizar, Casa Nova Street, Nazareth, 6 September 2003

I am sitting with Abu Nizar amongst the clusters of boxes of handicrafts and souvenirs at the back of his shop on the Casa Nova, the street going up to the Basilica, revered by Catholics as the site of the Annunciation to the Virgin Mary. Perched on a little stool next to friends who have brought me here, I explain that I am interested in knowing about the lives of the villagers of Saffuriyya.

The old man looked round slowly and smiled, taking in everything around him. "But if it is politics you want, why did you come here? I am not sure how I can help you. It is my brother you should be speaking to." Abu Nizar is the older brother of Abu 'Arab, the chair of the Saffuriyya Heritage Association. Abu Nizar is himself a poet, celebrated and published at home and abroad, translated into Hebrew and English. Formal education cut off with the 1948 occupation of Saffuriyya, he continued studying on the floor of his shop, reading classical Arabic texts, the works of Shakespeare and translations of Chekhov amongst the olivewood camels. Performing to Palestinian, Israeli and foreign audiences, today Abu Nizar (Taha Muhammad 'Ali) is known both at home and abroad.

One of his poems tells of the death of Sabha, a villager's cow that died by swallowing a rope.

> For a while,
> the village was choked
> in a muted sort of grief,
> like Abu Hashem's hoarse voice,
> and green as Sabha's eyes.
> Don't you see, Abu Muhammad,
> our village was pleasant.
> It's true there were hard times,
> but the bitterness was good,
> like chicory,
> or better!

You see what I mean …
wasn't it pleasant?
– Pleasant?!
Ha! …
Pleasant, he says, … pleasant.
Let me tell you,
by the book of Almighty Allah,
I swear to you,
I was prepared,
in fact I would have preferred,
and with all my heart I would have agreed,
to swallow a rope longer than Sabha's,
if only
we could have stayed in our village.

from "Sabha's Rope" (15 March 1988)[4]

Nazareth, 29 October 2000

They took my land, they took my home. Now they have taken my brother. What else have I got left to be frightened of losing?

Going against the Nazareth grain, Jamila is a boxer in her spare time. Every now and again I see her and Umm Ibrahim, her mother, at a demonstration, usually at the front holding the banner. Nothing left to lose.

I had been living in Nazareth for just two weeks when Jamila's brother was killed. It was the only time I have tasted fear. My landlord's family, living upstairs from my apartment, went into hysterics as the mosque announced, at around 7 p.m. one Sunday night, that the city's eastern neighbourhood in which we lived was under attack from a mob of Jewish residents of Natzeret 'Illit (Upper Nazareth). The daughter, in her twenties, flew into a panic, screaming, "The Russians are coming, they've got guns" in reference to the new immigrants to the surrounding settlement, which for years now has been encircling and choking Nazareth. Earlier in the week her uncle had been shot full of police bullets, so nothing now seemed beyond the realms of possibility. I went with the family to relatives on the eastern side of the city, leaving the elderly father pacing up and down and muttering loudly that he was going nowhere.

In the event, the 200-strong mob was held back at the borderline between Arab and Jewish city by police protecting the Jewish crowd. Two of the Palestinians gathered to defend the city were killed. The attack reinforced the vulnerability of the 1948 Palestinians, and the sense of threat permanently hanging in the air.

And so, on that Sunday 8 October 2000, Umm Ibrahim became the mother of a martyr. Jamila's 42-year-old brother 'Umar was unmarried, and lived at home with his mother and sister. "I thought he was just out at the shop or something," his mother said, "I didn't know what was going on outside. Only then a friend called from abroad and told me to turn on the television." Her son had joined the crowds of men going to the crossroads. He ended up the victim of a sniper's bullet. A small white memorial marks the spot against the wall where he died.

The two women live in a small house up the hill from the centre of town, an empty room where 'Umar should be. But this was not the hill 'Umar's mother played on as a child; Umm Ibrahim is a refugee from Tiberias.

Tiberias, 1948

The fall of Tiberias came early in the Zionist occupation of the Galilee.[5] A 1944 census states that of a population of 11,310 around 5,310 were Arabs, yet none remained after 1948. The Arab population had been concentrated in the Old City area as new Jewish immigrants had settled around the outlying parts of the town.[6] During the Mandate period, relations between Arab and Jew were generally good, but following the Partition Plan, tensions emerged as Zionist propaganda campaigns began to encourage cooperation with Jewish forces.[7]

By February 1948, sniping and violence had become an everyday occurrence and Jews living in the Arab Old City moved out. At the beginning of April, aware of the fate of other Arab villages around, the Palestinian non-Jews of Tiberias found themselves under siege. All contact with the outside world was cut off, except during the British supervised truce. The Arabs of Tiberias had neither enough fighters, nor armaments to withstand the onslaught.[8] By 17 April Tiberias was in the hands of the pre-state army, the Haganah.[9]

Umm Ibrahim was newly married with a tiny baby when she and her family were piled onto a bus to Nazareth.[10] She was just one of over 500 refugees from Tiberias who ended up in exile in Nazareth and the surrounding areas.[11] The British gave safe passage to the Arabs of the city out to a life in exile. "We didn't know what was happening and so we didn't bring anything with us. We got to Nazareth and saw all the other refugees and my mother did not even have a blanket to cover the children in. She pleaded and begged the British soldiers to let her go back home just to fetch some possessions." When the British officials refused, Umm Ibrahim says, her mother stole onto a bus returning for more refugees, and was able to get back home to Tiberias to get a few blankets. "She hid between the back seats to reach our home … And then she got the last bus out of the city to Nazareth".

What's in a Name?

"Naming, as you know, is a powerful thing, a privilege given to those who have power."[12] In the period of military rule, as the stories of internally displaced people in Nazareth show, fear of the authorities and further displacement largely prevented public expression of Palestinian identity. Israeli policy isolated the Arabs "inside" from those beyond the borders, convincing the world that "Israeli Arabs" were an Israeli domestic issue. Even amongst those who express solidarity with the Palestinian cause abroad (Arabs included), there is widespread acceptance of the term "Israeli Arab", and a failure to grasp the dilemmas faced by Palestinians within the Jewish state. "Aren't they the ones who stayed behind because they agreed to collaborate?" one person asked, when I said I was working in a Nazareth human rights organisation.

Attempts to isolate the Palestinians inside the Green Line from the rest of the Palestinian community continue, but not without resistance. Research on collective self-identification among Palestinians revealed that over 75 per cent of high school and university students used the term "Palestinian" as part of the label with which they identified.[13]

Palestinians inside Israel are, of course, not facing the same militarily imposed curfew and dangers experienced by their compatriots in the West Bank and Gaza. Yet the exclusion that 1948 Palestinians experience daily is a result of the same Zionist ideology which dictates the situation in the 1967 Occupied Territories: the concept of a state for one ethnic group at the expense of another. The surreal oxymoron *present absentees*, reveals the denial of Palestinian rights inherent in the definition of an exclusively Jewish state, and demonstrates why there will be no just solution without recognition of the rights of those inside the Green Line. As the stories from Nazareth show, the dispossession of Palestinians living in the Galilee today is an inseparable part of the wider story.

Halissa Neighbourhood, Haifa, 1948

My mother became hysterical, "Don't you know we are never going back? Not your book, not us, nothing," she screamed.[14]

Thus a ten-year-old Umm Muhammad discovered from her mother that she was not going back. Not going back to the house that was still standing in Haifa less than an hour's drive from the small village she found herself in.

When Umm Muhammad was in the third grade, the nightly shooting and fighting in the Halissa neighbourhood of Haifa became too much. The family fled at night barefoot without their possessions. "We all thought someone else was carrying my sister," says Umm Muhammad, the oldest of five children. The baby almost got left behind where she had been hidden away from the windows and the danger of stray bullets.

On 21 April 1948, British forces withdrew from Haifa,[15] leaving in full progress a Haganah dawn assault against the Palestinian population, including heavy mortar shelling of residential areas. The Palestinian resistance had no power to stand up to such an attack, and by the end of April the majority of the Arab population had left. It was a crucial turning point in the Zionist campaign.[16]

When they reached the port the family was thrown onto a ship. "I can't remember the details of the boat, or who was urging us to get on. All I can see as I close my eyes today, is the other people crying and wailing 'We lost you, Haifa'."

Nazareth, 1948

An air of uncertainty and anxiety, not to say dread, hung over Nazareth with the approach of 15 May 1948, the deadline set for the end of the British Mandate ...[17]

Nazareth is situated in the heart of lower Galilee, seated amid seven hills that rise above the plain of Marj Ibn 'Amer, the start of a more northern hilly region reaching to Lebanon and Syria in the north. Despite Nazareth's relatively small size, it was accorded worldwide renown as the home of the Christian Messiah and thus housed large educational and medical establishments funded by the international Church. The British administration made their district headquarters here.

The importance of Nazareth in the popular Western Christian imagination did not escape the attention of various Zionist pre-state institutions planning the occupation of Palestine. Prior to the Second World War, many had concluded that it would be necessary to transfer or "cleanse" any potential Jewish state of Arabs, but attention also had to be paid to achieving minimal damage to the international face of the new Jewish state.[18]

"There is no way but to transfer the Arabs from here to the neigh-bouring countries, to transfer all of them, save perhaps for [the Arabs of] Bethlehem, Nazareth and old Jerusalem," wrote Yosef Weitz, director of the Jewish National Fund Lands Department and a key player in the planning and development of Jewish settlement before and after state establishment.[19] This diary entry, eight years before the main expulsion began, shows that it was no accident that the population of Nazareth was spared expulsion.

As 1948 progressed the hostilities in the Galilee increased. Financial concerns led to the flight of around 75,000 of the urban upper and middle classes from Jaffa, Haifa and Jerusalem by the end of March (representing a higher proportion of Christians than the whole popula-tion). Whilst many of those with assets in Lebanon or further afield left Palestine, others joined relatives in urban centres such as Nazareth or Nablus in the east which were deemed safer.[20] Refugees from attacked Galilee villages had begun to flee to Nazareth, counting on the impor-tance of the town to provide relative safety.

> By mid-May, thousands of refugees had poured into Nazareth. Some had been taken in by friends and relatives or were able to rent spare rooms, but many were housed in makeshift fashion in the halls of the local religious establishments or in vacated public buildings. No preparations had been made for the desperate need for relief and assistance.[21]

Later, the majority of wealthier, urban refugees who had family and homes outside the Jewish state left to join them. The internal refugees today are predominantly from the Muslim rural working classes, who did not have any viable financial options or life outside the new Jewish state.

The capture of Nazareth was swift and took place with little resistance. Ben-Gurion gave specific orders that there should be no looting or destruction of houses as the world would be watching. Morris says that there was talk of an order to destroy Nazareth from senior military, but this was overturned. [22] Relatively few Nazarenes fled; instead the town was swelled by up to 20,000 refugees during the first few days of occupation. After a few days some refugees from nearby towns such as Kafr Kanna and Shafa'amr were allowed to return home. [23] But Israeli estimates suggest that in April 1949, months after the occupation, over 5,000 refugees were still in Nazareth, and 7,334 were residing in the surrounding villages. [24]

Waleed Khleif was a small boy at the time of the occupation of Nazareth. He still lives today in the same house, close to the Mary's Well area. During the first days of the occupation he would sneak out of the house to run errands for his father, who thought a boy would be safer and less conspicuous out in the open. "I remember seeing people on the streets, in buildings, sitting on the floor. We knew something terrible had happened to them, but as Nazareth people we were not free ourselves to find out what was going on." [25]

Khleif recalls that all his neighbourhood (Nazarenes, not refugees) were forced to stand in the sun in an open yard while soldiers teased and refused to let them go to the toilet or fetch water. This was the "safe haven" of Nazareth that refugees had fled to.

Sulam Village, South of Nazareth, 1948

After a brief stay in Acre where their ship landed, Umm Muhammad's family went to Nazareth, and from there to the village of Sulam, south of the city in the plain of Marj Ibn 'Amer. The village of her father's birth, this would be her home until she married and settled in Nazareth to bring up her children.

My father had worked in the post office in Haifa. One day an army jeep came to Sulam, and the soldiers asked, "Where is Khalil Zo'abi?" My father was very afraid, but it turned out that a Jewish friend he had worked with at the post office knew he was hiding in the village. The Jewish man had arranged for my father to be able to make one last trip back to our home in Haifa. "If there is something in your house, come on!"

So Umm Muhammad's father went back to the house from which they had stumbled in the dark. He gathered clothes and some possessions.

And for me he brought my book, *The Little Red Hen*. I was so astonished that I had this book back in my hands. It was a library book, from the school which I loved so much.

Despite being separated from family members and friends, and dispossessed of their land and homes, most refugees who now live in Nazareth have at least had the small comfort of growing up among other refugees. Not so Umm Muhammad; growing up among the villagers of Sulam isolated her, despite her father's origins in the village.[26] She was a refugee town girl from Haifa, among her village kin who saw her as different.

In a village it was amazing to see such things, an English storybook. Everyone wanted to see it. One day another child grabbed it too roughly and tore a page. I was distraught because I knew I had to give it back. I went running and crying to my mother, "but I have to give it back to the school!"

My mother became hysterical, "Don't you know we are never going back? Not your book, not us, nothing," she screamed. "What did you think? We have nothing left." For the first time someone had told it to me straight. My mother told it to me in such a brutal way: "You've finished with Haifa and the school forever."[27]

Near the Ancient Well, Lands of Saffuriyya, 4 October 2002

"I was born under that tree over there. That's where the house would have been." Umm Ahmad pointed across the open field her husband was tilling. The tree is the marker because the building no longer stands. The land of Saffuriyya is still farmed, and in the case of this piece of land, by Saffuriyyans themselves. But the elderly couple cannot take the fruit of the land for their labour. Both are from the village, but Abu Ahmad is paid as a wage labourer by Tzippori's Jewish farmers. Every night he and his wife must return to a house in Nazareth.

For decades the couple have come to work on the land, sheltering from the hot midday sun under a small nylon awning. When I met them, the Israeli antiquities authority had a few days previously torn down their shelter, as it was judged to be "too close" to the ancient well of Saffuriyya. Despite the well's isolation and dilapidated state, apparently it was a matter of great import to the historical narrative and national defence of the state of Israel, such that it should be sealed off from former residents.[28]

Saffuriyya, 1948

The Galilean village of Saffuriyya was the largest village in the region. Famous in Roman times as Sepphoris, with the remains of a coliseum still visible, Saffuriyya's hilltop is today covered with a pine forest planted by the Jewish National Fund to commemorate Guatemalan Independence Day and, like in so many other destroyed villages, to mask the signs of any Palestinian past.[29] Daher al-'Umar's fortress still stands, but it is no longer surrounded by a Palestinian village. An Israeli *moshav* (farming settlement) named Tzippori now sits on the lands of Saffuriyya; its travel brochures welcome tourists to see its ancient Roman ruins, but fail to acknowledge the ethnic cleansing of an entire Palestinian village half a century ago.

Israeli forces occupied Saffuriyya, a town with 4,500 Palestinian residents and 55,000 *dunums* of land, on 15 July 1948. A few hundred residents remained after the bombing and occupation and initially were granted Israeli identity cards recognising Saffuriyya as their place of residence. Seven months after the original attack and occupation, the army came back to the village and demanded, "If you don't leave we will kill you."[30] The Saffuriyya Heritage Association has registered the names of the heads of 86 families who were given identity cards. The association estimates that about 1,500 people were living in the village at this stage; many had been sheltering in other villages and thus were given identity cards with these villages marked as their place of residence. They had only returned to their original homes later, believing they could now remain.

Many still hold the identity cards proving that fifty years ago the Israeli government recognised their place of residence as Saffuriyya. 'Ali al-Azhari today lives in Jaffa. It was only in recent years that he lost his identity card, the only document that recorded his birth in Saffuriyya. He wrote about his experience in Hebrew in an Israeli newspaper *Ma'ariv*, a challenge to the Zionist myths of state foundation.

My father, Shaykh Muhammad 'Abdel Majid al-Azhari, a graduate of the University of Al-Azhar in Cairo and a well-known religious authority, was recognised as such, and a sign saying "a holy place" in three languages was placed on our house. Six months later, on 7 January 1949, when the fighting was over, came the expulsion order. It was quite unequivocal – anyone found in the village 48 hours later would be shot.[31]

Despite these threats many held their ground. The Israeli military came to the village and forcibly loaded people onto trucks. Refugees were dumped in Nazareth and other villages around about. The village of Saffuriyya and its land was declared a military zone; *"mantiqa 'askariyya"*. Only those with a permit could enter. Some tried to go through the Israeli courts, but in vain:

> The answer was not long in coming … It was three or four that morning, when the village of al-Reineh, where we were living at the time, woke to the sounds of mighty explosions from the direction of Saffuriyeh [sic], some five kms away … Columns of smoke and dust rose to the heavens above Saffuriyeh [sic]. In the evening came the news; there would never be a return.[32]

Lands of Saffuriyya, 1 February 2002

A bright February day in the Galilee, and Saffuriyyans were out busy tilling the land. But only a few of them, and cultivating only a fraction of the original 27,000 *dunums* of cultivable land owned by villagers.

Over the years the government enacted legislation to try to persuade "internal refugees" to accept offers of compensation. Few applied because the offer of compensation was not equal to the value of the land lost and the loss of earnings incurred in the previous twenty-five years. Secondly, signing for compensation meant a signing away of any claim to the land in the future. This was an offer few were prepared to accept.[33] A similar strategy is still employed today following confiscation of land, e.g. in the West Bank for farmers dispossessed of land by the new wall. Accepting compensation means signing away claims to the land in the future.[34]

Those Saffuriyyans who accepted small plots of land within the old village boundaries know what is theirs by rights. One farmer stopped to speak with us, and discovered I was English. "I have the document at home that proves all the land I owned. It has the stamp of your King

George on it," he said surveying the tiny patch. The Israelis selectively use the laws of previous colonial overlords to maximum benefit, such as the 1943 British public land ordinance.[35] But Israeli land laws conveniently failed to incorporate Ottoman and Mandate laws that would recognise Palestinian ownership.

Nazareth, 2000

> Nazareth ... a place that is neither a village nor a city. It does not have the intimacy of a village, or the scope of a city. A place, just a place, which has lost its connection to the fields, the groves, and the smell of the earth, and which has also lost its connection to the clubs, the cinema, and the city square ...[36]

Nazareth. In a strange way it seems that years of neglect and lack of investment have done more to kill the spirit of the capital of the Galilee, than years of bloodshed and soldiers have achieved in Nablus and Ramallah. It is an odd type of depression that seizes hold of you. Visiting Bethlehem under curfew, Nablus under siege by settlements, or Qalqilya surrounded by the Wall you feel that people at least know what they are fighting for, a vision for the future however far away that may be. Sometimes it feels like Nazareth has forgotten how to dream.

The Cinema in the Old Souq, Nazareth, 8 September 2003

We are drinking tea one evening in a small cinema café created in a deserted grainhouse in the old Nazareth souq. The last mainstream cinema in Nazareth disappeared several years ago, and until recently Nazareth folk who wished to see a film on the big screen had to traipse up the hill to the multiplex in Natzeret 'Illit. Earlier this year a group of young professionals, among them Ziad from Saffuriyya, decided to try and at least realise some of a dream, using an old building belonging to a relative. This group of Nazarenes, in their late twenties, are some of the few who have returned after studying outside. It takes some commitment for those who have the opportunity to be outside to return. The project now has a café, shows films at the weekend, and hosts cultural political events in the form of art shows, music and discussion.

Sitting at the small café table, Abu 'Arab isn't quite sure where to start. As head of Saffuriyya Heritage Association, he has countless stories about dispossession, decades of struggle, and recent commemorative events and campaigning within the community.

In the early days, the people of Saffuriyya who remained as internal refugees were dotted all over Nazareth and the area. "We were not thinking or knowing what would happen."[37] The 1948 Palestinians went from a majority in a British-ruled colony to a minority in a Jewish settled state in a matter of weeks and months. Thousands lost their homes. The effect of this trauma cannot be underestimated.

Those who were left behind were largely *fellahin* (peasants) with little political awareness and few links to political organisations. Most Palestinian leaders and the educated elites had become external refugees under the *Nakba*, and people were fearful of forming new groups. In this climate of fear people did not talk openly about politics; "anyone who was just listening to the speeches of [Gamal] 'Abdul Nasser [of Egypt] on the radio was informed on. The Israelis would send for you …"[38]

Abu Arab recalls that in the early years, two Jewish settlers in the area were killed, and eight Palestinian refugees from Saffuriyya were arrested. "The High Court case about Saffuriyya came up at the same time, but the people of Saffuriyya were too busy worrying about how to get their sons out of jail. This detracted from the interest in the land court case. I can't believe this was a coincidence." Fear of collaborators and informers successfully stifled most early political activity. "The atmosphere was, Don't talk about Saffuriyya, forget about Saffuriyya, forget your demands." Everyone was under suspicion.

Fear: Michel Khleifi's *Ma'loul Celebrates Its Destruction*

Dispossession itself was a dangerous topic. Umm Muhammad's parents never spoke of what had befallen them in Haifa. One day, the children from her school had to sit with the Jewish children of the kibbutz and the teacher asked, "Who can sing a nice song?" "I put up my hand and started to sing a nationalist song in Arabic. The smile immediately dropped from the Arab teacher's face and she silenced me in anger. I was ten years old and I just thought it was a pretty song. I didn't know it was dangerous talk."[39]

The terror of speaking out became ingrained in a whole generation. I met Umm Muhammad at the invitation of her daughter Heba, after she told me of her mother who had not spoken in Heba's entire childhood about what she had been through. "I didn't have any idea what she had suffered. One day she broke down and told us. I couldn't believe she had hidden it, not even spoken to her own children about what she went through."[40]

"Why didn't we speak?" asks Umm Muhammad. "We couldn't talk about this thing, they didn't even let us say the word *Filastin* [Palestine]. I couldn't … later as a teacher myself I couldn't. Even in my family we didn't talk about it. Everywhere it was forbidden to talk about it. Too many people were arrested when they spoke about it."

Umm Muhammad was a teacher in an Arab school which, like all others, was governed by the Israeli curriculum. She describes how, as a teacher, on the day that the Israelis celebrate Independence Day, she and her colleagues would have to raise the Israeli flag. "If the flag fell we would be interrogated as to why. We were slaves without thinking."

Michel Khleifi's film, *Ma'loul Celebrates Its Destruction* documents the tangible fear that still remained amongst the villagers in the 1980s. A wave of fear and agitation suddenly crosses the face of the old man he is accompanying to the site of the destroyed village.

> Villager: "This interview is probably illegal. I am convinced it is. What could you do for me if they were to arrest me?"
> Interviewer: "They won't."
> "They will! And they will squash my tongue as well!"
> "What are you scared of?"
> "Nothing! But to be thrown into prison at sixty-five and be humiliated is out of the question! What would I get out of it? I tell myself, Hold your tongue as you would your horse … I am telling you, I'll never sell! The land belongs to Ma'loul."

Saffuriyya – The National Park – 4 October 2002

Today Ziad from the cinema is taking a couple of BBC documentary makers to Saffuriyya to "see how it all started". Before we reach Saffuriyya itself, we stand on the sunny road looking out over the Galilee hills towards Lebanon as Ziad starts explaining something of the history. "Excuse me," the documentary maker, on her first trip to Palestine-Israel, whispers in my ear, "Did he say that it was the Israelis bombing this village? Why were they doing that?"

I tear the knee of my trousers trying to get over the barbed wire fence into the closed area that was once Saffuriyya. I take a picture of some unrecognisable stones on the ground that once belonged to the mosque. Ziad points amongst the trees to the place where his family used to live. He describes himself as "pure Saffuri", since all four of his grandparents were born in the village.

While many Saffurians fled to Lebanon or farther afield, a large number found themselves closer to home. Saffafri houses refugees from Saffuriyya who initially were spread across Nazareth city and surrounding areas, believing that they were only taking up temporary residence. While they never abandoned faith in return, around fifteen years after the occupation the neighbourhood of Saffafri began to develop. Some refugees grudgingly accepted token compensatory land from the government, while others purchased land in the same area. To the north of the city of Nazareth, it was ideal for Saffuriyyans, as it actually looked out upon their lands, symbolising the hope of return.[41] The neighbourhood neither forgets its roots nor its kinfolk. After the killings in Lebanon in 1982 in which many refugees from the Galilee and Saffuriyya died, the neighbourhood named a street "Sabra and Shatilla".[42]

It is not just the BBC that came filming here. Ziad, along with other villagers, had recently organised the annual festival, held in Nazareth's Saffafri neighbourhood for the people of Saffuriyya who remain so near, but so distant. There was poetry, theatre and music, and of course, the three evenings would not be complete without the traditional *debke* dancing. For this year's new contribution, the organisers decided to film testimonies of the older generation who can still remember the days before the exile.

"We brought people back to the site of the village to film their reactions, and people remembered every little shape and detail, irrespective of how the landscape had changed," said Ziad. "We brought an old man back here ... He knew everything by the stones and shape of land." The people filmed by Michel Khleifi in Ma'loul find their homes in the same way. Those who remember, do so by the shape of the land, the trunk of a tree. The old man Khleifi is accompanying finds his house by the olive trees, the cactus and the almond. He looks for the walls and they have crumbled, but he knows his home for he sees his neighbour's plants. Not even the non-indigenous fir trees, planted by the Israelis to cover the scene, can stop the cactus from continuing to mark the boundaries of long-gone homes.

But visits by refugees are not trouble-free. As the Saffuriyyans were filming, police and security were called three times by today's occupying Jewish residents. Refugees have been arrested trying to see where they used to live, or to visit a family grave. "One Romanian living here started accusing us of trying to set fire to his house. But when we talked further, I saw that it was not this that he was afraid of. Looking at us, he was afraid that we wanted to come and take back our homes."

The Saffuriyya Heritage Association began to develop seriously in response to the Oslo process which took no interest in the situation of the *"present absentees"*. The committee organises a whole range of activities, from political meetings to literacy classes, providing a focus on the future of the community as well as the past. It has published books, magazines and even a calendar, with the aim of informing and encouraging an interest in the village across all generations. Primary among activities is taking the old and new generations to the site of the village. It took a long battle with the Israeli authorities, but now the villagers have been allowed to fence off the old cemetery (*al-Maqbara*) which had already been damaged from years of neglect. The struggle has now moved to a second cemetery close to Daher al-'Umar's castle.

The group has a vast collection of old pictures, tools and household items used at the time of the *Nakba* and hurriedly brought away. Abu Arab describes how some cried on seeing these items at the recent festival: "by these we had lived ... our source of income". To try and mobilise the community, the group delivered a picture and a small bag of sand taken from the village to all the houses in the Saffafri neighbourhood.

Arguably even more important, the group is collecting oral history and stories about the *Nakba*, about village life before the catastrophe, and names and geography long gone by. Despite the stifling Nazareth air, Saffuriyyans have a dream and a vision. With all the data and artifacts collected, if funds can be found, they want to open a centre that will serve all the activities of the organisation in the future: a building that will be a small museum, a data collection point, a library and meeting room, a centre providing a focus for visitors from other villages and abroad.

Memory is more than direct recollection. In a recent interview, a twenty-year-old refugee from a Lebanese camp was asked what was her worst memory. "The *Nakba* of course."[43] Whether it be learning about the plants and fruit of the land or cleaning the graveyards in the village, the group wants the younger generation to plant Saffuriyya in their memories. Ziad recalls the making of the festival film as a special moment for the younger generation who were filming as well as for the older ones recalling the past. "Our aim is to keep the memory of what had remained from our village in the minds and memories of the second and third generation."[44]

Ziad regularly takes guests to Saffuriyya, pointing out the pine forest where once stood the houses of Saffuriyya. He holds up to the horizon an old photo of the village which is the cover page to the Saffuriyya calendar, comparing today and yesterday. Anger focused on the forests planted to cover the past is a recurring theme in the accounts of the internally displaced. In the recent film *500 Dunam on the Moon*, Muhammad Abu al-Haija, from the destroyed village of 'Ayn Hawd, expresses his hatred of the trees that state institutions plant to cover the village land.[45] "To this day I hate cypress trees, because they killed our fruit trees and were planted right in front of our houses to close us in, to shut out the air, to block the view of the sea … Cypresses for me are a Jewish symbol – when I see them I think of what the Jews have done to us since 1948."[46]

There is still a working convent there that in the past served the people of Saffuriyya as a clinic and a school for girls. It is a strange living link with the past. Until recently even some of the same nuns were living in the place from which they had assisted Saffuriyyans over half a century ago.

On one visit, just as we were leaving the convent, which gives stunning views over the confiscated lands of Saffuriyya, a huge coach swung into the driveway with a woman standing at the front, microphone in hand. "Hang on," said Ziad, "I'll just have a word. That's my mother bringing a Jewish women's group to see the village she comes from."

While some refugees refuse to take part in Arab-Jewish forums, believing that such groups merely offer Israeli Jewish liberals a chance to salve an uneasy conscience, others see taking part as an essential part of the struggle. A decade ago Umm Muhammad finally started talking. Talking to her own children about what happened when she was a child. Like Ziad's mother, she wanted to tell Israelis exactly what she had been through, and where she came from.

I listened to what Jewish women told me about their suffering. And then I told them about mine. I told them that when they had passed through all that they went through, they arrived to Israel to my house, my clothes. All of them. And now I have reached nothing.

"Cactus" Shop, Ruins of Roman Baths, Mary's Well Square, Nazareth

Every year on the *Nakba* anniversary, a large demonstration is organised to take internal refugees and others in the community, including some foreigners and Jewish citizens, to visit a destroyed village. Others of course prefer to go and picnic and wander on the site of their own village.

But some refugees have no wish to remember or visit. Elias knew that I was interested in talking about such things, but for the first few months I knew him he never mentioned that he came from Ma'lul. For him, the fact that his tourist business was crumbling before his eyes was a more immediate concern to tell a foreigner, or in fact anyone who would listen. Whether he would be able to support his family today was his urgent question.

Thirteen years ago, Elias and his Belgian wife Martina returned to Nazareth after years in Europe. After buying a new shop for their cosmetics business in the Mary's Well area of Nazareth, Elias uncovered the foundations and found himself on the site of an ancient Roman bathhouse. Potentially Jesus of Nazareth could have bathed here in the only source of water for the Nazarenes of two millennia ago. Yet until today, the Israeli authorities have not given any financial support to this Arab family to support the heritage of the Holy Land. Having invested all their money, the family are now heavily in debt as few tourists come to Arab Nazareth.

As I drank Arab coffee from the stove with Martina in the lovingly restored bathhouse, the conversation happened to turn to the destroyed villages. "You should talk to Elias about that. Didn't he tell you that his grandfather was a *mukhtar* [village headman] in Ma'lul? His mother came to Nazareth but her father was killed on his doorstep."

"He was killed in front of his own house, trying to defend his family home," said Elias when I asked him. The rest of the family came to Nazareth having lost everything.

Does he ever go back? "No, why should I? They built a Jewish kibbutz or something there," he said with a shrug. He looked away, a sign that the conversation was over.

Ma'lul, 1948

On 14 July the second village in the Nazareth district to be destroyed was Ma'lul, situated just 6 kilometres west of the city. The 1945 census registered a couple of hundred Christians and just less than 500 Muslims living there.[47]

> Narrator: "Abu Zeid, why did you leave Ma'loul [sic]?"
> Abu Zeid: "I was scared of dying. Terrified. I had no weapons. Nothing, no rifle or anything. I never hurt anyone. I never went to prison."[48]

Michel Khleifi's *Ma'loul Celebrates Its Destruction* (1985) films an older generation remembering life in the village, nearly forty years earlier.

> Man: "The war broke out and people fled to save their children."
> Narrator: "How did they attack?"
> Woman: "They kept shooting from the opposite hill. So how could we fight back? With stones? No! Some of us were killed by bullets others by bombs. Leave or die? We had to choose. So we left."
> Narrator: "Didn't they tell you to come back?"
> Woman: "Sure. But the next day, they destroyed everything! The day after we left, they arrived with their bulldozers! We took nothing, neither our clothes nor crockery, neither chickens nor pigeons! We abandoned everything, as God is my witness! I had left some water for my chickens, but the water and the chickens had disappeared under the rubble!"[49]

The villagers of Ma'lul were no strangers to Zionist interest in their lands. At the turn of the twentieth century the land was owned by the wealthy Lebanese Sursuq family, but in 1921 most of it was sold to the Zionist "Palestine Land Company". The residents of Ma'lul were left with only 2,000 *dunums*, insufficient for village needs. Following a request by the mandatory authorities, the villagers were allowed to lease the land for six years with the possibility of buying it back within that time. However later the company refused, saying that it had now been transferred to the Jewish National Fund which constitutionally would not sell. The case dragged on undecided through the Mandate, until the matter was settled by the Zionist expulsion of the whole village in 1948.[50] Many of the refugees found themselves living in Nazareth.

"Cactus" Shop, Nazareth, 12 April 2003

Months after Elias had first spoken about his grandfather in Ma'lul, on a stop by for coffee, the conversation suddenly swung round again to land. "Elias went back, you know. Ask him," said Martina.

"Yes I went back. And it was horrible. They were using the church for a cowshed. A cowshed! It is totally shameful. I can't tell you. And the settlers have dogs. Snapping and barking. It is disgraceful. Disgraceful."

Elias was not the only one left speechless by the desecration of the church. Michel Khleifi's camera panned around the same building:

Old Man: "This church is filled with cattle and the other with garbage. And the mosque. It's even worse! What can I say? In their eyes I am just a contemptible insect that must be crushed" (tears of anger and hopelessness) ...

"So where's the solution?"

"It's in God's hands. If He wanted it that way. What's the solution? The solution is Justice. Let every man respect the rights of others. Recognise mine and I'll recognise yours."

Learning something of the lives of internal refugees reinforces my understanding of the personal as political. With the limitations of party political action for Palestinian citizens of the Jewish state, actions of memory and networking can be more directly political than voting. For "present absentees" the perpetuation of the community's very existence is a political act.

As I sit with families in downtown Nazareth, drinking coffee, talking about the price of tomatoes or the building of the son's new apartment, the television is always on in the background. A scene of massive destruction and suffering in a West Bank city flashes across the screen. Then someone flicks channels to a Lebanese gameshow or an Egyptian comedy. In three years living in Nazareth I was regularly frustrated by the fact that many of my friends did not want to talk about the daily horrors outside the tiny borders of Nazareth, shrugging and sighing that there was no longer anything to say. Perhaps discussion of "the situation" is a luxury for outsiders who have not grown up with it.

And yet if someone asks me what my research interest is, immediately everyone wants to talk, volunteering a friend, neighbour or relative who is an internal refugee. "You must speak with Zuhayr, he is from al-Mujaydil"; "I can take you to people who have maps and pictures and stories. When can you come over?" or "You can't do your research without talking to Heba upstairs. Her grandfather is from Samakh."

In Nazareth, dispossession is indivisible from life, even when on an everyday basis it may go unspoken. Palestinians inside the Green Line watch their television screens with their hands tied, as Israel decimates the West Bank and Gaza. Current affairs programmes in Hebrew demonstrate that the topic of Arab "transfer" becomes an increasingly acceptable subject for mainstream Israeli politicians and academics. There may be no bulldozers on the streets of Nazareth, but as the struggles of the internally displaced to hold their community together show, the *Nakba* is not a memory that Palestinians can afford to lay to rest.

Notes

1 Line from Taha Muhammad 'Ali, "Sabha's Rope", *Never Mind: Twenty Poems and a Story,* trans. Peter Cole, Yahya Hijazi, Gabriel Levin (Jerusalem: Ibis, 2000), p.83.

2 For instance, Benny Morris, *The Birth of the Palestinian Refugee Problem, 1947-1949* (Cambridge: Cambridge University Press, 1987), p.2.

3 See works such as Rosemary Sayigh, *Palestinians: From Peasants to Revolutionaries* (London: Zed Books, 1979); Ted Swedenburg, *Memories of Revolt: The 1936-1939 Rebellion and the Palestinian National Past* (Minneapolis: University of Minnesota Press, 1995); Randa Farah, "The Significance of Oral Narratives and Life-Histories", *Al-Jana 2002 File on Palestinian Oral History,* ARCPA: Beirut, pp.24-7.

4 Taha Muhammad 'Ali, "Sabha's Rope", pp.83-4.

5 Nafez Nazzal, *The Palestinian Exodus from the Galilee, 1948* (Beirut: Institute for Palestine Studies, 1978), pp.28-30.

6 This pattern can be seen today in the "mixed" city of Acre (Akka), where the remaining Arab population (many of whom are internal refugees from other areas living in the homes of external Acre refugees) are packed into the rundown and poorer old city, while the new Jewish neighbourhoods of the city surround them.

7 Interview with eyewitness Khalil al-Tabari, a landowner from Tiberias, conducted in Beirut, Lebanon, 22 January 1973, by Nazzal. Nazzal, *The Palestinian Exodus from the Galilee,* p.28.

8 See Nazzal, *The Palestinian Exodus from the Galilee,* p.29, for details of weaponry.

9 Detailed in Nazzal, *The Palestinian Exodus from the Galilee,* and Morris, *The Birth of the Palestinian Refugee Problem,* pp.70-3.

10 Interview conducted by the author, 29 October 2000, at the home of the interviewee, Nazareth.

11 Charles S. Kamen, "After the Catastrophe II: The Arabs in Israel, 1948–51", *Middle Eastern Studies 24,* No. 1 (January 1988), pp.78-9.

12 Anton Shammas, "Palestinians in Israel: You Ain't Seen Nothin' Yet", *Journal of*

the International Institute, 1995, University of Michigan, Michigan (internet version).

13 Nadim Rouhana examines the issue of community identity in detail. This specific reference is to a 1989 survey. Nadim Rouhana, *Palestinian Citizens in an Ethnic Jewish State: Identities in Conflict* (New Haven: Yale University Press, 1997), p.122.

14 Author's interview with Umm Muhammad, 13 September 2003, in her Nazareth home.

15 In fact British General Stockwell gave orders for his forces to pull out of their positions in the town and redeploy in the Haifa region to safeguard critical routes and areas for British forces.

16 Morris, *The Birth of the Palestinian Refugee Problem*, p.73.

17 Elias Srouji, "The Last Days of 'Free Galilee': Memories of 1948", *Journal of Palestine Studies* 33, no.1 (Fall 2003), p.55.

18 For examination of the development of transfer policy pre-1948, see Nur Masalha, *Expulsion of the Palestinians: The Concept of 'Transfer' in Zionist Political Thought, 1882–1948,* (Washington DC: Institute for Palestine Studies, 1992).

19 Yosef Weitz, *Yomani Ve'igrotai Labanim* [My Diary and Letters to the Children], Vol. II, p.181, entry for 20 December 1940, cited in Morris, *The Birth of the Palestinian Refugee Problem*, p.27.

20 Morris, *The Birth of the Palestinian Refugee Problem*, p.30.

21 Srouji, "The Last Days of 'Free Galilee' ", p.57.

22 Morris, *The Birth of the Palestinian Refugee Problem*, p.201.

23 Ibid, p.202.

24 Kamen, "After the Catastrophe II", p.78.

25 Waleed Khlief, interview with researcher, 11 April 2003, Nazareth home.

26 The village of Sulam had survived along with six other villages of the Zo'abi family, owing to a secret deal on the part of a leading member of the family with the invading forces.

27 Interview with Umm Muhammad, 13 September 2003.

28 Interview with Umm Ahmad in the fields of the former lands of Saffuriyya, 4 October 2002.

29 See Swedenburg, *Memories of Revolt,* pp.60-63 on Israeli reforestation policy.

30 Interview with Abu 'Arab, Nazareth, 8 September 2003.

31 Ali Al-Azhari, "Saffuriyeh: A Short Story by Ali Al-Azhari", *Palestine–Israel Journal of Politics, Economics and Culture* 3, no.1 (Winter 1996) (originally published in Hebrew in *Ma'ariv*, 15 October 1995, translated by Yael Lotan).

32 Ibid.

33 Hussein Abu Hussein and Fiona McKay, *Access Denied: Palestinian Land Rights in Israel* (London: Zed Books, 2003), p.73.

34 Ahdaf Soueif, "The Waiting Game", *Guardian*, 24 November 2003.

35 Abu Hussein and McKay, *Access Denied,* pp.86-96.

36 Raif Zraiq, "Through Arab Eyes", *News from Within*, Vol. XV, no.8 (August 1999).

37 Interview with Abu 'Arab, 8 September 2003.

38 Interview with Abu 'Arab, Nazareth, 8 September 2003.

39 Interview with Umm Muhammad, 13 September 2003.

40 Heba, daughter of Umm Muhammad, in conversation with researcher 12 September 2003.
41 Interview with Abu 'Arab, 8 September 2003.
42 Laurie King-Irani, "Land, Identity and the Limits of Resistance in the Galilee", in "Losing Ground? The Politics of Environment and Space", *Middle East Report* 216 (Fall 2000).
43 Laleh Khalili, *Citizens of an Unborn Kingdom: Stateless Refugees, Commemoration and Contention*. Unpublished draft dissertation, University of Columbia, 2004, p.20.
44 Personal communication from Ziad 'Awaisy, 18 December 2002.
45 Rachel Leah Jones, (dir.), *500 Dunam on the Moon* (France/USA/UK, Sindibad Films, 2002).
46 Riad Beidas, "'Ayn Hawd' and the Unrecognized Villages: An Interview with Muhammad Al-Hayja", *Journal of Palestine Studies* 31, no.1 (Autumn 2001), p.45.
47 Walid Khalidi, (ed.), *All That Remains: The Palestinian Villages Occupied and Depopulated by Israel in 1948* (Washington, DC: Institute for Palestine Studies, 1992), p.347.
48 Interviews in film by Michel Khleifi, (dir.) *Ma'loul Celebrates Its Destruction* (Belgium/Palestine, Sindibad Films, 1985).
49 Interviews in Khleifi's *Ma'loul Celebrates Its Destruction*.
50 Khalidi, *All That Remains*, p.347.

6
Kafr Bir'im
William Dalrymple

On a visit to Beirut in 1994, I met the Daous, a Christian Palestinian family. After half a century of exile, they now had found shelter in the squalid Mar Elias refugee camp on the southern outskirts of the city. Like so many other Palestinians they had fled their old village – in their case Kafr Bir'im – in 1948, during the upheavals and expulsions that marked the violent birth of the state of Israel. The Daous had decided they would be safer if they temporarily left their homes in the northern Galilee, and as a direct result of that decision had spent forty-six years in exile in a succession of refugee camps. What would have happened to them, I wondered, if they had decided to stay? Would their life have been any easier in the new state of Israel? In November 1994, while in Israel, I went to try and find out.

In a general sense I already knew the answer to these questions. Compared to their compatriots who were expelled – or indeed those on the West Bank who had been conquered by the Israelis in 1967 and were still under military rule years later – the Christians who had stayed on and become citizens of Israel in 1948 had been very lucky. They had Israeli passports, and could vote in Israeli elections. They had access to Israeli educational facilities, enjoyed civil Israeli justice and could even, if they so wished, join the Israeli army. True, there were complaints about land expropriation and discrimination: the councils of Arab towns were said to receive less than a third of the funds available to those with Jewish populations. Yet compared to the dismal fate of those who still languished in refugee camps, the Israeli Arabs had been very fortunate indeed. Unlike their counterparts on the West Bank, relatively few have emigrated abroad and since the foundation of Israel their numbers have almost quadrupled.

But what I wanted to compare with what I had heard in Beirut was more specific: the fate of the Daous' neighbours in Kafr Bir'im who had stayed on. Samira Daous had told me that when Israeli planes had bombed Kafr Bir'im, her friends and neighbours had taken shelter in the nearby town of Jish. What had happened to them?

The drive led past the Sea of Galilee, with its ancient Byzantine churches clustering around the lake shore, and up, over stark hillsides of black volcanic stone, on towards the North and the Lebanese border. The countryside was dotted with Israeli kibbutzim and moshavim, energetically scratching out a living from the harsh soil. But as we drove, my Palestinian taxi driver Sami, pointed out the sites of some of the 418 Arab villages that had preceded such Israeli settlements in Galilee and elsewhere, until they were systematically depopulated and destroyed by the Jewish Haganah during the war of 1948. It was the cactus plants that always gave the old villages away: however efficiently the Israelis had bulldozed the buildings and erased the Palestinian communities from the map, the old villages' cactus hedges had deep roots and kept sprouting again and again to mark the sites of the former house boundaries and the shadows of former fields.

"That was the village of Farradiyya," said Sami at one stage, pointing to a few blocks of stone and some cactus plants lying by the side of the road at the bottom of a hill. "Now the kibbutz of Farud farms that land."

As we climbed the hill, Sami's battered old Mercedes labouring behind a convoy of slow military trucks, the kibbutz's cowsheds and farm buildings came into view, their solar panels glinting in the morning light. Beyond, the low hills and plains of Galilee spread out before us. Despite the mass immigration of the 1920s and 1930s, in 1948 the Jews had still formed less than a quarter of the population of this area, and the displacement of the Arab majority had been achieved only by a process which Yigal Allon, the commander of the Jewish military forces in Galilee (and later deputy prime minister of Israel), himself described as [ethnic] cleansing: "We saw a need to clean the Inner Galilee," he wrote in his memoirs, "and to create a Jewish territorial succession in the entire area of Upper Galilee. We therefore looked for means to cause the tens of thousands of sulky Arabs who remained in Galilee to flee ... Wide areas were [thus] cleansed."

In the process of this "cleansing" of the Galilee, the Christian Palestinians offered less resistance than the Muslims and were consequently better treated. Moreover Israel was careful not to offend public opinion in the Christian West by committing atrocities in Christian towns and villages: special instructions were issued by David Ben-Gurion himself not to loot Christian holy places such as Nazareth. As the brigade commander who captured the city later wrote: "the conquest of Nazareth has political importance – the behaviour of the [Israeli] occupation forces in the city could serve as a factor in determining the prestige of the young state abroad".

In nearby Beit Shean (then known by its Arabic name, Baysan) the inhabitants were divided in two: Muslims were bussed across the Jordan into exile, but the Christians were given the option of fleeing to Nazareth. Canon Na'im 'Ateek, whom I had met in Jerusalem where he was archdeacon of St George's Anglican Cathedral, was eleven when he was expelled from his family home in Baysan: "When the Israeli army came into the town there was no resistance," he told me when I visited him at St George's. "Then quite suddenly a fortnight later we were given two hours to pack up and leave: the soldiers came around from house to house and said 'if you don't leave we will kill you'. We were allowed to take only what we could carry." Ten years later, in 1958, when travel restrictions on the Israeli Arabs were lifted, 'Ateek's father took the family back to see their old house. They knocked on the door, but were sent roughly away by a Polish man armed with a rifle. They never went back again.

An hour's drive beyond Nazareth, the road turned a corner and we found ourselves looking down over thick conifer forests to the tower blocks of Safad: "Before 1948 it was a mixed town," said Sami. "There were Muslims, Jews and Christians. Now it's exclusively Jewish. The Christians and the Muslims were driven out by force and were never allowed back again. My mother had cousins there, but most of her family were killed when the Haganah bombarded the Arab part of the town with mortars. A few made it to Lebanon, but we haven't heard from them since the invasion of '82. We don't know whether they are alive or dead."

Jish lay a short distance beyond Safad, a little higher into the hills. It was a scrappy-looking place, the few old stone houses surrounded by many more new bungalows, among them, the minaret of a mosque and the spires of two churches. Unsure where to begin my inquiries, I asked an Arab woman in a pinafore the way to the priest's house. I was directed a short distance down the street.

The door was opened by Father Bishara Suleiman, the Maronite parish priest. He was a tall man with a short clipped goatee beard, and he spoke excellent English (and French, as I later discovered: he had studied theology at the Sorbonne). Unusually for a Middle Eastern clergyman he was dressed not in formal black robes, but in a T-shirt and slacks. I explained the reason for my visit to the town and he immediately invited me in. At the same time he called to his nephew, John Suleiman, to go and fetch some of the old men from Kafr Bir'im.

We took seats on a balcony, looking out onto the village's olive groves. Father Suleiman's wife produced a thermos of strong Turkish coffee from the kitchen and while we sipped the scalding liquid, I asked the priest if he would tell me the full story of what had happened to Kafr Bir'im after the Daous had left it in 1948. Would they have been better advised to stay?

"Very few of our villagers did flee in '48", said Father Suleiman. "We had always had good relations with the Jews and the British: so much so that in 1936 [during the Palestinian revolt] we were accused of collaboration and had to beg the British to protect us. They sent some Tommies who set up camp on the edge of the village, and after that we had no trouble. We had always helped the Jews entering Palestine from Lebanon, and we thought that if there was any trouble they would help us. That was why most of the villagers stayed on, despite all the stories we heard about Dayr Yasin and other massacres nearer here ..."

"Such as?"

"The Haganah massacred seventy Arab prisoners at 'Ayn al-Zaytun near Safad. They tied their hands behind their backs. Then they shot them. But we thought nothing like that would happen here, partly because we were Christians and partly because we had always been friendly towards the Jews."

At this moment Father Suleiman's nephew returned with the old village schoolmaster of Bir'im, Elias Jacob.

Elias was a thin, wizened old man. At seventy-five he was a little uncertain on his legs, but still absolutely clear in his mind. He was, said Father Suleiman, the best authority on the history of Kafr Bir'im; and as if to prove it, Elias produced from his pocket a slip of paper on which were written the main dates and facts of the story. He didn't want anyone getting anything wrong, he said. The old teacher took a seat, threw back a small cup of Turkish coffee and at Father Suleiman's invitation began to talk:

"The Haganah soldiers arrived in our village on October the 29th 1948", he said, checking the date against his notes. "Most of us remained in our houses, but the old men and the priest received the troops at the entrance of the village with a white flag. We offered them bread and salt, the symbol of friendship and peace."

"Were they equally friendly?" I asked.

"They were," said the old man. "They were very good, very polite. We gave them food and they occupied some houses. They stayed for fifteen days. Then on the 13th of November 1948 an order arrived that we all had to leave."

"Were you surprised?"

"We were amazed. At first we refused to go. But then a new officer arrived and he was very different. He said we had twenty-four hours to get out. Then we were afraid. He gave no reasons. He just said that we had to be five kilometres from the village or we would be shot."

As Elias was speaking we were joined on the balcony by another old man, Wadeer Ferhat. He was a big, high-spirited man with a huge walrus moustache. When he discovered what we were talking about he began shouting in a series of angry outbursts of guttural Arabic. Sami, the taxi driver, translated: "Mr. Wadeer says that they threw the people out from their homes into the countryside. They had no tents. Some found shelter in caves. Everyone else just squatted under trees or in the fields. It was November, but much colder than this year. By December there was thick snow. He said many babies died from exposure."

Wadeer continued shouting, hands flying in the air in a series of graphic gestures.

"He says he was thirty-five at the time, but that both his parents were very old, over seventy. He says that they cried for many days because they had lost their homes and their land."

"What Wadeer has not said," pointed out Elias Jacob, calmly consulting his fact sheet, "was that before we left, each of the 1050 villagers was given a number, granting them Israeli citizenship. We tidied and cleaned our houses because we thought we would soon be allowed back. After a time the Minister for Minorities, Mr Bechor Shitrit, came here. He saw that we were living under trees and ordered that we be given those houses here in Jish which had been vacated by fleeing Muslims. He said that we should wait for just fifteen days, and after that, when the area was calm, we could go back to Kafr Bir'im. In the meantime he allowed a few old men to stay in the village to guard the houses and the crops."

"What happened then?" I asked.

"Six months later the old men were ordered out of the village, and it became clear that we were not going to get our houses back. So we decided to take the matter to the Israeli High Court."

"The people of Bir'im have never resorted to violence," added Father Suleiman. "We have always fought by law and by Christian principles."

"In 1953 we finally won the case," continued Elias. "The court ordered that the evictions were unjust and said that we should all be allowed back to our homes and to farm our fields."

"So why aren't you back there now?" I asked.

"Because the next day the Israeli army declared the area a military zone and banned us from entering it. That afternoon they destroyed Kafr Bir'im by aerial bombardment. We had won the case but they tricked us all the same. There was nothing we could do."

Wadeer frowned and banged his fist on the table. Again Sami translated:

"He says: All the villagers went up onto that hill and watched the bombing of their homes. They call it the Crying Hill now, because everyone from Kafr Bir'im wept that day. Everything they owned was still in those houses."

"My father told me that they didn't know what was going to happen until they heard the planes begin their bombing," said Father Suleiman. "It was the 16th of September 1953. They thought it was going to be the day that they returned to their homes. But it was the day we lost them – and our fields – forever."

"I had built a house with my own hands," said Elias. "It had five rooms. But I lived in it only five months. Everything went. My furniture, cupboards, beds, icons. Worst of all I lost my books."

"I remember my father telling me what a wonderful village it was," said Father Suleiman. "The climate was very good. The soil was fertile. The air was fresh …"

"There were figs, olives, grapes, apples, springs of fresh water …" said Elias.

"And many wells," added Wadeer in Arabic. "I can see the whole village very clearly when I close my eyes. I remember every house, every building."

"But when the Israeli air force began bombing there was nothing we could do," said the old teacher. "We could do nothing – nothing but go up to the hill and spend the whole day weeping like children."

"We were betrayed," said Wadeer.

"We still feel betrayed," added Father Suleiman.

A silence fell over the balcony.

"So what happened to your land?" I asked eventually.

"In 1949 they gave some of our fields to a new kibbutz, Kibbutz Bar'am," said the teacher, consulting his precious list of facts and figures. "The kibbutz was built on 350 *dunums* of our land. Then in 1963 they established Moshav Dovev with another 2,000 *dunums.*"

"The site of the village is now a national park," said Father Suleiman. "At the entrance to it they have put up a sign saying that 'Bar'am Antiquities' date from the Second Temple Period. It's true that there are the ruins of a Roman-period synagogue in the middle of our village. But the sign deliberately gives the impression that the remains of our houses are all Roman ruins. The schoolchildren who are taken around it think that our old buildings – our stables and schools and houses – are like the ones you see in Pompeii."

"We've been edited out of history," said the old teacher. "They don't admit to our existence. Or to the existence of our fathers and grand-fathers and great-grandfathers."

"I and my father dug a well," said Wadeer. "There is a sign there now saying that it was built by someone called Yohanan of Bar'am at the time of the Romans."

"Who is Yohanan of Bar'am?"

"Apparently a leader of the Jewish Revolt in AD 66," said the teacher. "Though we in the village had never heard of him until the park was built."

"They've made it as if my well is part of ancient Jewish history," said Wadeer. "But we dug that well with our own labour!"

"Another man, a friend of mine called Farah Laqzaly, made a sculpture of the Madonna," said Elias. "I remember seeing him making it. But now they say it is centuries old. They took it to Kibbutz Sasa and put it on display."

"If the village is now a park does that mean I could go and visit it?" I asked.

"Of course," said Father Suleiman. "And we will come too. No one from Bir'im misses a chance to return."

Everyone rose. Wadeer and Father Suleiman's nephew John went in the priest's old station wagon, while Sami and I followed with Elias the schoolteacher. It was a short drive from Jish to Kafr Bir'im, less than ten minutes.

At the entrance to the park new Israeli flags were flying above a neat parking lot. In it sat two enormous tour buses. A large sign next to the ticket office, did indeed read BAR'AM ANTIQUITIES, just as Father Suleiman had said. In English and Hebrew – though again not Arabic – it told the ancient Jewish history of the site. No mention was made of the mediaeval and modern Arab history of the ruins, and there was no reference to the bombing of the village in 1953. The brochure available at the ticket office was a little more forthcoming, remarking at the end of a long description of the synagogue that "until 1948 Bar'am was a Maronite Christian village. During the War of Independence, the villagers were evacuated and the site is now under the auspices of the National Parks Authority." I liked the way the writer had used the word "evacuated," as if the villagers expulsion had somehow been an act of kindness, intended to ensure their own safety and well being, giving the very opposite impression of what had actually taken place.

Father Suleiman shrugged when I showed him the leaflet. "Of course they do not tell the truth of what really happened to us," he said, adding proudly, and without irony: "But at least they don't make me pay to get in. It's because I'm a priest, you see."

Meanwhile the two old men were already half way across the ruins. Far from being depressed at seeing the flattened ruins of their childhood village they were almost skipping with excitement: "It always makes us happy to breathe the air of Bir'im," said Wadeer.

"The Daous house stood over there," said Elias pointing to some foundations sticking out of the carefully manicured grass. "The family of Ghattas lived beside them in that house, beside the pine trees. After 1948 two of their boys ended up in Brazil where they became famous footballers. You haven't heard of Rai and Socrates? They played in the World Cup. Now, see over there: where those American tourists are standing? Yes those two with the baseball caps. Those are the ruins of the old synagogue. And over here: that's our church. It was the one building the Israelis left standing when they flattened our homes."

"And those gothic arches?" I asked. "To the side of the church. Are they Crusader?"

"No, no," said Elias, frowning. "Those arches are all that remains of my school. This was my classroom."

Elias stood in the middle of what was now a carefully tended patch of grass.

"For four years I taught in here, from 1944 to 1948. This was the door. The blackboard was here. But that was forty-five years ago now."

Wadeer began rattling away in Arabic; this time it was Father Suleiman who translated. "He says he was taught in here. In his day it was a Jesuit school. The teacher afterwards became the Maronite Patriarch, Cardinal Khreish.[1] He was very strict. He would beat the children with a canvas shoe and sometimes also with a stick."

Wadeer walked over to the corner of the plot, making whacking gestures with his wrist.

"He says the stick was kept here. Everyone in the class tasted the stick. No one dared to play tricks."

Father Suleiman had got out his keys and was now opening the door into the church tower. We all followed him up the winding stairs. Halfway up, Wadeer began to gesture excitedly at the wall of the staircase:

"Look! Look!" he said. "Yes here: here is my name. I was fifteen when I wrote that."

At the top, a grille on the roof looked down into the nave below. Through it you could see two graves:

"That was the grave of the parish priest. They let us bury him here in 1956. It was the first time we had been allowed back into the village since the bombing. The military gave us authorisation, as long as we didn't take more than three hours."

"Between 1948 and 1967 there were soldiers everywhere," said Elias. "We were not allowed to come here at all."

"Once my goats escaped and came here," said Wadeer. "I came to get them back and was caught. They took me to the military tribunal in Nazareth. I spent a month in prison and had to pay a large fine."

"Now it is much better," said Father Suleiman. "If we pay we can come as often as we like. And they let us use the church for free on Easter, Christmas, Palm Sunday and Pentecost. Also for burials. They do not charge us for that."

All six of us were now standing against the parapet looking out over the countryside around us.

"When we come here we are happy," said Elias. "All the old memories

come back. We remember many things: the streets, the homes, the neighbours. Everything. My house was over there: at the end of the village to
the right. But it was completely destroyed."

"Over there," said Wadeer, pointing to the horizon. "That is the hill
where we stood when they destroyed the village."

"See through those trees?" said Father Suleiman, pointing into the
distance. "That is Kibbutz Bar'am. And over there: to the North? That's
Moshav Dovev. They took two parts of our land, but this, to the South:
that is free. Where the forest is now growing: that used to be our fig trees
and our vineyards. There are 10,000 *dunums* which are not used. That is all
we want."

"It would be so easy," said Elias. "We don't even need 10,000 *dunums*.
Five thousand *dunums* would do. We would accept anything."

We began to file down the stairs. The priest closed and locked the
door behind us.

"But you see they are worried it would be a precedent," said Father
Suleiman as we walked back to the car park, past the American tourists
now eating a picnic at a wooden tables by the ticket office. "They say that
once you let one Arab back, you admit the others have rights too. That is
why, despite everything, they dare not give us back what is ours. Israel
says it is a democracy and it is true. But it seems that for us Palestinians
there is no justice."

"We've told the government that Kafr Bir'am is like a house of three
rooms," said Elias, looking back at his old village. "One is now the
kibbutz. One is the moshav. One is empty. We don't ask much. But that
we must have."

Note

1   Cardinal Antonious Butros Khreish, Lebanon's most senior Maronite cleric, died
    August 1994 in Bkirki, the traditional mountain seat of the Maronite patriarchs,
    at the age of eighty-seven. He began his religious career in 1936, and was acting
    bishop of Haifa's Maronite community in Palestine. Elected Maronite patriarch
    in 1975, he resigned for health reasons in 1985, when he became the only
    Maronite to be made a cardinal by the Vatican.

7
The *Nakba,* Oral History and the Palestinian Peasantry: The Case of Lubya

Mahmoud 'Issa

Oral History: From Classical Islam to Modern Methodology

Oral history was and remains one of the main sources for our conceptions and understanding of different social and historical experiences is specific periods. One can argue forcefully that oral history is as old as history itself, and its importance was particularly great before the advent of writing as a means of communication, and the subsequent reliance on it as a main source for material. In the early years of Islam, particularly from the seventh century onwards, a huge controversy surrounded the interpretation and the authenticity of the collected *hadiths* (the oral sayings of the Prophet Muhammad) as relayed by leading *Sahaba* figures, the Prophet's companions. Compiling authentic *hadiths* of the Prophet from oral sources which had been communicated by the Prophet's companions, and after such long periods, posed a serious problem concerning the value and authenticity of the collected accounts. It took Arab historians and Muslim scholars many years of investigation, analysis, and comparative research to identify what was believed to be the accepted version of the authentic sayings of the Prophet.

The prominent Arab Muslim historian Al-Bukhari was one of the best-known literary figure of the classical age of Islam, who critically examined and challenged the authenticity of hundreds of different versions of the *hadiths* that had been cited by various people after the death of the Prophet. Al-Bukhari eventually reduced the number of authentic *hadiths* to fewer than two-thirds of their original number, after spending years of collecting, analysing and comparing various versions. This process of analysis and comparative research reflected the scholarly approaches of classical Islam and the scientific methodology employed by Muslim scholars used in critically scrutinising oral accounts and traditions closely associated with the Prophet and his companions. In many cases, Al-Bukhari would travel hundreds of miles on his horse to hear someone who had been recommended by others as a reliable source for the *hadiths*. One could say that Al-Bukhari was a pioneer in the field of establishing the best techniques and modes of verifying Muslim oral accounts and oral histories before establishing their credibility as a source of documentation.

With the advent and advancement of printing, the role of the written document and the validity of its testimony took on an almost sacred connotation in terms of plausibility and authenticity and as a vital, reliable source of history. In recent years, however, and with the emergence of post-colonial and post-modern studies, question marks began to be raised concerning the validity of the written document as the only source for recovering and constructing the past. Post-modern historians began questioning the "objectivity" of historical accounts, and the influence of the "subjective" when recording and reconstructing "objective" realities. Furthermore, it is worth posing the following questions. Who makes history? What about the experiences and the accounts of the "illiterate", the "marginal", the "colonised" and the "oppressed"? Shouldn't these groups be inclusively considered as important factors in history? What are the best means of recording and preserving their versions of history?

"Subjectivity" and the personal tendency of those "in power" to present and emphasise their version of events and facts raise serious doubt about the whole notion of "total objectivity". However, only recently – following the realisation of the inadequacy of traditional historical methods – has oral history begun to establish itself as an independent discipline with its own theories and specific research methodologies. In November 2003, while I was touring South Africa with a group of Palestinian researchers seeking to study closely the country's policies towards restitution of property and land issues in the post-apartheid period, we heard the chief land claims commissioner, Tozi Gwanya, telling us – at a meeting in Pretoria – that his government sought to employ oral history techniques to identify the lands of indigenous black people who had no written documentation or title deeds for their expropriated land. This would be in addition to other techniques such as family genealogical trees and even the cemeteries of ancestors.

Oral History and Rural Palestine

The use of oral history is an even more crucial and fundamental issue when we consider Palestinian historiography, and the lack of information on major periods of modern history. Furthermore Palestinian oral history is critical because of the dominant Zionist discourse in the West – a discourse whose prevalence has also contributed to the marginalisation of the indigenous inhabitants of Palestine, their history and their narrative.

Hundreds of books have been written on Palestine-Israel from a variety of angles: historical, social, economic, psychological, and political. But, with a few exceptions, one major aspect is still absent from the discourse: namely the recording of Palestinian history on the basis of Palestinian "voices" and "actors" (to use the language of the theatre). Throughout much of the twentieth century the majority of the Palestinians were *fellahin*, peasants. Their experiences in the fields, in their villages, in wars, and in exile are almost totally absent from history writing and much of recent historiography; in this sense they are, to use the Kafkaesque term coined by the Israelis, *"present absentees"*. Not only men's voices, but women's too are absent, neglected and marginalised. The narrative of the refugee and the marginalised is almost totally absent from Palestinian historiography.

Moreover the Palestinian nationalist narrative was always an elite narrative; until recently we have heard only the voices of Palestinian elite groups, urban notables and official spokespersons, on the one hand, and Israeli versions of the events and the orthodox Zionist discourse, on the other. The questions that should be posed are: why is it that Palestinians have not yet articulated and narrated their own history? And why is it that Palestinians are still, by and large, represented by others? Is it a question of "illiteracy" among the vast majority of the rural population of Palestine? I myself have my own doubts, but let us assume that this is plausible, the questions then would necessarily be: what happened to all Palestinian intellectuals and revolutionaries? Why did Chinese and Vietnamese intellectuals write many books on the involvement of Chinese and Vietnamese peasants in the struggles and revolutions of the twentieth century, while Palestinian authors chose to ignore the role of the Palestinian peasantry? Do we really expect to understand Palestinian history without any real knowledge of the Palestinian peasantry and its oral history? And should we construct new definitions of culture and history more inclusively, not just accept those derived from elite concepts and versions of history?

The following anecdote illustrates the point I am trying to make on oral history and the Palestinian peasantry. When Professor Sharif Kana'ana, of Beir Zeit University in Palestine, first came up with the idea of setting up a university project to record the history of the 1948 destroyed villages, the reaction of some of his colleagues was apparently a mixture of cynicism and mockery: "why look for the debris of the past?"[1] Kana'ana nevertheless persisted and kept sending his students to the remains of the 1948 Palestinian villages (in Israel), and also managed to interview survivors of the 1948 *Nakba* (catastrophe) and record their accounts. The cumulative results were impressive, and twenty-seven monographs on the destroyed villages were published in Arabic. The project was carried out with the help of Saleh 'Abdel Jawwad and other colleagues at Beir Zeit University, who had eventually been won over. Others followed, and Palestinian researcher Sahira Dirbas wrote three monographs on three destroyed villages in the Haifa and Jaffa districts (Salama, al-Tira and al-Birwa). At least five other monographs have been published on destroyed villages in Galilee using the oral history methods of interviewing refugees and recording their recollections. However, the question is whether these relatively small-scale and local initiatives are adequate in terms of achieving the goal of writing the history of an uprooted people and recording the experiences of millions of Palestinian refugees.[2]

After 57 years of *Nakba*, dispossession and exile, in one of the biggest ethnic cleansing operations in modern times, we have only about forty monographs on the destroyed villages, while the rest – as many as 531, according to one authority – are still to be documented.[3] Given the immense loss of documents due to the sudden uprooting of the population from their homes and lands, there is only one way to fill the gap: to record the lives of the pre-1948 generation through oral history methods as quickly as possible. According to one estimate by a Palestinian demographer, Palestinians aged 68 and over are between 3.3 and 3.9 per cent of the whole population. This would make the pool around 210,000 (counting only Palestine and the Arab host countries, as social historian Rosemary Sayigh wrote in the editorial to the Arab-language magazine *Al-Jana*, which recently devoted a whole issue to

Palestinian oral history).[4] More than fifteen old men and women from the village of Lubya whom I interviewed in the last five years have since died. Without their accounts and words, part of this work would have been impossible.

Of course there are many theoretical and methodological problems which need to be examined by those working in the field of oral history. I myself have encountered a series of problems since I began my research project of recording the accounts of the *fellahin* of Lubya. These problems include: methods of interviews, preparation of questionnaires, choices of place and time, verification and cross-questioning, the psychological impact of remembering past memories, especially when marked by trauma and tragic events, the lapse of time of more than half a century between the event and its newly recorded oral accounts, fear of persecution as a hindrance to vividly remembering the past – in one case one Lubyan man was called in by the police of an Arab country after giving an interview on what happened in 1948 and warned not to give more interviews.

When I began my oral history and *Nakba* project on Lubya in 1994 it was on a modest scale, and concerned primarily with Lubyan refugees living in Denmark. I was surprised to discover that from one Palestinian village (Lubya) there were about one thousand people living in Denmark. This encouraged me to go one step further, to try to visit the destroyed site of Lubya (in Israel), something I could do only after becoming a Danish citizen. I travelled there with my parents and a crew from the main Danish television company. The trip resulted in a forty-five-minute documentary, entitled *The Ancestors Land*, that covered our journey from Denmark to Lubya, and interviews with the internally displaced Palestinian families still living nearby in Dayr Hanna, Nazareth, and Acre.

Social Life Disrupted by the *Nakba*

Weddings, songs and celebrations in pre-1948 Lubya

Traditional society was riddled with cleavages, and subaltern studies tend to highlight the social, economic, gender and clan (*hamula*) conflicts that bedevilled peasant societies. Most elderly Lubyans I interviewed, however, tended to portray peasant life in pre-1948 Palestine in rosy terms. For these elderly Lubyans the trauma of the *Nakba* had silenced all fond memories of life in the village, including celebration and wedding days. Tamam 'Ajaini, also known as Umm Hassan, was born in 1898 in Lubya. She died in 1997 in Dayr Hanna, Galilee, without visiting Lubya even once after 1948. The interview I conducted with her had the tone of past memories that refused to wither or die. Her attitude towards people had undertones of tenderness and love. "May God compensate you for your trouble," she said in Arabic when she knew that I had two daughters. In the two months during which I saw her many times for the purpose of this research project, she refused to talk about Lubya. "Lubya is gone [*rahat*]," were the only words she uttered. But I did not give up. I continued encouraging her to speak, and she continued to ask me only about the few old people who had left for Lebanon and Syria. One day, unexpectedly, Umm Hassan began to talk. She started with the story of a wedding in the al-'Atwat neighbourhood of Lubya. She recounted how she lived with six brothers and their wives in the same house and how reconciliation took place between families following disputes. She recalled wedding songs and other broken bits and pieces from her memory. Her first story was about a dispute between two singers.

The two popular singers (*haddayi*) from Dayr al-Asad and Hittin were assaulting one another with verse. One is personifying the female voice, mainly dealing with kinship relations, and the priority of the cousin to get married to girls from the *hamula*, otherwise a feud would ensue. The dispute revolves around kinship relations, and respect for the rules of marriage. Generally, villagers would marry within the same *hamula*. The following is a *haddayi* song:

A cup was poured
don't antagonise me
Hijazi coffee is poured
only to the noble
Take care and don't antagonise me
my cousin will protect me
She carries a sword and a knife
with one blow she'll shed your
blood
Stand up and don't be afraid
let speech only be between us
I'll turn your anger into peace
My brother would interrupt
and crush with stones your head

Let your brother meet me
if he dares to speak
I have a sword and a knife
I will scatter your blood
Stand up and don't be afraid
let speech only be between us.

Umm Hassan went on to share romanticised memories of her own wedding in Lubya and to tell her story in her own lovely way, recounting how the two poets reconciled after having attacked one another, reflecting the modes of reconciliation among the *fellahin*, if disputes started:

We lived in one house with my husband 'Abdel-Rahman and his five brothers 'Issa, 'Abdel-Rahim, Muhammad, 'Eid and 'Ayid. All of them were married and had their wives and children in that same house. When people came to visit, they thought that we were sisters. The six brothers were married to women from different families. One of them, Ghazali al-Wahsh was from al-Mughar. In the house there was also an inner patio [*qa' al-dar*] and above it there was an open attic [*siddi*]. When you sat there, you felt as if you were sitting in the sky [*bil'alali*]. The entire village was jealous of the six brothers. I was married to the youngest who also happened to be the strongest among them. Our *mukhtar* was Mahmoud Hussein [the father of Abu Tal'at who was also *mukhtar* in Irbid, Jordan, until his recent death]. He had four wives, while Yusif al-Musa had six.[5] Lubya was the mother of all the land [*umm al-bilad*]. There was a struggle between the al-'Atwat and al-Shihabi families, but al-'Ajaini were the best because they were sensible.

Abu Tal'at, the Lubyan *mukhtar* in Irbid, however, gave a more realistic picture of kinship and social life in pre-1948 Lubya:

My marriage was the result of an exchange with the family of my sister's husband, Muhammad Ibrahim ... The big wedding celebration [*al-'urs*], in which all the village and other neighbours participated, lasted for a whole week. The village at that time was living in the shadow of a large dispute between its two biggest families, al-Shihabi and al-'Atwat. The al-Shihabi family was poor in comparison with the al-'Atwat, which had large property holdings and owned different small factories. I remember how this dispute started in the 1930s as a result of having forced a beautiful young girl from al-'Atwat to marry an old man from al-Shihabi tribe. The girl had refused the arrangement, especially because she had already fallen in love with Fayiz al-Fawaz. The couple eloped to Jordan and then settled in Tiberias. However, the girl's uncle, Hassan Taha, managed to locate their house and to avenge the family honour. He burned the house as well as the woman with it. The British [mandatory] Government later executed Hassan in Acre prison. This incident had already poisoned the social life of the village. This sort of incident happened as a result of people's ignorance at that time.

Harvest time

Romanticised memories of harvest time are designed to illustrate the kind of social solidarity that prevailed in the pre-1948 village. Those peasants who did not own land or other means of production also had the possibility of earning a decent living. People helped one another. The shepherd, barber, merchant, teacher, and imam of the mosque, as well as every other villager, were connected to one another either socially or by virtue of their shared interests. Usually the entire village – men, women and children – all participated in the harvest. Each had a role to play. Normally, the men were responsible for cutting the grain with scythes. Grain crops primarily consisted of barley and wheat. The women collected and transported the sheaves to the threshing floor.

> Sa'diyya Yunis, sixty-seven years old, now living in Copenhagen, still remembers the harvest days: We used to collect the cut grain in a place called *hilli*, a gathering place for sheaves. We made many *hillis* depending on the size of the field [*maris al-ard*]. Then a man from the family came with a camel and transported the sheaves to the threshing floor.
>
> In April we began picking by hand: beans, lentils … When it was dry we sent it to be threshed. Then in May as usual, we started reaping the wheat and barley.

During the interview her husband Yusif interrupted to add a well-remembered phrase, which used to announce the beginning of the harvest season: "On the 15th of May carry your scythe and start working."[6]

Normally one mule, cow or horse with a threshing sledge was used to thresh the grain. The type of animal used depended on the financial situation of the family. According to Yusif 'Issa:

> Children were mainly used to drive the animals. After we separated the grain from the straw with wooden pitchforks, we would put each in

different sacks. Our family used to produce about 15 to 20 *kail* (one *kail* is about 60 kilograms) and store what it needed in clay bins for the year. The rest we would sell. The extra straw we sold as animal fodder.

As a child Yusif 'Issa participated in the 1936–39 Arab Great Rebellion and was imprisoned by the British for three months until the outbreak of the Second World War. He visited Lubya in 1994 for the first time since leaving the village in 1948. There was not a piece of land or place that escaped his memory after forty-six years in exile. While I accompanied him on this first visit, and as he walked in the ruins of the village homes, Yusif started showing me the remains of the five wells in the area. He found four; then he started looking for the fifth. After digging a few centimetres with his fingers, he located the fifth well in Wadi al-'Ayn near his own household. I was astonished at the extraordinary power of his memory, his recall of the use of a piece of stone and an iron nail as a cover for the well. He commented: "Even after one hundred years, and however much they have done to the land, they will never succeed in erasing my memory of the land I lived in for twenty-eight years of my youth."

Yusif continued his story about the harvest time. The work day started early in the morning.

> First I would pray, then we would prepare the donkeys and horses and start our journey to the fields. It took us one hour or a little more to arrive at our plots of land [*mawarisna*]. Normally we would be five to six from our family. The few people who had no children hired a sharecropper [*muzari'*], who would be paid 5 *qirsh*[7] for his trouble. We started by harvesting the beans … After we completed the harvest, we gathered the sheaves, which took four days to accomplish, and then camels transported it to the threshing floor in Lubya. The families who did not have enough men to do the work used to hire boys to do the threshing. The boys would work from eleven until four and we would give each of them one *kail*, about 60 kilograms, for threshing the whole threshing floor [*baydar*]. It took about twenty days to finish the beans and lentils. Then we started collecting the wheat. All during the month of May we would harvest the wheat, and the work lasted well into August.

Every day and every month had its full agenda of work, from the early morning to the late evening, especially the summer days of harvest. On their departure from Lubya in 1948, residents of the village left everything in their villages, deprived of the benefits of their hard work. Overnight, village life was exchanged for life in a refugee camp, and the endless queue for basic necessities such as flour and oil, which the villagers had once provided for themselves as the product of their hard work. "There we were lords of our life; here in Denmark, we are no more than refugees, stateless refugees," lamented 'Issa.

At the end of September the olive season began and we normally did not have enough olive oil, so we bought what we needed from 'Eilabun and Rami. There were two oil mills in Lubya, one owned by Hassan Abu Dhais and the other by Qwateen. They used to halter a horse to the main stone, and it would circle around the stone. Normally the owners of the mill took one pitcher of oil for every twelve pitchers produced. Al-Sharkasi – his real name was Sa'id al-Shami and he originally hailed from Kafr Kama (his brother was an officer in the British border police) – owned a grain mill. For every *kail*, he took two or three *qirsh*, or a rub'iyyi (a pot used by villagers to weigh the grain), which is one quarter of the *saa'* [one *saa'* = 5kg].

The millstone can still be seen, though the mill was demolished in 1948. There were those who lived well and earned a good income, those in the middle, and those who were poor which meant that they had no land to plant and no permanent job. (There were only two families in Lubya who did not have land of their own. That was because they arrived late in Lubya after the land was distributed among its people.) Those people used to work on the land of others. Their salary was four *kail*, while their wives received 1½ *kail*. This meant that a couple could earn 5½ *kail*, or about 75 kilograms of flour. This was enough to cover the family's needs for the whole year. Many transient workers came with their camels from Joulis, Kafr Yassif and al-Bi'ni to work at transporting the sheaves. For every twelve *kails*[8] they transported, they would be given one. In the late thirties two *hamulas*, about twelve families from al-Asafra and Samallote in Lubya, bought a tractor and used it for their own benefit as well as rented it out at the usual rate, which was one *kail* for every 12.[9]

Sa'diyya 'Ali, Yusif's wife, refused to be photographed during her first trip to Lubya. She did not want to reveal herself to the others, especially among the ruins of Lubya and her childhood. Sa'diyya wept most of the time, and sometimes attacked us for convincing her to come back to see Lubya. "Why did you bring me here, to torture me by seeing the ruins of my house. To hell with all the Arab leaders who didn't move to help us". Only after she had seen the film on television, and when it was too late, Sa'diyya said: "Now I want to be interviewed."

Sa'diyya was unlike Umm al-'Abid – whom we will meet later when dealing with the internally displaced Lubyans in Israel – who was not afraid to be interviewed, speaking about the past without any hesitation. As with all the women in Lubya, Sa'diyya's narrative is more warm and more detailed when remembering the daily life of her youth. In winter, the people prepared for spring by sowing and planting. Sa'diyya Yunis remembered a proverb about the necessity of being ready to work in December: "He who does not work hard in December will be sorry when harvest time comes."[10] "Village women made braziers, which were the stoves of that time, from clay and water that would then be dried in the sun. They used a kind of soil called *hizria* to make jars, vessels and vats. I remember that when I was a child, we did not have a primus, or kerosene cooker. We used to cook and warm ourselves on the brazier for which we collected wood from the nearby villages of 'Eilabun and al-Mughar. The primus was used in Lubya only later, just before our expulsion in 1948."

Modes of social reconciliation

When one villager was killed by another from a different *hamula* or another village the accused was required to bow in front of an assembly of the victim's family and offer his neck as the price of reconciliation. Usually, the victim's family would grant mercy to the accused in front of all the people gathered to witness the reconciliation process. Sometimes, however, the enmity continued as illustrated in the following account by Tamam 'Ajaini. She describes how residents of the village of Sakhnin were not allowed to marry girls from Lubya even though they had not been involved directly in the following feud:

> One day two men from Sakhnin killed Hussein Hajjo near 'Eilabun. First his kin suspected that people from 'Eilabun did the killing, but later on everyone knew who the killer was. He arrived one day in Lubya holding a handkerchief, stood in front of 100 men and said: "Kill me if you will, I committed a mistake and ask for your mercy."

Reconciliation had then taken place. Later, however, a man from Sakhnin proposed to a girl, Khadra, from Lubya, but my [future] husband objected to the marriage saying that we will not give one of our daughters to the enemy. I must have been ten years old then. I was married when I was twelve but they didn't hold a party for me. I had three sons and two daughters in all. Two of my sons died early, one from snakebite and the other fell from the horse. I worked in the fields for many years. All my family is living together now as they did in Lubya.

Before I left Dayr Hanna, Umm Hassan insisted on giving me 2,000 shekels from her savings as a present for my daughters. To avoid upsetting her, I took the money and gave it to her son-in-law, to give back to her.

Mythologies of the past

Ramzia (living currently in Nazareth), the daughter of *mukhtar* Hassan Abu Dhais, was born in 1925. She is the mother of ten children, eight boys and two girls. When asked to recount what she remembers about pre-1948 Lubya, she chose to begin with the battle against 'Arab al-Subeih.

The battle against 'Arab al-Subeih (a Bedouin tribe well-known in the whole area), was mentioned by many of the elderly Lubyans I interviewed. The story, in which the tribe revenges the killing of the head of their *hamula*, is part of the mythology that Lubyans bestowed upon themselves as brave people. While the account is real, there is an exaggerated dimension to the story because al-Subeih was a powerful tribe and the source of fear among other villages. Abu Dhais, the man killed in the story, was Ramzia's grandfather. It is likely that she heard the story in her house while a young girl.

> The battle between Lubya and the Subeih took place long ago in the time of my grandfather during the Ottoman period. Apparently the al-Subeihs came to Lubya, ate, slept, and were accorded all the usual hospitality, but left the village stealthily at night after stealing a few cows from the *fellahin*. Accompanied by a small group of men including my father, my grandfather followed them. A well-known fighter from the al-Subeih, named Jalmud, and my grandfather were killed in the ensuing battle. Subsequently my father came back home, vowing to disperse the entire Subeih tribe, which is exactly what actually happened later on.

As most elderly Lubyans did, Ahmad, Ramzia's son recited the events that took place against the al-Subeih tribe during the Ottoman period. This story is part of the family heritage, especially since the man murdered by the al-Subeih tribe was his grandfather. He referred to an unconfirmed rumour that the Abu Dhais *hamula* descended from Druze leadership.[11]

It is worth adding my own family information to what has already been said concerning the battle with Subeih. My grandfather was fourteen years old when his father was killed. One year after the first battle with Subeih, the latter tried again to invade Lubya, but the Lubyans this time were ready for them. The Subeih had a brave fighter named Jalmud, and among the Lubyans was a man named Kayid who was so blind that he sometimes rode his horse in the wrong direction. After the battle, the Ottoman Turks put the rest of the Subeih leadership in prison. The son of Subeih, Nimr, came back a few years ago. There is also a very well-known story about a dispute that occurred between the inhabitants of Hittin and the Druze community living there.[12]

Abu Muhamamd Kilani (an internally displaced refugee living in al-Makr, near Acre)[13] is blind. But it was an amazing experience for me to accompany him on a visit in Lubya where he began telling me about his house, the cave beside the house, and his *hamula* members in Lubya. He talked as if he was still living in Lubya. About Lubya's fights with the Bedouin of Subeih, he recounted almost the same story I had heard from other Lubyans, but with more details).[14] Saleh Effendi (a title for a landowner) who owned 8,000 *dunums*, including the entire village of al-Makr village, had supported the Lubyans in their war against the Subeih, and he was buried in al-Makr. Now there are "internal refugees" from Lubya living in Tur'an,[15] al-Mashhad[16] and Kafr Kanna, as well as al-Makr.

Concerning *fellahin* disputes and the way they were dealt with, Zahra reflected on her earlier experiences by saying:

> This was the domain of men, my uncle personally used to solve disagreements that used to occur in the village from time to time. I still remember well when Fayiz al-Fawaz, the son of Shaykh al-Shihabi, eloped with a Sa'da, a woman from al-'Atwat. Her uncle had burned her and he was later executed by the British in Acre. I also heard that he was released after serving only six months in jail because his brother bribed the British police.

Memories of the *Nakba* and Internal Refuge

Subhiyya Muhsin Gouda is currently living in Dayr Hanna, Galilee. She is a hard-working woman who worked for all the past fifty years, side by side with her husband of twenty-four years, to help bring up a family of twelve children. Even after the death of her husband, she continued working every day, including holidays, to support her family. Her memory of the past is as fresh and clear as her active engagement today. She used to accompany us every time we visited Lubya. She accompanied the Danish team who were filming for the documentary *The Ancestors Land* in 1995.

Unlike some women of Lubya, Subhiyya has a strong character, is highly confident and unafraid of anything concerning memories of the *Nakba*, her personal life, or her attack on Mustafa Abu Dhais when he returned to Dayr Hanna and refused to sell them the plot of land that he had taken from the Israeli authorities as an exchange for his land in Lubya. In fact Subhiyya knew more than other, much older people about all the corners and alleyways of her neighbourhood (*hara*), where she lived until 1948. She was lucky to remain in Galilee because of an accidental and distant connection with a relative in Dayr Hanna. But life at that time was not easy. Here are a few memories of the harsh times following Lubya's occupation in 1948:

> I was born in 1942, but I still remember the day when we left Lubya. I was very hungry and when I asked a woman in Nimrin, a nearby village, to give me bread, she refused. We continued on our way to 'Eilabun where my mother baked for us loaves of bread on a piece of corroded metal. We arrived in Dayr Hanna and slept in a cottage, then moved to another village where we stayed for three years. We rented one room for seven people and when my brothers started working, we were able to build an additional room. I still remember how the water penetrated through the roof, and when it rained it sounded as if a herd of goats was running on the roof. I got married at seventeen and it was, and still is, our habit to marry from within the same family, not outside. I worked with my husband for twenty-four years, picking fruits, olives, and vegetables from our land and selling them. In spite of that, I managed to have nine daughters and three sons.

"The struggle of people against power is the struggle of memory against forgetting," Milan Kundera wrote. In my interviews with exiled

Lubyans I was surprised to discover how fresh memories of the *Nakba* memory still were among the old people, even after more than fifty years of exile. Lubya had been totally demolished by the Israelis, and planted over with trees (named as "South Africa Forest"), to cover the crime. One of the two Jewish kibbutzim built on its lands had been given the Hebrew name Lavi, a distortion of the Arabic word *Lubya*, as usual invoking the Old Testament, where "Lavi" occurs; the renaming was a decision made by an Israeli official committee. Yet after all the years my father and mother managed to find the remains of our house as well as five trees my father had planted during the Mandate period. Now the trees are high in the sky. After tasting the leaves from one tree, he carved his name on its trunk, but only his name and the date of his visit. Afterwards he said to the television reporter, "I wouldn't exchange a tent on the ruins of my house for all the palaces of the queen of Denmark." His remarks were published the next day in some major Danish newspapers.

In November 2003 I was a member of a Palestinian delegation which visited South Africa to study land issues and reconciliation processes affecting blacks and whites in that country. A year earlier, in September 2002, during the South Africa Earth Summit, a significant event took place in South Africa: the planting of a memorial tree in the name of my village of Lubya by the South African Water Affairs and Forestry Minister Ronnie Kasrils. The act of planting a memorial tree and commemorating Lubya by a South African minister – a former African National Congress (ANC) guerrilla fighter of the Jewish faith – was in itself highly symbolic in recognising the injustices of the Palestinian *Nakba*. The South African memorial reads:

> Lubya: dedicated by the honourable minister, Ronnie Kasrils (minister of water affairs and forestry), to the Palestinian village of Lubya upon whose ruins a forest was built where cows were permitted to graze but the displaced occupants are not allowed to return.[17]

One of the refugees from Lubya I interviewed was Khaled Sa'id, who visited Lubya after forty years in exile. Although he was eight years old when he left the village, nevertheless the memory of the *Nakba* was still fresh in his mind. He had this to say:

> You may ask how I discovered my family's home when I arrived in Lubya on the morning of the 5th August 1990. I left Lubya when I was

eight years old. I asked my companions to just take me to Bir Judi (Judi's well) and the flat big rock beside that well where I used to play marbles with my mates; and I asked them to leave me to discover my grandfather's house; which I found easily. If you ask me how I could remember I will say: there was something in me through all my life that persisted and insisted that I come back one day. It was a great dream.[18]

In addition to conducting extensive interviews with old, middle and young generations of exiled Lubyans, I also found it useful to carry out archival research in Israel, at institutions such as the Central Zionist Archives in Jerusalem, the Haganah museum in Tel Aviv, and the land registration offices in Nazareth. There I came across valuable documents on Lubya, in Hebrew, Arabic and English, including lists of names; statistics on the numbers of wells, olive trees, donkeys, camels; plans of the village; one British aerial photo of Lubya taken in 1945; a photograph of Lubya's club; names of Lubyans whose land was confiscated; and personal accounts of those who fought in battles in and around Lubya. The Israeli archival material provided detailed Israeli accounts of what took place in 1948 in Lubya, how the village was attacked by the Haganah and fierce resistance was put up by the villagers.

In Israel I also conducted interviews with two former Haganah officers who were involved in the occupation of Lubya in 1948. Their accounts show that in 1948 the Lubyans fought with only old and outdated weaponry[19] against a modern and well-equipped army supported by canons and armoured vehicles. In his assessment, the Jewish commander of the Haganah force at Lubya, Ya'acov Dror, recorded that the villagers themselves, with no support from the Arab Salvation Army, had initially succeeded in repulsing the first Jewish attack on the village. According to the Israeli military assessment of the battle of Lubya, the village was the first Arab community in Palestine to repulse the Jewish forces. Only at the third attempt, and only after the occupation of the nearby towns of Tiberias and Nazareth, was Lubya captured, and only after four consecutive days of shelling (18–21 July 1948). The official Israeli account of the fall of Lubya that appeared in *The History of the War of Independence* erroneously reads: "Lubya fell without fighting, and the road to Tiberias was open to us."[20]

I found other interesting documents in Palestinian libraries in Nablus and Jerusalem. All these were valuable for the construction of the history of Lubya before, during and after 1948. I later used the documentation collected in Palestine-Israel in an effort to stimulate discussion among refugees and gather more oral history from them. Subsequently an old man, named Karzoon, in the Yarmuk refugee camp in Syria made a drawing of the village with all the houses and the names of their owners. When I placed the 1945 aerial photo over his drawing, I found that his drawing was fairly accurate. Several old refugees from the same village who turned up at the meeting in Yarmuk also confirmed the drawing.

It is only through training that one can adequately master the recording and editing of interviews, and there is a desperate need to train Palestinians in the methods and methodology of oral history. The oral history project needs to be sponsored by an academic institution if substantial progress is to be made. Recording stories of the hundreds of villages destroyed in 1948 is only one angle of research to be pursued; there are many dimensions to the Palestinian *Nakba*.[21] Furthermore the success of the Dar al-Shajara project of Ghassan Shihabi, who is at Yarmuk refugee camp, is a good example of refugees from *fellahi* origins taking the initiative "from below" to record their own *Nakba* experiences and to contribute to books on the subject. Shihabi published a book about Tantura before Israeli student Teddy Katz carried out his study of the infamous massacre. However, because Shihabi's monograph was in Arabic, only a few knew about it, while Katz's study became widely publicised.[22] The Israeli "new historians" have done a great deal to reveal the ethnic cleansing policies during the 1948 *Nakba*. But the main task remains for the Palestinian themselves to take the initiative and produce their own memories of the *Nakba*.

Notes

1 Personal communication by Kana'na at a conference on "Palestinian Refugees in Europe: Challenges of Adaptation and Identity", St Antony's College, University of Oxford, 6 May 2000.

2 There are fewer than forty monographs on the destroyed villages (out of 531 villages). Salman Abu Sitta, *Sijil al Nakba 1948* (London: Palestinian Return Centre, 1998 [Arabic]). It is also worth mentioning the work of Ghassan Shihabi, who published many monographs on destroyed villages (published by Dar al-Shajara, Damascus).

3 For nearly forty years many academics cited the figure of 418 for the number of villages destroyed in or after 1948. In 1998 Salman Abu Sitta came up with the figure of 531 localities, including many localities and hamlets in Negev desert. Abu Sitta, *Sijil al Nakba 1948*.

4 *Al-Jana* (Beirut, Lebanon: Arab Resource Centre for Popular Arts, 2002).

5 Other researchers confirmed that Mahmoud Hussein married four women, but not at the same time.

6 *fi khamistash ayyar ihmil minjalak wa ghar.*

7 One *lira* = 100 *qirsh* (Palestinian piastre).

8 *Fellahi* measures of weight in Arabic are: one *saa'* = 5kg; one *kail* = 12 *saa'*, one *'ulba* = 6 *saa'* one *mid* = two *saa'*.

9 During the Mandate period one Palestinian *jinaih* = approx. one English pound; One *kail* was sold for 20 Palestinian qirsh (piastre).

10 *al-ajrad: illi ma bishid bilijrad, 'ind al-salayib bihrad.*

11 Professor Kais Firro, of Haifa University and a Druze specialist, had also heard of the same episode, but has not found concrete evidence to support these claims,

12 Abu Dhais made the Druze leader dismount from his horse from the right side and not from the left. This was considered an insult at that time.

13 Interviews with Abu Muhammad Kilani, Yusif Muhammad Ibrahim Yusif, on 19 October 1995, in Lubya.

14 The additional details he provided concerned the four men from Subeih who came to Abu Dhais farm. Those four, after spending the night in Lubya, followed farmers to the east side of the village, to Karim al-Shaykh Saleh, where they stole some cows. Abu Dhais and his cousin 'Abdel-Rahman Mutlak called after them to return the cows, but the Subeihs refused, and Abu Dhais shot and killed one of them. Abu Dhais himself was later killed in revenge.

15 Zahra 'Azzam and her sons, and Khadija al-Shaykh from Samallote who has a brother, Sa'id, in Sweden. Umm 'Ali, Rashida, from Tur'an, who married Yahya Shihabi in Damascus, visited her family two years ago and came to Abu Muhammad's house in al-Makr.

16 The interviewer contacted Hilala's son Hassan 'Issa in the Galilee village of Al-Mashhad and confirmed that his mother had been 105 years old when she had died two years earlier.

17 I would like to thank the following persons who helped with the interviews and the South African tour: Zakiya Fareed, who arranged all our interviews and the main engagements during the tour; the chairman of the Media Review Network (MRN), Iqbal Jassat, who was in charge of the whole tour; Dr Uri Davies, who presented the MRN, and Deputy Minister Aziz Pahad with "an Eyewitness Report: Visit to the South African Forest, Golani Junction, planted by the Jewish National Fund, the friends of JNF and the women's Zionist organisation of SA to cover up the Remains of the 1948 Destroyed Palestinian Arab Village of Lubya." The report was based on a manuscript I have written about Lubya's historiography. Both Iqbal and Davis complained to South African officials about the Israelis using the name of South Africa to cover up remains of the Palestinian village of Lubya.

18 An interview with Khalid Sa'id (born in 1940) on 12 November 1998 in Burj al-Barajneh refugee camp Beirut.

19 "There were between 100 and 120 men, including a small infantry detachment

from the Arab Salvation Army, armed with 100 rifles, two machine guns, two Bren guns, two mortars with only two shells, and between 70 to 100 rounds of ammunition for each rifle." This account is based on an interview with both Haj Sa'id al-'Abid and Fawzi Mahmoud Abu 'Alul, conducted by Nafez Nazzal, in 'Ayn al-Hilwi refugee camp, Lebanon, on 18 and 19 February 1973. See Nafez Nazzal, *The Palestinian Exodus from the Galilee, 1948* (Beirut: Institute for Palestine Studies, 1978), p.81.

20 Walid Khalidi (ed.), *All That Remains* (Washington DC: Institute for Palestine Studies, 1992), p.527.

21 This project on the destroyed village will be promoted with a planned museum exhibition that will display all the documents, the transcripts of 700 interviews, photographs, and a model of Lubya before its destruction in 1948. It is hoped that the planned exhibition will be displayed in various European cities, but will eventually be permanently based in Palestine.

22 Ilan Pappé, "The Tantura Case in Israel: The Katz Research and Trial", *Journal of Palestine Studies* 30 (no.3), 2001, pp.19-39; Ilan Pappé, "Historical Truth, Modern Historiography, and Ethical Obligations: The Challenge of the Tantura Case", *Holy Land Studies: A Multidisciplinary Journal* 3.2 (November 2004), pp.171–94.

8
Unrecognised Villages: Indigenous 'Ayn Hawd *versus* Artists' Colony 'Ein Hod

Jonathan Cook

First Encounter: Nir 'Etzion (July 2000)

An uncomfortable silence separated the two of us. In a small fish restaurant, one of Dalia's favourite haunts yards from the beach at 'Atlit, a few miles south of the northern Israeli city of Haifa, we had ventured on to the combustible topics of land ownership and military service. It was the summer of 2000, two months before the outbreak of the second uprising (al-Aqsa Intifada), in the dying days of the more optimistic Oslo era, and the air was sweating tension – even at this peaceful spot by the Mediterranean, far from the traditional confrontation lines between Israelis and Palestinians. Yasser 'Arafat, the Palestinian leader, was threatening to declare unilaterally a state in the West Bank and Gaza by mid-September should Israel refuse to be midwife to its birth.

I was on a solo press trip to the Jewish state – oblivious to the trouble brewing – arranged by a British travel agency. Although the itinerary was my own, the nightly resting places had been selected by the company. That was the reason I found myself seated opposite Dalia, the public relations officer for kibbutz Nir 'Etzion, one of a number of farming collectives that had fallen on the idea of opening hotels and tourist apartments as a way to revive their flagging fortunes from farming. The Orthodox kibbutz, Dalia proudly told me, was one of the most religiously observant in Israel, had its own private synagogue and a restaurant that had been awarded the highest kosher rating possible for its food.

Maybe Dalia was tired of Nir 'Etzion's purity standards, for she suggested that evening that the two of us try the fish restaurant a few miles away. In her early thirties, thin and pale, with a husband and three young children sharing her life on the kibbutz, Dalia seemed in confessional mood. The drive to the restaurant was heavy with thoughts she needed to unburden to a stranger. Later, over plates of denise fish, I listened as Dalia told me what she thought of Palestinians. It was a familiar rhetoric, today articulated by many Israelis but then given voice more rarely. She was convinced that the Palestinians wanted to take the kibbutz from her and her friends, that they would not stop at a Palestinian state and that given the chance they would drive all the Jews into the sea. "This is our homeland, we suffered as a people and it is our right to be here. I won't apologise to anyone for living here," she said. I hadn't asked for an apology.

Israelis, she added, had a duty to fight to protect what was theirs. Two months earlier, the Israeli prime minister, Ehud Barak, had withdrawn Israeli soldiers from south Lebanon, from what Israel liked to term its "security buffer zone", returning to the international border that separates the two countries. With the border only thirty miles or so to the north, Dalia did not approve. Her brother, she told me with a moist stare, had died as a soldier defending Israel from Hizbullah. The Shi'ite militia could not be trusted. And leaving Lebanon would be seen as weakness by the Palestinians. One day it would inspire them to try to take back Haifa and Jaffa, Israeli cities that were Palestinian before the war of 1948.

Then, lowering her voice, Dalia revealed her greatest, and most troubling, confidence. The problem was not just the Palestinians, she said, but "the Arabs". At first I wasn't sure what she meant. But as she continued it became clear she was referring not to the Arab leaders, or the neighbouring Arab publics. She was talking about a small community of Arab citizens, neighbours of hers, living somewhere on the wooded slopes of the Carmel mountain by the kibbutz. In the two days I spent at Nir 'Etzion I never saw these Arabs but Dalia mentioned them several times on different occasions. While escorting me around the dairy sheds, showing me the advanced milking system, she said that once the kibbutz had employed some of the Arabs to help on the farm but it did not trust them now. Later, while we strolled on the manicured lawn at the heart of the kibbutz, past the swimming pool and immaculate flowerbeds, she supplied the reason. Pointing down from our lofty location to the tangle of trees below, she said: "Two summers ago they started a fire to kill us, to drive us from here and into the sea. It took a long time to repair all the damage. Many of the houses at the edge of the wood were singed by the flames before the firefighters got the blaze under control. They wanted us dead." Who are "they", I asked. "The Arabs," she said impassively. "They live in the trees there."

I left Nir 'Etzion shortly afterwards, no clearer about who these faceless Arabs living "in the trees" were.

Paradoxically, in the fish restaurant Dalia had presented me with a chance to begin unravelling the mystery. At the end of her monologue, she paused and, possibly remembering it was rude not to seem interested in other people, asked me precisely what I was writing about for my travel article. I told her: I was interested in Arab sites of interest. Like what, she asked suspiciously. Like the holy city of Nazareth, I told her. Like the Crusader port of Acre. Like the Druze villages of the Carmel. Like the Syrian Golan Heights, occupied by Israel since 1967. The list did not impress her and silence descended.

Finally breaking it, I asked where she would recommend I visit instead. Her eyes lit up. Excitedly she told me of a wonderful Jewish artists' village, 'Ein Hod, at the entrance to the kibbutz, that I simply must visit. It is the only artists' village in Israel and one of the few in the world, she added. She loved to walk through it in the late afternoon, watching the shadows lengthen, admiring the sculptures that adorn its narrow lanes and public square. The next day she would take me there and we would walk together. It's built in a Turkish style, she added decisively.

Our date was never kept. I ran out of time and, with the more pressing need to visit my chosen Arab – rather than Jewish – tourist sites, I hurried off to my next destination.

Second Encounter: 'Ayn Hawd (April 2001)

In fact, Dalia had misled me. There are two 'Ein Hods next to Nir 'Etzion – or, depending on how you look at it, three. Dalia thought she knew of only one, her Jewish artists' colony, but much later I would realise that at some level she was aware of all three. The two of them she did not talk about – both Palestinian – had been consciously exorcised from her memory, as well as from the memory of her kibbutz and nation. She could refer to the other 'Ein Hods simply in metaphor, and then only because they haunted her like corpses she could not quite bury.

I came to reassess my encounter with Dalia after I began working in

Israel as a journalist nearly a year later. I was researching a newspaper article on the phenomenon of what are called in Israel the "unrecognised villages" and contacted the Association of Forty, a non-profit organisation that seeks to publicise their plight. These communities, a handful in the north, in the Galilee, and many more in the southern semi-desert area of the Negev, are home to a tenth of Israel's Arab population, some 100,000 Palestinian citizens. A substantial proportion of them, particularly in the Negev, are also internal refugees, communities forced from their historic lands during or after the 1948 war to make way for Jewish development.[1]

The unrecognised villages are the legacy of the Planning and Construction Law of 1965, which established for the first time a comprehensive system of planning authorities, dominated by Jewish officials, that were required to zone all land inside Israel, either for construction (residential and industrial use) or for non-development (agricultural or green belt use). As part of this system, the law also set up mechanisms to bring Israeli towns and villages under the control of a specific municipality.

These new planning bodies recognised only 123 Arab localities, effectively setting in stone where Palestinians could live inside Israel.[2] Overnight Arab communities that were not on the list became invisible to the planning authorities: they had no rights to land, housing or any service provided by state bodies. Instead, these unrecognised villages were classified as illegal, built on land where all construction was banned. They became visible again only when the state wanted to enforce punishment. Demolition teams were sent in to raze every concrete or stone structure in most of the villages, whether or not the families had been living there since before the creation of Israel or had title deeds to their homes. There was no recourse to appeal either. The law meant that no planning authorities existed for the unrecognised villagers so there was no one they could apply to for a building permit. After 1965 all building work in the unrecognised villages was by definition illegal, and demolition could be enforced without a court order.

Today the threat of demolition immediately hangs over every house, mosque, school, shed, road or playground as soon as it is built. Even alterations, repairs and renovations are illegal. As a result, most of the unrecognised villages look like slums: the inhabitants live in battered, rusting corrugated iron shacks or in weather-beaten tents, sometimes just yards from wealthy Jewish settlements that have full access to state services.[3] Any sign of improvements in the unrecognised villages, or the building of more permanent structures, risks provoking a visit from Israeli wrecking crews. At least 12,000 homes in the villages are currently under threat of destruction.

The criminalisation of large segments of the Palestinian minority reached its peak in 1986 with the publication of the report of the Markovitch committee into unlicenced building. Despite ostensibly seeking solutions to the problem, the Markovitch report calls for an iron-fist policy towards illegal building by Palestinian citizens, suggesting a range of punitive measures such as heavy fines, imprisonment and making lawbreakers pay for the demolition of their own homes.[4] The committee's recommendations, which were accepted by the government, were directed against "unlicensed" construction anywhere in the Arab sector but by implication the new measures were bound to fall most heavily on the unrecognised villages, where building legally was impossible.

The creation of the Association of Forty was in part a response to the Markovitch report. The organisation launched a vigorous publicity campaign which has slowly shunted the unrecognised villages out of the shadows, if not yet into the spotlight. An immediate consequence was what appeared to be a stunning success in the early 1990s, during the more image-conscious years of Yitzhak Rabin's premiership. The Association secured recognition for eight of the villages in northern Israel, although the ethnic cleansing of the Bedouin in the Negev region continued apace.

Victory in the Galilee has proved hollow, however. A decade on, recognition appears to have been a cynical ploy to remove the issue from the international agenda. In practice almost nothing has changed for the villagers. Israeli planning authorities continue to refuse to issue local master plans for any of the communities, meaning that all construction and infrastructure projects remain illegal. In true kafkaesque style, Israel has declared the villages legal but judged all the buildings inside them to be illegal.

I wanted to meet the chairman of the Association of Forty, Muhammad Abu al-Haija, in his unrecognised village, 'Ayn Hawd al-Jadida, the place where the organisation was launched. What had recognition, in 1992, meant in practice for his village? One of the Association's officials, Khaled, met me in Haifa to drive me the ten miles south. He said I would never locate the village by myself as it was not marked on any map and there were no road signs. "Israel agrees to recognise us as long as no one can find us," he quipped.

Only as we turned off the main road by 'Atlit and followed the sign for Nir 'Etzion, did I start to make connections. Close to the entrance I saw the path leading to the artists' village of 'Ein Hod that Dalia had wanted to show me. Finally the moment had arrived when I was to begin weaving together the different narratives of 1948 – one Jewish, one Palestinian – to understand how the stories of modern 'Ein Hod and modern 'Ayn Hawd were inextricably tied by the trauma of Israel's founding and by the ghost of a much older place, the original village of 'Ayn Hawd.

"Isn't 'Ein Hod where we are heading?" I asked Khaled as he drove past the artists' village on towards the kibbutz. The names 'Ayn Hawd and 'Ein Hod sound almost identical to an ear untrained in Semitic languages. In Arabic the words mean "Spring of the Trough" and in Hebrew "Spring of Glory".[5] It must have been a happy coincidence for the Jewish artists who took over the deserted 'Ayn Hawd five years after the war, in 1953, to discover that usurping the village's original name would prove as easy as cleansing it of its 900-year Arab history. The story of 'Ayn Hawd's loss is addressed senstively and in great detail in Susan Slyomovics's award-winning book *The Object of Memory: Arab and Jew Narrate the Palestinian Village*. That book also examines the Palestinian collective and individual memory of the *Nakba* using ethnography, architecture, memory books, and other artifacts of memory.

In 1948 'Ayn Hawd was inhabited by seven hundred members of the Abu al-Haija clan, Muslims who had come to this part of what is now northern Israel in the twelfth century. Emir Hussam al-Din Abu al-Haija, the commander of Kurdish forces loyal to Salah al-Din (Saladin), withstood a three-year siege of nearby Acre before the port fell to the Crusaders in 1192. When the emir returned to Iraq, several members of his clan were rewarded with farming lands in the Carmel region and the Galilee, one tract becoming a village known as 'Ayn Hawd.[6] The farmers were given approximately 12,000 *dunums* (3,000 acres), much of it pastureland on which they grazed cattle, sheep and goats, and grew cereal crops and sesame, as well as harvesting the plentiful olive, carob and fruit trees.

Accounts differ as to when 'Ayn Hawd fell to the advancing Israeli army. Some say in May 1948, others July. It appears that the villagers put up some resistance as divisions of Golani, Carmeli and Alexandroni Brigades launched their assaults from Haifa. According to Walid Khalidi, 'Ayn Hawd only fell when the Israeli navy joined the assault, bombarding the village from the sea.[7] In typical fashion, the Israeli army occupied the village, sealing it off as "a closed military zone". Most of the villagers fled to the banks of the River Jordan, mainly to Irbid in what is today Jordan or to Jenin in what is now the occupied Palestinian territory of the West Bank, to sit out the war. One family, however, refused to leave. Less than a mile from his original home, Muhammad Mahmoud Abu al-Haija (known as "Abu Hilmi") set up an encampment close to the traditional winter shelters used for the cattle and sheep.

Doubtless all the village refugees expected soon to hear the news that they were being allowed back, but only Abu Hilmi was able to keep a watch from afar on the fate of their 85 village homes. The chance to return never came for either the far-flung refugees or Abu Hilmi's family. Instead the army only released its vice-like grip in 1949 to allow the Moshav Movement, which had been offered the village as a farming collective, to send a group of newly arrived immigrants from Tunisia and Algeria. They did not last long. According to one of Abu Hilmi's descendants: "They believe all sorts of superstitions and they used to say that at night they could see eyes watching them from the hills, or that rocks fell on them from the sky, or all sorts of ghosts, or that the earth was crying out to them, or that they could see the village people returning to take back their houses."[8]

The village was briefly inhabited again by Jewish refugees from the 'Etzion bloc of settlements in the Hebron Hills, which along with the rest of the West Bank had been taken by Jordan in the 1948 war. But 'Ein Hod was only a temporary shelter for these Jews while they built their new homes a short distance away. They called their new settlement Nir 'Etzion. The authorities soon gave control of a vast tract of land around the kibbutz to the members of Nir 'Etzion, which today farms much of the pastureland once grazed by the Abu al-Haija clan.

Again empty, the village was due for demolition by the army when the Romanian painter Marcel Janco began lobbying to turn the "aesthetic gem" into an artists' colony, a campaign similar to one he had earlier waged to save Old Jaffa. In 1953 he was given permission, and dozens of Jewish artists poured into the village, converting the stone houses into art galleries, studios and their new homes. All this took place under the eyes of Abu Hilmi's family who, resigned to the loss of their lands to Nir 'Etzion and their homes to the artists, began rebuilding their village. They called it 'Ayn Hawd al-Jadida (the new 'Ayn Hawd).

Today the huddle of thirty-five buildings that comprises 'Ayn Hawd, home to about two hundred residents, can just be glimpsed among the trees from the artists' village of 'Ein Hod. But despite the proximity, and their common ancestry, they are a universe apart. Both 'Ein Hod and 'Ayn Hawd lie close to the main No. 4 road running south from Haifa, but only the Jewish village is connected by an access road. There is one way to reach 'Ayn Hawd and that is via a road that passes through Nir 'Etzion. The road through Dalia's kibbutz may have been built on land stolen from the Abu al-Haija clan, but nowadays the Jewish kibbutzniks appear to feel little obligation towards their unrecognised neighbours. Whenever the mood takes Nir 'Etzion, it seals off access to and from the village with a large electronic metal gate of the kind that can be seen guarding entry to kibbutzim around the country. The mood always takes the strictly observant inhabitants of Nir 'Etzion on Friday afternoons when they lock the gate to mark the beginning of *shabat* (the holy day that serves as the Jewish weekend), opening it again on Saturday night. Effectively, the villagers of 'Ayn Hawd have to live with a weekly 24-hour curfew, imposed by Nir 'Etzion.

But that is the least of their troubles. The road through Nir 'Etzion is metalled until it reaches the back of the cowsheds, where it becomes a dirt track. Through a gate and the route's only destination is 'Ayn Hawd. The deterioration is dramatic. Potholed would be too kind a description: the deeply cratered path winds along the top of the ridge in the Carmel national park, above the woods, before plunging down into a clearing where the huddle of 'Ayn Hawd's houses is to be found. After winter rains the track becomes treacherous, with the danger of mudslides. The grossly circuitous route, maybe two miles long, takes something in the order of twenty minutes to complete. The villagers are forbidden to improve the track themselves: they would contravene the Planning Law and the new road would be torn up.

Muhammad Abu al-Haija, the grandson of Abu Hilmi, greets us by the mosque at the entrance to the village. To anyone familiar with unrecognised villages, 'Ayn Hawd al-Jadida makes a mildly pleasant change. Some of the buildings are made of concrete or stone, exactly as they were originally constructed in the 1950s before the advent of the

Planning Law. There are few of the makeshift tin huts and tents that can be seen all over the Negev, where a paramilitary police force known as the Green Patrol strictly enforces demolition of any permanent structures. The reason is that 'Ayn Hawd has benefited from an unusual combination of factors which have privileged it over other unrecognised villages.

First, its residents are not just victims of the Planning Law that created the unrecognised villages. Like thousands of other internal refugees, they are also struggling against the dispossession of their original homes under the Absentee Property Law. Israel appears to have been wary of too visibly compounding the injustice of the villagers' classification as "present absentees", and the consequent loss of their right to their historic lands, by enforcing the wholesale demolition of the new village. Second, the proximity of 'Ein Hod, the artists' colony, has offered an unintentional protection to 'Ayn Hawd. Israel has no interest in highlighting the war crime of 1948 – ethnic cleansing – by repeating it again now, in a more media-saturated era. Third, the residents of 'Ayn Hawd, unusually, are Palestinian Muslims. Other major unrecognised villages are Bedouin, communities which are the most marginalised and weakest in Israel. The Abu al-Haija clan has therefore been able to use its, admittedly limited, political clout, both inside Israel and outside, more effectively to win publicity and support.[9]

But make no mistake: Israel has been quietly persecuting Ayn Hawd's inhabitants as systematically as it has the Bedouin.

During the guided tour by Abu al-Haija I hear a familiar story: none of the houses is connected to the water and sewerage system, electricity must be self-generated and rationed to certain parts of the day, there are no telephone lines. In the early years the villagers relied on their spring, renowned for its healing qualities, but the Jewish National Fund soon blocked it up. Eventually, after years of drinking rainwater and sewage water from the kibbutz, the villagers persuaded Nir 'Etzion to pipe in water, at inflated prices. The supply, however, can be shut off at any time and for no reason, as it has been on many occasions in the past, says Abu al-Haija. The arrival of cellphones has at least eased the problem of modern communication. Still, the two hundred inhabitants must travel huge distances to receive either health care or schooling beyond primary level. At least two inhabitants have died while ambulances tried to negotiate the potholed track.[10] It goes without saying that all the houses are under threat of demolition, although in 'Ayn Hawd's case the threats have not been carried out. The villagers even lack a postal address, Abu al-Haija tells me, with their Israeli identity cards assigning them to the Jewish kibbutz rather than admit their true provenance.

The state has not been shy about delivering other, coded messages to the villagers reminding them that they are not welcome on their historic lands. As Abu al-Haija observes, the state has concurrently zoned the land on which 'Ayn Hawd stands for agricultural, forestry and military use. The only status it has not been given is residential, which would finally make the homes legal.

The military has had unrestricted access to the lands around 'Ayn Hawd al-Jadida since they occupied the older village in 1948. On regular occasions, soldiers have used the area around the new village as a firing range. The most recent incident occurred in January 2001 when the army erected signs on the only track by which the village can be reached warning that the area was a closed military zone. At the time, several villagers complained that their homes had been hit by bullets. They also said soldiers were using heavy artillery nearby that was frightening the children.[11]

But the most traumatic moment arrived for the new village in 1964 when the Jewish National Fund chopped down the Abu al-Haija clan's fruit trees and tore up the pastures that for hundreds of years its animals had grazed on. In their place were planted thousands of pines and cypresses to create a national forest. At the same time Israeli officials arrived to tightly fence in the villagers and their fifteen homes with barbed wire – and to fence off their historic lands. Today 'Ayn Hawd has access to only 19 of its original 12,000 *dunums*.[12] Animals straying outside the cordon were confiscated on the grounds that they posed a threat to the young trees that were planted up to the very boundaries of the village.

The story of Israel's forestation programmes is of more than historic interest. The cypress and pine are visible all over the Galilee, shaping the local topography and its Jewish citizens' understanding of the country's past. According to the Israeli government, some 200 million pines were planted across the country in its first few decades. The objective, according to official accounts, was to provide wood for the country.[13] Other, less material, goals may have motivated Israel's early planners too. One theory is that the trees were planted to make the landscape of Israel more familiar to the east European Jews who arrived after 1948. Subliminally, by filling in what appeared to be empty space, they also doubtless reinforced to the newcomers the Zionist myth of a "land without people for a people without land".[14] But the pines offered another advantage: their fast-growing habits meant they could quickly produce a canopy of year-round greenery to conceal the remains of hundreds of Palestinian villages the army destroyed during and after the war.

In 'Ayn Hawd al-Jadida's case, however, the forest served a different purpose: to bury the living, breathing body of a Palestinian village, rather the inert, diminished remains of one, under the weight of vegetation. This was how the trees were viewed by the families of 'Ayn Hawd al-Jadida, as the wooden bars of a monstrous cage which not only imprisoned them but deprived them of any livelihood should they ever break free. The pines both barred access to 'Ayn Hawd's farmland and stripped it irreversibly of its value to the inhabitants, by turning it into Judaised non-farmland.

In more recent times, the forest has contributed to a further souring of relations between the Palestinians of 'Ayn Hawd and the Jewish residents of Nir 'Etzion and 'Ein Hod. In 1998 a fire swept the slopes of Mount Carmel licking at the homes of all three communities. The fire destroyed twelve artists' homes, provoking anguished comments from residents such as Ora Lahav-Chaaltiel. "Many people lost everything. For them, it means not just economic loss, or possessions, but their life's work. They have nothing left of their past, their careers. Nothing."[15] From other residents there were veiled accusations against their Arab neighbours, which were picked up and amplified by the Hebrew media. Few seemed to notice that the fire posed an even more serious threat to the homes of 'Ayn Hawd, from which it was harder to evacuate the inhabitants and which was closely surrounded on all sides by the trees. During the firefighting operation, the Arab residents were also deprived of any means to battle the flames, as the water supply from Nir 'Etzion was redirected to fight the blaze there.

A more likely reason for the outbreak of the blaze was posited at the end of a news report in the *Jerusalem Post*, which while claiming that the local pine tree was "suited to the topography and terrain of the Carmel" continued that it "was one of the main reasons for the spread of the fire. The tree is highly flammable."[16] No one stopped to ask a deeper question. Why had the mass planting of pines and cypresses been deemed suitable in the Carmel, as it had for much of the Galilee? And why had it been judged necessary to change the landscape of the Carmel, replacing centuries-old pastureland and olive and carob trees, with a thick forest of pines?

Third Encounter: 'Ein Hod (April 2003)

'Ein Hod, according to the village's official website, was saved from destruction by the Israeli army because of the vision of one man, the Romanian architect and painter Marcel Janco, who was one of the founders of Dadaism. He reinvented it as an artists' colony, a safe haven for Jewish art. Today 'Ein Hod hosts the world-renowned Sculpture Biennale, offers artist exchange programmes and stages regular exhibitions, plays, festivals and concerts. Since 1983 it has housed the Janco-Dada Museum, which has collected Janco's works. Among 'Ein Hod's ninety artists are several winners of the Israel Prize, the most prestigious cultural award given by the Jewish state. It is, in other words, an important international centre for art and a jewel in the crown of Israel's admittedly now beleaguered tourist industry.

Janco, like other Dadaists, rejected the conventions of bourgeois art, seeking authenticity through a return to more primitive and indigenous forms of expression, including the use of paradox and satire. He selected 'Ein Hod for its aesthetic qualities: its rustic charm, Arab primitivism and views of the Mediterranean. But he was also driven by a vision. He wanted to create a safe haven in which he and other artists could realise the idea of an intuitive and instinctual art and nurture each other. The need for such a community was framed in his mind in entirely Zionist terms. Just as the Jewish people needed a national homeland to realise their true potential, Jewish artists needed a protected space – inside that homeland – to be creative. He rejected requests from friends to join them in New York or Paris, later telling one interviewer: "I didn't want to be another wandering Jew. I wanted to settle in my own land, so I went to Israel. I brought here the ideas we started in Zurich and Romania. And I helped to build art in Israel."[17]

It is unclear what Janco knew of or thought about the Palestinian inhabitants who had been displaced so that he and his colleagues could stop wandering. It is reported that close to the end of his life he viewed the founding of 'Ein Hod as a historic mistake and something he regretted. But over the decades since its founding 'Ein Hod has thrived, becoming integral to Israel's view of itself as sensitive, aesthetic, demo-cratic, cultured. It is a self-image promoted today as relentlessly by its artist inhabitants as it is by the tourism board. On the official website no light is allowed to penetrate that might cast doubt on the provenance of the artists' village, or question its authenticity. It is packaged for consumers in a language that could as easily be selling a holiday in Tuscany.

> Ein Hod is characterized by the special setting of a village sitting on a hillside, surrounded by olive groves, with a view of the Mediterranean Sea where baroque sunsets end each day. Despite lack of funds and development resources, the village has managed to preserve its original, historic nature and the romantic and simple charm of Israel in its first years of independence. Very few places in Israel have managed to retain the authentic quality of the Mediterranean. One can still discern in the old structures the many textures and architectural forms of earlier occupants from the Christian Crusades to the Turkish Empire. The roads and byways, a mixture of ancient and modern, all add to a very special atmosphere.[18]

It feels almost mean-spirited to point out that the reason why so few places in Israel have retained "the authentic quality of the Mediter-ranean" is because almost all of them – more than 400 Palestinian villages – were destroyed by the Israeli army. Such self-deluding sentiments are clearly passed on to and shared by most of the tourists who visit 'Ein Hod. A couple identified as Aron and Judith Hirt-Manheimer describe their trip to 'Ein Hod in a 1997 article for the *Reform Judaism Magazine*. Under the title "Art Lovers' Paradise", they use the same bland, unques-tioning language: in this "storybook" village, we learn, "historic and modern stone homes are wrapped with cascading vines and surrounded by works of art" while "an 'old-country style' restaurant near the village entrance serves as a place for social gathering and merriment".[19]

The "Disneyfication" of 'Ein Hod and its Mediterranean charms sits uneasily with its inhabitants' claims to be innovative artists seeking inspiration from all that is authentic in their environment. It suggests that what is primitive and indigenous about the village has been avoided rather than confronted. Eyes have been averted for fear of what they might see. The celebration of 'Ein Hod's true heritage would more than likely be an unsettling experience for the artists.

This might explain why, when I strolled around 'Ein Hod's alleyways one day in the spring of 2003, I was struck less by the cascading vines and more by the furious frivolity of the art, a forced mood of jocularity that seemed to hide much more than it revealed. Dada may have been the inspiration but desperate distraction seemed to be the underlying theme. "Jewish art" littered every open space, perched on every ancient surface, as if to reclaim it from its Arab past. A series of postboxes lined the exterior wall of one old house close to the central square, with toy farmyard animals randomly placed inside the boxes in place of letters. Ancient stone milling wheels were propped up on their sides, as if vaguely discarded, next to human forms shaped out of bits of metal. Balustrades on balconies had been painted in crazy, vivid colours. The artists seemed to have plundered and distorted every last scrap of what remained of old 'Ayn Hawd to reinvent it. Even the building that was once the Dahir al-'Umar mosque had been converted into a restaurant-bar called the Bonanza (since renamed the Dona Rosa), with a sculpture of a naked woman in front of the patio. Apparently it is modelled on the Café Voltaire in Zurich, where the Dadaism movement was conceived.

It is intriguing to speculate on what effect such self-deception has had on the creative process. Most of the artists are reluctant to talk too intimately of their relationship with the former inhabitants of 'Ayn Hawd. It is not a question of ignorance: they know who the former inhabitants are, and how and where they live. Many of the Arab villagers have worked for 'Ein Hod, as gardeners and handymen. Some of them have been employed to reapply the skills they learnt when they originally built their stone houses to sympathetically restore or extend them for the new owners. So the Arabs of 'Ayn Hawd are not faceless to the Jewish artists of 'Ein Hod: they have simply been stripped of their significance, turned into figures like the metal matchstick sculptures – without substance or history.

One online review of an art exhibition in the summer of 1999 by 'Ein Hod artist Yuval Shaul seems to encapsulate the traumatic, unresolved relationship between the old and new 'Ein Hods. Raya Zommer, the village's museum director, tells us of Shaul's examination of moral issues in man's exploitation of animals. Working only with animal hides, Shaul hopes to show that the artist can treat more sympathetically and sensitively what is left of an animal – its skin – after its flesh and bones have been taken and exploited for the baser benefit of mankind. Zommer writes: "The artist's gentle handling of the cattle's hide is rather unlike man's rough handling of animals." But Zommer appears finally unconvinced, concluding that a darker purpose may lie behind Shaul's art: "Ultimately we are left with a question whether a work of art made of the skin of animals is not in itself an act of exploitation."[20]

Is it too much to see in Shaul's art and Zommer's analysis a more primitive and troubling Zionist debate, its principal participants both choosing to reinterpret it, in their different ways, in a less threatening form? Are the leftover animal skins not symbolically the stone structures that Israel discarded and wanted to destroy but which they as artists fought to save? Is the "rough handling" of the animals by ordinary men criticism of the Zionist mainstream – people like the kibbutzniks of Nir 'Etzion – who were allowed to steal the land and exploit it for their own commercial benefit? Conversely, is the "gentle handling" of the hides the artists' sympathetic attachment to the stone houses after the land had been consumed? And is the final observation not a rare moment of confession, when Zommer understands that as artists they are no less exploiters than their kibbutznik neighbours? The theft, whether of the land or homes, is no less a dispossession for the refugees of 'Ayn Hawd.

Maybe, instead, this is an exercise in Dada paradox. As possibly is the homepage of Zvi Garti, who offers an innocent photograph of himself, dressed in attire reminiscent of a comic French onion seller, with his young daughter Maya.[21] He reports that his acrylic paintings have been influenced by "the pristine nature that is characteristic of the rural setting" of 'Ein Hod. How does he square that "pristine nature" with the fact that the visitors to his studio park their cars on a tarmac surface covering the Muslim cemetery of 'Ayn Hawd? Or that the building now converted into the village's public toilets were once home to the family of Husayn Hasan Husayn? Or that the kindergarten his daughter once attended was the property of 'Uthman Khalil Ibrahim? Or that the grocery store rightfully belongs to Ibrahim Khalil 'Ali?[22]

The inhabitants of 'Ein Hod have persuaded themselves that the narrative of their predecessors must be supplanted and displaced by their own. There is only room for one set of memories in 'Ein Hod, as there is only room for one historical narrative in the rest of Israel. The cruellest evidence of this is to be found on the homepage of Gedalia Ben-Zvi, a 78-year-old Czech painter who was among the first wave of artists to join 'Ein Hod, taking as his home the property of 'Ata Najib and as his studio the home of Hikmat Sa'id.[23] Miraculously, Ben-Zvi writes in his short online biography, he escaped from a Polish concentration camp in 1945 and for weeks hid in the forests of northern Poland awaiting liberation by the Russian army.[24] His story has more than a faint echo of those long years spent in the woods of the Carmel mountains by Abu Hilmi and his family awaiting their village's liberation from the Israeli army. Ben Zvi's freedom, however, could only be bought at the price of Abu Hilmi's dispossession.

Reading the biographical accounts, throwaway remarks and philosophical views of 'Ein Hod's new residents reminded me of that evening in an 'Atlit fish restaurant. Like Dalia's confessions, the observations of the artists unwittingly suggest an enduring unease with their environment little different from those Algerian immigrants who in 1949 felt that eyes were watching them from the hills. Both the artists and kibbutzniks stand in a peculiarly discomfiting relationship to their Arab neighbours. Whereas the 1948 dispossession of the Palestinian people, the *Nakba*, was erased from view and memory for many Israelis – that after all was the point of the destruction of the villages and the later forestation programmes – the old and new Arab 'Ayn Hawds stand as enduring accusations. They make burying those memories much harder for the artists of 'Ein Hod and the kibbutzniks of Nir 'Etzion. The old dead village and the new living one stand as harsh reminders not only of what was done to the Abu al-Haija clan but of what befell the whole Palestinian people. The artists' desperate reinvention of their stolen homes, and the kibbutzniks' hostility towards their indigenous neighbours, are the story of Israel.

Perhaps the artists and kibbutzniks have convinced themselves that they can only put down roots, both spiritually and physically, when such ghosts are exorcised. This is their curse. For the "Arabs in the trees" do not look ready to leave.

Notes

1 Jonathan Cook, "Bedouin in the Negev face new transfer", *Middle East Report* online, 10 May 2003, at: http://www.merip.org/mero/mero051003.html
2 Association of Forty at: http://www.assoc40.org/
3 Jonathan Cook, "Unwanted Citizens", *Al-Ahram Weekly* online, 1-16 January 2002.
4 Association of Forty at: http://www.assoc40.org/

5   Susan Slyomovics, *The Object of Memory: Arab and Jew Narrate the Palestinian Village* (Philadelphia: University of Pennsylvania Press, 1998), p.66.

6   Meron Benvenisti, *Sacred Landscape: The Buried History of the Holy Land Since 1948* (Berkeley: University of California Press, 2000), p.194.

7   Walid Khalidi (ed.), *All That Remains: The Palestinian Villages Occupied and Depopulated by Israel in 1948* (Washington DC: Institute of Palestine Studies, 1992), p.150.

8   David Grossman, *Sleeping on a Wire: Conversations with Palestinians in Israel* (New York: Farrar, Straus and Giroux, 1993), p.86.

9   Slyomovics, *The Object of Memory*, p.118.

10   "Never Mind Now: An Interview with Mohammed Abu al-Haija", Ittijah website, undated, at: http://www.ittijah.org/inside/abuelheija.html

11   "Military Siege on Ein Hod - the Army Closes the Access Road to the village", Ittijah website, 11 January 2001 at:
   http://www.ittijah.org/press/pr_01_01_11.html

12   Susan Slyomovics, *The Object of Memory*, p.102.

13   Daniella Ashkenazy, "The Greening of Israel Takes a New Turn", December 1999, Israel Magazine on-web, at:
   http://www.mfa.gov.il/mfa/go.asp?MFAH0hv10

14   For further discussion of this myth see, Nur Masalha, *A Land Without a People* (London: Faber and Faber, 1997).

15   Sam Orbaum, "Ein Hod, blackly", 26 January 1999, at:
   http://www.samorbaum.com/places/Ein%20Hod.html.

16   David Rudge, "Fires rage for fourth day", *Jerusalem Post*, 14 October 1998.

17   Quoted in Susan Slyomovics, *The Object of Memory*, p.32.

18   "Ein Hod artists' village" at: http://www.ein-hod.israel.net/about/aboutus.htm

19   Aron and Judith Hirt-Manheimer, "Romancing Israel", *Reform Judaism Magazine*, undated at: http://www.uahc.org/rjmag/997ajhm.html. Aron Hirt-Manheimer was identified as editor of *Reform Judaism Magazine* and co-author with Rabbi Arthur Hertzberg of the book, *Jews: The Essence and Character of a People* (HarperCollins). Judith Hirt-Manheimer was identified as copyeditor of *Reform Judaism Magazine*.

20   Yuval Shaul homepage at: http://shaulyuval.com/text.htm

21   Zvi Garti homepage at:
   http://www.geocities.com/soho/canvas/7190/page16.htm

22   Slyomovics, *The Object of Memory*, pp.214-18.

23   Ibid.

24   Gdalia Ben Zvi homepage at: http://www.inter.net.il/~ben_zvi/

9
The *Nakba* in Hebrew: Israeli-Jewish Awareness of the Palestinian Catastrophe and Internal Refugees
Eitan Bronstein

Introduction: A Tour of Another Place

One Saturday, 20 September 2003, Shadiah Hijazi went to visit the remnants of her family's town, al-Majdal, today a part of the Jewish city of Ashkelon.[1]

Shadiah was born in Gaza as a Palestinian refugee. Her family had been forced out of al-Majdal in 1948. She married Bassam, from the mixed Jewish–Arab city of Lydda, Israel. Bassam's family had also been forced out of al-Majdal in 1950, but had ended up internally displaced within the boundaries of the state of Israel.[2]

Shadiah, Bassam and their family go to visit al-Majdal every year. They go to the cemetery, where their loved ones are buried. They have asked the city council of Ashkelon many times to take care of the old graveyard, but to no avail. They go and see the remnants of al-Majdal, have a picnic in the town and return home to Lydda. On previous visits the family never made contact with the Jewish residents of Ashkelon, and no Jew was a partner in the annual visits.

Shadiah did not think that the 20 September visit would be any different. She thought that, as always, this would be a trip of Palestinian families displaced from al-Majdal. But she was wrong. This time two buses came to visit: the first was of al-Majdal's refugees and their descendants; the passengers of the second bus were all Israeli Jews, who came to learn about the story of al-Majdal, support the displaced families and express solidarity with the Palestinian refugees. These Israeli Jews are members of an organisation called Zochrot whose aim is to make Israeli-Jewish society aware of the 1948 Palestinian catastrophe and to encourage *Nakba* remembrance among Israeli Jews. Zochrot organised and sponsored the tour, which was attended by some 150 people. Before that day, Shadiah had never heard of Zochrot.

Moshe Cohen lives in Ashkelon. His family immigrated to Israel from Iraq when he was three. Upon arrival, the family was given a house that had belonged to a Palestinian Arab family until 1948. Moshe lives in that house to this day. That Saturday, 20 September, when the Arab community of al-Majdal came to visit Ashkelon, Moshe was in this house, with his family. He knew nothing of the visit. But the rumour that Arabs had come to visit al-Majdal soon spread around the neighbourhood, and Moshe decided to go and see what was going on.

The unexpected encounter between Moshe Cohen and Shadiah Hijazi during a visit organised by Zochrot is the focus of this chapter. This encounter will be used as a metonym, helping us understand what goes on in interactions between Jews and internally displaced Palestinians in Israel, and also to examine Israeli-Jewish attitudes towards the Palestinian *Nakba*. The main objective of this chapter is to try to comprehend what exactly happened in the encounter between the refugees of al-Majdal and the current Jewish residents of Ashkelon that took place in September 2003. Its central argument is that the events organised by Zochrot created a "displacement", occurring at several levels, each of which will be interpreted below.

As a general point, I would argue that a person's identity is not something "fixed", but rather a cultural construction, always undergoing changes. During the tour of Ashkelon, and in the aftermath of the visit, there was some change in the so-called "fixed identity" of all those who took part and those who witnessed it. Every single person experienced some sort of "displacement", extraction, or even a sense of confusion regarding his or her initial political attitudes, and then an emplacement into a new identity or position, sometimes unexpected and surprising. The chapter will also examine the effects of Zochrot's activities on reconstructing the "space" in which Jews and Arabs operate, and also examine the modes of ideological hegemony which we all need to overcome.

The general Israeli-Jewish public is represented in this text by the people of Ashkelon. The Jewish groups that identify with the Palestinian refugees are represented by the Jewish participants of the tour and members of Zochrot. The internally displaced Palestinians inside Israel are represented by the people who once lived in the town of al-Majdal. It is obvious that in categorising the three groups we are minimising the actual complexity of the Palestinian refugee question. Nonetheless, viewing matters from this perspective might shed new light on the processes and challenges that these three groups face, and how these processes and challenges are affected by the activities of Zochrot.

On the theoretical level, this chapter will attempt to use the works of Henri Lefebvre[3] and Michel Foucault[4] in order to understand the spheres in which people operate. Both philosophers refused to accept the notion that reality is a vessel containing people and other objects; rather they perceived reality as the outcome of cultural developments and symbolic constructions. Human beings, according to their views, construct space and are themselves reconstructed by it. I shall examine how the space of Ashkelon is reconstructed through the actions of Zochrot. Exploring the remnants of al-Majdal brings to the surface a kind of spatial unconsciousness in the city of Ashkelon. I shall also attempt to explore this process by using terms developed by the psychoanalyst Jacques Lacan.

Present Absentees and *Nakba* Memorial Day

About a quarter of Israel's Palestinian citizens are internally displaced, also known as *"present absentees"*. They were forced out of their homes and prohibited from returning. Israel declared them *"absentees"*. From a legal point of view, these people are *"present"* as Israeli citizens but *"absent"* in regard to their lands and properties, which were confiscated along with the property of all Palestinian refugees, in accordance with the Absentees' Property Law of 1950. The internally displaced originate from eighty villages that were either taken over by Jewish settlers or completely destroyed.

Following the 1991 Madrid peace conference – at which issues concerning the Palestinian internal refugees were never brought up – local activists from the internally displaced felt that their agenda was pushed into a corner. The result was the foundation of the Association for the Defense of the Rights of the Internally Displaced in Israel.[5] This grassroots organisation campaigns for the return of the internally displaced to their homes, lands and villages. Its main mission is to place this issue on the Israeli public agenda. For the past seven years, the association has organised an annual March of Return, taking place on Israel's "Independence Day". A different village is chosen every year, and the march is organised and led by the association together with people who originated from the chosen village.

Nakba Memorial Day, furthermore, which is commemorated widely by Palestinians, also takes place on Israel's Independence Day. The official Palestinian *Nakba* Day was set for 15 May, the day that the State of Israel was declared. However, Israel's Independence Day is set according to the Hebrew calendar, and that date is when the country holds its celebrations. Interestingly, during the period of military rule (1948–1966), Israel's Independence Day was the only day of the year when Israeli Palestinians were allowed to leave their place of residence without permits. During this period the internally displaced took advantage of their one day of freedom to go and visit their abandoned and destroyed villages. Attorney Wakim Wakim, from the destroyed village of al-Bassa in western Galilee, and a leading member of the Association for the Defense of the Rights of the Internally Displaced, stated during the Return March of 2003: "*The day when Israel celebrates is the day when we mourn.*" [6]

Due to the close cooperation between the Association for the Defense of the Rights of the Internally Displaced in Israel and Zochrot, which began in 2002, hundreds of Israeli Jews began joining the Return March. Furthermore, for the first time a sermon in Hebrew was given by one of the Jewish women attending the event. Another Jewish woman, who spoke at the depopulated village of Umm al-Zinat during the seventh Return March of 2003, stated that she supported the Palestinian "right of return".

Expulsion of the Palestinians from their Own Homeland: Israeli-Jewish Attitudes Towards the *Nakba*

A combination of indifference and hostility characterises the general attitude of the Jewish public in Israel towards the 1948 Palestinian *Nakba*. Indifference, because the Jewish public is largely unaware of this issue. The *Nakba* is not taught in Israeli schools and is almost universally ignored by the Hebrew media. The hostility, on the other hand, surfaces every time someone – Palestinian or Jewish – attempts to put the issue on the public agenda. The roots of the hostility stem from Israeli-Jewish paranoia and the overall Israeli perception of the relations between the state of Israel and of the Palestinians living inside Israel as a zero-sum game.

It is true that the price for the zero-sum attainment of Israeli independence in 1948 was an almost total destruction of Palestinian society. More than 80 per cent of the Palestinians were driven out and over 75 per cent of their villages were either destroyed or taken over by Jewish settlers. Therefore the acknowledgement of the *Nakba* and Palestinian suffering, and of a sense of responsibility towards the refugees, appears in Jewish eyes to be turning over the wheel of history. Following the same logic, the Jewish perception is that the outcome of acknowledging the Palestinian *Nakba* would be an exile of the Jews from the land. This deeply rooted paranoia is also partly reflected in the widely used propagandistic phrase about "throwing the Jews into the sea".

The political and mental control of Zionism over Israeli society goes far beyond the legal measures of state confiscation of Palestinian land and property and their distribution almost exclusively among Jews. The "Judaisation of the landscape"[7] has also been carried out through the official changing of placenames from Arabic to Hebrew and the elimination of the physical remnants of Arab villages from the country's scenery. It is somewhat surprising, however, that across Israel there still remain remnants of the 1948 villages, reminders of the Arab life that existed prior to 1948. Yet only a few remains are actually identified by signs, displayed by those who had once lived there. The depopulated Palestinian Arab town of al-Majdal in the south is a good example of such a place. The area is called Migdal, and that name is written on the signposts. The name al-Majdal is a reminder of the biblical Migdal Gad. The remnants of the Arab town of al-Majdal, some of which are very impressive, are not signposted and there is no indication of the Arab origin of the town.

During our first visit to al-Majdal we met a Jewish woman who sells burgers in a luxurious Arab building. Although the arches along the front of the building are an example of classical Arab architecture, the woman working there knew nothing about Arab al-Majdal. This total ignorance is common amongst many Jews, who know nothing of the Palestinian history of the country, even in relation to places in which they work or live. This typical attitude of ignorance is also reflected by the fact that the presence of al-Majdal in today's city landscape is completely overlooked. A typical example of this Israeli attitude is found in the Museum of the History of Ashkelon, which was built inside what until 1948 used to be al-Majdal's largest mosque. It is only reasonable to assume that a history museum would tell the story of al-Majdal, especially since it is located in a building that was central to al-Majdal. Yet there is no mention of the mosque in the museum. In one of the exhibitions there is a great deal about "the liberation of Ashkelon".

In the light of Edward Said's seminal work on Orientalism,[8] this Israeli denial of the *Nakba* – and of al-Majdal – can best be described as typical "Israeli Orientalism": using the so-called "oriental" sites and scenery to give a place a feeling of aesthetics and authenticity, but without reference to the realities and lives of those Palestinians who had once lived in what became Israel and are now refugees scattered all over the world. The Israeli-Jewish domination of this space is symbolised by the keeping of the mosque of al-Majdal standing. This gives the impression that the place is ancient, deeply-rooted in the soil – even though the roots belong to people who no longer share this space; they simply remain faceless.

Zochrot

Zochrot was established in 2002 as a non-profit organisation. Its main goal is to promote awareness and knowledge of the Palestinian *Nakba* among the Jewish population of Israel. Its founders are Israeli Jews who believe that the Arab–Israeli conflict is prolonged by overlooking the Palestinian catastrophe of 1948. Jewish acknowledgment of this historical tragedy and the development of a sense of responsibility for Zionist "ethnic cleansing", massacres and property confiscation are essential for bringing about an end to the conflict and promoting true reconciliation between the two peoples. Zochrot operates in several ways. Its unique method of action is found in organising tours to Palestinian villages and towns that were destroyed during and after the 1948 war.

Both Jews and Arabs take part in the tours, during which clearly visible signs are posted to commemorate the sites and to provide the Israeli public with basic information on the *Nakba* and the history of the destroyed villages. The tours include the distribution of printed material by the former inhabitants of the Arab villages and members of their families and the unveiling of the often-masked remnants of the village. For the Palestinians involved, the tour is a journey in memory, to places they lived in or from where members of their families came. For the Jews who sympathise with them, the experience uncovers a kind of memory that was deliberately and systematically hidden from them. An alternative culture is thus created to the predominant, hegemonic collective memory that oppresses the Palestinians and suppresses their *Nakba*, and that suppresses the reality of historic Palestine and Palestinian life before 1948.

Another significant and indeed unique part of the tours organised by Zochrot is the simultaneous publication of a booklet – written in both Hebrew and Arabic – on the specific village chosen and the tour itself. Up until now four such booklets have been produced: on Dayr Yasin; 'Ayn al-Ghazal; al-Majdal and Isdud (in one booklet); and Shaykh Muwanis. In addition, a brochure has been compiled about the three villages of the Latrun area ('Imwas, Yalu and Bayt Nuba) that were destroyed in 1967. This publication was undertaken in collaboration with Neve Shalom/Wahat al-Salam, an Arab–Jewish village which was founded in the 1970s to promote coexistence and equality in Israel. The various booklets published by Zochrot also include interviews with former residents of the destroyed villages, pictures and academic and research material.[9]

The demand for these booklets is high. This is not because of any original research in history or geography, but because of the uniqueness of the mostly Jewish group that brings into the present the stories of the indigenous people and places from the past. The booklet on 'Ayn al-Ghazal and the tour of the destroyed village were accomplished in collaboration with an internal refugee from the village, 'Ali Hamude, who currently lives in the Arab village of Furaydis. Hamude has distributed hundreds of copies of the booklet, and a village school has used the booklet during class trips to 'Ayn al-Ghazal to educate the students about the history of the village.

Another key objective of Zochrot is to "Hebrewise the *Nakba*": that is, to create a space for it in the written, spoken and public discourse of Hebrew Israel. For this reason a Hebrew-language Internet site has been established, *www.nakbainhebrew.org*. The website documents all the Palestinian villages and towns that have been destroyed and/or resettled by Jews since 1948; it lists the names of the Jewish settlements and neighbourhoods that were built on these Arab lands. There is also additional information, in Hebrew, about the villages as well as detailed maps. The website also publishes reports on the activities of Zochrot, in words and pictures. The website is important in that it places the Palestinian *Nakba* in the virtual space of the Internet for Hebrew readers.

The establishment of Zochrot in 2002 can be placed in the context of two evolving processes taking place in recent years. The first relates to the fact that since the beginning of the 1990s the production of the memory of the *Nakba* has been given a greater emphasis within the public sphere of the Arab citizens in Israel. Until the early 1990s public and nationwide commemoration of the *Nakba* by the Israeli Palestinians was relatively weak. The memory of the 1948 catastrophe was primarily personal and communal, but largely confined to single villages or towns. However the internally displaced have been going on visits to their destroyed villages on *Nakba* Day for decades, and more visibly since the Land Day (*Yawm al-Ard* in Arabic; *Yom Haadama* in Hebrew) of 1976. With the growing activity around the *Nakba* and its annual commemoration since the early 1990s by Israeli Palestinians, more and more Israeli Jews have become exposed to the event. The second process that gave rise to the "*Nakba* in Hebrew" campaign was the aftermath of the October 2000 events – which took place against the background of the Al-Aqsa Intifada – in which thirteen unarmed Israeli-Palestinian demonstrators were killed by the Israeli security forces. Following these events there was growing understanding among some Jews in Israel that joint Arab–Jewish activities were not enough to win the struggle for peace and equality. There was a need for Jews to take responsibility for the Palestinian catastrophe and work towards changing the discourse within the Israeli-Jewish public.

The word "Zochrot" uses the Hebrew verb meaning "remember" in its feminine plural form. Why call the organisation Zochrot–*women who remember*? In the Hebrew language, it is customary to use a verb in its masculine form when referring to a group of people, even if that group consists of men and women. The name Zochrot, in the feminine, on the other hand, consciously articulates a fundamentally different approach towards the public sphere and towards collective memory. The hegemonic Zionist discourse conjures up images of a violent memory, invariably exclusive and masculine, and leaves no room for the (Palestinian) "other". Zochrot seeks to promote an alternative discourse on memory, one that strives towards true reconciliation and is openly inclusive and compassionate towards the Palestinian side. Zochrot also attempts to create a space for the memory of women in commemoration of the Palestinian *Nakba*, thus challenging the historical narrative monopolised by men.

When Shadiah Meets Moshe in Al-Majdal

On 20 September 2003 The bus carrying the internal refugees of al-Majdal stop at Ramle, where some of its passengers move to the second bus, containing mostly Jews who have come to hear the story of al-Majdal. At Ramle booklets are distributed, telling the story – in Hebrew and Arabic – of the town of al-Majdal and Isdud, a large Arab village that was destroyed in 1948, not far from where the Jewish city of Ashdod was built.

For Shadiah, this visit to al-Majdal is already different. A group of Israeli Jews who are organising the tour have brought people she has never met, and who have produced a booklet about the village her family once lived in. Naturally this is both surprising and pleasant. A group of outsiders (in this case Zochrot) is intervening with Shadiah's personal memory and with the collective memory of the internal refugees from al-Majdal. The outside group is trying to collect that memory of al-Majdal and then distribute it to Hebrew readers. If the Hebrew-speaking public chooses, this memory can also become a part of its heritage.

Upon arrival in al-Majdal, the group of about 150 participants walks towards the Museum of the History of Ashkelon, which is located in what was the great mosque of the Arab town. The group seeks to enter the closed plaza, right next to the museum. Every Saturday, the museum and plaza are open to the public, along with a restaurant operating in the place. But that Saturday, probably because of the group's visit, the entire place is closed. One of the participants has the entrance door slammed in his face, and he is told, "you lot should be sunk in the sea". Having been blocked, the participants move to the market, which is located behind the mosque but empty at the weekend. In the course of the visit two Palestinian men tell the story of the expulsion from al-Majdal. In line with prior arrangements made by Zochrot, two women who had lived in al-Majdal are given the stage, and they are followed by a woman from Lydda, who belongs to the second generation of the *Nakba*.

Meanwhile two television crews are recording the event. The gathering becomes very crowded and it is difficult to hear the speakers. However, the excitement in the air is palpable and there is a real desire to tell and hear the stories. After about half an hour the group moves on to a small square located on the street that today bears the name of (Theodor) "Herzl". In this square, in 1950, the remaining residents of al-

Majdal, all living by then in a ghetto surrounded by barbed wire, were gathered and driven out to the Gaza Strip. A small minority of them were expelled to Lydda, inside Israel. Some of the visiting families today are internal refugees living in Lydda.

In the course of the visit Zochrot, together with the people of al-Majdal, puts up a signpost onto a regular street sign. It reads: "*The square where the Arabs of al-Majdal were assembled, to be deported to Gaza, 1950.*" No speeches are given, no ceremony is taking place. But the audience is very moved by the action, and applauds. The event takes place in a shopping area, and on Saturday, *shabbat*, few local Jews are present. Those locals who turn up don't really understand at first what is going on and who these people are who are invading their space.

For Shadiah, however, it has become clear by this stage that this is a totally different kind of visit to al-Majdal. Even the signpost attests to a different kind of al-Majdal than the one she has experienced on previous visits. A small part of the story of her memory appears now to the public eye, in both Hebrew and in Arabic. A detailed story has also been told to the gathering. Suddenly, the story of her family and her own life is echoed, spread out, even recorded to be shown on television.

For a brief moment, this space, this street in Ashkelon, reverts back to being the place where Shadiah and her family once lived and from which they were expelled to Gaza and Lydda. This is not the al-Majdal that she has encountered on previous visits, the al-Majdal that was hidden from the eye, despite the remaining impressive Arab buildings. In the whole area there had been no mention of the Arab town. Now, as if it were a ghost, al-Majdal is revealed in the landscape of the town that became Jewish. The new sign that was posted is not intended to conceal or to replace the existing sign bearing the Hebrew street name. It is added onto it. It points to another layer of existence in this space, pointing also to another time in history. The new sign aims at being a reminder of the destruction of Palestinian life. Paradoxically, by doing so it also reiterates their defeat.

The group continues on Herzl Street to the corner of Eli Cohen Street, where more signs will be posted, bearing the past names of these streets: Market Street and Teacher Street, in Arabic Al-Suk and Al-Ustath. The new names are posted next to the existing street names, not over them. This is a kind of coexistence, or a sharing of life. The physical space of the city becomes a symbolic space where the existing power relations, of total Jewish dominance, are challenged. However, the local Jewish existence is not eliminated but a Palestinian existence is added alongside it. This hints at the possibility of a "return" of the al-Majdal exiles, which should not necessarily happen at the expense of Ashkelon's residents but beside them.

Shadiah stays behind the group for a short while. Moshe Cohen hears about the unexpected visit of Arabs and Jews in his town and rushes to the place. He sees the new signpost, and without thinking twice he immediately takes it down. The sign has been up for only ten minutes before it is removed.

Shadiah, who witnesses the act, walks towards Moshe and starts yelling at him and even pushing him. Her son, Salih, tries to make her stop, but she refuses to let go. "What are you doing? Why are you doing this?" She wrestles with Moshe and even makes a small rip in his shirt. She does not give up. The sign is thrown to the ground and she picks it up. "This bothers you?" she yells, pointing at the words on the sign. "My house was here, my father lived right here where the mosque is." "My house is also here," Moshe yells back, sounding insulted. He points to the house where he lives. The two curse and threaten each other.

"Space of Uprising": The Space is Disturbed, the Sign is Removed

The action initiated by Zochrot, of posting signs of another place, or of the same place at a different time, causes disorder in space. Disturbing the space raises questions of belonging and, in our case, a question regarding the name of the place. Shadiah Hijazi suddenly experiences this space as something which belongs to her, or at least something she belongs to. She now feels a sense of responsibility to guard and protect it. Moshe Cohen, on the other hand, feels like his space has been taken away from him. "I live here," he says, in the most clear and simple way. This situation brings to mind a book by Irit Rogoff called *Terra Infirma*, or Shaky Ground.[10] Rogoff introduces and problematises the question, "Where do I belong?" This is not a naïve question, for there is no ultimate and final belonging to a nation, ethnic group, gender or any other identity. The question brings us to notice the presence of politics in that space and action.[11]

The political action of Zochrot brings to the surface the question of identity and connection to this place called Ashkelon today and al-Majdal in 1948. The two are put in direct confrontation, which challenges the exclusive and predominant presence of Ashkelon in the landscape. The possibility of a space in conflict is not easy for the people present. Shadiah Hijazi and the other internal refugees from al-Majdal are surprised to see the memory of their town appear in reality, as if a phantom. This experience causes much excitement, and Shadiah wants to hang on to it and not let it fade away. She is probably aware that the action of Zochrot is mostly symbolic, a kind of protest, and yet she wants to cling on to it even for one brief moment. It is a sort of fantasy, hinting at "what could have happened if we were not forced out", or maybe "what could have happened if we all were to return to our homes".

In any event, once the sign is posted and the audience gives it legitimisation, Shadiah "forgets" the existing surroundings, "forgets" that this is present-day Ashkelon and is delighted to be once again in al-Majdal. She takes this political action seriously; not necessarily in terms of returning to this place tomorrow morning, but to say to herself and to those living here: I too belong to this place – and this sign that we have just put up proves that.

Moshe Cohen and the other Jews in the area are not indifferent to the signposting. Especially not when this symbolic act is carried out by a group of Arabs and their Jewish supporters. For Moshe, al-Majdal is a place that threatens Ashkelon, threatens "his" place. The feeling of threat can be understood through the Hebrew word "*shelet*", sign, which is similar to the Hebrew word "*shlita*", control. The sign makes a statement, and through it gains control over that space. In this case, the sign declares that this place is, or was, al-Majdal, and therefore places in question the connection of the Jews living here to this space. If the city that they live in was created through the destruction of al-Majdal, then the "return" of al-Majdal – however symbolic and temporary, even alongside Ashkelon – shakes the ground on which the residents of Ashkelon live.

Though this ground is symbolic, the sign gives an indication of the lives that had once been here and are now gone; it is very powerful, especially when it is publicly supported by a significant number of Jews and Arabs. In the words of Dr Sylvaine Bulle, the new sign "desecrates the borders of the ruling, legitimate, normative city and constructs new territorial borders".[12] The territory of the ruling city, Ashkelon, is perforated. Through the action of Zochrot, it changes and becomes a different territory. The names of the streets are no longer exclusively "Eli

Cohen" and "Herzl". Other names are added, written in Arabic, "*Al-Ustath*" and "*Al-Suk*". The presence of Arabic opens the Hebrew city's "closet", and lets the demons out. These are the spirits of some 10,000 men and women from al-Majdal who were forced to leave their town in 1948 and some 2,000 who were viciously locked away in a ghetto and eventually expelled in 1950.

The sign is a testimony to the deportation that took place here. It desecrates this territory by testifying to the unholy act of the "ancestors" of the local residents, the founders of the city. Through this act, a "space of uprising"[13] is created, in which the indigenous people who were expelled signify their protest. The signifying act writes a new language in the space. It does not fit the hegemonic language, that constructs that space, a language that got rid of anything that would remind us of al-Majdal.

Desecrating the border also undermines the time in the space. Posting alongside signs of present-day life, a sign that refers to past lives shakes the routine sense of linear time. This might seems surprising, since Jewish culture is characterised by placing the past and the present together. In the feast of Passover, every Jew is commanded to perceive himself or herself as if they too had just journeyed out of Egypt. When Israelis are killed by Palestinians, the killers are compared to the Nazis and are presented as their disciples.[14]

In the joint visit of Palestinians from al-Majdal and Jews from Zochrot time is challenged; the dominant, Zionist, Israeli-Jewish time is called into question. Into the exclusiveness of Zionism in the realm of history, into the glorious history of the establishment of the state in "*tashakh*" (the Jewish calendar year of 1948), the history of the 1948 *Nakba* enters. *Tashakh* and the 1948 *Nakba* are precisely the same time in history, but they represent two opposite concepts of that time. The abyss that lies between *tashakh* and the 1948 *Nakba* endangers all Jews living here – that is how many Jews feel. That is why they insist on getting rid of all signs addressing the 1948 *Nakba* and not *tashakh*. They are quick to remove the obstacle (sign) that creates an abyss they cannot face. At this point, the only way of closing this gap is by removing the sign.

The gap between *tashakh* and the 1948 *Nakba* is made visible through terms we use when relating to that period in time: the "War of Independence", on the one hand, and the *Nakba*, on the other hand. In historiographical writing, the writer chooses whether to use terms from one discourse or the other; the two are not mixed together. This is the case in Ashkelon, as well as in any other space that is under Israeli control. The time concept is *tashakh*; the monuments commemorate those who died in *tashakh*; the foundation of the state was in *tashakh*. 1948 signifies the desecration of the Zionist time. It is the sign of the Palestinian *Nakba*; the massacres and expulsions caused by the Zionist forces; Palestinian exile, loss of homeland and refugeedom. The time of 1948 was cast away from the dominant, ruling Israeli time. The action of Zochrot intends to bring back that time into the Israeli landscape, to put back the presence that was removed.

The time of the 1948 *Nakba* is marginalised, but it does not cease to exist. It is put outside of the Israeli time of *tashakh*, but its persistence, even from the margins, can realise Michel Foucault's assertion that "we live in the age of duality, when two times can exist one beside the other, when the close and the distant are besides each other, are with each other".[15] The action of Zochrot does not create something new. The footprints of the 1948 generation and Palestinian lives before the *Nakba* are still present in the time and space of 2004 Ashkelon, as elsewhere around the country. Zochrot takes those footprints and posts signs on them, reminding the observer of what existed in the past.

In Ashkelon, the remnants of the Palestinian Arab landscape are vividly visible to this day, and are used as shops, homes and offices for various Israeli institutions. Time does not "stand still" in them, perhaps the opposite can be said. The remnants of al-Majdal have been renovated and modernised. Sometimes it is difficult to spot the original Arabic building style. The remnants also do not appear as a graveyard of the Palestinian life that existed here until 1948. They are full of life, filled with people who came here from the four corners of the earth. Some of them speak foreign languages, and know nothing of the people who lived here till 1948.

The visit to al-Majdal, or today's Ashkelon, and the posting of geographical signs of al-Majdal force us to look into a hidden aspect of al-Majdal's time and space. The action of Zochrot brings back into view what was taken out, "what is seen is strengthened by the illusion of transparent space".[16] The visit brings back into space the time and the signs that existed in the past and even the actual people who lived here in the past, they and their descendents. These men and women, the internally displaced Palestinians, are part of the scenery. When they step off the bus and onto the parking lot in Ashkelon, the scenery is not the same any more, it is not (only) a Jewish space.

Those who were expelled return to the space, perhaps invade it. The refugees return to their place of birth. Their physical presence brings up the political question of "return" of the refugees. They force the observer to see something that does not go well with the regular, dominant scenery; a picture of conflict that is different from the dominant point of view, that point of view that "Judaises" space. The visit to al-Majdal is a moment of critical observation upon space, a moment when nothing is accepted as it is. It is not a tourists' visit, of people who used to live there and are returning for a visit; these people are interfering in this space in an effort to gain some control over it, even if that control is only on the surface for a short while. Their tool is using the signposts – they place new signs to tell the story of the past.

Al-Majdal's sign is a metaphor for the face of Palestinian life in the past, for lives that represent the *Other* for the people of Ashkelon, though they are defined by it. The sign posted by Zochrot represents the face of the *Other*, the Palestinian, in the heart of the Israeli-Jewish space. The face has substance, and it takes up space, but, it also has an ethical meaning. The philosopher Emmanuel Levinas once stated that the face of the *Other* who stands in front of us "intends to say: Thou shall not murder … The response and the responsibility are the authentic approach to the (face of the) other."[17]

Zochrot's act puts up the sign/face of the *Other*, of the Palestinian, and interacts with it, listens to its stories. The reaction, or response, to the Palestinian refugees and their collective and individual memories is what Zochrot strives to create through its activities. Moshe, a resident of Ashkelon, removes the sign, and thus symbolically "murders" the *Other*, the Palestinian. Shadiah's insistence that the sign should go back up is an expression of her demand that her face be recognised in this place, an expression of profound objection to the removal of her presence.

The truth is that all the signs that Zochrot posted together with internally displaced Palestinians in more than twelve destroyed villages were all taken down. The confrontation of Shadiah and Moshe was actually the first time that a direct encounter happened and that a struggle over the signs took place. The confrontation testifies to the possible outcomes an action of sign posting can have. The clash between those who wish to post the sign and those who wish to remove it is an inevitable result of the efforts made to gain control of space. Zochrot seeks to add to the space a reminder of what had been taken away, and the people who take down the signs seek to maintain the illusion of transparency, the purely Jewish-Israeli nature of the space.

The confrontation described above also shows how Zochrot's actions are a major challenge to the Jewish public. The challenge is to look at the Palestinian past in the country, straight in the eye, not in a condescending manner; to look at it by using signs (and booklets and an Internet website) which have a presence in space. Often, harsh responses from the Jewish public are reflected through hostile writing in the Hebrew newspapers or through e-mails sent to the Zochrot website. In al-Majdal, the confrontation happened in broad daylight, in front of cameras, in the city square – the square from which the al-Majdal community was deported in 1948. The drama between Shadiah and Moshe was not only a personal encounter. It contained years of Israeli-Jewish animosity towards the Palestinians. Zochrot insists on commemorating the *Nakba* and remembering Palestinian lives in this place. The Palestinians from al-Majdal demand to return and say: "Our lives here have not been wiped away from the face of history."

Removing the sign, which proclaims the existence of Palestinian life here, is also a way of relating to that past and its traces. When someone relates, in any form or way, to people who were here and are now gone, somehow, through this action, they are brought back. If I say, "she was here once and is no longer present", I unavoidably make her existence in this place present, at least as someone who was here and then driven out. Even a minimised saying, "she is not here", brings back the fact that she was here. For one brief moment at least, her memory, her smell, her words are brought back. When she – who was forced out – returns, even if she is only perceived as "the one who was expelled", this opens the possibility of perceiving her as "she who will return", or as "she, who may return, under certain circumstances".[18]

Thinking of her return, and of the significance that it might have on my surroundings and myself, depends to a large extent on how intense the representation of the 1948 expulsion is. Zochrot's main goal is to make Palestinian life prior to 1948 present, and it is using signposts to achieve that objective. When Israeli Jews remove those signs, they are also compelled to take notice of the lives that were once here. In most cases, they relate to them in a violent way, without any empathy.

However, there is always the potential that this may turn into a different experience, the kind that accepts the presence of the other. The practice of Zochrot also places in front of Israeli Jews the idea of the "return" of Palestinians as an actual possibility. It is actual even if only in the sense that this possibility of return should be eliminated. This elimination is exactly what places the Palestinian life here as an option that always exists.

A Surprising Twist in the Plot: The Return of the Sign

The dramatic encounter between Shadiah and Moshe does not come to an end with the removal of the sign; the story takes a surprising twist: Moshe is persuaded and helps Shadiah put the sign back where it was. The sign seems to belong to the place, even though it hung there for only a few minutes as a parasite on a pole carrying the legal street sign. It gained acknowledgement by the residents of al-Majdal who had never before posted a sign marking the place from where they were deported. Now, even a resident of Ashkelon acknowledges the appropriate place for the sign, even though this might be just for a short while, for the time of the tour. Moshe helps Shadiah put the sign back up. To a reporter recording this unexpected incident, he explains that he is helping her "so she would be satisfied". Following the re-posting of the signpost, Moshe brings a glass of water and urges Shadiah to drink. She said that, in her eyes, the glass of water was a sign of reconciliation, and she immediately responded to the hand that reached out to her.

It is difficult to know what made Moshe change his mind and be persuaded to put the sign back up. Perhaps it was the television camera that made him realise how bad his behaviour towards this woman, who is weaker then him, looks. We shall leave the question of the reason for this change open, and let psychologists or mystics try to answer it. But the meaning of this change, or shift, is valuable in understanding the practice of Zochrot and the encounters with Jews who are living on lands that belonged to Palestinians prior to their expulsion in 1948.

By returning the sign back to "its" place, in the presence of Arabs from al-Majdal and the television camera, there is some acknowledgement of the possibility of Palestinians returning to the places they once lived in. Even if the "right of return" is not accepted by Israelis, and even if Moshe strongly objects to it, his willingness to put back the sign, following the quarrel with Shadiah in the town square in a sense brings back to the square Palestinian life. Through the conflict with Shadiah, Moshe changes his position. From a proud Israeli Jew who wishes to reassert Zionist rule over this space, he changes into a compassionate man who helps a Palestinian woman to put back "her" sign, in "her" town, even though she was not born there. There is something odd about this short drama. In one moment, years of Zionist rule over space and efforts to "cleanse" the space of any hint of the possibility of return of Palestinians to their homes have crumbled. Moshe had a change of mind, and he puts the sign back up, just so that Shadiah would "be satisfied".

The sudden change in Moshe's behaviour and the strangeness of his actions testify to the possibility of change also in the larger scheme of things. Some may think that this is a naïve way of looking at things, on the writer's part, because Moshe did not "really" change his standpoint and he still objects to the "right of return". Reviving the memory of Palestinian life in the Israeli-Jewish space through the actions of Zochrot holds in it a potential of acknowledgement of the possibility that Palestinians might return to Palestine. At least, it holds the potential of acknowledging the "right of return" (even if not necessarily the actual act of returning). Even this seems today far-fetched. The large majority of Israeli Jews do not see this as an acceptable solution.

Maybe one day, removal of signposts by Jews will come to a surprising end, and a larger number of people will have a change of heart, like Moshe Cohen from Ashkelon. Maybe the Israeli-Jewish public will even be willing, like Moshe, to put up signs and bring back the memory of Palestinian lives, to look at them straight in the eye and even take some responsibility for their destruction. It is not possible for us to know what really caused Moshe to change his mind following his stubborn struggle with Shadiah. What is clear, however, is that his behaviour is surprising, because it is different from the common pattern of behaviour that the majority of Jews in the country would show in similar situations. His initial reaction – taking off the sign – seems "ordinary" in Israeli society, despite its bluntness. This is the "required Zionist reaction" towards an attempt to undermine the premisses and fundamentals of the Jewish state.

The change in Moshe's behaviour, the returning of the sign, compels us to ask what the significance is of this change for the different players in this arena: the internally displaced Palestinians in Israel, the Israeli Jews who object to the commemoration of Palestinian lives and those who support Zochrot's activities. In their visits to their destroyed villages, the internally displaced Palestinians do not publicly express towards Jews their claim to return or at least their claims for acknowledgement of their internal exile. They refrain from expressing this, probably because they are worried that such an expression might draw a harsh and even violent response from the Israeli police and the local Jewish community. The visits of the internally displaced were usually similar to the previous visits of Shadiah and her family: they toured the remnants of their town, had a picnic and returned to Lydda. This time, the visit was different. The Arabs of al-Majdal, through the initiative of Zochrot, put up signs in Hebrew and Arabic that attested to the Arab town that stood here till 1948. The internally displaced gave a message of presence in al-Majdal: We are here. They gave the message not only in Arabic but also in Hebrew, so that the Jews of Ashkelon would understand. This message can be interpreted in different ways. It is clear, though, that it includes at least one cry: Al-Majdal was here, and we, its refugees and descendants, are still here.

Posting up the sign creates much excitement for the people of al-Majdal, and they break out in applause. This time, the visit is not hidden from the eye. The visitors do not conceal their *majdalinian* identity, they empower it. They place it out in the open, for the Jewish public to see, in front of the eyes of the dominant majority in the space and the state. This is unexpected conduct on behalf of the Palestinian community in Israel, which is systematically discriminated against. It disturbs and upsets the existing power relations in the country. The Arabs are daring to act in front of the Israeli-Jewish public – in the same manner as they do when they demonstrate inside their villages – in front of those that are the masters of this land, in reality and in the eyes of both Jews and Arabs. The people of al-Majdal demand that their past existence in this place be acknowledged, and this is new for the residents of Ashkelon.

The internally displaced Palestinians are not alone in their demand. Alongside them stands a not-so-small group of Jews who identify with them and even lead the initiative of demanding that the Israeli-Jewish population recognise, or acknowledge, the Palestinian *Nakba*. Zochrot posts the signs of the destruction of Palestinian life in this country, both jointly with the internally displaced and also independently of them. In other words, the actions of Zochrot are not an example of Jewish–Arab coexistence. They are a plea for a recognition of the moral responsibility Israeli Jews have towards the Palestinians, upon the rubble of whose world the Jewish state was founded. For this reason, the practice of Zochrot does not depend upon the consent or the approval of the Arabs in Israel, even those internally displaced. Its is aimed at changing the dominant discourse amongst Israeli Jews, and not at displaying Jewish–Arab cooperation.

To some extent, Zochrot's action might even exclude Palestinian groups in Israel, because its main target is to change fundamentally the discourse in the "national Jewish camp". In reality and in practice, however, Zochrot's activities are largely dependent on cooperation with Palestinians who live in the country. The Palestinians possess the memory that Zochrot is trying to promote.

Zochrot's objectives – which include changing the status of Palestinians inside Israel, promoting the return of the Palestinian refugees and acknowledging their catastrophe – are all largely directed towards the Jewish public. Israeli Jews who put up a sign in partnership with Palestinian refugees are saying something new to the Jewish people of Ashkelon. The exclusive control over Ashkelon's space has been penetrated, it is now also al-Majdal's space, and those penetrating the space are not only Arabs but also Jews, who play a leading role in this event.

Moshe Cohen had changed his behaviour, and some remarks on this have been made earlier in this chapter. However, the burden that has been put on the shoulders of this one man from Ashkelon might be overstated, and presenting him as a kind of prototype for all Israeli Jews might be unfair. To "help" Moshe carry that burden, we shall give a few more examples of Israeli-Jewish reactions to activities run by Zochrot. As has been noted, all the signs that were posted up by Zochrot were taken down after a while. However, there have also been other responses. When Zochrot organised a tour of 'Ayn al-Ghazal, a village on the Carmel mountain whose inhabitants were forced to flee in 1948, a woman from the nearby Jewish town of 'Ein Ayala wrote back to say that when reading Zochrot's publicity she realised for the first time why her town was given its name. Though she had lived there most of her life, she was not aware that the name "*ayala*", Hebrew for female deer, is a translation of the Arabic word *ghazal*, and her town was called that after the Arab village which no longer exists. Despite this new finding, the woman from 'Ein Ayala did not attend the tour organised by Zochrot to 'Ayn al-Ghazal. She said, simply, that she was not yet ready.

In another example, Zochrot asked a Jewish man who lives in an Arab house in north Tel Aviv to put up a sign on his house saying that here once stood the Arab village of Shaykh Muwanis. The man agreed to this and also attended a talk at which the stories of life in Shaykh Muwanis were told. That event, taking place in Tel Aviv University, which also is partially built on lands belonging to Shaykh Muwanis, was also attended by other Jewish people who live in the area, on property that belonged to the people of the village, who also heard at the meeting the tale of Shaykh Muwanis.

Visiting the Real Areas of Ashkelon

Visiting al-Majdal, and especially putting up the signs that bring back into the picture the Palestinian past, raises the "subconsciousness" of space. According to Freud, the subconscious is full of demons and ghosts that the soul wishes to push away so as to avoid confrontation.[19] Lacan interprets Freud but rejects this construction of the soul and the distinction Freud makes between the inner and the outer parts of the soul. Instead of the subconscious, Lacan places the "real order", which erupts and disturbs the symbolic structure of language.[20] The "Judaised" space of al-Majdal-Ashkelon is articulated through the Hebrew language and the Zionist ideology. In al-Majdal, as in most places in which Palestinians lived up to 1948, there is hardly any indication of those lives. When something is indicated, it is placed as part of the Zionist narrative.[21] Zochrot upsets the symbolic order in the city by the posting of signs. In Moshe's words, "of course this [the sign] disturbs me, because I live here".

The sign goes against the spoken and written language of Ashkelon's space. However, it does not desecrate the space or penetrate it as something external but rather as something that "belongs" to this space and to its past. The previous Palestinian existence in the city floats in like a ghost from the past, which had been suppressed and now returns to the conscious and the spatial language of the city. Eli Cohen Street is all of a sudden also Al-Ustath Street. There is a gap in the symbolic order of the language, and this demands a quick closing of the gap – executed through the removal of the signs from their poles and the city's scenery.

The symbolic order is thus restored – but not entirely. Now there is a memory of the disturbance that was caused in the symbolic order. This memory is well documented on video, still photos, reports in the newspapers and in the bodies of those visiting Ashkelon as well as the residents of the city observing the tour. The police also took part in the efforts to minimise that gap in the disturbed symbolic order. Two policemen were called in and demanded that Zochrot take off the signs. The representatives of law and order thus aligned the state law, which it is up to them to enforce, with the "law" of the local language, which is enforced or maintained by many. Moshe from Ashkelon and the policemen are both part of the effort to restore the disturbed symbolic order. Zochrot is for Ashkelon what Morfias is for the hero in the movie *Matrix* (actor Keanu Reeves): they uncover the "real reality" of the destruction of al-Majdal/Chicago. When showing the destruction, Morfias blesses the hero, as Zochrot would perhaps say: "Welcome to the 'Desert of Real'."[22] The reality of life in Ashkelon is the life of those who were driven out of al-Majdal in 1948, and have missed their town ever since.

This real, this subconscious, space, is not the Subconscious of Ashkelon.[23] I do not claim that the city has one subconscious, embodied in al-Majdal and its refugees. The destruction of al-Majdal's remnants is also a kind of subconscious that exists in the city's landscape, and one day might resurface, destroying whatever is on the surface and reconstructing it. The "real" that Zochrot is exposing, the representation of the *Nakba* and of al-Majdal, is one possible interpretation of Ashkelon's space. The city has other possible interpretations. The practice of Zochrot, however, demands a moral say on the issue of the victim in that space. The face of al-Majdal, which Levinas demands be addressed, is the face of which Zochrot offers to be the addressee. This interpretation of space has an ethical dimension.

Would it be fair to say that Zochrot takes part in the operation to bring freedom to the indigenous, conquered, oppressed population? To some extent, yes. Through the actions of Zochrot, the internally displaced, who had their homes and lands destroyed and confiscated, are able to get some acknowledgement and recognition of their distress from an Israeli-Jewish crowd. This crowd even joins the Palestinians in their demand to return to their lands. But what Zochrot does also affirms the occupation, the deportation and the confiscation, which have been taking place since

1948. The representation of the victims and their sufferings portrays the displaced Palestinians once again as victims of the *Nakba*. This is perhaps why some internally displaced Palestinians are not interested in joining such activities. They wish to open a new page, to face the future and forget the past.

An even greater danger lies in the activities organised by Zochrot: yet another removal, once again, of the representation of the memory of the *Nakba*. This is what Moshe Cohen from Ashkelon did in the first part of the plot, and this is what was done many times by Israeli Jews after signs were posted in Palestinian villages and towns. The sign points to what once was – and to what was removed from the scene once again. Over and over again, the presence of the *Nakba* is uncovered by Zochrot and than covered again, removed from view. The act of remembering thus turns into an act of forgetting and silencing what is unpleasant to bear; this is done against the will of the agents of the act, it is beyond their control.

The routine repetitiveness of Zochrot's actions enables the creation of new, non-oppressive practices. There is always the potential that this time, when signs are posted and refugees return, they will be warmly greeted. There is no guarantee that this will happen, and for the moment it seems that there is practically no chance of this happening. In fact, in most cases the visit duplicates the pain caused by the deportation. The Palestinians experience a trauma that holds in it their collective memory of the *Nakba* with the ongoing discrimination against them as second-class and displaced citizens. The repetitiveness of these actions, their obsessive fixation, allows an alteration from the depressing pattern of denial and silencing. The repetitiveness creates opportunities for the forming of a new pattern; denial is not the determined pattern, and it can be changed. For example, when a sign is put back on the pole the fixed pattern is shaken. This is true even if the explanation for the change is just "so she [a specific Palestinian] would be happy". This experience is new; this Israeli Jew joins the posting of the sign "in its place". Returning the sign is a kind of change of heart, perhaps even conversion, which is made possible through the expression of the *Nakba's* trauma.[24]

In that context, the *Nakba* "belongs" to the Palestinians; but is also a trauma for Israeli Jews. It is not surprising that they find it hard to speak of the *Nakba* as well as to remember it. The repetitive action of putting up signs might bring greater parts of the Israeli-Jewish public – as it brought Moshe from Ashkelon – to put up geographical signs of the catastrophe of 1948 and to put up signs on the "mental map" of the (forgetful) Israeli collective.

Michel's Foucault's Heterotopian Space: New Relations Between Israeli Jews and Palestinian Arabs

Through the activity of Zochrot, the space is doubled and it becomes a "heterogeneous space".[25] Al-Majdal and Ashkelon appear in it in a way that does not allow one to be reduced to the other or the granting of superiority or exclusiveness to either of them. In the words of Foucault: "our lives span around a compound of relations which outline spaces that cannot be reduced to each other".[26] In the specific context of the political activity of Zochrot and the people of al-Majdal, there is a "preference" for al-Majdal since the people visiting are not interested in the city of Ashkelon. For the time of the tour, the presence of Ashkelon in that space is suspended. However, in the larger context of space and time, Ashkelon has a preference. Outside and around where the activity is taking place, Ashkelon remains peaceful. The presence of al-Majdal does not disrupt or doubt Ashkelon's existence, at least not on the surface of the existing power relations.

The action of Zochrot may have the advantage of a phenomenon that steps out from the margins and casts a different light upon space and time; like a sting that leaves a scar. That scar damages the well-kept complexion of the Hebrew city of Ashkelon. It hints at what once was in this very place, and what could have been here today. These possibilities, of "what the past was and what it could have been" are the continuing present of this city. They are leftovers, which cannot be removed, and will prevail there forever. Foucault calls this doubled space "*heterotopia*", a different space that "has the power to put in one place several opposing spaces, one confronting the other".[27] The space of Ashkelon is opposed to the space of al-Majdal, and this is reflected in a most accurate way through the encounter between Shadiah from al-Majdal and Moshe from Ashkelon. She cries out that her father was born here, and he cries back that he himself was born here. The sign posted by Zochrot bothers Moshe because, in his words, "I live here".

In this opposition, both Moshe and Shadiah appear in the space. There is a certain homogeneous quality that appears to exist in this space

– as long as Shadiah does not step in. The moment she enters into this space and revolts against her previous exclusion from it is the moment when the space is doubled. At that moment, an inner contradiction appears within it.

It is important to note that the double quality of that space exists all the time. The difference is that usually it is well hidden from the eye. The political action brings back what was taken out of that space; it does not create it. For example, the most apparent remnants of al-Majdal are part of the "authentic" museum of Ashkelon, where al-Majdal is not mentioned, as we have already learned. This does not mean, though, that al-Majdal does not "exist" there. This *heterotopia*, hybrid space, enables individuals from al-Majdal and Ashkelon to identify and construct that space as "theirs", even though it is not only theirs, is not only al-Majdal or Ashkelon. The *heterotopia* of the space where remnants of Palestinian existence remained after 1948 enabled the foundation of Israeli-Jewish existence, stemming out of the logic of an "ethnocratic" space, to use Oren Yiftachel's term. "The complete heterotopia begins when people are in a state of total separation from their traditional time."[28] The identity of individual Jews in Israel was constructed in accordance with the *ethnocratic* Zionist logic, that is, a total disconnection from the time prior to 1948. The museum in Ashkelon turns to ancient history, where there is supposedly no Arab existence. It makes a huge leap over the time period of al-Majdal, straight into the Israeli-Jewish time period. The result is a heterotopia combined with a "heterochronia"[29] (of different times), in which the Jew is separated from the time in which his space belongs.[30] By returning the sign, Moshe Cohen acknowledges the "traditional time" of the city in which he lives. His reconnection to the traditional time embodies the possibility of eliminating the ethnocratic logic of the city of Ashkelon.

The encounter that we have brought forward in this chapter describes this possibility in an ideal, maybe even romantic, way, because the story ends in a "*sulha*", reconciliation. He (Moshe) brings her (Shadiah) water; she sees in his hand that reaches out to her a plea for peace and resolution, in her own words. The heterotopic space is also the place of reconciliation, where different identities can have their unique articulation; where no one can claim to dismiss the other. The visit to al-Majdal, during which the internally displaced Palestinians re-marked their presence there, created also a new encounter for the Jews of Ashkelon.

Shadiah, who till then took no interest in Ashkelon's residents, was suddenly reconciled with Moshe. She now acknowledges his presence in this space and is not asking for his removal.

Shadiah demands that her presence will be a part of that place, which should be called – Al-Majdal? Ashkelon? Can it ever be al-Majdal again? Can one really "return" to al-Majdal? It seems that the answer is no. Nonetheless, the claim of return cannot be dismissed, the dream of Palestinian refugees of returning to their home. A "return" - such as that which took place in this event, where Jews and Arabs alike were given place in this space – seems perhaps imaginary today. But not impossible. What took place on the street in al-Majdal/Ashkelon in the encounter between Moshe and Shadiah can happen also on a larger scale, given the suitable political conditions. Abolishing the exclusivist, ethnic Zionist logic of space is a central political condition that will enable this process. The private reconciliation in the town square can become a legacy to the lives of all men and women living in the Middle East, in this space. A symbolic return and an actual return are essential for this to happen.

Notes

1 The author would like to thank Ronit Sela' for translating this chapter from Hebrew into English.

2 The town of al-Majdal suffered two expulsions. The first eviction took place during the 1948 war, when about 10,000 people were forced to flee. The second took place in 1950, when the remaining 2,000 residents, who had been confined to a ghetto, were deported, mostly to Gaza and some to Lydda. Benny Morris, *The Birth of the Palestinian Refugee Problem 1947–1949* (Tel Aviv: 'Am 'Oved, 1991 [in Hebrew]), pp.149-74.

3 Henri Lefebvre, *The Production of Space*, translated by Donald Nicholson-Smith (Oxford: Blackwell, 1991).

4 Michel Foucault, *Heterotopia* (translated into Hebrew by Ariela Azulay) (Tel Aviv: Resling, 2003 [Hebrew]).

5 Lecture by Muhammad Kayyal, The Association for the Defense of the Rights of the Internally Displaced in Israel, at:
http://www.nakbainhebrew.org/index.php?id=130 (accessed on 12 June 2004 [in Hebrew]).

6 It is important to note that not all of the internally displaced are active in the struggle to return to the destroyed villages. There is no exact data on this matter, but taking into account the actual number of people who participate in the marches and visit the destroyed villages, it seems that many internally displaced are not active members of this struggle.

7   See Oren Yiftachel's term at:
    http://www.geog.bgu.ac.il/members/yiftachel/new_papers_heb/alpayim-
    print.htm (accessed on 12 June 2004 [in Hebrew]).

8   Edward W. Said, *Orientalism: Western Conceptions of the Orient* (London: Penguin,
    2003).

9   The academic material includes articles published by historians Walid Khalidi
    and Benny Morris. See also Walid Khalidi (ed.), *All That Remains: The Palestinian
    Villages Occupied and Depopulated by Israel in 1948* (Washington DC: Institute for
    Palestine Studies, 1992).

10 Irit Rogoff, *Terra Infirma: Geography's Visual Culture* (London and New York:
    Routledge, 2000).

11 Rogoff, *Terra Infirma*, p.14.

12 Sylvaine Bulle: "Indiscipline et Insurrection en Architecture" ["Disobedience
    and Uprising in Architecture: Regarding the Appearances of Disorder and Dis-
    shape in Middle East Architecture", translated by Yael Bergstein, *Resling* 4, 1998,
    p.16 [Hebrew]. Bulle borrows the term "desecrating the borders" from Foucault,
    at: http://www.resling.co.il/articles/resling4/resling_bul-archit.doc (accessed
    on 12 June 2004 [in Hebrew]).

13 Bulle, "Indiscipline et Insurrection en Architecture".

14 See, for example, Idith Zartal, *Nation and Death: History, Memory, Politics* (Or
    Yehuda: Dvir, 2002 [Hebrew]).

15 Foucault, *Heterotopia*, p.10.

16 Rogoff, *Terra Infirma*, p.34.

17 Emmanuel Levinas, *Ethics and Infinity* (translated into Hebrew by Efraim Meir
    (Jerusalem: Magnes, Hebrew University, 1996 [Hebrew]), p.68.

18 Perhaps the most dramatic example for this is the passing away of a loved one.
    Knowing that someone is dead does not "free" the mind from thinking about
    how it could have been if he or she were here, beside me. This thought brings
    back the deceased and the memory of him or her.

19 Sigmund Freud, *Beyond the Pleasure Principle* (1920), pp.218-68 in The Essentials of
    Psycho-analysis: The Definitive Collection of Sigmund Freud's Writing, edited
    by Anna Freud (London: Penguin, Harmondsworth, 1991).

20 Jacques Lacan, *Écrits* (London: Routledge, 2001).

21 See, for example, a description of Ashkelon from the city's website. "New
    Ashkelon was established by *'olim* (new immigrants). Following the War of
    Independence, with the freeing of the city in November 1948, the first families
    arrived in the town of al-Majdal – new *'olim*, the remaining few from the refugee
    camps in Europe and refugees from the Arab countries who had just arrived in
    the country. They took hold of the abandoned houses, made roots, built a new
    town that in a short time developed into a large, thriving city." at:
    http://www.ashkelon.muni.il/MainMenu.asp?MenuId=145   (accessed   on   12
    June 2004).

22 Slavoj Žižek, *Welcome to the Desert of the Real* (translated into Hebrew by Rina
    Marks) (Tel Aviv: Resling, 2002 [in Hebrew]), p.23.

23 This notion of the subconscious is opposed to that of Freud, founder of

psychoanalysis, who related the subconscious to matters of sexuality alone.

24 Here, as well as in many other parts of this chapter, the argument is influenced by the work of Ariela Azulay, a researcher who is also my teacher at the deparment of Hermeneutics Studies, Bar Ilan University.

25 Foucault, *Heterotopia*, p.10.

26 Foucault, *Heterotopia*, p.10.

27 Foucault, *Heterotopia*, p.15.

28 Foucault, *Heterotopia*, p.16.

29 Foucault, *Heterotopia*, p.16.

30 It is interesting to think in this context of the double rejection, in Zionist ideology, of both time and space: (a) the rejection of the Jewish existence in the Diaspora ("*golah*") and (b) the rejection of the Palestinian Arab reality that existed prior to the founding of the Jewish state in 1948.

PART THREE
Human Rights and International Protection

10
The Real Road Map to Peace: International Dimensions of the Internal Refugee Question
Ilan Pappé

The United Nations took over the issue of Palestine from Britain in February 1947. Its proposals for the future of the land and the subsequent tragedy they generated are a well-known story and there is no need to repeat it here. The 1947 Partition Plan proposed by the UN, the 1948 war, the uprooting of the indigenous inhabitants of Palestine and the creation of Israel are all issues with which historians have dealt extensively. What has been neglected in the historiography of 1948, however, is the issue of the UN's responsibility and accountability regarding the future of the people of Palestine and their fate in view of the international organisation's involvement and subsequent policies.

In its Resolution 181 of 29 November 1947, the UN not only charted the proposed map for a post-mandatory Palestine, but also determined the international body's own responsibility for the fate of the Palestinians. The UN pledged to protect the rights, the well-being and the property of the local population. The expulsion and uprooting of many of the indigenous people in 1948 and the consequent Israeli takeover of their land and property demonstrated that the UN failed miserably to keep its pledges and to shoulder its responsibility.[1]

The UN in a way recognised its own failure in UN Resolution 194. Approved in December 1948, a year after the dismal failure of the Partition Plan, the new resolution attempted to rectify the catastrophe brought about by the 1947 UN peace plan. Resolution 194 affirmed unequivocally the fundamental right of the uprooted people to return to their homes, villages and towns. But this was not implemented for two main reasons. The first was Israel's anti-repatriation policy which had begun in earnest in August 1948 when the evicted Arab villages and neighbourhoods were largely demolished in order to create a new physical reality designed to make repatriation impractical. Although Israeli policies did not deter the UN from reiterating its repatriation demands in the years to come – by reaffirming Resolution 194 – they did weaken the international organisation's willingness to confront Israel. More significant, however, was the second reason: the waning of American support for the principle of refugee repatriation. The US government at first supported the right of return but, by the spring of 1949, greater interest in other parts of the world loosened the American pressure on Israel to repatriate refugees.[2] In that year, the refugee camps as we know them were built, replacing the tent camps in which about three-quarters of a million refugees lived.

So the UN failed twice to keep its promises to the Palestinian population, and its subsequent efforts have been neither impressive nor significant. However there is still a theoretical hope for a deeper UN involvement on behalf of the refugees and their right of return. The international organisation still has a committee named "the committee for the inalienable rights of the Palestinian refugees", supposedly the body that would supervise the implementation of Resolution 194. Nothing has happened as yet, since the UN currently is a junior, almost insignificant, player in peace-making in Israel and Palestine.

Those who were and still are in charge of the "peace process" excluded the refugees from the peace agenda, although this has changed somewhat in recent years. In the Oslo negotiations, the Taba talks and the Road Map, the refugees are mentioned as an item for negotiation. However, in all three instances the issue of refugees was "allowed" onto the negotiating table by the Israelis only after they had guarantees from the Americans or Palestinian negotiators that the issue would not be discussed within the framework of the Right of Return.

Given the dismal contemporary scene on the Palestinian side, the ideological orientations of recent Israeli governments, the current orientation of American Middle East policies under George W. Bush, and the huge disarray in the Arab world, it is difficult to imagine any significant changes in the official peace agenda in the near future. But even if the refugee issue were to be dealt within the peace process, one particular group of refugees is likely to be excluded from the international protection and from any future negotiated settlement: *the Palestinian internal refugees inside Israel.* This chapter will attempt to show that the cause of the internal refugees and its inclusion in the peace process is, in fact, the only way forward towards a comprehensive solution in Israel-Palestine. The exclusion of the internal refugees, on the other hand, is an assured recipe for continued deadlock and failure to bring peace to both peoples.

The Palestinian internal refugees' unique role and significance can only be understood adequately within the wider context of the international dimensions of the conflict in Palestine. These dimensions are explored here within two specific contexts: as an aspect relating to a distinct group within the Palestinian minority in Israel and as another dimension relating to a community belonging to the larger communities of Palestinian refugees in the world. In both contexts the internal refugees inside Israel can potentially play a crucial role, one that would affect the future of both the Palestinians inside Israel and the Palestinian refugee community at large.

The Palestinian Internal Refugees in Israel: A Conscience and Compass

The Palestinian minority in Israel has gone through two major phases in its relationship with the Israeli-Jewish state. Roughly until 1966, Israeli governments regarded the minority as a "fifth column" that had to be put under a severe military regime. Under such harsh conditions there was no room to develop discrete political agendas, and the struggle for survival among Israeli Palestinians dominated their everyday lives. Consequently, during the same period, the relationship between the Palestinians inside Israel and other Palestinian groups was tense, as the dominant discourse among the Palestinians in Israel was defensive; they were the ones who had not become external refugees and they had to accept a marginal role within the Palestinian people as whole. Those who were not driven out – namely, the Palestinians of Israel – were depicted by other Palestinians as (and quite often felt themselves to be) people who either had not resisted or had simply succumbed too easily to Jewish domination and rule.[3] Outside the boundaries of the state of Israel, Palestinian nationality was reconstituted on the basis of refugeedom and refugee identity. The Palestinian refugee communities produced a new generation of national leadership and reorientated the Palestinian national struggle on the basis of an agenda closely related to their rights and demands. The fact that there was a significant community of refugees inside Israeli itself, resulting both from the "ethnic cleansing" of 1948 and from the evictions which continued into the 1950s, did not hugely affect, then, the political orientation of the Palestinian minority in Israel either in its relationship with the Jewish state or in its relations with other Palestinian communities.[4]

In 1966 Israel abolished its military rule within the Green Line and, as a result, some of the *de jure* features of discrimination against the Palestinian minority diminished, although many of the *de facto* policies of discrimination remained intact. However the new legal situation allowed for the development of a more sophisticated and diverse political agenda among the Palestinians in Israel. The new situation also brought to the fore an explicitly articulated collective national Palestinian identity, which recognised the limits of living as second-class citizens in a state that continued to exercise apartheid and discrimination policies against them. The Palestinian national identity, more than any other sphere of identity or association, was now openly and publicly stated; there was no need to hide, for instance, behind communist or other internationalist labels. This new reality led, on the one hand, to a more tense political relationship between the Israeli Palestinians and the Israeli state – whose successive governments felt that their policies of co-option and coercion were not reaping the desired results – and, on the other, to a significant improvement in the relationship between Israeli Palestinians and other Palestinian communities.

There was, however, a common ground between the Israeli state and the Palestinian political elite inside Israel concerning the domestic nature of the Arab–Jewish relationship in Israel. Consequently this question was not a subject for peace negotiations between Israel and the Palestinian national movement. According to this tacit understanding, this internal relationship was affected by the overall conflict with the Palestinians, but was not, however, a major component of that conflict. Although some Israeli-Palestinian politicians and intellectuals have challenged that tacit understanding, in practice very little has changed in this respect. In reality the principal issues of debate and even confrontation inside Israel were almost exclusively related to the conditions of the Palestinian minority in Israel: land expropriation, economic deprivation, and social and political discrimination. At the same time, however, since the 1970s, the same political and intellectual elite has insisted on referring to the Israeli-

Palestinian citizens as a "Palestinian constituency" and has demonstrated greater solidarity with the Palestinian struggle as whole – especially on issues to do with the Israeli invasion of Lebanon in 1982 and the Palestinian Intifadas in the Occupied Territories (1987–93, and since September 2000). This shift in struggle, however, stopped short of the demand to include the Palestinian question inside Israel within the general Middle East peace process. Within the Israeli-Jewish academic and political establishment the treatment of this subject was far worse: at first the Jewish–Arab relationship inside Israel was analysed within the context of "modernisation theories", and later as part of the "clash of civilisations" between the "barbaric world", to which many of the Palestinians in Israel belonged, and the "civilised world", spearheaded in the Middle East by Israel.[5]

The Palestinian internal refugee struggle that emerged within Israel in the late 1980s and early 1990s challenged both the elitist view within the Palestinian minority and that of the Israeli state and its agencies. The new refugee struggle inside Israel was firmly rooted in the traumatic events of 1948 and therefore could not possibly be treated as an issue separate from other issues of Palestinian refugee communities in the world. Moreover, the character of its activities, operating in the form of NGOs and within a civil society struggle, indicated the close link between the Palestinian question inside Israel and the overall Palestinian question.

What the internal refugees did in this context was to translate a vague political and intellectual discourse about the "Palestinians in Israel" into a clear message and direct action.[6] Their highly symbolic marches into their villages of origin, their ongoing protests and their publications clearly show that the struggle of the Palestinians in Israel – like that of other Palestinian constituencies – has highlighted collective memories of the 1948 *Nakba* (catastrophe). This line of struggle began in earnest in 1988, when the fortieth anniversary of the state of Israel coincided with the first Palestinian Intifada. While the actual support provided by the Palestinians inside Israel to the uprising was limited, the confrontation between the Israeli army and the Palestinians under occupation helped to expand the agenda of the Palestinians in Israel beyond their traditional narrow issues and grievances. While the Israeli state was using the Independence Day celebration of May 1988 as a show of internal solidarity to combat the Palestinian uprising, it was the Palestinian internal refugees who fought back against this Israeli symbolism by articulating a new discourse and "inventing" a new tradition: the "return" visits and marches to destroyed Palestinian villages. The new phenomenon was soon consolidated and institutionalised as a major annual event commemorating the Palestinian catastrophe: the *Nakba* Day.

Further crystallisation of the "commemoration" struggle took place in the 1990s, during the years of the Oslo process. The catalyst was once again the Israeli overemphasis on the celebration of Independence Day in May. Another catalyst was the 1998 Israeli jubilee festivities, which were extended by the Likud government of Benyamin Netanyahu from the traditional one-day to three-days of celebrations. The internal refugees began, with the support of other NGOs and local activists, organising trips and processions to the various sites where Palestinian villages and neighbourhoods had existed until 1948. Even on Israeli university campuses the *Nakba* Day was marked at seminars and symposia which were encouraged by Israeli-Palestinian students.

The plight both of those who were living in "unrecognised villages" and of those who had lived for over fifty years next door to the homes and villages that had been theirs until 1948 and now were either inhabited by Jews or completely destroyed, emerged as an issue on the political agenda of the Palestinians in Israel, although it did not dominate that agenda. The status of the Palestinians (and the nature of their citizenship) within the Jewish state and support for the PLO in its struggle against the Israeli occupation were still top of the political agenda. This is why it is so difficult to find explicit references to the question of the "right of return" in the platforms of the main Palestinian parties in Israel or in the discourse of leading politicians. But the internal refugees' "politics from below" – with its main focus on civil society, including weekly trips to the destroyed villages and combined with the legal struggle for recognition – was one of the few ongoing activities, as opposed to the annual demonstration organised "from above" on the Land Day, conducted by Palestinians in Israel.

The internal refugees, partly because of who they were, but mainly because of their stated agenda – including the "right of return" – became the conscience of the Palestinian citizens in Israel; they also represented the strongest link between the Palestinians in Israel and the 1948 catastrophe. Quite a few Palestinians in Israel do not encounter this nexus, or even are unaware of the connection between Israel's 1948 "ethnic cleansing" policies and current official Israeli attitudes towards them, including the threat of future "transfer" policies.

The link between the past and the present is so acute since Zionist premises, fundamentals and perceptions have not changed essentially in the past 120 years. Since the beginning of the Zionist project in Palestine, two basic Zionist strategies have remained intact: territorial expansionism and demographic domination. The territorial ambition has been to grab as much of historic Palestine as possible in order to make the Jewish state viable. The demographic premiss was to de-Arabise the territory as much as possible – and in the process to de-Arabise the Arab Jews who had been brought into Palestine in order to tip the demographic balance in favour of the Israeli Jews.

The Palestinian internal refugees are the human reminders of these twin policies of the past and of the dangers of their further implementation in the future. In fact the internal refugees are more than that: they are the compass that can reorient Palestinian politics inside Israel beyond the constraints of its present boundaries and agenda and beyond the narrow calculations of Palestinian politicians inside Israel, who are competing – with diminishing returns – for the Arab vote under various labels: neo-communist, nationalist and Islamist. The internal refugee cause connects the local Palestinian scene in Israel to the overall question of peace and reconciliation in Palestine-Israel. In fact the internal refugees are the only group among the Palestinian minority in Israel that demands international intervention on behalf of the Palestinian citizens on the basis of UN resolutions dating back to 1947. The internal refugees were the first group in Israel to ask for the implementation of UN Resolution 194 as part of a future peace agreement. Even a partial implementation of that resolution would potentially result in far-reaching structural changes in Israel and Palestine.

Put differently, if the internal refugees' quest for repatriation – for both internal and external refugees – were to be adopted as a major issue by the Palestinians inside Israel, it would force the Jewish public to deal with the question of Palestine as a problem born out of the catastrophic events of 1948, rather than as a conflict that began in 1967, in line with the misleading narrative of the Israeli "peace camp". A host of new questions would then arise as part of the overall search for peace and reconciliation. Prominent among these questions are the moral basis of the Jewish state in view of the war crimes committed in its name in 1948. In this context, bringing the fate of the internal refugees into the open and onto the agenda for negotiations would raise awareness among both Palestinians and Jews in Israel and raise serious political questions about the nature of the Israeli state and the victims of its Zionist ideology.

The internal refugees repudiate the Israeli claim, which has been tacitly accepted by the PLO since the signing the Oslo Accord, that the issue of Palestinians inside Israel is an internal Israeli affair. The placing of this issue on the negotiating table would highlight the exclusion of the Palestinians in Israel not only from the question of a comprehensive settlement, but also from the question of the Palestinian refugees as whole.

The "Exclusion" Groups of the Palestine Peace Process

The internal refugees are also part of the larger Palestinian refugee community. Within this sphere of politics, the internal refugees have not played, and cannot play, a major role, the reason being their relatively small numbers and unique political circumstances. In fact, among those groups excluded from the negotiations were also the Palestinian minority inside Israel. But the internal refugees are a very significant group. In fact, together with two other communities, the inhabitants of the refugee camps and various diaspora communities, they are an integral part of the majority of the Palestinian people, which has so far been sidelined by the peace process. Potentially the same majority has the power to reorient the peace process onto a different track and away from its past and current failures. As I have tried to demonstrate elsewhere, ever since 1948 the peace process in Palestine has failed, largely because it bypassed the issue of the Palestinian refugees.[7] Therefore it would be futile to continue in the same effort, without addressing the overall relationship between Jews and Palestinians, beginning with the need for Israel to acknowledge its own accountability for the 1948 "ethnic cleansing".

The best way to illustrate the internal refugees' significance for future negotiations and their possible contribution to them, is to consider the realities today on the ground and how these affect the Palestinians in general and those living in Israel and the Occupied Territories in particular.

The major drive in Israeli politics ever since the outbreak of the second (Al-Aqsa) Intifada has been to demarcate unilaterally the eastern border of the Jewish state on the basis of the formula mentioned above: *having as much of the land as possible with as few Palestinians as possible*. This

Zionist premiss informed the strategic thinking of the late Yitzhak Rabin and those prime ministers who came after him: Benyamin Netanyahu, Ehud Barak and Ariel Sharon. The three prime ministers differed in their territorial outlook, but they all shared several principles: they wished to retain under Israeli control the major settlement blocs in the West Bank, greater Jerusalem and part of the Jordan Valley. They also viewed the areas left in Palestinian hands as part of an entity that could be called a Palestinian state (only Netanyahu never openly stated such an opinion). They also viewed such a formulation as an end of the conflict situation. This meant a very narrow and inflexible ethnic redefinition of the new Israel as a Jewish state. As many Labourites in Israel put it: we are doves on the question of the Occupied Territories, but hawks with regard to the Palestinian minority in Israel. "Hawkishness" meant, in this context, that the demographic balance inside the final borders of Israel was still posing, in the eyes of most Zionists, a grave danger to the existence of the Jewish state – even after an agreed settlement with the Palestinians.

It is therefore not surprising that two processes intertwined: the almost total disappearance of any ideological debates within the Zionist political centre – particularly within the Labour and Likud parties – with regard to the Occupied Territories, while, at the same time, the same political centre legitimised the racist public "transfer" discourse, in fact moving it from the extreme right-wing margins of society into centre-stage politics.

There were several manifestations of the new public legitimacy bestowed on "transfer" plans and rhetoric. It began in 2001, when a very distinguished academic institute, the centre for interdisciplinary studies in Herzeliya, published reports on the "Arabs in Israel", describing them as constituting a "demographic danger" to Israel. This body serves as a strategic think-tank for the Israeli government, as well as reflecting faithfully mainstream national thought in Israel.[8] Once a year, the institute produces a strategic outlook for the state of Israel. Ever since 2001, the Palestinians inside Israel have been depicted as a major demographic problem tantamount to a strategic threat to Israel's survival, a problem that required radical and "revolutionary" measures by the state.

These reports were followed by more random suggestions made by mainstream academics and politicians (Shlomo Avineri, of the Hebrew University of Jerusalem, and Ephraim Sneh of the Labour party) for annexation of the Wadi 'Ara area – a small strip of land along the West

Bank, but inhabited by the second largest concentration of Palestinians inside Israel – to a future Palestinian state in return for the annexation to Israel of the large Jewish settlement blocs in the occupied West Bank.[9] The worst aspect of these extraordinary proposals was not just that they were derived from the assumption that such a settlement should be imposed unilaterally on hundred of thousands of Israeli-Palestinian citizens. Far worse was the total annulment of the very concept of citizenship when it comes to Palestinians inside Israel. These proposals were just another indication of how dangerous would become the lives of those Palestinians remaining in Galilee, for instance, within the Jewish state of Israel. Their citizenship would always be "conditional" and "temporary" as long as the state continued to be a Jewish "ethnocracy". And we should not forget for one moment that we are not talking about a group of immigrants, but rather the indigenous (Arab) inhabitants of the land to which Jews had only immigrated in recent decades.

Furthermore, after 2001 the work of the official "demographic council" in Israel was renewed.[10] This is an inter-ministerial council of "experts", which has been mandated to keep a watchful eye on the "demographic balance" between Israeli Jews and Israeli Palestinians inside Israel and to come up with strategies and recommendations for maintaining the present balance. Among its major remits has been the issue of devising strategies for the Israeli state, including encouraging fertility and reproduction among Jewish families.

More recently, another worrying indication of the new racist trends in Israel emerged from an interview given by "new historian" Benny Morris to the daily *Haaretz* in which he explicitly justified the "ethnic cleansing" of 1948 and condoned similar actions in the future.[11] This public support for "transfer" by a leading university professor in Israel would not have received huge coverage in a major newspaper – nor would Morris himself have dared to air such extraordinary views in public – had the political culture and public mood not deteriorated so sharply. In the late 1980s and early 1990s, when rewriting Israel's history became fashionable – and endorsing greater understanding of the Palestinian plight was encouraged – Morris had managed to conceal his controversial views on "ethnic cleansing" fairly successfully. This was evident in his now-famous article "The New Historiography: Israel Confronts its Past",[12] which saw the rewriting of Israeli history contributing to Israeli–Palestinian reconciliation. The Israeli public mood has clearly changed since September 2000

– the same transformation has been seen in the United States after 11 September 2001. Israeli opinions regarded as fanatical and repugnant before September 2000 have now become "sane", "acceptable" and a "legitimate" response to the al-Aqsa Intifada in Israel – or the Bin Laden attacks in the United States. In both cases, however, the events in Palestine and the US were only pretexts for reviving old deeply rooted dreams and colonial enterprises. That is why at the beginning of the twenty-first century one should hardly be surprised by the revival of the concept of "ethnic cleansing" and expulsion in Israel.[13]

The" Fence", Internal Displacement and "Ethnic Cleansing"

It is within this context that one should view the "fence" that already surrounds the Gaza Strip and the "Apartheid Wall" currently being built around those areas in the West Bank designated as part of a future Palestinian entity, or so-called "state". Two issues come to mind in this respect. First: around the Wall there is a security zone which would involve the displacement and "transfer" of a large number of Palestinians who live in villages and towns within that zone. Second: the Wall would eventually create two "west banks": a "Jewish west bank" for the settlers, which also would include Palestinian residents in it, and a "Palestinian west bank" for the natives. As the Wall is a major demographic marker, it would also mean that the Palestinians within the "Jewish west bank" would be in grave danger of being "transferred" eastwards to the "Palestinian west bank", either in a massive military operation – as a "retaliation" against what the Israelis call mega-terrorist attacks – or by more gradual means that would include economic deprivation, unemployment and daily harassment.

The Wall has already added more refugees and internal displaced persons to the large communities of Palestinian refugees victimised by Zionism and the state of Israel. But the Wall is not just an another cruel device in the Zionist arsenal of oppression and destruction. It represents a typical Zionist peace plan. In essence the Wall typifies the cartographic vision of much of the Israeli-Zionist "peace camp": fragmenting Palestine into areas which would be roughly 15 per cent of historic Palestine – and the other half of the West Bank which would be annexed to Israel. That Zionist vision conceives Israel as in control of 85 per cent of historic Palestine.

Unfortunately the Palestinian Authority, the United Nations, the US administration, the European Community and leading states in the Arab world – as well as various groups within the Palestinian community inside Israel – seem to endorse this vision of a truncated and fragmented Palestine. We can see from the most recent efforts at peace-making, namely the Road Map – which was endorsed by the quartet of the UN, the USA, the EU and Russia – that this vision of the future has now gained international "legitimacy". It has also received regional Arab support in the form of the Saudi peace proposals, and those will almost certainly become the official peace plans of the Arab League.

Edward Said's *Community of Consciousness* and Future Prospects

The majority of the Palestinians do not live in those areas designated to be a fragmented "mini-Palestine"; the same majority is unlikely to accept "Palestinian bantustans" even if a formidable international coalition were to sanction them. The alternative suggested here would a real road map for peace which would unite the Palestinian refugee communities and NGOs operating in different Palestinian constituencies: inside Israel, in the Occupied Territories, in the refugee camps and in the diaspora. This alternative vision should be based on what the late Edward W. Said called a *community of consciousness*. Indeed it is the immense legacy of Said and his moral stature that could underpin the demands of the Palestinian refugees, whether inside Israel or in the Occupied Territories and the diaspora. Morality and justice are weapons in the hands of the dispossessed and marginalised, particularly in the light of recent developments and the unjust nature of the current peace process.

This alternative approach is also deeply rooted in international law and justice. And this point brings us back to the argument made at the beginning of this chapter. The UN took on itself the task of replacing the colonial power in Palestine (Britain) as an international guarantor of Palestine and its people. Its endorsement of the 1947 partition resolution was among the main causes of the 1948 Palestinian *Nakba*. Subsequent UN resolutions aimed at addressing the Palestine refugee problem remain legally valid and internationally binding. The most important of these was Resolution 194 which affirmed the right of uprooted people to return to their homes. This resolution was not confined geographically.

Wherever the uprooted people lived, and wherever their previous houses existed, they were accorded the right to choose between return and compensation for lost property and land.

The same right is also a matter of *Realpolitik*. Israeli attempts to carve up historic Palestine and create purely Zionist-Jewish territories will not bring peace to the region – as the last thirty-five years have shown. Moreover, Israeli politics of denial[14] and the exclusion of the "right of return" remain major obstacles creating frustration and despair which inevitably fuel the vicious cycles of violence and destruction.

The blatant attempts to bypass the central issue at the heart of the Palestine problem – the *ethnic cleansing* of 1948 – are no longer challenged by political elites in the region and internationally. Therefore it is the "politics from below" of civil society, on both sides of Palestine-Israel, that has to create the real road map for peace and reconciliation. This has to be based on Israeli acknowledgment of the 1948 expulsions and the Israeli state's readiness to accept responsibility for the *Nakba* and to endorse the Palestinian "right of return". However if this were to become the basis for a future comprehensive settlement in Palestine-Israel, then one would have to ensure that adequate political structures were in place to accommodate the new realities in Israel and Palestine. The political options have always been the same: *either a two-state solution or a one-state solution*.

As I have already pointed out above in the discussion on the "Apartheid Wall", the two-state solution is now being endorsed by mainstream Israeli political parties. The historical roots of this idea as an Israeli solution are quite intriguing. It was first mentioned by the Jewish Agency in 1947; after 1967 the idea of a two-state solution became exclusively the position of the Israeli communist party and this situation lasted until the mid 1970s. During the same period, the communist slogan was "two states for two peoples" without a clear definition of the nature of each state and with only a vague commitment to the "right of return". After 1977, the two-state solution was endorsed by the Peace Now movement which also envisaged a demilitarised Palestinian state in the Occupied Territories, but without a "right of return" and without a Palestinian capital in Jerusalem. Subsequently, during the Oslo process, the idea of a two-state solution was backed by the Israel political centre; this would entail a "mini-state" established in parts of the West Bank and most of the Gaza Strip. (The Labour Party was willing to cede 90 per cent of the

Occupied Territories to a Palestinian state, while the Likud envisaged only 60 per cent). However this would be a fragmented Palestinian entity, without territorial continuity and without a capital in Jerusalem; most of the refugees would be excluded.

Acceptance of the "right of return" will indicate a radical departure from this framework. It will probably go hand in hand with the abandonment of the two-state solution. The implementation in full, or even partially, of the "right of return" will also indicate an Israeli acknowledgement of past ethnic cleansing and the beginning of a genuine reconciliation between the two peoples. Some "de-zionisation" of Israeli political culture and policies would have to precede such developments. But all these ideas would eventually reinforce the need to build inclusive institutions and unitary political structures in Palestine-Israel. The contemporary demographic map – where various ethnic communities are intertwined – the local and regional balance of power and the principle of ensuring repatriation can all be combined to undermine the exclusionist two-state solution.

Coming back to the question of the Palestinian internal refugees in Israel, it seems that any support for their cause and "right of return" can no longer be advanced as merely part of the local and domestic agenda in Israel. Many local attempts were made, but most failed. The legal struggle for return by the people of Iqrit and Kafr Bir'im has recently failed to get backing from the Israeli Supreme Court. More successful, however, was the legal struggle to grant legal status to some unrecognised villages – communities of internally displaced persons that eventually became villages. However the bulk of those who became internal refugees between 1948 and 1956 will not be able to exercise their rights within the present political power structure in Israel – a structure deeply committed to exclusionist Zionism and Jewish "ethnocracy". The only chance of success is within a new comprehensive solution for the Palestine conflict based on inclusive political structures.

In conclusion, two additional points ought to be highlighted: (a) without a just solution more Palestinians are likely to become displaced persons in their homeland; (b) those who are the ultimate victims of Zionism – the Palestinian refugees – are the only ones who can facilitate genuine reconciliation with the Jewish community in Israel. Without such reconciliation, even an Israeli withdrawal from most of the territories occupied in 1967 would not bring about an end to the conflict.

Notes

1 For further discussion, see Ilan Pappé, *The Making of the Arab-Israeli Conflict, 1947–1951* (London and New York: I. B. Tauris: 1992), pp.16-46.

2 For the change in US policy see Pappé, *The Making of the Arab-Israeli Conflict*, pp.203-44.

3 See Nadim Rouhana and Asad Ghanem, "The Democratization of a Traditional Minority in an Ethnic Democracy: The Palestinians in Israel" in Edi Kaufman, Shukri B. Abed, and Robert L. Rothestien (eds.), *Democracy, Peace, and the Israeli– Palestinian Conflict* (London and New York: Lynne Reinner, 1993), pp.163-88.

4 Nur Masalha, *A Land Without a People: Israel, Transfer and the Palestinians 1949–96* (London: Faber and Faber, 1997), pp.1-34.

5 For a good analysis on this issue, see Dan Rabinowitz, "Oriental Nostalgia: The Transformation of Palestinians into Israeli Arabs", *Teoriya Ve-Bekoret* [*Theory and Criticism*] 4 (Fall 1993), pp.141-51 [Hebrew]).

6 Among them are Sa'id Zaydani and 'Azmi Bishara.

7 Ilan Pappé, "The Post-territorial Dimensions of a Future Homeland in Israel and Palestine", in Ron Robin and Bo Strath (eds.), *Homelands: Poetic Power and the Politics of Space* (Brussels: Peter Lang, 2003), pp.189-208.

8 *Haaretz*, 27 March 2001.

9 Shlomo Avineri in *Haaretz*, 6 September 2002.

10 The council was behind the law passed in the Israeli Knesset on 31 July 2003, entitled The Nationality and Entry Law (Temporary Order), prohibiting citizenship, permanent residence and/or temporary residency status to West Bank/Gaza Palestinians married to Israeli citizens.

11 *Haaretz*, 16 January 2004.

12 Benny Morris, "The New Historiography: Israel Confronts its Past", *Tikkun* 4 (November/December 1988), pp.19-23, 99-102.

13 For a further discussion of the idea of "transfer" in Zionism, see Nur Masalha, *Expulsion of the Palestinians: The Concept of 'Transfer' in Zionist Political Thought, 1882– 1948* (Washington DC: Institute for Palestine Studies, 1992).

14 Nur Masalha, *The Politics of Denial: Israel and the Palestinian Refugee Problem* (London: Pluto Press, 2003).

11
International Protection and Durable Solutions[1]
Terry Rempel

Internally displaced persons (IDPs) comprise the largest group of displaced persons around the world today. Of an estimated 40 million displaced persons worldwide (December 2003), some two-thirds are IDPs. Like refugees, the internally displaced are persons or groups of persons who have been forced or obliged to flee or to leave their homes or places of habitual residence as a result of or in order to avoid the effects of armed conflict, situations of generalised violence, and violations of human rights. The defining characteristic of internally displaced persons, however, is that they have not crossed an internationally recognised border.[2]

The overwhelming majority of IDPs are members of minority groups. They are also predominantly women, children, and the poor. Over half the world's internally displaced persons reside in Africa. The Middle East is the region with the least IDPs, numbering around 1.5 million. Arab states with large IDP populations include Iraq, Lebanon, Syria, and Algeria. Unlike other regions, the refugee population in the Middle East, including more than 6 million Palestinian refugees (December 2003), exceeds that of the internally displaced.[3] Root causes of internal displacement in the Middle East include ethno-national conflict, competition over land and resources, foreign occupation, and colonisation.[4]

One of the often neglected groups of internally displaced persons in the Middle East is internally displaced Palestinians. This neglect stems, in part, from the fact that internal displacement is difficult to conceptualise in the context of the Palestinian/Arab–Israeli conflict, which is rooted in the ongoing struggle over control of land and sovereignty thereon. In the course of the more than 57-year-old conflict, wars and military occupation have frequently changed ceasefire lines and so-called borders. An internationally recognised border between Palestinians and Israel has not yet been established. Concepts like "Palestinian minority" and "internally displaced Palestinians" are therefore extremely fluid and subject to changes. They can only be applied pragmatically in order to describe the phenomenon of internal displacement in a specific period of time.

One of the major problems faced by internally displaced persons worldwide is the lack of protection. National authorities, which have the primary responsibility for the protection of IDPs within their borders, often lack the resources and/or political will to provide protection, particularly when internal displacement is a result of competition over control of land and resources or ethno-national conflict. The international community, moreover, often fails to respond adequately to the protection needs of internally displaced persons due to unresolved issues of UN mandate and institutional responsibility for IDPs; the lack of a binding legal instrument that delineates the rights of IDPs and the concomitant obligations of signatory states; and overriding concerns about sovereignty and non-interference in the internal affairs of states.

Over the past decade, the international community has attempted to address institutional and legal gaps concerning IDP protection through a collaborative inter-agency approach bringing together resources and expertise of key UN agencies and other international actors. The UN also commissioned the drafting of a set of universal principles on internal displacement. The 1998 *Guiding Principles on Internal Displacement* identifies rights and guarantees relevant to the protection of persons from forced displacement; protection during displacement; provision of humanitarian assistance; as well as protection during return or resettlement and reintegration.[5] The *Guiding Principles on Internal Displacement* restate already recognised rights under international human rights and humanitarian law and their applicability to internally displaced persons. The international community opted for a set of "guiding principles" rather than an international convention in order to circumvent state concerns about sovereignty and to ensure greater international acceptance.

One of the defining characteristics of internally displaced Palestinians, similar to IDPs worldwide, is the lack of both national and international protection. Israel is able but not willing to extend comprehensive national protection to internally displaced Palestinians inside Israel. Internally displaced Palestinians in the 1967 Occupied Territories lack national protection by virtue of the absence of a state obligated to provide such protection.[6] Israel, the occupying power, has refused to abide by its obligations under the Fourth Geneva Convention to provide protection to the civilian population.[7] Israel also refuses direct responsibility for international human rights law in the 1967 occupied Palestinian territories.[8] The self-governing Palestinian Authority, a non-sovereign entity established during the 1990s under the Oslo political process, has not been able to provide full protection for the civilian population in the 1967 Occupied Territories, including IDPs. Since the second Palestinian Intifada began in September 2000, the Palestinian Authority has come under severe attack by Israeli military forces further hampering its limited ability to protect the civilian population in the Occupied Territories. Israeli practices inside Israel and in the 1967 Occupied Territories, including land expropriation, house demolition, revocation of residency rights, military closure and the construction of a wall leading to forced separation according to ethnic, religious and national origins continues to generate internal displacement.

The international community has largely ignored the protection needs of internally displaced Palestinians inside Israel and in the 1967 Occupied Territories. No single international agency is currently recognised as having an explicit protection mandate for internally displaced Palestinians. The United Nations Conciliation Commission for Palestine (UNCCP), mandated to provide international protection for 1948 Palestinian refugees and internally displaced, ceased to provide effective protection in the early 1950s. The UN Relief and Works Agency for Palestine Refugees (UNRWA) does not have an explicit mandate to provide comprehensive protection to refugees and internally displaced Palestinians in the 1967 Occupied Territories. Various UN organs have addressed the protection needs of the Palestinian population in the 1967 Occupied Territories, which would include internally displaced persons, but the lack of international political will has prevented an effective response.

Internally displaced Palestinians thus experience multiple forms of marginalisation relative to national and international protection. As with other IDPs worldwide, they experience general marginalisation due to shortcomings in the institutional setup and legal framework for international protection of internally displaced persons. Internally displaced Palestinians inside Israel are further marginalised as members of a non-

Jewish ethno-national minority in a Jewish state. Internally displaced Palestinians in the 1967 Occupied Territories are further marginalised by Israel's illegal occupation and the absence of a state that is obligated, able and willing to provide protection. Generally, Palestinian IDPs have been marginalised due to the exclusion of the issue of internally displaced persons from the Oslo political process. Unlike most other peace agreements, the Oslo agreements do not include provisions for durable solutions for IDPs.

The *Guiding Principles on Internal Displacement* provides the legal framework for this chapter. The chapter first examines the day-to-day protection needs of internally displaced Palestinians. The second section examines protection from displacement and durable solutions for internal displacement. The final section examines mechanisms for implementation. Concluding recommendations are provided at the end of the chapter.

Protection of IDPs During Displacement

The *Guiding Principles on Internal Displacement* delineates a set of universal principles relative to the protection of human rights of internally displaced persons during displacement. Discrimination against internally displaced persons is strictly prohibited. Principle 1 prohibits discrimination on the grounds that persons are internally displaced. Principle 4 provides a broader prohibition against discrimination on the basis of race, sex, language, religion or belief, political or other opinion, national, ethnic or social origin, legal or social status, age, disability, property, birth or any other similar criteria.

Discrimination against Palestinians inside Israel, including IDPs, is primarily based on nationality, ethnicity, and religion. Deeply embedded discriminatory social attitudes, practices, and laws are rooted in Israel's definition of itself as a "Jewish state".[9] "A main reason for the prevalence of racism in Israeli society is that State institutions, including the Government, the Legislature, the Judiciary, the Army, and the Religious Bodies, consistently emphasise the national-religious character of the State."[10] Public opinion surveys reveal significant levels of intolerance towards Palestinian citizens of the state. Surveys conducted in 2003 by Israeli think-tanks and universities, for example, revealed that half or more of Israeli Jews polled supported limiting the rights of Palestinian

264 · Catastrophe Remembered

citizens.[11] Since the beginning of the second Palestinian uprising in September 2000, "[s]tatements of collective hatred toward Arab citizens on the part of some [Israeli-Jewish] politicians have garnered increasingly broad influence among the Jewish public".[12]

Institutionalised discrimination takes shape in the form of quasi-government bodies – namely, the World Zionist Organisation, the Jewish Agency, and the Jewish National Fund – authorised by the government to provide public (that is, government) services to the Jewish community.[13] There is no parallel government agency that provides similar services for Palestinians inside Israel. Per capita government investment in Palestinian communities in Israel is significantly lower than similar investment in Jewish communities. The 2002 development budget for Israel's Health Ministry, for example, was NIS277 million (US$59 million) but it has allocated just NIS1.6 million (US$340,000) for development in the Palestinian sector, which comprises 20 per cent of the population.[14] According to the same plan, Palestinian localities were allocated NIS104 (US$23) per resident compared to the Jewish city of Modi'in which received NIS11,554 (US$2,500) per resident. Only 4 per cent of the 2002 budget for culture was targeted for Palestinian communities.[15] In order to protect the Jewish character of the state, Israeli law does not provide for the constitutional protection of the right to equality of all citizens of the state.[16]

Palestinians in the 1967 Occupied Territories, including IDPs, are also discriminated against based on their national, ethnic, and religious origins. Israel's illegal military occupation is characterised by overt discrimination between Jewish colonists (that is, settlers) resident in the West Bank, including eastern Jerusalem, and the Gaza Strip, and the indigenous Palestinian population. Israel applies two different sets of laws to these areas. "The annexation's direct effect is the application of different legal systems, and different protections to the Jewish and Palestinian populations living in the same territory. Whereas the settlers benefit from their status as citizens of a democratic state and enjoy all the rights that accompany citizenship, the Palestinians live under a military occupation that denies them these rights."[17]

Discrimination takes shape in the form of the "Civil Administration", Israel's military government, which protects and promotes the interests of Israel (that is, as a Jewish state), in the Occupied Territories.[18] Israel has issued over 1,200 military orders introducing extensive changes in the administrative structures and substantive laws according to powers set forth under Proclamation No. 2 (Proclamation on Law and Administration) of 7 June 1967. Under the Oslo agreements[19] Israel's military government was withdrawn but not abolished. Jewish colonists fall within the jurisdiction of Israeli domestic law. Palestinians fall under Israeli military law. Israeli citizenship law, for example, is applicable to all Jews residing in the Occupied Territories.[20] Palestinians, however, are considered to be resident aliens.[21] Thus, while Jewish colonists enjoy protection of basic rights as citizens of Israel, Palestinians are denied many of the same basic rights.

In addition to the general prohibition against discrimination, the *Guiding Principles on Internal Displacement* also delineate specific principles concerning the protection of basic human rights (Principles 10 through 23). Relevant principles include:

the right to life;

the right to dignity and physical, mental and moral integrity, including the prohibition against torture, cruel, inhuman or degrading treatment or punishment;

the right to liberty and security of person, including the prohibition against arbitrary arrest and detention;

the right to liberty of movement and freedom to choose one's residence;

the right to seek safety in another part of the country and the right to leave one's country;

the right to know the whereabouts of missing relatives, including protection of and access to grave sites;

the right to respect of family life, including family reunification;

the right to an adequate standard of living;

the right to medical attention and care;

the right to recognition as a person before the law, including the issuance of documents such as passports and ID cards without unreasonable conditions;

the prohibition against arbitrary deprivation of property and possessions; and

the right to education.

The right to liberty of movement and freedom to choose one's residence, the right to respect of family life, the right to an adequate standard of living, including health and education, and the prohibition against arbitrary deprivation of property are particularly relevant to internally displaced Palestinians inside Israel.

The geographical distribution of IDPs inside Israel today is a function of severe restrictions on freedom of movement and the right to choose one's place of residence. Between 1948 and 1966, Palestinians inside Israel were placed under military rule.[22] IDPs were not only prevented from returning to their villages of origin, as addressed below; resettlement was largely restricted to government-designated areas with the aim or result of "freeing" temporarily abandoned Palestinian land for permanent Jewish colonisation, clearing large swaths of land in border zones, and concentrating Palestinians within Arab towns and villages not destroyed during the war. Approximately 200 IDP families, for example, were "relocated" to targeted resettlement areas referred to as "shelter villages".[23] Public access to numerous official documents and records held in state archives concerning internal transfer of the Palestinian population is still prohibited. The majority of the Palestinian population was placed under a tight dusk-till-dawn curfew that lasted until the early 1960s. Today Palestinians are generally not permitted to reside in Jewish communities established by quasi-government bodies such as the Jewish Agency.[24]

Respect for family life and reunification of divided Palestinian families is largely conditioned on arbitrary criteria that screen out and limit the number of displaced Palestinians eligible to rejoin families inside Israel. The primary aim of the policy is to preserve the demographic outcome of the 1948 war – namely, a Jewish majority. Early family reunification programmes for displaced Palestinians, for example, were limited to minor sons, single daughters and women. Palestinian women whose husbands were displaced outside the state were expected to join their husbands abroad. Many applications for family reunification were rejected due to the fact that displaced Palestinians could not produce required documentation, including marriage and birth certificates, lost during the 1948 war.[25] In May 2002, Israel suspended family reunification procedures for Palestinians whose spouses are residents of the 1967 occupied Palestinian territories. In July 2003 the Israeli government adopted a temporary law – Nationality and Entry into Israel Law (Temporary Order) – prohibiting family reunification for Palestinians married to Palestinian spouses from the West Bank and Gaza Strip.[26] In 2003 two UN human rights treaty committees called upon Israel to revoke the law and reconsider its family unification policy.[27] In addition, internally displaced Palestinians are often denied access to gravesites in their villages of origin.

Displacement, dispossession, and discrimination undermine the right to an adequate standard of living. Internally displaced Palestinians inside Israel experience higher levels of unemployment than the national average. The 18 cities and villages in Israel where unemployment is highest are all Palestinian.[28] More than half has a significant IDP population. Unemployment levels are even higher among internally displaced Palestinians residing in "unrecognised villages" – villages not recognised by the government as "legal" settlements and therefore denied government services – and among displaced Bedouin forced into government-constructed townships.[29] The number of Palestinians, including internally displaced, living below the poverty line is significantly higher than the national average. Over 50 per cent of all Palestinians inside Israel live below the poverty line. Infant mortality among Palestinians is more than double that of the Jewish population; in unrecognised villages, infant mortality rates in 2001 were triple that of Jews.[30] The dropout rate for Palestinian students is more than twice that of Jewish students. All but 5.7 per cent of the students receiving their first university degree in the 1998–99 school year were Jewish even though Palestinians comprise 20 per cent of the population.[31]

One of the most widespread violations of the universal principles concerning the protection of IDPs during displacement, as set forth in the *Guiding Principles on Internal Displacement*, is the prohibition against arbitrary deprivation of property. Homes temporarily abandoned during the 1948 war, primarily in villages, were subsequently destroyed in order to prevent the return of internally displaced Palestinians. Israel appropriated IDP homes in cities in order to resettle new Jewish immigrants primarily from Europe. This policy towards the indigenous Palestinian population was referred to as "retroactive transfer".[32] Privately owned Palestinian land, including land still held by IDPs, has been targeted for expropriation to facilitate Jewish colonisation (settlement).[33] This expropriation includes land from Palestinian villages that provided shelter to IDPs in 1948, such as Tamra, Judayda, Jish, Furaydis, and Mazra'a, among others. In 2003, the Israeli government expropriated land from the Palestinian villages of Baqa al-Gharbiyya and Jitt in order to construct a massive barrier to wall off Palestinians in the West Bank from Jewish settlers and from Israelis living inside Israel.[34] Since 1948 Israel has destroyed hundreds of Palestinian homes it says were built without permits. Stringent enforcement is rarely applied to Israeli Jews. During

2002, for example, Israel demolished an estimated 125 Palestinian homes, the majority belonging to IDPs residing in unrecognised villages in the Naqab. By the end of 2003, the Israeli Ministry of the Interior had demolished more than 500 Palestinian homes inside Israel. In September 2003, the Israeli press reported that the Israeli government intended to increase the rate of house demolitions in the Palestinian sector.[35] Israel refuses to release information on the status of movable and immovable IDP property based on claims that it lacks the necessary resources to carry out a complete inventory and because release of the information would harm Israel's foreign relations.[36]

The full panoply of rights set forth in the *Guiding Principles on Internal Displacement* are currently relevant to the situation of internally displaced Palestinians in the 1967 occupied Palestinian territories.

Israel's violation of these rights does not distinguish between internally displaced Palestinians and the general Palestinian population. Torture, collective punishment, extra-judicial killings, administrative detention, revocation of residency rights, denial of family reunification, house demolition, economic policies (referred to as "de-development"[37]) that have created extreme economic dependency on Israel, military closure and curfews, as well as military attacks on civilian areas, extensively documented by local and international human rights organisations, violate the rights of the Palestinian population in the Occupied Territories without distinction. The impact of these violations is especially severe in the context of the second Palestinian Intifada. As of the end of 2004, three years after the beginning of the uprising, some 3,500 Palestinians, primarily civilians, have been killed and tens of thousands injured.[38] Unemployment is hovering at 50 percent.[39] Over 60 per cent of the population is living below the poverty line.[40] On average between 500,000 and 1 million Palestinians were placed under military curfew during 2002. While there are no statistics on the specific impact of these practices on internally displaced Palestinians it can be assumed that the internally displaced, like refugees, are more vulnerable due to their situation of displacement, particularly those IDPs residing in areas close to Israeli military installations, settlements and "border areas".

As with internally displaced Palestinians inside Israel, one of the most widespread violations of the universal principles set forth in the *Guiding Principles on Internal Displacement* is the prohibition against arbitrary deprivation of property. Similar to the situation inside Israel, Palestinians from areas targeted for Jewish colonisation or in "border areas" have been particularly vulnerable to arbitrary dispossession. It is estimated that following the 1967 war Israel immediately expropriated some 400 square kilometres from internally displaced Palestinians and refugees.[41] This expropriation included IDPs from the destroyed villages of Imwas, Yalu and Beit Nuba in the Latrun salient, the entire Moghrabi quarter of the old city of Jerusalem, which was demolished to create a large public plaza adjacent to the Western Wall, and areas adjacent to eastern Jerusalem. An additional 1,048 Palestinian apartments were expropriated to expand the Jewish quarter of the old city.[42] More recently, Israel has expropriated an estimated 3,000 acres of privately owned Palestinian land to construct the separation wall fencing off Palestinians from Israeli settlers and Israelis living inside Israel. Thousands of Palestinians are expected to be displaced as a result of the wall.[43] House demolition is another source of arbitrary property deprivation. It is estimated that Israel has demolished more than 20,000 Palestinian homes in the West Bank, including eastern Jerusalem, and the Gaza Strip since 1967.[44] More than 1,000 homes have been demolished during the second Palestinian Intifada. During the first two years of the conflict, the average number of homes demolished in Gaza was 32 per month. Since the start of 2003 that average has risen to 72.[45]

Finally, the *Guiding Principles* provide a set of principles concerning humanitarian assistance for IDPs (Principles 24-27). The primary duty and responsibility for providing humanitarian assistance to internally displaced persons lies with national authorities (Principle 25.1). International humanitarian organisations and other appropriate actors have the right to offer their services in support of the internally displaced. Such an offer shall not be regarded as an unfriendly act or interference in a state's internal affairs and shall be considered in good faith. Consent thereto shall not be arbitrarily withheld, particularly when authorities concerned are unable or unwilling to provide the required humanitarian assistance (Principle 25.2). The *Guiding Principles* further provide for the free passage of humanitarian assistance and protection from acts of violence.

Inside Israel, UNRWA transferred responsibility for emergency relief and assistance for IDPs to the government of Israel in 1952. Israel does not provide special assistance to internally displaced Palestinians, despite the distinct vulnerability of this sector of the Palestinian community inside Israel. In the 1967 Occupied Territories, where Israel has not fulfilled obligations under international humanitarian law to provide and facilitate the delivery of humanitarian assistance to the civilian population, the Palestinian Authority is not able to cope with the humanitarian crisis created by Israel's occupation and military campaign in the West Bank and Gaza Strip, especially over the past three years. International agencies providing humanitarian assistance in the 1967 Occupied Territories face administrative obstacles and physical barriers (including military closure, curfew, and destruction of infrastructure) imposed by Israel.[46] This includes denial of access for emergency and regular medical assistance, evacuation of the wounded and dead, and delivery of medicines, food, water, and temporary shelter.

Durable Solutions Protection

The *Guiding Principles on Internal Displacement* also provide a set of universal principles governing protection from displacement and remedies to displacement.

Individuals are protected against arbitrary displacement from their home or place of habitual residence. Displacement is considered arbitrary when it is based on policies of apartheid, "ethnic cleansing" or similar practices aimed at/or resulting in altering the ethnic, religious or racial composition of the affected population; in cases of large-scale development projects, which are not justified by compelling and overriding public interests; and when it is used as collective punishment. Arbitrary displacement includes displacement in situations of armed conflict, unless the security of the civilians involved or imperative military reasons so demand. (Principle 6.2).

The majority of Palestinian IDPs inside Israel were displaced during armed conflict and war in 1948 by a combination of tactics that violated basic principles of international law relative to the conduct of war. Tactics included targeted attacks on civilians, expulsion, massacres, looting, and the destruction of property without military necessity. Approximately 80 per cent of the IDP and refugee population were displaced as a result of military attack.[47] Reviewing the legislative history of UN Resolution 194 (1948), paragraph 11, calling for the return of Palestinian refugees and displaced persons to their homes and compensation for losses and damages, a legal advisor to the UN Conciliation Commission for

Palestine (UNCCP) commented that the General Assembly intended that paragraph 11 function as a legal remedy to the "violation of the laws and customs of war on land laid down in the Hague Convention of 18 October 1907, the rules of which, as stated in the Nuremberg Judgement of 1939, were recognised by all civilised nations and were regarded as being declaratory of the laws and customs of war".[48]

The geographic distribution of the internally displaced inside Israel draws a map of mostly forced resettlement based on policies of forced separation or apartheid and "ethnic cleansing" aimed at or resulting in altering the demographic composition of Israel. As mentioned above, territory identified as security zones or targeted for exclusive Jewish settlement and development were rendered clean [*naki*] and empty [*reik*].[49] Cleaning operations are documented in numerous documents held in state archives; others remain inaccessible to the public based on concerns that release of the documents would harm Israel's foreign relations.[50] The remaining inhabitants of the villages of Iqrit, Kafr Bir'im, al-Faluja, Iraq al-Manshiya, Farraddiya, 'Inan, Saffurriya, al-Khisa, Qeitiya, Khirbet Muntar, al-Ghabisiyya and al-Hamma, for example, were evicted and the villages razed to facilitate the development of pure Jewish areas. Planning and building laws[51] effectively contain the remaining indigenous Palestinian population by maintaining "public" (Jewish) control over vast areas of land. Since 1948, Israel has also gradually carried out a policy of forced resettlement of the Bedouin population in the Naqab (Negev) in seven "townships". The programme of "sedentarisation" aims to make lands held by Bedouin in customary ownership available for Jewish settlement and development, and provide a cheap source of wage labour for the Jewish sector. More recently the Israeli government has proposed targeting US$1.75 billion to implement a five-year plan to extinguish Bedouin land claims and concentrate the remaining Bedouin in so-called development towns.[52]

Palestinian displacement during the 1967 war is also the result of military practices that violate the laws of war, including targeted attacks on civilians, expulsion, and destruction of property without military necessity. It is estimated that 60 per cent of those displaced were displaced as a result of direct military attack.[53] Unlike the situation inside Israel, the majority of internally displaced Palestinians in the 1967 Occupied Territories were displaced after rather than during armed conflict. Internal displacement is primarily the result of policies that aim or result in the alteration of the demographic composition of the Occupied Territories. Israel's 37-year military occupation, characterised by land expropriation, house demolition, and colonisation, draws a pattern of forced segregation along ethnic, religious and national lines. Palestinians residing in "border areas", areas identified by Israel as security zones, and areas targeted for Jewish colonies have been displaced in order to prevent the establishment of contiguous Palestinian built-up areas, and, at the same time, to create territorial contiguity between Jewish colonies and link them to the territory of Israel.[54] Today, the Gaza Strip is totally isolated from the West Bank. The West Bank is divided into some 64 non-contiguous zones surrounded by roadblocks and permanent Israeli checkpoints. As of May 2002 Palestinian residents require special permits issued by the Civil Administration, Israel's military government, for travel between Palestinian-controlled zones. The system of ethnic/religious separation is culminating in the building of a massive wall inside the West Bank separating Palestinians therein from Israel while maintaining links between Jewish colonies and Israel proper. It is estimated that approximately 10 per cent of the West Bank and more than 350,000 Palestinians, including those residing in eastern Jerusalem, will be effectively annexed to Israel. Palestinians unlawfully transferred to the direct control of Israel will not be granted residency or citizenship. In October 2003, the Israeli government declared extensive areas adjacent to the wall in the northern West Bank a closed military zone. Palestinians residing in the military zone, along with all persons entering the zone, will require special permits.[55]

Under the *Guiding Principles on Internal Displacement* individuals are provided with further guarantees against displacement in situations other than during emergency stages of armed conflicts and disasters. Guarantees include the free and informed consent of those to be displaced and the right to an effective remedy, including the review of decisions resulting in displacement by appropriate judicial authorities (Principle 7.3).

Internal displacement of Palestinians inside Israel is almost never a function of free and informed consent. IDPs have organised popular demonstrations and filed legal petitions to express explicit opposition to internal displacement. Popular protests have failed to secure a fundamental change in state policies and practices. Protests have also been met with state violence. In March 1976, for example, Israeli security forces killed six Palestinians during a mass protest against land expropriation in the Galilee. To this day, IDPs and other victims of dispossession consider 30 March – Land Day – as a day of commemoration and protest against ongoing displacement and dispossession inside Israel. Other forms of protest include the refusal of IDPs to accept government offers of compensation as a form of protest against displacement and dispossession. In 2002, for example, Israel offered IDPs from the villages of Iqrit and Kafr Bir'im compensation in lieu of return. The offer was rejected. "We reject compensation and we are not even interested in discussing it with the government," stated an IDP from Iqrit. "The only solution for our cases is not material; we are looking to return the people to their father's lands."[56]

Israel's judicial system effectively underwrites displacement rather than affording IDPs effective legal remedy. Israeli courts refuse to rule on cases where displacement is the result of alleged national security considerations.[57] Appeals committees have never cancelled an order for Palestinian inhabitants to leave their villages in areas closed under the Emergency Regulations of 1949.[58] In cases where displacement stems from arbitrary deprivation of property, transactions undertaken by the state and its organs "in good faith" are considered legal even if found by the courts to be illegal in fact.[59] In cases where petitions seeking redress from expropriation are accepted at the District Court level they are always rejected when they reach the High Court.[60] For Bedouin IDPs, the legal process appears to be a no-win situation; no Bedouin has ever won a land claim in any of the more than 3,000 lawsuits filed over the past several decades.[61]

In several cases where Palestinians have consented to temporary displacement based on Israeli security considerations, Israel has either reneged on agreements or failed to uphold judicial rulings allowing IDPs to return to their villages of origin. Despite a 1951 court ruling allowing IDPs from Kafr Bir'im and Iqrit to return to their villages, for example, successive Israeli governments continue to block implementation of the ruling.[62] In 2003 the Israeli Supreme Court rejected a fourth petition filed by IDPs from Iqrit stating, in part, that the return of the villagers might set a precedent that could harm the state's interests. The Israeli military has also played an active role in blocking implementation of judicial rulings. Inhabitants of the village of al-Ghabisiyya, for example, were expelled in February 1950 by order of the Military Governor who then declared the village a closed area. An Israeli court decided that the declaration was a legislative act and "only valid if it is published in the Official Gazette" (at the time the declaration had not been published) and ordered that the inhabitants be permitted to return. The Israeli military prevented the villagers from returning and a few days later the Military Governor published a declaration in the Official Gazette. Inhabitants of the village went back to court, which subsequently ruled against them.[63]

In the 1967 Occupied Territories displacement is never a function of free and informed consent. For example, Israel has unilaterally revoked the residency rights of more than 6,000 Palestinian Jerusalemites, affecting some 24,000 individuals if family members are included. Palestinians have protested against ongoing displacement through public protest and through the courts and administrative bodies established by Israel in the Occupied Territories. Public protest by Palestinians, including displaced persons, is most often met with harsh military repression including mass arrest, detention, and the killing of civilian protesters. Since the beginning of the second Palestinian Intifada, which erupted in response to continued expropriation of land, settlement construction and denial of the right to self-determination and the right of return, for example, more than 8,000 Palestinians have been arrested and detained and several thousand have been killed as of October 2003.

Legal mechanisms established by Israel's military government in the Occupied Territories do not provide effective remedy to displacement. The so-called Civil Administration is responsible for policies and practices that lead to internal displacement; in most cases, it is also the sole arbitrator and judge for IDPs seeking legal remedy. In cases of displacement resulting from arbitrary deprivation of property, Israel's Supreme Court only accepts cases related to private property. In some cases the court itself removes all legal avenues for redress. In August 2002, for example, the High Court ruled that homes belonging to families of persons who are believed to have carried out attacks against Israelis could be demolished without the right to judicial review.

The majority of legal petitions of Palestinian IDPs in the 1967 Occupied Territories are handled by the special military objection committees established by the Civil Administration (Military Order 172). The Committees are staffed and administered by the same military authorities responsible for issuing expropriation orders. Israeli officials often fail to deliver a copy of the expropriation order to the affected landowner; Palestinians are restricted from inspecting records of the special registration department established to register land sold to Jews or expropriated as state land or for military purposes; land transactions undertaken by the state and its organs in "good faith" are considered legal even if the expropriation was found to be illegal; the burden of proof rests with the plaintiff rather than the expropriating power; the military objections committee is authorised to hold hearings partially or totally in camera and may excuse witnesses from identifying themselves; and decisions of the appeals committee are not published and are not accessible for public viewing. In August 2002, the Civil Administration adopted an amendment to Military Order 378 (1970) allowing for the forcible transfer of Palestinians from the West Bank to the Gaza Strip.

Under the *Guiding Principles on Internal Displacement* States are under an obligation to protect against the displacement of indigenous peoples, minorities, peasants, pastoralists and other groups with a special dependency on and attachment to their lands (Principle 9).

Israel has not fulfilled its obligation to protect Bedouin and the general Palestinian population from displacement as far as they constitute indigenous peoples, minorities, and groups with a special attachment to their lands. Until 1948, Palestinian Arabs comprised the vast majority of the indigenous inhabitants of mandatory Palestine. More than two-thirds of those Palestinians displaced in 1948 were peasants (*fellahin*). Of the 95 Bedouin tribes living in the Naqab before 1948, only 11 remained after the war. Those who were not expelled were transferred to the northern part of the Bir al-Sabi' (Beersheba) Sub-District and forced to settle in an area one-tenth the size of the former area in which they lived. Land in this area is of poorer quality and not as amenable to traditional grazing and rain-fed agriculture. During the 1980s a further 750 Bedouin families were displaced to facilitate the construction of an Israeli military base.[64] More recently Israeli military forces have displaced Bedouin in the West Bank who reside primarily in "Area C" – that part of the West Bank (60 per cent) where Israel retained full military and administrative control under the Oslo agreements. All but a few of Israel's illegal colonies (settlements) are located in this area. Displacement has intensified over the past six years, affecting numerous tribes, including Froush Bayt Dajan near Tamoun, Jahalin Salamat near Ma'ale Adumim colony, Qa'abneh near Dayr Dibwan, al-Rashayda south of Bethlehem, Azameh near

Nablus, Da'is near Jiftlik, Jahalin Saray'an Wad Abu Hindi, and Jahalin Abu Dahouk at Bir al-Maskoub.[65]

The *Guiding Principles on Internal Displacement* also elaborate the right of IDPs and the obligation of national and international authorities to facilitate durable solutions. Competent authorities have the primary duty and responsibility to establish conditions, as well as provide the means, that allow internally displaced persons to return voluntarily, in safety and with dignity, to their homes or places of habitual residence, or to resettle voluntarily in another part of the country (Principle 28). The *Guiding Principles* further state that displacement shall last no longer than required by the circumstances (Principle 6.3). Competent authorities also have the duty and responsibility to assist returned and/or resettled internally displaced persons to recover, to the extent possible, their property and possessions which they left behind or were dispossessed of upon their displacement (Principle 29).

These principles are consistent with the framework set forth in UN General Assembly Resolution 194 applicable to 1948 Palestinian refugees and internally displaced persons. Resolution 194 affirms the right of all persons displaced during the 1948 war to return *to their homes of origin* and repossess their properties.[66] The drafters of the resolution intended that displaced persons should be permitted to return following the establishment of stable conditions with the signing of armistice agreements between Israel and neighbouring Arab states in 1949. The United States delegate at the UN stated that the US "could not accept the proclamation of peace as a prerequisite for the return of refugees … [The refugees] should not be made pawns in the negotiations for a final settlement."[67] Resolution 194 also recognises the principle of safe return. Commenting on the drafting history of the Resolution, the UNCCP Secretariat noted that Resolution 194 "impose[d] a [governmental] obligation … to ensure the peace of the returning refugees and protect them from any elements seeking to disturb that peace". Since 1967, resolutions adopted by the UN General Assembly and the Commission on Human Rights call upon Israel to facilitate the return of those persons displaced during the 1967 war. Various local and international NGOs, as well as UN human rights treaty committees, have reaffirmed the right of internally displaced Palestinians to return to their homes of origin and repossess their properties.

While an internationally recognised border does not separate internally displaced Palestinians from their homes and properties, the obstacles they face in returning and repossessing their properties are as difficult to overcome as those faced by Palestinian refugees displaced and expelled to neighbouring Arab states. Apart from a number of minor exceptions, Israel has not and does not permit internally displaced Palestinians to return to their villages of origin. Few IDPs from Haifa, for example, were permitted to return to the city. In the 1960s and 1970s, some IDPs from Sha'ab were permitted to return. As mentioned above, even in the few cases where Israeli courts have ruled in favour of IDP return, such as Iqrit and Kafr Bir'im, successive governments have blocked implementation of the court rulings. Generally requests for IDP return are rejected for several reasons: (1) alleged security considerations; (2) transfer of IDP property to the state for the development of Jewish [colonies] settlements; and (3) the fear of setting a precedent for the individual return of all IDPs and refugees choosing to do so. Israel, moreover, has prevented over 70,000 internally displaced Palestinians who spontaneously resettled in other parts of the country in so-called unrecognised villages from being reintegrated in their new places of residence. Israel does not recognise these new villages as "legal" settlements and does not provide services, including water, sewage, electricity, health and education.

Internally displaced Palestinians inside Israel are also prevented from repossessing their homes and properties. A complex system of property laws, including a series of abandoned property regulations, emergency regulations, and a set of absentees' property laws, among others, has been used to expropriate refugee and IDP properties and transfer them to the state for exclusive and inalienable Jewish use. It is estimated that since 1948 Israel has expropriated close to 1,000 square kilometres of land owned by Palestinian citizens of Israel, not including internally displaced Bedouin, in addition to thousands of homes.[68] In the few cases where internally displaced persons were permitted to return to their cities and villages of origin, such as Haifa and Sha'ab, they have not been permitted to repossess their properties, which were allocated to Israeli soldiers and new Jewish immigrants. Bedouin IDPs face further obstacles to property restitution due to the traditional or customary system of land rights prevalent in the community similar to that of other indigenous peoples.[69] Housing and property restitution is rejected to ensure permanent Jewish use and control of IDP and refugee properties, and to prevent the return of IDPs and refugees.

Many internally displaced Palestinians in the 1967 Occupied Territories are also prevented from returning to their homes and villages of origin. Of the more than 6,000 Palestinian Jerusalemites who were displaced when Israel revoked their right of residence in Jerusalem, it is estimated that fewer than one-fifth have been able to reacquire residency status in the city. Military occupation effectively precludes return. Palestinians are not permitted to reside in areas expropriated for the construction and expansion of Jewish colonies. In cases of house demolition where homes are not located in areas targeted for use by Jewish colonies, IDPs are often able to return to rebuild homes; in many cases, however, homes have been demolished for a second and third time.

Palestinian IDPs in the 1967 Occupied Territories are also prevented from repossessing housing and property. Israel has expropriated or acquired control of more than 3,000 square kilometres of Palestinian-owned land in the 1967 occupied Palestinian territories.[70] Domestic law and military orders promulgated by Israel in the 1967 Occupied Territories effectively apply many of the same property laws employed inside Israel to acquire Palestinian property for Jewish colonisation. Palestinian land in eastern Jerusalem is acquired for so-called "public" purpose, while land in the occupied West Bank and Gaza Strip is acquired under a complex set of military orders dealing with "abandoned" land, "state" property, military use, and public purpose, among others. While expropriated Palestinian property held by the state is not considered inalienable, the use of land acquired under these military orders (namely, for construction of Jewish colonies, including related infrastructure such as "bypass roads"), suggests *de facto* permanent acquisition. Even in cases where IDPs are willing to purchase expropriated property, they have been excluded from placing a bid to buy back their own property. In 1977, for example, Israel expropriated the home of the Burqan family in the expanded Jewish quarter of the old city of Jerusalem on the basis of public purpose (that is, development of the Jewish quarter). The family was later prevented from bidding for their home at a public auction on the basis of their ethnic, national and religious origins.[71] The majority of the land in the Occupied Territories was not registered by cadastral survey prior to Israel's 1967 military occupation of the area, making it difficult for most persons to prove ownership of land.

Mechanisms

National authorities have the primary responsibility for the protection of the basic rights of internally displaced persons within their borders (Principle 3.1). National and international authorities are required to respect and ensure respect for their obligations under international law, including human rights and humanitarian law, in all circumstances, so as to prevent and avoid conditions that might lead to displacement of persons (Principle 5). The right of internally displaced persons to request and receive protection and humanitarian assistance is the corollary of the state's duty to provide protection and assistance to IDPs (Principle 3.2).

The Israeli government and judiciary, as discussed above, does not provide adequate protection for IDPs inside Israel. During the early years of internal displacement, Israel provided limited targeted assistance to internally displaced Palestinians, either through regular government services, or through the Refugee Rehabilitation Authority (RRA), which operated during the early 1950s primarily in official and semi-official "shelter villages".[72] RRA programmes, however, were guided by two basic criteria: preservation of the demographic changes that took place during the 1948 war; and, preservation of Jewish control of Palestinian land temporarily abandoned during the war. Services were conditioned on cancellation of IDP claims to properties and lands in the villages of origin.

In the 1967 Occupied Territories, Israel does not fulfil its obligations under international humanitarian law (namely, the Fourth Geneva Convention) to protect the civilian population. The absence of a state, moreover, means that there is no national entity obligated, able and willing to provide protection to Palestinian IDPs. Israel's military assault on the Palestinian Authority, which in any case does not have the powers of a sovereign entity, has made it all but impossible to provide effective protection of Palestinians in the Occupied Territories.

International protection is often required when national authorities are either unwilling or unable to protect the basic rights of internally displaced persons. Unresolved issues of UN mandate and institutional responsibility for internal displacement continue to hamper effective provision of international protection of IDPs. No single agency is recognised as having an explicit mandate to provide international protection for internally displaced persons. State concerns about sovereignty and

non-interference in internal state affairs have further impeded international efforts to resolve the problem of providing protection for IDPs.
International agencies that do provide some level of protection to
internally displaced people are at times reluctant to do so, fearing it would
damage relations with government authorities and impair humanitarian
programmes.

In the absence of a single agency mandated to provide protection to
internally displaced people, various UN agencies and other international
humanitarian organisations have provided some form of protection on a
case-by-case basis worldwide. They include the Office of the UN High
Commissioner for Refugees (UNHCR), the UN Development
Programme (UNDP), the United Nation's Children's Fund (UNICEF),
the World Health Organisation (WHO), and the Office of the UN High
Commissioner for Human Rights (UNHCHR). During the late 1980s,
the UNDP was delegated responsibility for coordination of relief
programmes for IDPs. UNDP programmes also focused on reintegration of uprooted persons following the cessation of hostilities and
resolution of political crises leading to displacement. The UNHCR,
however, has historically born the brunt of most aid and protection to
internally displaced persons. The UNHCR does not have an explicit
mandate to provide protection and assistance to IDPs, but the agency
may carry out expanded functions by request of the UN Secretary
General and the UN General Assembly. For example, the UNHCR has
been delegated the responsibility for assisting the displaced in countries
such as Sierra Leone, Angola and Azerbaijan, and more recently Bosnia-
Herzegovina.

International opposition to the establishment of a new agency with a
specific mandate for internally displaced people and opposition to the
inclusion of IDPs within the mandate of existing agencies has led to a so-
called collaborative approach to international protection and assistance
for the internally displaced. In 1992 the UN Commission on Human
Rights asked the Secretary General to appoint a special representative for
internally displaced persons. The Special Representative focused, in
particular, on the development of a doctrine specifically tailored to the
needs of the internally displaced, resulting in the adoption of the *Guiding
Principles on Internal Displacement*. In 1994 the UN emergency relief coordinator (ERC), created to promote a more rapid and coherent response
to all emergency situations, was formally designated as "reference point"

for requests for assistance and protection in situations of internal displacement. The preliminary outcome of the international debate on the UN responsibilities towards IDPs was the establishment in 2001 of a small unit within the UN Office for the Coordination of Humanitarian Affairs (OCHA). The unit is staffed with personnel seconded from the major humanitarian UN agencies and the NGO community and is tasked with providing expertise, training and guidance to humanitarian agencies working in IDP crises.

No single agency has an explicit mandate to provide international protection for internally displaced Palestinians in Israel and the 1967 Occupied Territories. The UNCCP, which has a protection mandate for 1948 Palestinian refugees *and* 1948 internally displaced Palestinians, ceased to provide effective international protection in the early 1950s. UNRWA, the International Committee of the Red Cross, and UNDP, and other UN agencies provide case-by-case assistance to Palestinian IDPs in the 1967 Occupied Territories, but there is no single agency with an explicit mandate to provide comprehensive protection.

Conclusion

Internally displaced Palestinians lack effective national and international protection in relation to protection from displacement, respect for basic human rights during displacement, provision of humanitarian assistance, and the search for durable solutions, including the right of return and housing and property restitution. No international body or mechanism, moreover, is currently recognised as having an explicit mandate to provide comprehensive protection for Palestinian IDPs.

Awareness about the existence and problems faced by Palestinian IDPs is poor. Until recently, major non-governmental and UN agencies did not recognise internally displaced Palestinians. Local, regional and international NGOs, UN agencies and solidarity organisations should include information about Palestinian IDPs in education and information material. The recent inclusion of all categories of Palestinian IDPs in the Global IDP Database sponsored by the Norwegian Refugee Council is one positive development. The award of the 2001 Body Shop Human Rights Award to the National Society for the Rights of the Internally Displaced in Israel is another. Organisations and agencies should also disseminate widely the 1998 *Guiding Principles on Internal Displacement.*

Based on the inter-agency collaborative approach established by the United Nations in response to IDPs worldwide, relevant UN agencies, including the UNHCR, UNRWA, and the UNHCHR, should initiate inter-agency discussions to determine the most effective approach to day-to-day protection for internally displaced Palestinians in addition to externally displaced refugees. The situation is particularly critical for internally displaced Palestinians and refugees in the 1967 Occupied Territories. Further discussion should focus on protection and the search for durable solutions. In particular, these agencies should closely monitor the status of IDPs, as well as refugees, in any future agreements between the PLO and Israel. Durable solutions, including the right of return and housing and property restitution, for Palestinian IDPs should be addressed within same international legal framework and mechanisms as Palestinian refugees. Critical attention should be given to peace plans and proposals that suggest solving the Palestinian refugee question at the expense of the right to return of and property restitution to Palestinian citizens, including IDPs in Israel, for example, "land swaps" and refugee resettlement on IDP lands.

Local NGOs are encouraged to address the specific situation of internally displaced Palestinians, as a particularly vulnerable category of the Palestinian people. This includes documentation of human rights violations, education, health, employment status, and other socio-economic indicators. Special attention should focus on arbitrary deprivation of property affecting IDPs. Local NGOs and IDP associations should also spearhead efforts, in coordination with international organisations, for the establishment of a comprehensive registration system for internally displaced persons, followed by a comprehensive field survey on the current status of IDPs.

International organisations should provide political, capacity building, and financial support to IDP associations and initiatives working to raise awareness and lobbying for durable solutions for internally displaced Palestinians.

Israel should incorporate the *Guiding Principles on Internal Displacement* within its domestic law and remove legal and other obstacles to durable solutions for Palestinian IDPs – for example, implementation of its obligations under international humanitarian law, the Geneva Convention and human rights conventions pertaining to the protection of Palestinian residents in the 1967 Occupied Territories. Israel should also open all files in state archives relevant to IDPs for public access and scrutiny. Civil society organisations and others inside Israel should raise awareness among Israeli Jews about Palestinian IDPs, their current status, and requirements for durable solutions. Israel should also end its thirty-seven-year illegal military occupation of the West Bank, eastern Jerusalem, and the Gaza Strip, which is the primary source of internal displacement in these territories, and facilitate durable solutions for all Palestinian IDPs.

Notes

1 The author would like to acknowledge the research and drafting assistance provided by Bassam 'Awad and Lama Habel. A version of this chapter was published as BADIL Information and Discussion Brief No. 9, November 2002, by Badil Resource Center for Palestinian Residency and Refugee Rights.

2 See the IDP definition in *The Guiding Principles on Internal Displacement*. Addendum to: Report of the Representative of the Secretary-General, Mr. Francis M. Deng, submitted pursuant to Commission resolution 1997/39, UN Doc. E/CN.4/1998/53/Add.2, 11 February 1998, Further Promotion and Encouragement of Human Rights and Fundamental Freedoms, including the Question of the Programme and Methods of Works of the Commission Human Rights, Mass Exoduses and Displaced Persons. Available at: http://www.reliefweb.int/ocha_ol/pub/idp_gp/idp.html (accessed on 28 September 2004).

3 This includes approximately 4.1 million 1948 refugees registered with the UN Relief and Works Agency for Palestine Refugees (UNRWA); an estimated 1.6 million non-registered 1948 refugees; 779,000 1967 refugees; and 838,000 refugees displaced for the first time after 1967. There is no single authoritative source for the global Palestinian refugee population. With the exception of registered refugees, the figures are estimates. See Table 2.1 "Palestinian Refugees, Internally Displaced Palestinians, and Convention Refugees, 1950-2002", *Survey of Palestinian Refugees and Internally Displaced Persons 2003*, Bethlehem: Badil Resource Center for Palestinian Residency & Refugee Rights, 2003), p.33.

4 For more details on internal displacement in the Middle East *see, Internally Displaced People: Global Survey 2002* (London: Earthscan Publications, 2002).

5 See note 1. For an annotated analysis of *The Guiding Principles on Internal Displacement*, see Walter Kalin, *Guiding Principles on Internal Displacement, Annotations*. Studies in Transnational Legal Policy No. 32 (Washington, DC: The American Society of International Law and the Brookings Institution Project on Internal Displacement, 2000).

6 Lex Takkenberg, *The Status of Palestinian Refugees in International Law* (Oxford: Clarendon Press, 1998), p.181, stating, "Although there can be no doubt that the entity 'Palestine' should be considered a state *in statu nascendi* [...] the entity

'Palestine' currently does not fully satisfy the international legal criteria of statehood: a permanent population, a defined territory, government, and the capacity to enter into relations with other states." For recent commentary on protection and the limited role of the Palestinian Authority in the context of the second Palestinian uprising *see*, for example, *Question of the Violation of Human Rights in the Occupied Arab Territories, including Palestine, Report of the Human Rights Inquiry Commission established pursuant to Commission Resolution 3-5/1, of 19 October 2000*, U.N. Doc. E/CN.4/2001/121 (2001), IV. The Legal Status of the Conflict, Section 7.

7 International consensus affirms the *de jure* applicability of the Fourth Geneva Convention to the 1967 occupied Palestinian territories. For a recent commentary *see Report of the Human Rights Inquiry Commission*, pp.35-43. *Also see Report of the Special Rapporteur of the Commission of Human Rights, Mr. John Dugard, on the Situation of Human Rights in the Palestinian Territories Occupied by Israel since 1967*, U.N. Doc. E/CN.4/2002/32 (2002), pp.8-10. See also International Court of Justice, *Legal Consequences of the Construction of a Wall in the Occupied Palestinian Territories, Advisory Opinion*, 9 July 2004.

8 International consensus affirms Israel's responsibility for implementation of international human rights law in the 1967 Occupied Territories. Recently, see e.g., *Report of the Human Rights Inquiry Commission*, para. 37. Also see *Report of the Special Rapporteur of the Commission of Human Rights*, pp.8-9 and Committee on Economic, Social and Cultural Rights Concludes Twenty-Sixth Session, Releases Observations and Recommendations on [...] Israel. UN Doc. HR/4562, 31 August 2001.

9 According to the majority in Ben Shalom vs. Central Election Committee the definition of Israel as the State of the Jewish people is based on three fundamental principles: (1) that the Jews form the majority of the state; (2) that the Jews are entitled to preferential treatment such as the Law of Return; and (3) that a reciprocal relationship exists between the state and the Jewish people outside of Israel. *Ben Shalom vs. Central Election Committee*, 43 P.D. IV 221 (1988), in 25 Israel Law Review 219 (1991). For more analysis *see Legal Violations of Arab Minority Rights in Israel*. Shafa'amr: Adalah – the Legal Centre for Arab Minority Rights in Israel (March 1998). *Also see* Concluding Observations of the Committee on Economic, Social and Cultural Rights: Israel. 4/12/98. UN Doc. E/C.12/1/Add.27, 4 December 1998, para. 10. "The Committee expresses concern that a excessive emphasis upon the State as a "Jewish State" encourages discrimination and accords a second class status to its non-Jewish citizens".

10 *Legal Violations of Arab Minority Rights in Israel*, p.95. Also see *The Sikkuy Annual Report 2001-2002, Monitoring Civic Equality Between Arab and Jewish Citizens of Israel, edited by* Shalom Dichter and As'ad Ghanem (Jerusalem: Sikkuy, The Association for the Advancement of Civic Equality in Israel, July 2002), p.52, stating that racism "does not arise solely from the significance given to cultural differences between Jews and Arabs, but from the absence of a willingness to accept Arab citizens as citizens with equal rights, and as partners in shaping the image and the future of the state and its citizens".

11 Survey conducted by the National Security Studies Center, Haifa University, reported in *Sawt al-Haq Wal-Hurriyya*, 25 June 2004. Also see survey conducted by the Israel Democracy Inst. and the Guttman Center of Applied Social Research, reported in *Sawt al-Haq Wal-Hurriyya*, 2 January 2004. For further discussion of earlier polls, see *Legal Violations of Arab Minority Rights in Israel*, pp.95-107.

12 *The Sikkuy Annual Report 2001-2002*, p.44.

13 Israel cooperates and coordinates important government functions (including the establishment and development of new towns, immigrant absorption, and maintenance and support of cultural, educational, scientific, religious, recreational, and social welfare activities) with these agencies according to the 1952 World Zionist Organisation–Jewish Agency (Status) Law. *Laws of the State of Israel*, Vol. VII, p.3. The internal regulations of these bodies restrict services to Jews. The government is therefore able to channel resources to Jewish citizens of the state and avoid charges of overt discrimination. See *Legal Violations of Arab Minority Rights in Israel*, pp.50-54. See also, David Kretzmer, *The Legal Status of the Arabs in Israel* (Colorado: Westview Press, 1990), p.95; and Walter Lehn, *The Jewish National Fund* (London: Kegan Paul International, 1988).

14 During the first four months of 2002 when the Israeli government was supposed to begin implementing a four-year development plan for the Palestinian sector to address more than fifty years of inadequate and discriminatory investment, government ministry allocations actually dropped. Interestingly, the Public Security Ministry is the only government branch that has increased investment in Palestinian communities.

15 For a more detailed analysis of discrimination in government expenditures and service delivery to Palestinians inside Israel see the reports by Sikkuy, the Association for the Advancement of Civic Equality in Israel at: http://www.sikkuy.org.il (accessed on 28 September 2004).

16 The right to equality is upheld only so long as it is consistent with the character of the state as a Jewish state. The 1992 Basic Law: Human Dignity and Freedom 1992, for example, which empowers the Supreme Court to overturn Knesset laws that are incompatible with the right to dignity, life, freedom, privacy, property and the right to leave and enter the country, emphasises the character of the state as a Jewish state. The Law does not provide for equality because: (1) religious political parties insisted upon maintaining the status quo between the State and religion; and, (2) the majority sought to protect the character of the state as a Jewish state. J. Karp, "The Basic Law: Human Dignity and Freedom, History and Power Game", (1993) *Mishpat Umimshal* 342. Cited in *Legal Violations of Arab Minority Rights in Israel*, p.18. Israel does not have a constitution or a bill of rights. Israel's Declaration of Independence includes references to principles of equality, however, the Declaration is not considered constitutional law. Kretzmer, *The Legal Status of the Arabs in Israel*, pp.7-8.

17 Yehezkiel Lein, *Land Grab: Israel's Settlement Policy in the West Bank*. Jerusalem: B'tselem, The Israeli Information Center for Human Rights in the Occupied Territories (May 2002), p.27.

18 For more on the military government, see, e.g., Raja Shehadeh, *Occupier's Law: Israel and the West Bank* (Washington, DC: Institute for Palestine Studies, 1985), pp.63-75.

19 Declaration of Principles on Interim Self-Government Authority, Washington, 13 September 1993, *reprinted in* 31 I.L.M. 1525 (1993); Agreement on the Gaza Strip and the Jericho Area, Cairo, May 4th, 1994, *reprinted in* 33 I.L.M. 622 (1994); Interim Agreement on the West Bank and Gaza Strip, 28 September 1995, *reprinted in Palestine Yearbook of International Law* 353 (1994/95).

20 See *Ordinance 6B(A)*, Article 4, extension to the Law to Amend and Extend the Validity of the Emergency Regulations (Judea and Samaria, the Gaza Strip, Sinai and South Sinai – Prosecution of Offenses and Legal Aid), 5744-1984.

21 In the West Bank see Order Relating to Identity Cards and Population Registry (Judea and Samaria) (No. 234), 5728-1968, 17 March 1968; and, Order Relating to Identity Cards and Population Registry (Judea and Samaria) (No. 297), 5729-1969. Similar orders were issued in the Gaza Strip.

22 A military government was formally and legally established in January 1950, based on the 1945 (British) Defence (Emergency) Regulations. Under the military government, all matters relating to Palestinians living in cities were handled by the Israeli police; Israeli military governors were put in charge of Palestinians elsewhere. Judicial powers were entrusted to Israeli military courts appointed by the army chief of staff. For a more detailed description, see Sabri Jiryis, *The Arabs in Israel* (London: Monthly Review Press, 1976).

23 Cohen, *Hanifkadim Hanokhahim*, pp.26-27.

24 In a single case where the Israeli High Court ruled in favour of a Palestinian family seeking to live in a Jewish community established by the Jewish Agency, the community has refused to implement the ruling (8 March 2002, Supreme Court ruling in favour of Adel and Iman Qadan against the Jewish Agency and the Katzir Cooperation Society). As of mid-2003, the High Court decision had yet to be implemented.

25 For more details, see Don Peretz, *Israel and the Palestine Arabs* (Washington, DC: Middle East Institute, 1958), pp.50-55.

26 For analysis see Adalah – the Legal Center for Arab Minority Rights in Israel, *Family Reunification and Citizenship, UN Human Rights Committee - Information Sheet No. 3, (22* July 2003) available at: http://www.adalah.org (accessed on 29 October 2003).

27 *See* Concluding Observations of the Human Rights Committee: Israel. 21/08/2003. CCPR/CO/78/ISR. (Concluding Observations/Comments). On August 14, 2003 the Committee on the Elimination of Racial Discrimination (CERD/C/63/Misc.11/Rev.1, 14 August 2003) also called upon Israel to "revoke" the new ban on family unification law, and to "reconsider its policy with a view to facilitating family unification on a non-discriminatory basis".

28 *Al-Ahli*, 21 May 2004. The Peace and Social Justice Organisation published a report in February 2004 indicating unemployment rates in Palestinian cities and villages 50 per cent higher than the rate recorded by the Israel Central Bureau of Statistics. Al-Sinnara, 13 February 2004. According to Israel's Central Bureau of

Statistics, unemployment rates among Palestinians, including IDPs, inside Israel, are one-third higher than Jews. *Fasl al-Maqal,* 21 February 2001. *Also see Legal Violations of Arab Minority Rights in Israel,* pp.89-92; and Fiona MacKay, *The Palestinian Arab Minority in Israel: Economic, Social and Cultural Rights* (Nazareth: The Arab Association for Human Rights, November 1998), pp.62-76.

29 Approximately 70,000 Bedouin live in "unrecognised villages" in the Naqab and the Galilee. For more details, *see The Unrecognised Villages,* Fact Sheet, Arab Association for Human Rights; and *The Arab Bedouin of the Negev,* Fact Sheet, Arab Association for Human Rights. Available at, http://www.arabhra.org. Also see Regional Council for the Palestinian Bedouin of the Unrecognised Villages, at: http://www.arabhra.org/rcuv/index.htm.

30 *Haaretz,* 27 December 2001. The rate among Bedouin rises as high as 13 per 1,000. *al-Ittihad,* 3 May 2002. *Also see The Palestinian Minority in Israel,* pp.78-85.

31 *Second Class: Discrimination Against Palestinian Arab Children in Israel's Schools* (New York: Human Rights Watch, 2001). The situation is particularly grave in unrecognised villages.

32 See the "Retroactive Transfer Plan" prepared in early June 1948 and approved by Israeli Finance Minister Eleizar Kaplan and Prime Minister David Ben-Gurion. The plan is mentioned in Yosef Weitz, *Diary* III, p.294, entry for 20 May 1948, cited in Benny Morris, *The Birth of the Palestinian Refugee Problem, 1947–49.* (Cambridge: Cambridge University Press, 1987), p.136.

33 For example, 1,200 *dunums* was expropriated in 1957 from Palestinian land-owners of Nazareth to establish Nazareth Illit; land was expropriated from Tarshiha and Ma'iliya in 1957 to establish Ma'alot; 5,100 *dunums* was expropriated from Nahaf, Dayr al-Assad, Bi'neh and Majd al-Kurum in 1964 to establish Karmiel, while 20,103 *dunums* was expropriated in 1975 in the Galilee for twenty new Jewish settlements and expansion of existing settlements. It is estimated that Israel has expropriated as much as 1,000 square kilometres out of a total of 1,400 square kilometres of land from Palestinian citizens of Israel since 1948. Salman Abu Sitta, *The End of the Palestinian-Israeli Conflict: From Refugees to Citizens at Home* (London: Palestine Land Society and Palestinian Return Centre, 2001), p.13. This includes approximately 700 square kilometres of land expropriated from Palestinians by the early 1960s. The figure is based on a survey of 79 selected Palestinian villages. Table 5, "Land Lost by Some Arab Villages in Israel, 1945-1962 (in *dunums*)" in Jiryis, *The Arabs in Israel,* pp.292-6. See also Jack Cano, *The Question of Land in the National Conflict between Jews and Arabs 1917-1990* (Poalim Library, 1992), p.79.

34 For more details on the separation wall see the reports and maps prepared by the UN Office of the Coordinator of Humanitarian Affairs available at: http://www.reliefweb.int/hic-opt/ (accessed on 30 October 2003).

35 *Ma'ariv,* 29 September 2003. See also, "Adalah to Government: Plan to Demolish Arab Homes in the Naqab, the Galilee and the Triangle is Illegal", Adalah press release, 14 October 2003.

36 "Government Refuses to Provide Information on 'Moveable Property' of Palestinian Refugees", Adalah press release, 28 January 2002.

37 See Sara Roy, *The Gaza Strip: The Political Economy of De-Development.* (Washington, DC: The Institute for Palestine Studies), 1995.

38 See the Palestine Red Crescent Society, http://www.palestinercs.org (accessed on 30 October 2003).

39 World Bank, *Two Years of Intifada, Closures and Palestinian Economic Crisis: An Assessment,* March 2003, p.1.

40 Ibid., p.2.

41 A 1987 Israeli State Comptroller, *Annual Report,* lists a total of 430 square kilometres of Palestinian refugee land in the West Bank expropriated by Israel. Lein, *Land Grab: Israel's Settlement Policy in the West Bank,* p.45.

42 G. Dib and F. Jabber, *Israel's Violations of Human Rights in the Occupied Territories: A Documented Report* (Beirut, 1970), p.176.

43 Terry Rempel, "Are They Really New Refugees? The Hidden Reality Behind the Wall", *al-Majdal* 23 (September 2004), pp. 26-30.

44 The figure includes homes demolished for administrative and punitive reasons as well as thousands of refugee shelters demolished in the Gaza Strip on alleged security grounds. See al-Haq, Law in the Service of Man available at http://www.alhaq.org (accessed on 15 February 2002) and B'tselem – the Israeli Center for Human Rights in the Occupied Territories available at http://www.btselem.org (accessed on 20 May 2002). The figure also includes thousands of refugee shelters. *See* Norma Masriyeh Hazboun, *Israeli Resettlement Schemes for Palestinian Refugees in the West Bank and Gaza Strip Since 1967* (Ramallah: Shaml, The Palestinian Diaspora and Refugee Centre, 1996), p.32.

45 UNRWA, *Report on Emergency Activities in the West Bank and Gaza Strip,* April–June 2003.

46 For more details see the UN Relief and Works Agency for Palestine Refugees (UNRWA), http://www.unrwa.org and the Office of the UN Coordinator for Humanitarian Affairs (OCHA), http://www.reliefweb.int/hic-opt/ (accessed on 30 October 2003).

47 Table 3, "Assignment of Reasons for Exodus per each District", Salman Abu Sitta, *The Palestinian Nakba 1948: The Register of Depopulated Localities in Palestine.* (London: Palestinian Return Centre, 2000), p.11.

48 United Nations Conciliation Commission for Palestine, *Historical Survey of Efforts of the United Nations Conciliation Commission for Palestine to Secure the Implementation of Paragraph 11 of General Assembly Resolution 194 (III), Question of Compensation.* Working Paper prepared by the Secretariat. UN Doc. AC.25/W.81/Rev.2, 2 October 1961.

49 The terms were used by Israel's first Prime Minister David Ben-Gurion during a Cabinet meeting on 26 September 1948. Morris, *The Birth of the Palestinian Refugee Problem,* p.218.

50 Israeli State Archives, file: Ministry of Minority Affairs, 59/297, January 1949. Referring to fifteen villages in the Baysan district, for example, the document states: "These villages are located in an area which is now empty of Arab residents and in the middle of dense Jewish settlement. There is no possibility to settle or return refugees in these villages in order not to disturb the development

of settlement in a pure Jewish area which is located near the state borders". Cohen, *Hanifkadim Hanokhahim*, pp.48-52. On cleansing the Palestinian population, also see, e.g., Gabriel Piterberg, "Erasures", *New Left Review* 10 (July–August 2001), pp.31-46.

51 Inside Israel see 1965 Planning and Building Law, 19 *Laws of the State of Israel*, 1965, p.30. For a discussion of Israel's planning system inside Israel and its impact on the Palestinian population see, for example, Hussein Abu Hussein and Fiona McKay, *Access Denied: Palestinian Land Rights in Israel* (London: Zed Books, 2003).

52 See the Regional Council for the Palestinian Bedouin of the Unrecognised Villages website, http://www.arabhra.org/rcuv/index.htm (accessed on 30 October 2003).

53 Peter Dodd and Halim Barakat, *River Without Bridges: A Study of the Exodus of the 1967 Palestinian Arab Refugees* (Beirut: Institute for Palestine Studies, 1969), p.46.

54 For a discussion of the planning system in 1967-occupied Palestine see Shehadeh, *Occupier's Law*.

55 For more details, including translations of the Israeli military orders and permit criteria see the UN Office of the Coordinator of Human Affairs (OCHA), http://www.reliefweb.int/hic-opt/feat/trans1003.htm (accessed on 30 October 2003).

56 Statement by Ihassan Tuamee, member of the Committee of the Uprooted Residents of Iqrit, *al-Sinnara,* 8 March 2002.

57 Villagers of Khisas in upper Galilee appealed to the Supreme Court to return to their village in 1952. The Court ruled in their favour on 7 July 1952. Military authorities then served residents with orders to leave by virtue of the Defense (Emergency) Regulations and when the matter returned to court, it ruled it could not intervene in "security" issues. Judgments of the Supreme Court, Vol. 13, p.203, Ataya Jawwid *et al. vs.* the Minister of Defense, case no. 132/52.

58 It was later revealed that these regulations had been specially drafted to allow the authorities to confiscate lands on the frontiers or the adjacent areas so that they might be sold to the JNF, a policy agreed upon by the Judicial Adviser to the government and other Israeli officials. Sabri Jiryis, "The Legal Structure for the Expropriation and Absorption of Arab Lands in Israel", *Journal of Palestine Studies* 4 (Summer 1973), p.95.

59 See, e.g., Shikri Nicola *et. al vs.* Custodian of Absentees' Property *et al*, case 721/79, Judgement of 19 June 1980.

60 Effective legal remedy is further hampered by lack of procedural transparency, violation of due process, and arbitrary criteria including the passage of time. Israeli authorities have refused to release information related to the purpose of land expropriation and the status of expropriated property. The burden of proof rests with the plaintiff rather than the expropriating power. For a review of district and Supreme Court cases, see, e.g., Alexander Kedar, "The Jewish State and the Arab Possessor: 1948-67", in Ron Harris, *et al.* (eds.), *The History of Law in a Multicultural Society: Israel, 1917–1967* (Burlington, VT: Ashgate Publishing Company, 2002).

61 In 1976 Israel's Land Settlement Department offered to settle Bedouin land claims out of court. The offer included the following criteria: Israel would recognised 20 per cent of the total claim (with documented proof), offer compensation for 30 per cent of the total claim (at 65 per cent of its value), and expropriate 50 per cent of the total claim. Recent press reports indicate that Israel is considering restarting the legal process for land claims, suspended in 1976, in order to completely extinguish all Bedouin land claims and thereby ensure the full transfer of all Bedouin land to the state of Israel for exclusive and inalienable Jewish use.

62 The High Court ruled in July 1951 that the residents of Iqrit were entitled to return to their village since the reason for the temporary evacuation no longer existed, and there were no legal grounds for depriving them of their right to return. Judgments of the Supreme Court, Vol. 4, p.461, Mabada Dawud *et. al vs.* the Minister of Defense et al., case no. 64/51.

63 See Judgements of the Supreme Court, Vol. 6, p. 284, Jamal Aslan *et. al. vs.* the Military Governor of Galilee, case no. 220/51. Judgments of the Supreme Court, Vol. 9, p.689. Aslan, Mahmoud *et al. vs.* the Military Governor of Galilee, case nos. 288/51 and 33/52. Similar measures were applied to Iqrit and Kafr Bir'im.

64 The Negev Land Acquisition (Peace Treaty with Egypt) Law 1980 was used to expropriate 82,000 *dunums* of Bedouin land to relocate an airbase from the Sinai. The Bedouin landowners were given three months to be uprooted and the level of compensation was considerably lower than that paid to Jewish settlers relocated as part of the same peace process.

65 For more details, see, e.g., Rosemary Sayigh, "The West Bank Bedouin: The New Refugees?", *al-Majdal,* No. 5 (March 2000), pp.19-23.

66 For more details on the drafting history of UN Resolution 194, *see,* BADIL Occasional Bulletin No. 11, *The Meaning of UN General Assembly Resolution 194 (III), 11 December 1948 (The Right of Return),* April 2002.

67 United Nations Conciliation Commission for Palestine, *Analysis of paragraph 11 of the General Assembly's Resolution of 11 December 1948.* Working Paper prepared by the Secretariat. UN Doc. A/AC.25/W.45, 15 May 1950.

68 It is estimated that by the 1960s Israel had expropriated some 700 square km of land owned by Palestinian citizens of Israel. The figure is based on a survey of 79 selected Palestinian villages. Table 5, "Land Lost by Some Arab Villages in Israel, 1945–1962 (in *dunums*)" in Jiryis, *The Arabs in Israel,* at 292-96. As of 2002, it is estimated that Israel has expropriated approximately 80 per cent of the land owned by Palestinian citizens of the state. Salman Abu Sitta, *The End of the Palestinian–Israeli Conflict,* p.13.

69 As of 1948 the British administration in Palestine had not yet begun a land survey in the Bir al-Sabi' Sub-District. Only 64,000 *dunums* of Arab-owned land in the Sub-District were registered in the official Register of Deeds. (This land is included in registration records of the UN Conciliation Commission for Palestine.) In other words, most Bedouin do not possess land documents that identify ownership by cadastral survey. Maps of the Sub-District from the period, however, clearly identify tribal lands according to the name of the tribe.

70 It is estimated that as of the beginning of 2001 Israel had acquired control of 79 per cent of the land in the 1967 occupied Palestinian territories. *Passia Diary 2001* (Jerusalem: PASSIA, Palestinian Academic Society for the Study of International Affairs, 2001), p.257. See also Lein, *Land Grab.*

71 Allison B. Hodgkins, *Israeli Settlement Policy in Jerusalem, Facts on the Ground.* Jerusalem: PASSIA (December 1998), p.27. The family built a new home in an outlying area of the city and was evicted again when the land was expropriated for the Jewish colony of Pisgat Zeev.

72 For more on the RRA, see Cohen, *Hanifkadim Hanokhahim.*

Index

Arafat, Yasser, 50, 197
Armistice agreements, 1949, 24, 34;
    line(s), 9, 76
Ashdod, 222
Ashkar, Ahmad, 42
Ashkelon, 215-16, 223, 225, 227-8, 230-7,
    239; al-Majdal district, 214; Museum of
    the History of, 218, 222, 238
Association of Forty, 101, 200-1
Ateek, Na'im, 170
Authority for the Rehabilitation of
    Refugees, 59
Avineri, Shlomo, 253
Avner, Elimelech, 27, 29
'Ayn al-Ghazal, 233-4; village booklet, 220
'Ayn al-Helweh, refugee camp, 80
'Ayn al-Zaytun, massacre, 171
'Ayn Hawd, destroyed village, 161; 'Ayn
    Hawd al-Jadida , 201, 204-7, 210-11
Azameh, 275
Azerbaijan, UNHCR responsibility, 280
Azhari, Ali al-, 154
Azhari, Muhammad Abdel Majid al-, 155

Bader, Dawud, 84, 102
Badil Center for Palestinian Residency and
    Refugee Rights in Bethlehem, 10
Balata refugee camp, West Bank, 80
Baqa al-Gharbiyya, land expropriation, 27,
    267
Barak, Ehud, 40, 198, 253
Bat Shalom group, 98
Baysan district, 14
Bedouins, Negev Palestinians, 9, 113, 115,
    117, 120; collective punishment of, 76,
    118; criminalisation of, 124; crop
    destruction, 132; displaced/ forced
    relocation, 10, 91, 267, 271-3, 276-7;
    fifth column accusation, 58; Israeli
    dependence plan, 128; protection lack,
    275; spontaneous settlements, 119;
    urban transfer strategy, 125-8, 135
Bedouin Development Authority, Israeli,
    129-30
Bedouin Education Authority, Israeli,
    129-31
Beersheba (Bir al-Sabi); metropolitan area,

123, 127-8; Sub-District, 275
Beir Zeit University, 181
Ben-Gurion, David, 28-9, 58, 91, 114,
    117, 120-1, 152, 170
Ben-Zvi, Gedalia, 212
Benvenisti, Meron, 11
Bethlehem, 151, 156, 275; Badil Centre,
    10
Bir-al Moscoub, 276
Bishara, 'Azmi, 8
Bligh, Alexander, 65
Body Shop, Human Rights Award, 100,
    281
Boqai, Nihad, 2
Bosnia-Herzegovina, UNHCR, 280
Brazilai, Ronit, 88
British Mandate period, 25, 163; Public
    Land Ordinance 1943, 156
British Parliamentary Labour Council for
    the Middle East, 100
Bronstein, Eitan, 7, 15
Bulle, Sylvaine, 225
Burj al-Barajneh, refugee camp, 80
Burqan family, house expropriation, 278
Bush, George W., Administration, 246

Cabaha, Mustafa, 88
Camp David Summit: negotiations failure,
    68; refugee rights denial, 99
Carmel, Druze villages, 199
cellphones, importance of, 205
Central Zionist Archives, Jerusalem, 193
Chancellor, John, 115
Chekhov, Anton, 146
Christian churches, 38, 41
Citizinship Law, Occupied Territories,
    265
civil society organisations, Palestinians in
    Israel, 48, 100-1, 135, 257
Cohen, Hillel, 2, 11-12, 94
Cohen, Moshe, 215, 224-5, 228-31, 233,
    235-8
"closed military zones", 90, 92, 203, 271-2
collective punishments, 76, 118, 270
colonial laws, selective Israeli use, 156
Committee for the Defence of Arab
    Lands, 48

Committee for the Uprooted of Kafr
 Bir'im, 40, 48
community of consciousness, 256
Cook, Jonathan, 2
Council of Unrecognised Villages, 133
curfew, 266, 268
Custodian of Absentees' Property, 25, 31-
 2, 60
cypress trees, 206

Dadaism, 210-11; Zionist, 208
Dahaf Institute, 263
Daher al-'Umar castle, 160
Dalyrmple, William, 2
Daous family, 168; house of, 175
Daous, Samira, 169
Dar al-Shajara project, 194
Dayan, Moshe, 39, 92, 125
Dayr Hanna, Galilee, 182-3, 191
Dayr Yasin village, massacre, 7-8, 171;
 village booklet, 220
Defence (Emergency) Regulations, 25, 30-
 1, 33, 37, 92, 125
Dayr Dibwan, 275
Democratic Action Organisation, Israel
 (Da'im), 98
Democratic Front for Peace and Equality,
 Israel (DFPE), 84-5, 98
demography, 1948 war outcome, 266
Denmark, Lubyan refugees, 182, 187
Dimona town, Negev, 123, 128
Dirbas, Sahira, 181
"displacement narrative", 89
Diyya, 185
Dror, Ya'acopv, 193
Druze people, 14; villages, 57, 199

Egypt, Suez War defeat, 61
'Ein Ayala, 233-4
'Ein Hod, artists village, 199, 202, 204-5,
 207, 209-12; Disneyfication, 209;
 Sculpture Biennale, 208
elite(s), Palestinian political, Israel, 248-9,
 257; Western historians, 145
Elon, Amos, 39
Emergency Article for the Exploitation of
 Uncultivated Land, 25

Emergency Regulations 1949, 273
Endor village, *Nakba* commemoration, 48
ethnic cleansing, 154, 181, 205, 219, 248,
 252, 258, 270-1; Galilee, 169; 1948, 4;
 rationalisation, 254; transfer policy
 revived, 253, 255
Europe; European Community, 256;
 Jewish suffering, 3
external refugees, land confiscation, 24

Fahmawi, Suleiman, 100
Falah, G., 118, 123, 126
family reunification, rejected, 266
Furaydis, 267
fellahin, Palestinian peasantry, 2, 180, 275;
 culture, 78-9; dispute resolving
 methods, 184, 190
Ferhat, Wadeer, 172-3, 175-7
"Fifth column", Israeli
 assumptions/paranoia, 29, 58, 247
Flapan, Simha, 117
forestation, Israeli strategy, 161, 206, 208
Foucault, Michel, 216, 227, 237
Fourth Geneva Convention, Israeli non-
 observance, 262, 279
Freud, Sigmund, 234

Galilee area, 36, 48, 57, 60, 120, 254;
 destroyed villages, 181; eastern, 57;
 ethnic cleansing, 24, 148, 169; expul-
 sions from, 27-8; host villages, 75-6,
 80; Kafr Yasir village expulsions, 27;
 refugee communities, 46, 145; state
 killings March 1976, 272
Galilee Society, The, 101
Garti, Zvi, 211
Gaza Strip, 9, 149, 165, 197, 214, 223, 257,
 264, 266; "fence", 255;
Israeli military occupation, 88, 94, 270
Geneva Conventions, 262, 279, 282
Geneva Declaration of October 2003, 100
Global IDO Database, 281
Gouda, Subhiyya Mushin, 191
Green Line, 8, 149, 248; Nazareth, 150
Green Patrol, Israeli, 120, 129, 205; crop
 destruction, 132; expansion of, 133-4
Guatemalan Independence Day, 154